D1507092

The Guidebook for Performance Improvement:
Working with Individuals and Organizations

Jossey-Bass
Pfeiffer
San Francisco

Copyright © 1997 by Jossey-Bass/Pfeiffer

ISBN: 0-7879-0353-1
Library of Congress Catalog Card Number 96-077827

All rights reserved. No part of this publication may be reproduced, stored in a retrieval system, or transmitted, in any form or by any means, electronic, mechanical, photocopying, recording, or otherwise, without the prior written permission of the publisher.

Printed in the United States of America

Published by

350 Sansome Street, 5th Floor
San Francisco, California 94104-1342
(415) 433-1740; Fax (415) 433-0499
(800) 274-4434; Fax (800) 569-0443

Visit our website at: http://www.pfeiffer.com

Outside of the United States, Pfeiffer products can be purchased from the following Simon & Schuster International Offices:

Prentice Hall
Campus 400
Maylands Avenue
Hemel Hempstead
Hertfordshire HP2 7EZ
United Kingdom
44(0) 1442 881891; Fax 44(0) 1442 882074

Prentice Hall Professional
Locked Bag 507
Frenchs Forest PO NSW 2086
Australia
61 2 9454 2200; Fax 61 2 9453 0089

Simon & Schuster (Asia) Pte Ltd
317 Alexandra Road
#04–01 IKEA Building
Singapore 159965
Asia
65 476 4688; Fax 65 378 0370

Prentice Hall/Pfeiffer
P.O. Box 1636
Randburg 2125
South Africa
27 11 781 0780; Fax 27 11 781 0781

Printing 10 9 8 7 6 5 4 3 2

 This book is printed on acid-free, recycled stock that meets or exceeds the minimum GPO and EPA requirements for recycled paper.

TABLE OF CONTENTS

Introduction: The Changing Realities of Human and Organizational Performance Improvement

*Roger Kaufman,
Sivasailam Thiagarajan,
and Paula MacGillis*

Faster! Better! Cheaper!

We are constantly asked to be more competitive while working in an environment in which the time frame is shrinking so that we cannot take time to be responsive. High quality is expected. Demands and expectations are up; funding is down.

Our world is constantly changing. We may be masters of change or victims of it. Conventional knowledge and methods will not serve us well unless we focus on personal and organizational performance improvement—on fulfilling increased expectations, not just maintaining what is comfortable.

Unfortunately, our former predictions of the future are often inadequate, if not wrong. Peter Drucker's sage advice is, "If you cannot predict the future, create it." This book is about creating the future. It defines how and what successful human and organizational improvement professionals should do to create the future. Our success as individuals and organizations depends on doing what is right, not just doing things right (Drucker, 1973). We must make positive contributions to one another and to society.

A Look at Realities

We will begin by defining the arena for this book on human and organizational performance improvement.

A Learning Profession: Adding to Our Vistas

Our professional and technical focus has moved from micro-level interests—with individual performance as the primary core of organizational and human resource development—to a more inclusive one. Now our focus includes organizations and our shared society. To our expectations of faster, better, and cheaper for success today and tomorrow, we have to add another: societally responsible! Social contribution is no longer an extra; it is a requirement.

We are not alone in adopting this holistic perspective; many environmentalists advise us to think globally and act locally. Peter Drucker (1993) has endorsed the importance of society as primary client of all organizations.

We now understand that for all human and organizational performance improvement, although most activity is at the micro (individual performance) level, every change has larger implications and organizational (macro) and societal (mega) consequences. We are concerned with individual accomplishments and with their impact on the world. If the competence of workers at a nuclear power generator is defective, the implications could be global.

The mega◄──►micro link is an important consideration for anyone concerned with performance; it is vital for those involved in the areas of organizational and human performance, from industry to education, from government to politics. Let's review the evolution from micro- to macro- to mega-level activity in human and organizational performance systems and then identify several other evolutions in our field. These concepts characterize this book.[1]

The Beginnings

Our field has been growing and continuously improving for many years. We owe much of our origins to psychology and the understanding of human learning.

Learning Theory

If any one field provided an initial impetus, it is the psychology of learning. Performance-improvement pioneers experimented to find out how people acquire new behaviors that are not attributable to biological growth. Knowledge was amassed from several disciplines:

- Behaviorism: Performance was what was observable; that was the basis for understanding and developing human competence. Mental attributes were unseen and not subject to scientific study. Emphasis was on the importance of reinforcement (reward) in shaping behavior.

- Gestalt Psychology: Patterns, relationships, and understanding were the primary focus of study. The human brain and thought were also considered.

---

[1] The following summary is not intended as a scholarly or complete discussion of human and organizational performance. That is left to other authors.

- Developmental Psychology: The physiological and physical development of each individual was considered in designing learning opportunities.

- Adult Education: Adults learn differently from children because they bring experiences and values with them.

- Cognitive Sciences: Learning is understood in terms of psychological processing. This is an evolving field with many branches.

- Humanism: People, their uniqueness, and well-being are paramount over every other consideration or approach.

Other Contributions

Adding to the streams of knowledge useful for human and organizational performance improvement were contributions from the military and industry. They were interested in taking available human resources and improving their performance and contributions:

- The Military: Added assessment of mental attributes, the study of leadership, and systems analysis to the knowledge base. The military also studied instructional systems and, later, performance systems. The early applications of system engineering and system sciences to organizational improvement were done here.

- Industry: Early industrial studies were of the worker as a form of machine. Then industries became concerned with the human and humane side of management. This has evolved into understanding that people are an integral part of defining and achieving organizational health and success.

Some additional philosophical approaches have been used to understand people and how they learn and contribute:

- Constructivism: Everyone constructs his or her own knowledge based on his or her unique experiences and environment.

- Critical Theory: Society and societal well-being are paramount and must include the contributions and participation of all people, especially those who have not been included in the past.

- Semiotics: People respond to symbols and make sense of their environments based on the personal meanings of the symbols present.

Human resource development, organizational improvement, and human performance improvement as disciplines have emerged from these origins. More research and thinking will help us to create our future as these areas continue to evolve and interact. For example, there currently is a focus on strategic and tactical planning as a way to systematically and systemically improve the contributions that people make to their organizations and to external clients. In the public-service sector, this leads to citizen approval and continuation of funding; in the private sectors, it leads to client satisfaction and profits that continue over time.

Increasing Our Contributions

The concern for performance has been extending. It has grown from:

- A concern with individual reflexes to individual understanding, from physical behavior to mental processing;

- Assumed uniformity among people to understanding of individual differences, values, experiences, and interpretations;

- Individual performance to group performance and contributions;

- A focus on individuals to a focus on groups and organizations.

Recently, another tier has been added:

- From organizational improvement to societal contributions and consequences as well.

The study of performance systems has evolved from being concerned solely with individual workers to being concerned with the contributions of organizations to today's and tomorrow's worlds:

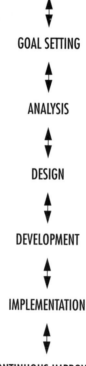

DIRECTION FINDING (INCLUDING SOCIETAL IMPROVEMENT AND CONSEQUENCES

GOAL SETTING

ANALYSIS

DESIGN

DEVELOPMENT

IMPLEMENTATION

EVALUATION, CONTINUOUS IMPROVEMENT, RENEWAL

Individual Competence and Performance

This book deals with all aspects and dimensions of human and organizational performance improvement. The core of the field, both historically and operationally, is individual competence and performance within the recognized framework of analysis, design, development, implementation, and evaluation/control. Most chapters deal with these fundamental building blocks of performance systems. In addition, the book links individual competence and performance to the larger frameworks of organizational success and contribution to society. It does not address the training aspects of human performance improvement.

Expanding Our Horizons

As part of defining the concepts and tools for improving human and organizational performance, this book provides the vehicles and concepts for *direction finding*—determining where an organization should be headed (and why). As we identify and justify where we are headed, we consider information, tools, and concepts for the other layers, including goal setting in a rapidly changing environment. Of particular interest is the interrelation of the aspects of performance systems, from defining the desired societal impact to evaluation and renewal.

The Elements of Organizational Success and Contribution

For any organization, public or private, to be successful, it must:

- Have useful *outcomes*—societal contributions;
- Efficiently deliver useful *outputs*—goods and/or services to external clients;

- Ensure that each functional unit within the organization contributes *products* to internal clients; and

- Ensure that each individual is competent and contributes to the *products* that are delivered to other internal clients.

If we delete, weaken, or discount any one of these elements of success, the organization will falter and fail. They are all equally important and must be linked.

Defining the Primary Client and Beneficiary of What Is Planned, Designed, Developed, and Delivered

There are three major clients for performance systems. Which one you select determines what you do and what you deliver. Table 1 defines the three levels.

Table 1. Levels of Planning and Associated Levels of Results

LEVEL OF PLANNING AND SCOPE OF RESULTS	PRIMARY CLIENT AND BENEFICIARY OF WHAT IS PLANNED AND DELIVERED	LEVEL OF RESULTS
Mega	External Clients and Society, Now and in the Future	Outcomes
Macro	The Organization Itself	Outputs
Micro	Individuals and/or Small Groups Within the Organization	Products

Based on Kaufman, 1996.

The questions each type of planning and related results poses are:

Mega/Outcomes: Do I commit to deliver desired and required positive social consequences?[2]

Macro/Outputs: Do I commit to deliver desired and required quality to external clients?

Micro/Products: Do I commit to deliver desired and required quality to internal clients?

Most current literature on performance systems deals with the micro level. Most attention is on being reactive. What we plan and do usually deals with problems that exist or what is believed to be important to a client. We realize that organizational reality includes reactivity; we also stress that creating one's future depends on being proactive.

Reactive and Proactive Approaches

Performance systems work has focused at the micro/individual level. After all, people are the basic fabric of organizations. In addition, performance specialists have tended to begin work *after* a problem has been identified. A basic flow is shown on page 10.

Reactive approaches are useful in *responding* to an existing problem. Applicable tools for dealing with the elements of this process include instructional systems, training, human resource development (HRD), quality improvement/total quality management, and excellence programs. Tools for improving current performance include systems analysis, training requirements analysis (sometimes misleadingly called training needs assessment), needs analysis, problem analysis, task analysis, methods-means-media analysis, and front-end analysis.

---

[2] For example, will the clearing of rain forests or the placement of dams in environmentally sensitive areas add to our profits in the short run, yet decrease or eliminate business in the medium and long run? Should we save a few dollars in production if it could lead to injuries or deaths?

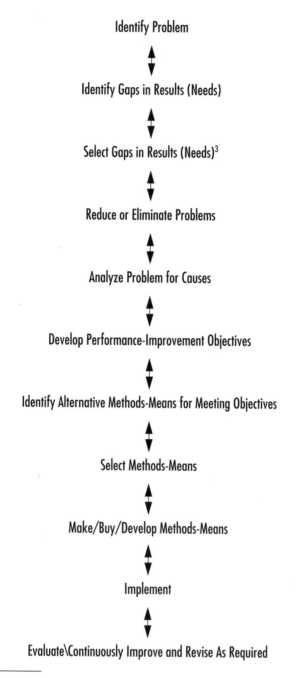

Identify Problem

Identify Gaps in Results (Needs)

Select Gaps in Results (Needs)[3]

Reduce or Eliminate Problems

Analyze Problem for Causes

Develop Performance-Improvement Objectives

Identify Alternative Methods-Means for Meeting Objectives

Select Methods-Means

Make/Buy/Develop Methods-Means

Implement

Evaluate\Continuously Improve and Revise As Required

---

[3] A need (gap in results) selected for reduction or elimination is defined as a problem.

They all start with an existing problem or performance deficit. This book deals with each of these topics and tools.

Proactive approaches provide an additional orientation (and set of concepts and tools) useful for the performance systems professional. Proactive concerns allow for systems to be designed to avoid deficits in the first place. Proactive approaches do not wait for problems to develop. Such a flow can be illustrated as:

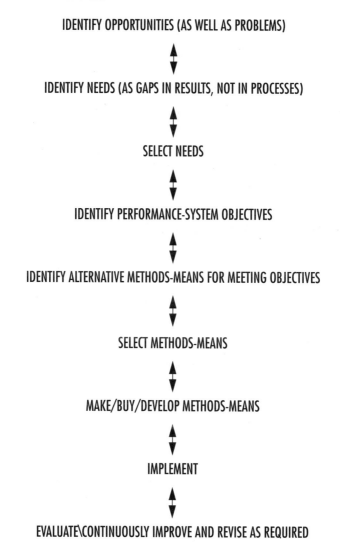

IDENTIFY OPPORTUNITIES (AS WELL AS PROBLEMS)

IDENTIFY NEEDS (AS GAPS IN RESULTS, NOT IN PROCESSES)

SELECT NEEDS

IDENTIFY PERFORMANCE-SYSTEM OBJECTIVES

IDENTIFY ALTERNATIVE METHODS-MEANS FOR MEETING OBJECTIVES

SELECT METHODS-MEANS

MAKE/BUY/DEVELOP METHODS-MEANS

IMPLEMENT

EVALUATE\CONTINUOUSLY IMPROVE AND REVISE AS REQUIRED

Creating the Future

Useful concepts for proactive approaches include mega-level tools such as strategic planning "plus," quality management plus, benchmarking plus, and reengineering plus. The "plus" is the inclusion of societal good as a primary focus (Kaufman, 1992, 1996; Kaufman & Swart, 1995). Adding the mega-level orientation to useful tools provides the opportunity to "create the future," not just to react to it. Thus, instead of trying only to be competitive, we can provide the performance and vision that others will want to emulate. This book covers each of these processes.

The basic difference between a *reactive* and a *proactive* approach is whether you accept a presenting problem as your starting point or whether you uncover what should be accomplished and delivered before a performance deficit appears. A successful performance systems professional does both. This book discusses both reactive and proactive approaches.

Starting a Performance-Improvement Effort

Planning for performance improvement may target the mega, macro, and/or micro levels. The most usual approach, if one is including all levels, is to "roll up" from the bottom to the top: from micro to macro to mega (although this level is infrequently considered).

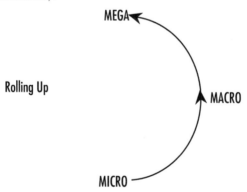

This rolling-up approach assumes that improving efficiency at the micro level will deliver useful organizational results (macro) and, thus, will lead to a positive societal contribution. This reactive tactic is hard to justify with performance data. The proactive approach "rolls down" from the mega to the macro to the micro.

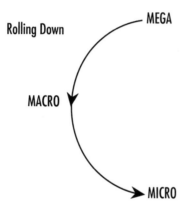

When both approaches are employed, comparison of the results of each can be made to ensure that all levels of performance are appropriate and contribute to one another.

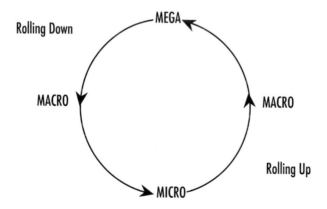

Basic Performance-Improvement Concepts and Terms

There are many useful tools and approaches for performance systems design, development, implementation, and evaluation. Unfortunately, most authors use their own vocabulary. However, most agree on several things:

1. Results are the basic "stuff" of performance-improvement systems. Accomplishments are primary, and methods are secondary.

2. People are the most important part of any organization. Investment in them is well rewarded.

3. People work best in an atmosphere of trust, sharing, and mutual contribution.

4. An ideal, common vision and common purposes among associates contribute to successful organizations.

5. Performance systems can and should be purposely designed to improve results.

6. The knowledge base exists for improving human performance and organizational efficiency and effectiveness.

Some of the terms that are used in this book are as follows:

Products: Results that are building blocks for larger results (test score, course passed, game won or lost, disk drives produced);

Outputs: Results that can be, or are, delivered to external clients and society; quality of contribution (delivered computer system, delivered service);

Outcomes: The social impact and payoffs of results (organizational and individual self-sufficiency, self-reliance, collective social payoffs, continuing profits, continuing funding);

Processes: The methods-means-media used to deliver a result. The how-to-do-its (training, organizational development, HRD, computer-assisted instruction);

Inputs: The ingredients or starting conditions under which one is expected to or will have to operate (laws, values, rules, regulations, existing personnel, resources);

Organizational Elements: The elements that every organization has and uses (inputs, processes, products, outputs, outcomes);

Ends: Results, contributions, and accomplishments;

Means: Methods, resources, processes, procedures, how-to-do-its;

Wishes (or Wants): Preferred or valued means;

Needs: Gaps in ends or in results, between "what is" and "what should be";

Needs Assessment: Identification of needs in order of priority, selection of the most important for reduction or elimination;

Problem: A need selected for reduction or elimination;

Evaluation: The retrospective determination of whether purposes were achieved and/or whether the methods and resources used were appropriate and efficient;

Continuous Improvement: The process of continuously improving the means, the resources and methods used within an organization to deliver increasingly useful and efficient results;

Mega-Level Planning: Planning that views the society and community, now and in the future, as the primary client and beneficiary of what is planned and delivered;

Macro-Level Planning: Planning that views the organization itself as the primary client and beneficiary of what is planned and delivered;

Micro-Level Planning: Planning that views an individual or small group as the primary client and beneficiary of what is planned and delivered.

Building a Common Vocabulary

A common vocabulary is vital to ensure that as we define and achieve human and organizational performance improvement, we know:

- What we intend to deliver;

- To whom we will deliver it;

- Why we benefit from what we accomplish; and

- That everyone knows and agrees on what is to be used, done, produced, and delivered, and on the payoffs.

Human and organizational performance improvement is a rewarding but complex process. To ensure that we all benefit from what we do, it is vital that we agree on our terms, tools, and destinations.

How This Book Is Organized

Because we believe that societal contributions—the mega level of planning and doing—are so important, this book relates the concepts, tools, and methods of organizational and human performance improvement to society as the primary client of what organizations, use, do, produce, and deliver. We have called on experts world-wide to provide information. Although each chapter stands on its own, each relates to societal/mega consequences and payoffs.

The book is organized as follows:

Section I. Origins: The origins of performance-improvement systems and a description of the field.

Section II. Direction Finding and Goal Setting: Where the field of performance improvement should be headed, strategic planning, and how to set useful objectives.

Section III. Analysis: How to define requirements and ensure that the requirements are correct and useful.

Section IV. Design and Development: What results we should deliver; how we design the interventions, programs, and activities.

Section V. Implementation: How to implement programs, projects, and activities; how to keep things on track.

Section VI. Evaluation: Examining what worked and what didn't, asking how we can continuously improve, and extracting the implications for the future.

References

Drucker, P.F. (1973). *Management: Tasks, responsibilities, practices.* New York: Harper & Row.

Drucker, P. (1993). *Post-capitalist society.* New York: HarperBusiness.

Kaufman, R. (1992). *Strategic planning plus: An organizational guide* (rev.). Newbury Park, CA: Sage.

Kaufman, R. (1996). *Strategic thinking: Identifying and solving problems.* Washington, DC: International Society for Performance Improvement / Alexandria, VA: American Society for Training and Development.

Kaufman, R., & Grise, P. (1995). *Auditing your educational strategic planning: Making a good thing better.* Thousand Oaks, CA: Corwin Press.

Kaufman, R., & Swart, W. (1995). Beyond conventional benchmarking: Integrating ideal visions, strategic planning, reengineering, and quality management. *Educational Technology.*

Section I

Origins

THE ORIGINS AND CRITICAL ATTRIBUTES OF HUMAN PERFORMANCE TECHNOLOGY

Odin Westgaard

The origins of human performance technology are either old or very recent. The thoughtful practitioner should explore all sources. For example, consider the behaviorists and the pragmatic applications personified by Mager (1975), Harless (1975), and Markle (1986). They swear by B.F. Skinner (1938), who derived most of what he had to say from Watson (1928) and Thorndike (1949). They, in turn, learned the basics from Dewey (1938), who formulated his thoughts with a great deal of help from Hegel.

A second source, cognitive theory or field psychology, emerges with Kaufman (1986) and Gagne (1985). They studied the Gestaltists and Kurt Lewin (1936). Lewin was a contemporary of Dewey and developed many of his precepts from Herbart (1904) and Jung. Herbart acknowledges his debt to Comenius, Kant, and Spinoza, although they held three very different points of view.

A third source is Gilbert (1996) and performance engineering. It travels back through Odiorne (1985) to Taylor and Gilbreth to the guilds of the Middle Ages and the German university. A stretch of the imagination takes us back to Aristotle.

A fourth source is "performance management." Perhaps our best examples are people like Fred Wells (AT&T and Mountain Bell), Roger Addison (Wells Fargo Bank), and Allison Rossett (professor), who owe much of their thinking to Drucker (1980), Odiorne (1985), and a host of others. These people relied on the thinking of Barnard (1938), Simon (1945), Smith (1776), and other turn-of-the-century theorists. Management is an ancient science; its beginnings can be traced back to the ancient Hebrews, Etruscans, and Chinese.

A fifth source is "consulting." The profession is rife with examples, including Judith Hale (Hale Associates), Sivalsailam Thiagarajan (Workshops by Thiagi), and Judy Springer (independent consultant). Their skill set is highly dependent on the thinking of sociologists, anthropologists, and interactive communicators like Satir (1972), Havighurst, and Peale.

Finally, there is measurement. Measurement theory derives from modern-topological mathematicians, theoretical statisticians and others. They are dependent on the thinking of pioneers like Bernoulli and Newton (1713) who, in turn, began with Euclid and Aristotle.

For the reader who would appreciate a historical account of philosophical approaches, I recommend Bigge and Hunt's *Psychological Foundations of Education* (1958). Most of the references above are explained and put in perspective. In my experience, this one source contains enough fundamental information for any practitioner who wants a solid grounding in the profession.

Thus, human performance technology (HPT) is a many-faceted profession with roots in several diverse areas. The most important development today may be the consolidation of these areas of expertise into a compatible field, melded by common interests. Another aspect also works to make the profession cohesive. To understand it, consider two constructs: "Brown Suiters" and the "Renaissance Person."

Brown Suiters

Hale (1993) describes "brown suiters" the way her father described them to her (circa 1960). He could always tell when a company was healthy. Typically, it was managed by a group of important-looking men who wore dark blue pin-stripe suits with white shirts and "power" ties. But there was one person who wore an old, wrinkled, brown suit; a poorly pressed shirt; and a flowered, gravy-stained tie (or no tie). The brown suiter was the key to success. Although the others were competent managers, they strayed little from accepted, traditional ways of doing things. The brown suiter, on the other hand, always tried new things, proposed unique solutions, and (in general) kept the company from becoming complacent in its success.

Successful HPT professionals are usually brown suiters. They examine evidence objectively and critically to identify problems and suggest solutions. More importantly, they do so without preconceived notions about what those solutions may be. They consider countless possibilities. Two examples are Jack Zigon and Greg Finnegan. They are respected by clients and colleagues for their willingness to apply systematic processes in new ways to solve unique problems.

Most of the current leaders in our field excelled in their early years because they were brown suiters. Joe Harless started the Harless Performance Guild, in part because he could not sell his ideas internally to his bosses (Harless, 1975). They were intent on using traditional methods. His current ambitions to reform public schools and contribute to the profession are also outside mainstream thinking. Seth Liebler quietly revolutionized the practices and results at the Center for Disease Control by implementing what, at the time, seemed to be strange procedures. Allison Rossett moves instruction outside the halls of academia (Rossett, 1987). Jim Russell directs his doctoral programs to practicing academicians. Ken Silber based an entire college curriculum on the needs and wants of a panel of professional managers. Judy Springer says mental constructs and psychological preferences are fundamental for successful interventions. Roger Addison uses a matrix organizational structure within a hierarchy because, for his organization, it is effective.

Perhaps the best examples of brown suiters in action are Judith Hale and Roger Kaufman. Hale's company, Hale Associates, is founded on and driven by her father's observation. She has incorporated it into the company's mission and constantly asks her people to employ it as they work with clients. As a result, each client is approached tabula rosa. There are no preconceived notions about where problems may lie or what solution(s) may be appropriate. Each client is considered unique. Therefore, the work is driven by clients' needs and wants.

Roger Kaufman fits the description in a different way. His is a life of continuous discovery. He goes from experience to experience with open eyes and ears for news. Every new datum is incorporated. Each new notion is respected. Each new insight is carefully incorporated into the body of his work, so the whole becomes an integrated construct. As a result, his work becomes more complex and meaningful (Kaufman, 1992).

Historically, we tend to classify the discoveries of those listed earlier in this article as serendipitous. However, from the perspective of their own time, they were classic brown suiters. John Dewey (1938), for example, wrote a series of books that figuratively stood the world on its ear. His discussions of reflective thinking and discovery were unique approaches to old (seemingly unsolvable) problems or impasses. Another, less wholesome, example is Machiavelli. *The Prince* is a primer for any would-be dictator and provides insights into autocratic rule. Many historical figures approached problems and solved them in unconventional ways.

Renaissance Person

The title "Renaissance person" describes someone who seems to be able to do anything well. It describes a person who takes on several critical roles and excels in them all. History abounds with examples, such as George Washington, Michelangelo, Thomas Jefferson, Rousseau, Ben Franklin, Shopenhauer, and Mahatma Ghandi. The stereotype of the modern entrepreneur includes an ability to do many things well.

The entrepreneurial spirit seems to be part of most of the people in our profession. Phil Tiemann dabbles in real estate and develops computer software. His coauthor, Susan Markle, is known as an expert in American jazz and blues music and their traditions. Jim Russel builds exquisite models and is sought as an expert in automobile races. Barry Boothe has developed such an expertise in ham radio transmission, he spends considerable time designing and building special antennas for fellow enthusiasts around the globe.

Perhaps the most renowned practitioner in the field is a consummate showman who tap dances, plays several instruments, and has an incredible repertoire of skits and comic sketches. Bob Mager has written the bellwether book about human performance technology (Mager, 1975). He teaches, consults, and presents with panache and skill.

So What?

I admit that there are thousands of people who can be called "brown suiters" and "Renaissance persons" who are not part of our profession. The point is that the traits seem to be important ingredients for ultimate success in human performance technology.

Those of us who bring well-established procedures and products to our clients and use them to solve whatever problems we find are, in my opinion, often doing our clients a disservice. Training will not solve every problem; neither will job aids, restructuring, or value modification. Practitioners with one or two (or a dozen) proven products that they apply to every problem may do more harm than good. Although such people are valuable and provide useful service to their clients, I doubt if they can be called fully competent human performance technologists.

Real HPTers come to their work with open minds. They rely on their ability to find real problems by clearing away obscuring symptoms. They are brown suiters. In addition, they hold themselves to high standards no matter what they are doing. Whether solving performance problems or building kites, they seek to excel. They are Renaissance people.

References

Barnard, C. (1938). *The functions of the executive.* Cambridge, MA: Harvard University Press.

Bernoulli, J. (1713). *Ars conjectandi.* Publisher unknown.

Bigge, M., & Hunt, H. (1958). *Psychological foundation of education.* New York: Harper & Row.

Dewey, J. (1938). *Experience and education.* New York: Macmillan.

Drucker, P.F. (1980). *Managing in turbulent times.* New York: Harper & Row.

Gagne, R. (1985). *The conditions of learning* (4th ed.). New York: Holt, Rinehart and Winston.

Gagne, R.L., Briggs, L.J., & Wager, W. (1988). *Principles of instructional design.* New York: Holt, Rinehart and Winston.

Gilbert, T.F. (1996). *Human competence: Engineering worthy performance* (2nd ed.). Washington, DC: NSPI.

Gilbreth, L. (1912). On Taylor's scientific management. *Industrial Engineering Magazine.*

Hale, J. (1993). The hierarchy of interventions. In R. Kaufman (ed.), *Handbook of human performance systems.* New York: University Press.

Harless, J.H. (1975). *An ounce of analysis is worth a pound of cure.* Newman, GA: Harless Performance Guild.

Herbart, J. (1904). *Outline of educational doctrine.* New York: Macmillan.

Kaufman, R. (1986). Introduction to performance technology. *Performance and Instruction Journal.*

Kaufman, R. (1992). *Strategic planning plus: An organizational guide* (rev.). Newbury Park, CA: Sage.

Lewin, K. (1936). *Principles of topological psychology.* New York: McGraw-Hill.

Mager, R.F. (1975). *Preparing instructional objectives* (2nd ed.). Belmont, CA: Pitman Learning.

Markle, S., & Tiemann, P. (1986). *Good frames and bad* (2nd ed.). Ann Arbor, MI: Books on Demand.

Odiorne, G. (1985, January). Human resource strategies for the 80s. *Training.*

Rossett, A. (1987). *Training needs assessment.* Englewood Cliffs, NJ: Educational Technology.

Satir, V. (1972). *Peoplemaking.* New York: Science and Behavior Books.

Simon, H.A. (1945). *Administrative behavior.* New York: Free Press.

Skinner, B.F. (1938). *Behavior of organism.* New York: Appleton-Century.

Smith, A. (1957). *Wealth of nations.* New York: Simon & Schuster. (Original work published 1776)

Thiagarajan, S., & Stolovitch, H.D. (1978). Instructional simulation games. In *The instructional design library, Vol. 12.* Englewood Cliffs, NJ: Educational Technology.

Thorndike, E.L. (1949). *Selected writings for a connectionist's psychology.* New York: Appleton-Century-Crofts.

Watson, J.B. (1928). *The ways of behaviorism.* New York: Harper & Row.

Watson, J.B., & Rayner, R. (1920, March). Conditioned emotional reactions. *Journal of Experimental Psychology.*

Research and Development Origins of Performance Systems

Dale M. Brethower

Introduction

Tracing origins of any intellectual paradigm is a task for fools rather than angels. The problem is that the only "truth" about intellectual history is that intellectual origins are as varied as the histories of the people involved. That's the truth, but it's not informative; on the other hand, a useful account will be untrue, except to a few individuals. An angel would be bound to silence, unable to say anything that is useful and true. A fool can press on to offer observations that, although too narrow for truth, might be useful as food for thought.

I offer food for thought, following the lead of the eminent historian of experimental psychology, E.G. Boring (1950), who frequently used the concept of the Zeitgeist in giving an account of intellectual history. "The Zeitgeist" translates literally as "time/spirit" and sensibly as "the intellectual spirit of the time." Boring's point was that, even in careful accounts of the origins of ideas, each person is influenced by the intellectual spirit of the times rather than by single ideas. Use of the term, "Zeitgeist," alerts the reader: I'm attempting to capture the essence of the matter by showing a few key influences; you might wish to add others.

Let's define performance systems—what are they? Performance, as all human performance technologists/performance systems consultants should know by now, is both behavior and the products or accomplishments of the behavior. The behavior may be inept or highly competent but it is always costly; the accomplishment may be trivial or valuable. The performance system is everything that supports or interferes with the behavior that generates the accomplishment (Brethower, 1982; Brethower & Smalley, 1992). "Everything that supports or interferes with the behavior that generates the accomplishment" covers a lot of territory including

- Tools, materials, and physical surroundings;

- Genetic histories tucked away in each performer's tissues;

- Performer's thoughts, feelings, and actions;

- Goals and cultures and political infighting of the organization;

- Data available to inform the performers;

- Fragments of management theories carried around by each manager and worker;

- Current marketing, management/union campaigns;

- Weather, the economy, and a zillion societal influences.

One thing that human performance technologists/performance systems consultants can do better than others, we often allege and sometimes demonstrate, is show how to manage the key variables that comprise the performance system. The know-how for finding and managing the key variables is the knowledge base from which we work. The know-how has been generated by several academic disciplines but no discipline, to date, has adopted the performance system as its domain of inquiry.

What are some of the words that performance technologists might use that offer clues about the knowledge base and its origins? What are some of the words that flow around us like chaff born on the intellectual winds of the Zeitgeist? Reinforcement schedules, feedback, rewards, punishers, goals, standards, measures, PERT charts, Gantt charts, flow charts, control charts, performance appraisal, pay, compensation systems, job analysis, task analysis, selection, quality control, total quality management, job models, function models, process maps, front-end analysis, needs assessment, instructional systems design, data, information, balance of consequences, multiple causation, total performance system, performance engineering, work redesign, ergonomics, intelligent systems, information maps, cognitive structures, human possibilities, teaming, transfer, behavior, accomplishment, performance improvement potential, value added, cost effectiveness, cost benefit, means-ends, cognitive science, information theory, operant conditioning, logistics, tactics, vantage levels, mega/macro/micro analysis, general systems theory, control theory, operations research, scientific management, Hawthorne effect, results, industrial engineering, efficiencies, strategic planning, etc. There are many more words that characterize the knowledge base; anyone who chooses is invited to modify the listing by addition or deletion, thereby giving it a better fit to her or his intellectual history.

Who are some of the people whose names we utter, sometimes in admiration, sometimes in vain? W.R. Ashby, S. Beer, K. Boulding, P. Drucker, J. Forrester, L. Gilbreth, E. Mayo, J.G. Miller, G.S. Odiorne, H. Simon, B.F. Skinner, F. Taylor, N. Weiner, and hundreds of others, mostly colleagues or intellectual descendants of one or more (but rarely several) of these. A few of the hundreds who readily come to my mind are K. Brethower, G. Geis, T. Gilbert, J. Harless, J. Holland, R. Malott, S. Markle, G. Rummler, C. Semmelroth, D.E.P. Smith, S. Thiagarajan, and D. Tosti. Other names could flow with nearly equal respect. Some of the names (on both lists) would be unfamiliar to other performance systems consultants, but those for whom most of the names on either list are new are in for a treat: they are either blessed with a high performance-improvement potential or else have learned important concepts from other sources—the Zeitgeist at work.

Threads of the Zeitgeist

A more organized attempt to capture the Zeitgeist is shown in Table 1. The first column shows several threads, characterized by a name and something that representatives of the movement might say. The second column shows a common form of misbehavior on the part of people who believe they are friends of the movement. With friends like these, a theory or movement requires no enemies but collects them anyway. The movement or theory gets discredited by sensible people who observe the foolish behavior and compound the foolery by attributing the foolishness to the movement as a whole. The third column represents what I hope we have learned from each movement or theory. The learning, of course, comes through the examples of successful application and the non-examples of misapplication.

Table 1. Movements or Theories, Misapplications, and Lessons Learned

Movement/Theory	Common Misapplication	Lessons Learned
Scientific Management: Taylor. "Take a scientific approach to productivity improvement; share the benefits with the workers."	Use scientific tactics to improve productivity but fail to consider other vantage levels, e.g., policy-level sharing of benefits.	Use scientific means in service of humanitarian ends, e.g., Lincoln Electric; discredit applications focused only on one level of vantage; require at least micro-, macro-, and mega-level analyses.

Scientific Psychology: Skinner. "Take a scientific approach to all human behavior."	Use scientific tactics to change behavior but fail to consider other vantage levels, e.g., cultural and philosophical.	Use scientific means in service of humanitarian ends; discredit applications focused only on one level of vantage; require at least micro-, macro-, and mega-level analyses.
Human Relations: "Pay attention to the needs and wants of humans, the human element."	Use tactics, e.g., "attention improves performance," but fail to evaluate effects; fail to consider other tactics and interpretations.	Use scientific means in service of humanitarian ends, e.g., Parsons' reinterpretation of Hawthorne studies; discredit applications focused on one level of vantage, i.e., humane intentions without evaluation of results.
Cognitive Science Movement: "Consider the computational or data/informational requirements of complex tasks."	Use computers as tactical or logistical models of human functioning.	Use computer models as strategy for analyzing information requirements of complex performance, e.g., Simon's work; discredit applications focused on one level of vantage, i.e., using computers as technological answers without considering humane questions.
General Systems Theory: "View each system as a whole, considering all the elements and relationships."	Become enamored of logistical complexity while doing detailed tactical analyses of parts and interrelationships.	Use analysis and synthesis together, considering parts in wholes, e.g., Miller's Living Systems approach to integration of matter/energy and information-processing functions; discredit applications focused on one level of vantage, e.g., simplistic analysis of parts without considering wholes or holistic rhetoric without integrating what's known about parts.

Instructional Systems Design (ISD): "Work in an orderly fashion."	Take a tactical-level, systematic approach to the means without considering the ends.	Build instructional systems only within context of macro- and mega-level analysis, i.e., always consider at least 3 vantage levels; discredit applications focused on one level of vantage, i.e., attending to means, instruction, without considering the ends, performance.
Operations Research and Operations Auditing: "Take a systematic approach to analyzing performance of necessary tasks."	Use logistical analyses and intuitive benchmarking without tactical, strategic, or policy-level analyses.	Do Gilbreth-like efficiency analyses but in context of several levels of vantage comprising micro-, macro-, and mega-level analyses; discredit applications focused on one level of vantage, i.e., treating efficiency or other bench marks as major goals.

The table, especially the "lessons learned" column, captures the major parts of the common intellectual heritage of those of us who do specialized work with performance systems. The major integrating concept for the table is what Gilbert (1996) refers to as "levels of vantage" and Kaufman (1992) refers to as "mega, macro, and micro analysis." The culture-at-large knows the problem that the concept attempts to solve as not seeing the forest because of the trees.

The problem is due to a property of humans and of theories. Humans can comprehend (i.e., keep in focus) only a few things at a time; theories are made up of many elements and relationships. Thus, to understand a complex theory, we must "take it in" in doses small enough to comprehend and then link the small doses into a complete picture. In other words, we understand a complex theory or movement only by taking several views of it and linking them. We must focus narrowly, on the details of a complex theory or movement, because unless we understand the details, we don't understand the movement. We must also focus broadly, on the whole movement and the context in which it operates. The broad focus is necessary because the details derive their meaning from the larger context: we cannot understand the parts (micro level) without knowing the whole (macro level), and we cannot understand the whole unless we understand the societal context (mega level) that composes the domain of applicability of the theory or movement.

Taylor's scientific management approach provides an example. I have characterized the movement as "take a scientific approach to productivity improvement; share benefits with the workers." Many of the applications became misapplications because they focused only on part of the theory, a scientific approach to productivity improvement. Neglecting to share the benefits with the workers results in misapplication. The logic of scientific management is that, if a company pays someone X dollars for a certain level of work, it can be considered a fair wage (since both parties have agreed to the implied performance contract). If the person performs a higher level of work, the company should benefit (having provided the opportunity) and the worker should benefit (having done the work). If X dollars were fair for the lower level of work, paying only X dollars for the higher level is exploitation. Thus, far too many attempts to apply scientific management resulted in exploiting workers rather than sharing the prosperity created by taking a scientific approach to work management.

The Lincoln Electric plant in Cleveland, Ohio, is an example of properly applying the spirit of scientific management. Lincoln (1951) believed in doing work efficiently and sharing the benefits with workers and customers. Consequently, at the Lincoln Electric plant, industrial engineering methods are used to establish fair pay rates, and workers who produce more are paid more. Workers typically are about three times as productive as the industry average and are paid about three times the industry average.

The approach advanced by Skinner is similar to Taylor's: take a scientific approach to all human behavior. The misapplications are also similar. Skinner demonstrated that performance can be controlled by controlling the environment in which organisms, including humans, perform (Skinner, 1938, 1976). The early research was designed to show that performance could be modified (a micro-level analysis). Little attention was given to either the macro level, the practical value of the performance, or the mega level, the social and ethical implications of widespread uses of the techniques. It was, in hindsight, inevitable that the specific control techniques would be more visible than the abstract notions of benefits to the individual and to society. Skinner later wrote extensively about social and ethical issues, but critics were already hard at work identifying both actual and fancied misapplications. The lesson to be learned from both the good applications and the fanciful and bad applications is that the techniques are powerful tools that can be used for good or evil purposes. Watkins (1988), for example, shows that the techniques have been used very practically in education and with great educational benefits to students.

The human relations movement (pay attention to the human element) came about in part as a reaction to misapplications of scientific management and scientific psychology. Unfortunately, concern for the human element (micro level) precluded many potentially valuable applications because proponents too often rejected efforts to apply macro-level economic and "bean counting" measures. For example, the famous Hawthorne studies described by Roethlisberger and Dickson (1939) were offered as evidence of the value of showing concern for the human element (Mayo, 1945). The evidence was there because the beans were counted. The

Hawthorne studies were never replicated so the human relations movement did not discover from them just how paying attention to the human element yielded the increased productivity. Ironically, when the Hawthorne data were analyzed to determine the probable reasons for the effect (Parsons, 1974), the results supported the scientific management and scientific psychology approaches. The lesson to be learned, I think, is that scientific means can be used effectively to support humanitarian ends.

The cognitive science movement can be characterized in a variety of ways. One has yielded misapplications: use the computer as the model for human cognition. Cognitive scientists and behavioral psychologists have shown that humans are very poor at what computers are very good at, i.e., precisely managing large amounts of detailed data. Another way is more promising: consider human abilities to process information. Work is now well-begun to devise computers that do what humans are very good at, i.e., forming fuzzy concepts and making fuzzy connections among items of sensory input. Performance technologists, educators, and equipment designers must consider the computational or data/informational requirements of complex tasks as we enter the age of the knowledge worker. Exemplary work in this area is being done by Simon (1981), among others, and by performance technologists who devise electronic performance support systems (Gery, 1991).

General systems theory—view each system as a whole, considering all the elements and relationships—was developed during and after the 1950s as an approach to integrating knowledge from multiple disciplines. The information explosion has produced a need to know more about any active area of inquiry. Consequently, "experts" are forced, given finite time and energy, to become idiots savants who know little beyond their areas of specialty. Furthermore, work on the frontiers of any specialty increasingly requires considerable knowledge of several other specialties. Many scientists know little beyond their specialties but now must know a lot about other specialties to advance their own. General systems theory offers two escape routes. In the short run, scientists must work in teams if knowledge is to advance; in the long run, similarities among disciplines must be discovered and exploited so that fundamental similarities emerge in place of apparent differences.

Misapplications of general systems theory abounded during the 1960s as people grappled with what it meant to "take a systems approach" and explored parts of general systems theory. Through the combination of good applications and misapplications, three meanings have emerged:

1. Work in teams.

2. Work in an orderly fashion.

3. View anything studied as a system (macro level) in interaction with other systems (mega level) composed of interacting elements (micro level).

In my view, the first two are sometimes-useful misapplications and the third is what exemplars in our profession must do to serve individuals, organizations, and society well in the future. We are just beginning to understand what a "performance system" is and how the many micro-level performance systems comprising a macro-level organization must interact if the organization is to prosper in its mega-level environment (Ashby, 1960; Beer, 1979; Gery, 1991; Gilbert, 1978; Rummler & Brache, 1990).

Instructional systems design (ISD)—work in an orderly fashion—is included in Table 1 as an outgrowth of application and misapplication of general systems theory during the 1960s. The approach can be enticing, even in misapplication, because it often gets better results than working haphazardly. Operations research/operations auditing—take a systematic approach to analyzing performance of necessary tasks—is included for the same reason. Both operations research/operations auditing and ISD have contributed significantly to where we are and will contribute in the future. The techniques are powerful and should be used more often; however, they should be used wisely.

The misapplications have been generated honestly in response to perceived requirements to "improve operation X" or "teach material X"; many of the applications have been generated in the same way. It is not necessary to change the techniques appreciably, but the techniques must be used in context to provide beneficial results. The context can be discovered by seeking answers to this question: How will "improving operation X/teaching material X" improve the functioning of the system at three levels of vantage, e.g., mega level, macro level, and micro level?

Why Threads Unravel

Each of the intellectual threads (Table 1) was begun by an individual or group facing a specific set of problems and looking for an approach that would help solve them. They were guided by a mega-level vision of what they were trying to accomplish. They were reaching for the vision and grasping whatever micro-level variables seemed to move them in the desired direction. The theory or movement grows as a macro-level integration of micro-level variables that move toward a mega-level vision. For example, Taylor and Skinner had visions of people working in harmony toward common purposes. Much of Skinner's writing (e.g., *Walden Two*) is visionary in that he reaches toward something that was clearly beyond the grasp of the psychological practice of the time. Taylor's scientific management is visionary in that scientific management had never been practiced—and still has not. But the means of science, he thought, would enable us to reach the ends of prosperous organizations that shared the prosperity with those who produced it.

The vision of innovators is directed toward mega-level ends and not clouded by specific examples of the micro-level means used to reach the ends. What followers see, however, is not the ethereal vision but the concrete efforts to move toward it. People saw Taylor's micro-level attempts to improve efficiency. Not understanding or knowing that science is a means and can never be anything else, people treated efforts to attain efficiency as if the specific effort or example were the concept of scientific management. Efficiency experts worked to improve efficiency, i.e., to get more work from labor, not realizing that the scientific management vision was to use such tools to increase prosperity and share it with the more productive workforce (Drucker, 1973, p. 24). Lacking the knowledge that science is the means, not the totality of scientific management, people attempting to practice scientific management simply failed to apply the concepts well. The misapplications, treating people as objects or resources to be exploited rather than as valued humans to be developed, set the stage for the human relations movement.

Some approaches thrive in spite of rejections and begin to blend into the Zeitgeist as the good applications show results. Blending has occurred with the scientific management approach as parts of it are built into management theory, in general, and into the total quality movement. The blending seems to be occurring with operations research, the human relations approach, and Skinner's scientific psychology. The good remains, though sometimes buried under mountains of misunderstanding.

A Glance Toward the Future

If we learn from history, the future of performance systems practice will be characterized by understanding rather than controversy. We will imagine that each attempt to accomplish something is an attempt, not the definitive example that defines an approach: a single instance cannot capture a complete vision. We know that when we work to create a reality that matches our own vision that the reality can be attained only when others understand the vision and the concepts and how these might be applied.

I doubt that we will learn the lesson. We are too good at forming fuzzy concepts and acting as if our concepts were accurate. Our ability to act on fuzzy concepts is a great strength that helps us survive in the messy reality we deal with daily. The strength is also a great weakness if we do not regularly step back and sharpen our fuzzy concepts to make sure that they are as accurate as possible and move us continuously toward our vision.

Academics are supposed to have the leisure to do that, but the academic world rewards picking apart other people's views. Nevertheless, we learn the rewards regardless of whether we accurately capture the view we criticize. As a result, we accidentally reward miscommunication and misunderstanding. That will happen in any performance system that cannot determine which accomplishments are worthy and which merely resemble worthy accomplishments.

I think history clearly shows that as a culture, and even as a profession, we must get better at identifying worthy accomplishments and discriminating them from counterfeits. Identifying worthy accomplishments requires looking at several levels of vantage, at looking at trees in the context of forests and forests in the context of ecologies.

References

Ashby, W.R. (1960). *Design for a brain* (2nd ed.). New York: John Wiley & Sons.

Beer, S. (1979). *The heart of enterprise.* New York: John Wiley & Sons.

Boring, E.G. (1950). *A story of experimental psychology* (2nd ed.). New York: Appleton-Century-Crofts.

Brethower, D.M. (1982). The total performance system. In R.M. O'Brien, A.M. Dickinson, & M.P. Rosow (Eds.), *Industrial behavior modification: A management handbook*. New York: Pergamon Press.

Brethower, D.M., & Smalley, K.A. (1992). Performance and instruction: Assuring that learning occurs and transfers to the job. *Performance & Instruction, 31*(6), 38-43.

Drucker, P.F. (1973). *Management: Tasks, responsibilities, practices.* New York: Harper & Row.

Gery, G. (1991). *Electronic performance support systems: How and why to remake the workplace through the strategic application of technology.* Boston, MA: Weingarten Press.

Gilbert, T.F., (1996). Human competence: Engineering worthy performance. Amherst, MA: HRD Press.

Kaufman, R. (1992). *Strategic planning plus: An organizational guide* (rev.). Newbury Park, CA: Sage.

Lincoln, J.R. (1951). *Incentive management.* Cleveland, OH: The Lincoln Electric Company.

Mayo, E. (1945). *The social problem of an industrial civilization.* Boston, MA: Harvard Business School. Cited in P.F. Drucker, (1973). *Management: Task, responsibilities, practices.* New York: Harper & Row.

Parsons, H.M. (1974). What happened at Hawthorne? *Science, 183,* 922-932.

Roethlisberger, F.J., & Dickson, W.J. (1939). *Management and the worker.* Cambridge, MA: Harvard University Press.

Rummler, G.A., & Brache, A.P. (1990). *Improving performance: How to manage the white space on the organization chart.* San Francisco, CA: Jossey-Bass.

Simon, H.A. (1981). *The sciences of the artificial* (2nd ed.). Cambridge, MA: The MIT Press.

Skinner, B.F. (1938). *Behavior of organism.* New York: Appleton-Century.

Skinner, B.F. (1948). *Walden two.* New York: Macmillan.

Skinner, B.F. (1976). *About behaviorism.* New York: Vintage Books.

Taylor, F.W. (1912). *The principles of scientific management.* New York: Harper's.

Watkins, C.L. (1988). Project follow through: A story of the identification and neglect of effective instruction. *Youth Policy, 10*(7), 7-11.

SOCIAL RESPONSIBILITY

Bette Madson

Social responsibility is a theme that can permeate all aspects of human performance systems, including recruitment, training, and benefits. Not only does it have an impact on the organization's outputs, such as trained graduates, but also it may have mega-level consequences for external clients including society. Why should we care about social responsibility? Aren't we supposed to make decisions to maximize profits for our stockholders? Perhaps. As we shall see, social responsibility and economic responsibility are not necessarily mutually exclusive concepts.

This chapter examines many facets of the corporate social responsibility debate that has taken place for decades without resolution. What is corporate social responsibility (CSR)? How does it impact various human performance systems? How can I, in whatever role, practice my personal values of social responsibility and communicate its worth to encourage others, perhaps even the organization itself, to embrace the value of incorporating social responsibility in the processes, decisions, outputs, and outcomes of the organization? This chapter addresses these and other issues as points to consider in approaching any task.

Viewpoints on Corporate Social Responsibility

Let's explore three commonly held viewpoints of CSR: fundamentalist (or capitalist), stakeholder, and societal.

Fundamentalist Viewpoint

The fundamentalist or capitalist viewpoint of CSR sees business as the turbine of economic production and distribution without reference to people. Defenders of this free-market approach, represented in the writings of Milton Friedman, hold that the only social responsibility of business is to increase profits and, therefore, please the stockholders. Beyond keeping contractual agreements, corporations and managers are not ethically required to be socially responsible. This narrow or fundamentalist view of CSR suggests that a corporation is socially responsible if it acts to

> provide jobs with good wages, sell wanted products of good quality at fair prices, provide reasonable service, pay bills on time, pay an equitable amount of taxes, and provide an adequate return on investment...not to eliminate poverty, racism, illiteracy, and social injustice. (Schick, Wokutch, & Conners, 1985, pp. 38, 39)

In this narrow view of CSR espoused by Friedman, the organization is the beneficiary and individual shareholders are its constituent group. The goal is profit maximization and the only constraints may be legal (Lee & McKenzie, 1994, p. 970).

A broader view of the fundamentalist perspective includes a place for ethics. Corporations have to abide by laws and regulations, some of which may protect the public. The role of government is seen as a regulator and protector or espouser of society's wishes. The feeling is that corporations would not voluntarily look out for society's good if it would compromise the corporation's responsibility to maximize shareholder's earnings. An example of a social issue is air pollution before emission controls were required for cars.

Stakeholder Viewpoint

The stakeholder viewpoint, part of the social contract approach, suggests that there is an interwoven web of human relationships that the corporation develops with diverse groups having a stake or vested interest in the corporation. This perspective, sometimes known as the managerial view of CSR, posits that a corporation may seek to satisfy these other constituent groups. These constituent groups may be internal or external to the organization; domestic or international stakeholders; and parties with direct or indirect economic ties. For example, stakeholders with direct economic ties to the corporation include employees, creditors, suppliers, and customers. Stakeholders with indirect ties that affect or are affected by the organization's policies and practices might include environmental groups, community constituencies, consumer advocacy groups, governmental units, representatives of neighboring communities, states, or countries, and trade unions. An example of a stakeholder with indirect economic ties might be Finland and other downwind countries after the Chernobyl nuclear reactor disaster. The corporation might respond to a challenge from one of these constituent groups (or an individual) that has a stake in the corporation's policies and practices. An example is McDonald's corporation's change to the use of paper packaging from styrofoam packaging to reduce the amount of nonbiodegradable landfill waste.

Societal Viewpoint

The last view of CSR presented here goes a step further than that in the stakeholder viewpoint. Independent of whether there is an actual advocate or stakeholder challenging the corporation, this "ethics of care" stance suggests that the corporation would act in such a manner that outcomes would help to create a better world. As Bowen said in Schick, Wokutch, and Conners (1985), business people should make decisions that "are desirable in terms of the objectives and values of society." Organizations make these decisions and take subsequent actions voluntarily, not because of a challenge or coercion by a stakeholder group. These behaviors, therefore, are not engaged in because of a regulation, mandate, or economic self-interest.

Several authors have developed arguments to support the societal viewpoint of CSR. Freeman and Liedtka (1991) note that corporations are places in which both individuals and communities engage in caring activities that are aimed at mutual support and unparalleled human achievement. This has an impact on the origin of CSR activities. It is not a responsibility of a foundation or an individual. As they point out, "rather than distancing managers from their altruistic selves, as the focus on rights does, the ethics of care reaffirms the self and its link to others." Klonoski (1991, p.15) continues to say that the virtue ethics approach (like the ethics of care) "focuses not on principles or contracts but on the development of good, morally virtuous people.... Good people are making the decisions."

Resolution of the Models' Differences

The wish is for corporations to form social partnerships with various constituencies to allow social responsibility and business goals to be achieved together rather than sacrificing one for the other. In spite of attempts in the fundamentalist view to see corporations in isolation, they are part of the world community. Business cannot make decisions based on purely economic reasons because businesses are intermingled with the whole social system. Business decisions do have social consequences. The resolution to some differences between profit maximization and social responsibility perspectives is to look for places in which they are compatible. Hiring "differently abled" employees (Marriott, AT&T, and Pizza Hut), abating pollution (car companies, Union Carbide, and McDonald's), and investing in the public school system (American Express and IBM) may have the economic result of increased profits. The social result may be, for example, that people with a good environment and sound education make satisfied neighbors. Plus, additional positive exposure may result from an awareness of a corporation's expression of values (from their outcomes) that are congruent with the expectations and wishes of society. It is most likely in the organization's self-interest to link its outputs to society. As Brice and Wegner (1989, pp. 163, 164) point out, "There has been a growing awareness in the private sector that by improving the quality of life in the broader socio-political environment, business can enhance the climate for its future survival and growth."

Corporate social responsibility can provide benefits that extend beyond considerations of profit maximization, e.g., positive influence on policy makers; changing a company image; or creating a positive relationship with the press. Through an integrated strategy of controlled communication, selective community service, and direct context-sensitive access to policy makers, corporations can maximize the benefits they derive from the good they do. And, they can indeed be perceived as socially responsible (Manheim & Pratt, 1986, p. 18). However, take care to consider why your organization undertook this endeavor. L'Etang (1995, p. 126) and others suggest if corporations at the outset are motivated only by the self-interested desire to achieve publicity instead of a desire to do good, they are acting immorally (per Kant). This can mislead the public.

In these times of scarce financial resources, many organizations are contributing to the community in volunteer hours and effort. EDS, Questar Corp., Helene Curtis, and Pillsbury, among others, have found substantial benefits other than profit maximization for their CSR efforts (Caudron, 1994, pp. 13-18). These internal benefits include morale boosts, teamwork improvements, skill development for employees, and company pride.

We should consider a word of caution here. What may sometimes result when corporations have social responsibility as one of their goals is a focus on efficiency and short-term outcomes rather than dealing with real problems. Solutions may be simplistic and sanitary. For example, contributing money toward fixing Thanksgiving dinner at a homeless shelter may be a corporation's way of addressing the homeless issue instead of providing these citizens with jobs, necessary training, and affordable housing, as Days Inn has done. This kind of simplistic approach (dinner) may encourage compartmentalizing the CSR efforts into the functions of a person or foundation, rather than integrating them as a daily business practice.

A more adequate approach is to tie the CSR effort into the corporate strategy and have it permeate the whole organization as Freeman and Liedtka (1991) have proposed. There "must be a deliberate and conscious attempt by senior corporate executives to guide their corporations towards the formulation of specific objectives, strategies, and plans with respect to CSR. Thus, CSR program formulation must be an integral component of the strategic management process within an organization" (Brice & Wegner, 1989, p. 164).

Epstein (1987, p. 107) has combined attributes of business ethics, corporate social responsibility, and corporate social responsiveness into what he refers to as the corporate social policy process. This process, which incorporates many of the issues addressed in this chapter, is defined as follows:

Institutionalization within the corporation of processes facilitating value-based individual and organizational reflection and choice regarding the moral significance of personal and corporate action. Individual and collective examination of likely overall consequences of such actions, thereby enabling the firm's leaders both individually and collectively within the organizational setting to anticipate, respond to, and manage dynamically evolving claims and expectations of internal and external stakeholders concerning the products (specific issues or problem-related consequences) of organizational policies and behaviors.

Impact on Human Performance Systems

The institutionalization of CSR suggests that it would permeate managers' proactive and reactive use of performance systems. This discussion examines the impact of a CSR orientation on selected performance and illustrates the impact with real-world examples. Emphasized is the interplay of various tools and systems, especially strategic planning, recruitment, training, and human resources division areas, such as benefits and compensation.

Strategic Planning Plus

Strongly suggested earlier in the chapter is the potential impact of CSR on strategic planning. Consistent with the view of Kaufman (1991) is the view that planning (direction finding and goal setting) can incorporate the current and future good of society as a primary focus. This approach acknowledges that what is good for society is also good for the organization and its people. Kaufman (1991) in mega-planning, a part of his

Strategic Planning Plus model includes a society-as-client perspective. His proposed outside-in planning seeks first to identify outcomes, societal payoffs, and contributions as the basis for responsible and responsive planning. Examples of results and consequences that supersede individuals or organizations include preserving wetlands and halting erosion. To illustrate this, let's consider Control Data. Control Data has chosen to build factories in run-down areas. It has provided jobs and training to local minority residents. In addition, it has helped to improve the infrastructure and environment of its employees. Specifically, the company helped to revitalize transportation and to create affordable housing (Reder, 1995, p. 39). This is a corporation that has included society in its planning. Small businesses, such as Stonyfield Farm, have embraced this approach as well (Davidson, 1993, p. 59).

The society-as-client perspective found in mega-planning contrasts with the organization-as-client perspective found in macro-planning. The macro-planning approach is similar to the fundamentalist view of CSR. The organization's survival is the ultimate goal, with the emphasis on making the system itself more successful not necessarily on improving the well-being of stakeholders such as employees, the community, or even stockholders. Examples of outputs, the collected results an organization delivers outside itself, might include graduates, computers delivered, and production quotas met. Salaries, prestige, span of control over employees, and facilities acquisition drive this planning to ensure survival of the organization.

Sometimes referred to as "tactical" planning, micro-planning focuses on the individual or small group. Typical products (the building blocks of performance) of micro-planning might be passing a course or test, meeting an educational objective, and improving employee skill mastery in, for example, sales.

Note that, underneath it, mega-planning may have nested appropriate products and outputs to support the meeting of the desired outcomes of mega-planning. Neither of the other two would necessarily incorporate societal goals.

Other Performance Systems

The results and consequences in Strategic Planning Plus directly include benefits for society. However, internal workings of an organization can benefit society even if they were not initially intended to do so. Here we look at performance systems other than strategic planning.

It is common knowledge that the composition of the workforce is changing (Jamieson & O'Mara, 1991). The workforce is aging. More people with disabilities (referred to here as "differently abled") are working, many more women are employed, the number of working retirees is swelling, plus many other changes. This era has also seen a decline in the pool of younger workers available for entry-level jobs. The demand for skilled workers continues to be high. Job requirements have become more technical and have required more worker flexibility to accommodate the swift changes occurring in technology.

This environment increasingly has stretched our conventional approaches to filling positions. Creatively fulfilling our staffing requirements has required new approaches. Searching out appropriate, often untraditional candidates (recruitment and selection), appropriately matching candidates to jobs or "skilling" the workers, and providing employee support can be key to performance systems. Organizations might reconsider and perhaps modify their one-size-fits-all approaches to some performance systems, including compensation, benefits programs, reward options, recruiting and assessment, job evaluation and design, and training. Ironically, in the process the corporation may be acting socially responsibly by helping to produce employed, skilled workers from under-used populations, such as the homeless or mothers reentering the workforce. Let's look at some examples to see the interplay of the human performance systems. The payoff is not only there for society but also financially for the corporation.

Days Inn and Marriott Corporation are well-known for their corporate policies of hiring senior citizens, a practice which, for example, has decreased turnover (average stay of 3 years versus 1 year for non-seniors) resulting in less time spent on training new workers. To attract this nontraditional worker, these corporations decided to provide flexible work schedules, complete on-the-job training with small classes, scholarship programs for children and grandchildren, incentives, and bonuses appropriate for this group.

Large corporations like Days Inn, Marriott, AT&T, and Pizza Hut have similar programs for differently abled employees. Adaptations to accommodate the requirements of these employees are usually minimal (Navran, 1992, p. 31). They, too, are good corporate investments. They are generally loyal, with low absenteeism and good productivity. In addition to some environmental changes, they may require changes in training and more support, such as a job coach for a mentally retarded employee, which is usually supplied by the placing agency (Geber, 1990, p. 31).

Smaller companies, such as Informania, Inc., a San Francisco consulting firm focused on performance support systems, also choose to accommodate special requirements because of socially responsible corporate values. For example, Informania, after assessing the traits of a developmentally delayed person they wished to employ, created job requirements to match the employee's abilities. This approach can capitalize on the employee's abilities and pay off economically. The task in this and other cases in the new environment, according to Jay Jamrog (personal communication, 1991) of the Human Resources Institute, is to "screen in" people for jobs (not screen them out), train the new employee, or redesign the job. Again, this has implications for interaction among the performance systems of recruitment/selection, job design and description, training, employee support, supervision including feedback, and others.

Implications of the CSR Literature

All of the examples illustrate the CSR literature in action. Kaufman's mega-planning is a reflection of the societal viewpoint with an emphasis on incorporating results to benefit society into strategic planning. The Days Inn initiatives in hiring seniors, homeless, and differently abled employees were based on a balance of profit maximization and CSR. A spokesperson is quoted as saying, "In no case were these companies motivated by compassion or social justice." They were motivated by profitability and the availability of skilled workers. The company literature's discussion of Senior Power, an older worker job fair, notes that benefits include being able to tap talented seniors, attract local media attention, promote a favorable community image, generate strong business and sales contacts, and show an "I care" philosophy. Other corporations, such as Pizza Hut and the Marriott Corporation, have had similar positive results, encouraging them to reach out to underused sources of employees, thus providing benefits not only for the corporations, but also for the employee and society.

Suggestions For Making CSR Work

Integration and institutionalization of CSR mean that you can have an impact on your corporation more often than you might suspect. This job aid offers some thoughts for you to consider.

Corporate Social Responsibility Job Aid

For Top Management to Promote CSR

To Institutionalize CSR Values:

- Include in strategic planning (corporate values, mission, or vision).

- Focus on issues. Select tasks that are specific and of societal value.

- Integrate performance systems to address issues.

- Evaluate the impact.

- Stay committed.

To Provide Top-Down Support:

- Encourage; don't punish the risk-taker.

- Maximize flexibility in supervisory implementation of policies.

- Minimize directives about policies to allow individual interpretation to support organizational values.

- Provide support for initiatives to thrive.

- Build in incentives and accountability to support CSR objectives.

For Others to Promote CSR to Top Management

- Present CSR plan with corporately valued benefits, e.g., profits; positive community relations; improved morale; better skills.

- Demonstrate effectiveness or value on a small scale initially.

Jamieson and O'Mara (1991) and Jamrog (personal communication, 1991) have emphasized the importance of creativity and flexibility in managing in today's environment. To capitalize on scarce available human resources will require the integration of performance systems that are centered on addressing issues such as aging, gender, elder care, diversity, and disabilities.

Summary

We have examined three perspectives of corporate social responsibility: fundamentalist, stakeholder, and societal. We have considered how to reconcile profit orientation with socially responsible values that at times promote different results. We considered CSR applications involving human performance systems and their interactions among the systems. Lastly, we examined the impact that you can have in encouraging the value of social responsibility within your organization.

Social responsibility has a place in many areas within organizations. Individuals can start receptive organizations thinking about and acting on incorporating these CSR values in their processes and outcomes to benefit the individual, organization, and society now and in the future.

References

Brice, H., & Wegner, T. (1989, June). A quantitative approach to corporate social responsibility programme formulation. *Managerial and Decision Economics.*

Caudron, S. (1994, February 21). Volunteerism and the bottom line. *Industry Week.*

Davidson, J. (1993, February). Responsibility reaps rewards. *Small Business Reports.*

Epstein, E.M. (1987, Spring). The corporate social policy process. Beyond business ethics, corporate social responsibility, and corporate social responsiveness. *California Management Review.*

Freeman, R.E., & Liedtka, J. (1991, July/August). Corporate social responsibility: A critical approach. *Business Horizons.*

Geber, B. (1990, December). The disabled: Ready, willing and able. *Training.*

Jamieson, D., & O'Mara, J. (1991). *Managing workforce 2000: Gaining the diversity advantage.* San Francisco, CA: Jossey-Bass.

Kaufman, R. (1991). *Strategic planning plus: An organizational guide.* Glenview, IL: Scott Foresman.

Klonoski, R.J. (1991, July/August). Foundational considerations in the corporate social responsibility debate. *Business Horizons.*

Lee, D.R., & McKenzie, R.B. (1994, December). Corporate failure as a means to corporate responsibility. *Journal of Business Ethics.*

L'Etang, J. (1995, February). Ethical corporate social responsibility: A framework for managers. *Journal of Business Ethics.*

Manheim, J.B., & Pratt, C.B. (1986, Summer). Communicating corporate social responsibility. *Public Relations Review.*

Navran, F.J. (1992, July). Hiring trainers with disabilities. *Training.*

Reder, A. (1995, Winter). The wide world of corporate philanthropy. *Business and Society Review.*

Schick, A.G., Wokutch, R.E., & Conners, S.B. (1985, Spring). An integrating framework for the teaching and researching of corporate social responsibility. *Business and Society.*

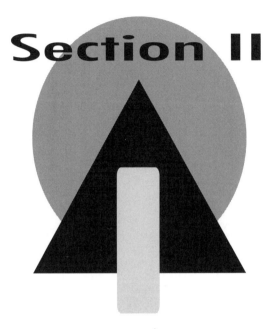

Section II

Direction Finding
and Goal Setting

A Strategic-Planning Framework: Mega Planning

Roger Kaufman

Introduction

Strategic planning has attracted the attention of serious per-formance improvement specialists and executives who want to ensure that the organization is doing things right as well as doing the right things (Drucker, 1973, 1993; Nanus, 1992). Strategic planning—deciding where to head and why—is essen-tial for any organization that must decide on what human, physical, and fiscal resources should be developed and used (Bryson, 1988; Kaufman, 1992, 1995a; Kaufman & Grise, 1995; Kaufman, Herman, & Watters, 1996; Nolan, Goodstein, & Pfeiffer 1993; Senge, 1990). Most organizations attempt strategic planning, but much of what gets done is closer to tac-tical and/or operational planning (Kaufman, 1992, 1995a, 1996). It fails to set a useful direction for the organization and, thus, provides faulty directions and intentions. If an organiza-tion does not have a useful direction, everything else that fol-lows will not be useful. Therefore, unfortunately, most strategic planning efforts have been longer on intentions than on useful results (Kaufman, 1992, 1996; Lloyd, 1992; Mintz-berg, 1994). Strategic planning, properly defined and accom-plished, provides the basic directions and rationale for determining where an organization should head and provides the specifications against which any organization may decide what to do and how to do it.

This chapter defines a basic framework for strategic planning[1]—a mega-planning focus—that better ensures that society, external clients, and organizational (internal) clients are well-served. This process identifies ways to provide a rational database for defining purposes and interventions, including responsive and responsible programs, projects, activities, and products. It is pragmatic and practical, but it presents a paradigm shift (Barker, 1989, 1992, 1993) that will challenge the "comfort zone" of many who would rather continue to operate conventionally regardless of the risks. The central focus of mega-planning is adding value through the organization to society.

Strategic planning, in its most powerful use, identifies measurable results based on an "ideal vision." The type of world we want and are willing to help create for and with the future generation becomes the basis for linked achievements at three levels: societal, organizational, and individual/small group (Kaufman, 1996).

Conventional strategic and performance improvement planners often are apprehensive in addressing societal outcomes and usually ignore or assume them. In such instances, so-called strategic planning actually stops at short-term, stop-gap objectives, and a practical and useful strategic plan is never developed (Kaufman, 1995b, 1996; Mintzberg, 1994). Instead of defining—in measurable performance terms—an ideal vision of the world in which we want the future generation to live, attention is immediately diverted to products, services, departments, and activities with the blind assump-

---

[1] Because of its characteristics, it allows the integration of other performance improvement processes, such as quality management, benchmarking, and reengineering, which, when used alone, may stop short of being as powerful as possible.

tion that socially useful results will follow.[2] Effective strategic planning depends on people being able to enlarge—even shift—their paradigms. This is so important that it forms strategic planning's first critical success factor:

Critical Success Factor #1: Shift your paradigm about organizations to one which is larger and more inclusive—think globally as you act locally.

The mega-level focus on society—defining and continuously improving the kind of society we want for tomorrow's children as the primary client and beneficiary—is obtaining increasing support (Drucker, 1992, 1993, 1994, 1995; Kaufman, 1972, 1988, 1992, 1995a, 1996; Kaufman, Herman, & Watters, 1996; Popcorn, 1991; Senge, 1990). This future-oriented societal focus provides the second critical success factor:

Critical Success Factor #2: Link all planning, development, implementation, and evaluation to societal requirements and payoffs—to the mega level and ideal vision. Don't restrict your ideal vision to the organization itself.

Defining an organization's mission without linking it to social consequences and payoffs denies that the organization must make a positive contribution to its external clients as well as society to be successful.[3] Organizations are only possible means to societal ends. An organization (or indeed nation) that is not a "good neighbor" has gloomy prospects for the future.

---

[2] Recent attention is growing concerning why executives "can't" learn and continue to use the same thinking that brought them previous success even though the world has changed and there are new realities for which old paradigms are destructive (Argyris, 1991; Barker, 1992, 1993; Martin, 1993). This unwillingness to change even though the realities dictate change provides one of the basic challenges to new approaches to strategic planning such as this (Barker, 1992, 1993; Martin, 1993).

[3] This is a weakness that is usually missed and might account for Mintzberg's (1994) critique, although he seems to also miss this point and societal referent.

Because practical planning, management, and evaluation[4] depend on defining the right destination in the first place, let's turn to strategic planning and what is called Strategic Planning Plus, or SP+.

A Strategic Planning Framework[5]

The strategic planning process for defining useful objectives and linking them with tactics is applicable to all organizations —public and private—that intend to define and deliver useful contributions. It also provides the basis on which to define and justify programs, projects, and operations at all levels.

This strategic planning framework has a number of steps (see Figure 1), starting with the decision concerning the primary focus or frame of reference: who is to be the primary client and beneficiary of what gets planned and delivered. The framework has three major clusters:

- Scoping

- Planning

- Implementation and Continuous Improvement (Evaluation)

There are three possible client groups that planners might select: (1) the community and society that the organization serves, (2) the organization itself, and (3) individuals or

---

[4] Although "evaluation" is the more recognized term, I use it more in the quality-management sense of "continuous improvement." Evaluation identifies the gaps between accomplishments and intentions; continuous improvement takes those data and finds ways to close the gaps.

[5] Based on Kaufman, 1972, 1992, 1995a, 1996; Kaufman & Grise, 1995; Kaufman, Herman, & Watters, 1996.

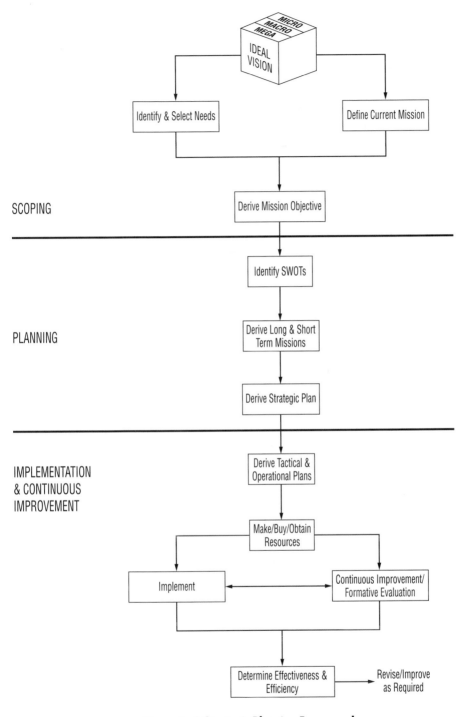

Figure 1. A Strategic Planning Framework

small groups (such as desired competencies of associates or supplier relations). *Practical* strategic planning targets the current and future well-being of one's community and society as the primary client. If your organization does not intend to make a direct and positive contribution to society, just what does it have in mind?

By first defining desired societal payoffs—such as healthy, self-sufficient, and self-reliant citizens, safe environment, businesses that legally and ethically prosper—sensible organizational and operational decisions may be made and justified. The safest and most practical point at which to start strategic planning is at the mega level; after all, there is life after the delivery of your organization's outputs to your clients.

Any strategic plan has to have a tangible and useful purpose. The questions any organization can (and should) address are listed in Table 1.

Table 1. Basic Questions an Organization Should Ask and Answer

QUESTIONS	LEVEL OF PLANNING	ORGANIZATIONAL ELEMENT
1. Do you commit to the delivery of outputs that have a positive and desired impact on what your organization contributes to society?	Mega	Outcome
2. Do you commit to providing the required and desired quality of what your organization delivers to external clients?	Macro	Output
3. Do you commit to providing the required quality of what your organization delivers to internal clients?	Micro	Product
4. Do you commit to providing the required efficiency of the programs, projects, and activities used by your organization?	Operations	Process

5. Do you commit to providing the required quality and appropriateness of the human, capital, and physical resources available to your organization?	Resources	Input
6. Do you commit to providing and reporting the required a. value and worth of your methods and procedures; b. achievement of your identified and accomplished objectives?	Evaluation and Continuous Improvement	Evaluation and Continuous Improvement

Based on Kaufman, 1992, 1995a, 1996.

When strategic planning starts at the mega level and includes the macro and micro levels (as defined in Table 1), there will be a linking of and synergy among all the elements, actions, and activities of the organization. This approach avoids a linear, lock-step, and narrow approach in favor of a dynamic human-centered process, which is built on synergy among levels. Table 2 shows the relationship among levels of planning, the type of person who champions each level, and the result each delivers. Note that under this definition, anyone may be a leader.

Table 2. Relationships Among Levels of Planning and the Results

LEVEL OF PLANNING	TYPE OF SPONSOR	TYPE OF RESULT
Mega	Leader[1]	Outcome
Macro	Executive	Output
Micro	Supervisor/Manager	Product

[1] "Leader" as used here requires a formal consideration of the payoffs and usefulness of what the organization contributes to society. This use seems to be compatible with Block's (1993) term "stewardship." However, Block seems to be most concerned with the macro level. I am extending his definition of steward to make certain it encompasses the mega level.

The use and linking of these three levels of results form the third critical success factor:

Critical Success Factor #3: Use and link all three levels of planning (mega, macro, micro) and the three related levels of results (outcomes, outputs, products).

Mega-level planning incorporates micro and macro planning. When selected, the three types of planning are aligned and integrated, and we increase the likelihood of achieving organizational success. When the mega level is included in strategic planning, it becomes Strategic Planning Plus (Kaufman, 1992, 1996).

A Focus on Results, Consequences, and Payoffs

This strategic planning framework is results-based and results-centered. Confusing means (how) and ends (what) has profound implications for success, or lack of it. When resources and methods (collectively called means) are selected before relating them to the results, one risks jumping to solutions before knowing the problems and opportunities.

Ends are results, accomplishments, and consequences. Means are the ways and resources to deliver ends. When one selects a means (TQM, CAD/CAM, etc.) before knowing the ends, the results are most always disappointing and expensive.

The ends/means distinction is so important that it is the fourth critical success factor:

Critical Success Factor #4: Distinguish between ends and means (between what and how).

Strategic Planning Plus Framework and Descriptions of the Basics

Each of the three phases and associated elements of SP+ (Figure 1) is described as follows.

Scoping

Select the scope of strategic planning from among three alternatives. Select the mega level (the safest option) from the three types based on who is to be the primary client and who benefits from what is planned and delivered: mega, macro, or micro. The mega-level option includes the macro and micro. When you select mega, the others automatically follow.

If you—and all your planning partners—don't select the mega level, you are assuming that positive societal consequences will flow. Failure to formally select and target the mega level leaves the organization and everyone in it vulnerable to legitimate claims of selecting means and resources that cannot be justified. It is the mega-level focus that gives rise to the label *"Strategic Planning Plus"* (SP+), which is unique in strategic planning approaches (Kaufman, 1992, 1996), although more experts are calling attention to the importance of a societal-payoff focus (Drucker, 1992, 1993, 1994, 1995; Popcorn, 1991; Senge, 1990).

The mega level is the most pragmatic choice because our organizations are means to societal ends. If an organization does not provide external clients with safe, cost-effective, and cost-efficient outputs so that they will be satisfied, successful, and self-sustaining today and tomorrow, everyone's future is threatened (Marshall & Tucker, 1992; Naisbitt & Aburdene, 1990; Toffler, 1990). The current strident demands on public and private sector organizations to be responsive and responsible signal that we must improve the extent to which we are making useful societal contributions.

Basic to selection of the mega level is the development of a *shared* ideal vision (see Kaufman, 1996, for a sample), which is an integral part of the first phase of strategic planning: the *scoping* process. The ideal vision defines the mega-level choice and commitment. Strategic planning is long-range planning. At the scoping step, the planning partners identify

---

and define "what should be" and "what could be" in an ideal society.

1. Define the Ideal Vision

It is important to set an ideal vision *before* restricting oneself with "real-world" data. The ideal vision should be developed by all people who are involved, internally and externally, with the organization.[6] It is not a task for the board of directors, the founder, or the CEO because their vision might not be "our" vision. Ownership is obtained from being active participants in defining and realizing the vision.

An ideal vision should be related to contributions, not to procedures, resources, or methods. It defines ends, not means. If we want a world where there is peace from armed hostilities, no deaths from illegal drugs, no requirement for welfare, no crime, and where there are no diseases that cause disability or loss of life, those should form the ideal vision. Issues of "practicality" should not be considered here.

An ideal vision should not be avoided because "we can't do *everything* in our society, and we cannot control everything in the world." An ideal vision forms a basic framework for any organization through its partnership with its associates, community members, governments, regulatory agencies, and business. The partners will select the part of the total vision that they will commit to deliver.

By first identifying an ideal vision and selecting its contribution to the vision, an organization can also identify other

---

[6] Peter Block, in *Stewardship*, (1993) identifies the risks of letting the "patriarch" (or boss, or leader) define the organization's purpose. He proposes a shift from "leadership" (someone else tells us what to do and we follow) and "stewardship," which involves a shared commitment to a worthy future. Developing a shared ideal vision may be a tool for providing stewardship and extending Block's definition by adding the "plus" of becoming active stewards for the organization and our shared world.

agencies and agents and what each will contribute to the total. Thus, synergies among and between societal partners are identified and delivered. It is an essential ingredient in creating the future, not reacting to it.

An ideal vision is stated in terms of measurable performance. We might not achieve it in our lifetime, but we must set our compass to that destination. The selection of the primary organizational mission (based on the ideal vision) is a commitment to a future and discourages drifting in the same direction the organization or current operations are heading.

What about beliefs, values, and wishes? They all drive the ways in which partners will address the strategic planning process. Usually, without questioning private frames of reference and biases, people apply existing paradigms in dealing with their life, associates, clients, competitors, families, neighbors, and, thus, planning. Beliefs and values are strongly held and unexamined and commonly focus on means and resources. (Some people call these their "philosophy" or "core values.")

Deriving an ideal vision allows the partners *in the context of future societal good* to compare their beliefs and values with the ideal vision. The success of the entire strategic planning process might hinge on the planning partners' ability to consider new outlooks and/or basic beliefs about people, prejudice, business, government, health, and what the organization should accomplish.

Unfortunately, many popular approaches to strategic planning start with harvesting and using the partners' beliefs and values with the naive view that "everyone's values are important and should be included." There are people who seek to have others shoulder a disproportionate share of contribution and demand rights without appropriate responsibilities. When one begins strategic planning with "naked" beliefs and values, processes, interventions, or programs, the means (such as "profits are evil," "setting objectives is too rigid," "computers are dehumanizing," or "pay is the primary motivator") are imposed before the useful ends are identified and justified. Thus, organizations head off prematurely to work with solutions that do not adequately meet the problems and opportunities.

It is imperative that both the ideal vision and the mission objective focus only on results, or ends, and are in measurable performance terms (Critical Success Factors #4 and #5) and that it all is based on outside-the-organization payoffs and consequences. Much of the deserved critique of so-called strategic planning (Adams, 1996; Mintzberg, 1994; Watkins, Triner,& Kaufman, 1996; Kaufman & Watkins, 1996) can be traced to (a) not having a primary focus on the mega level of results and payoffs; (b) including means, processes, and favored solutions (means) as part of the vision and/or mission; and (c) confusing *strategic planning*—where one may identify new objectives as well as delete existing ones—with *tactical planning*—identifying and selecting possible ways and means to meet accepted objectives—and *operational planning*— keeping eveything on track.

An ideal vision, which is cooperatively derived and shared, will allow partners to revise their current beliefs and values. Be patient and allow the planning partners to grow, develop, and change. The results will pay handsomely in terms of what the organization will be able to develop and contribute to our clients, shared communities, and society.

2. Identify and Define the Current Mission

While doing steps 1 and 3 (which follows) the current mission is obtained and, as is usually necessary, rewritten in terms of results. These revisions include developing measurable indicators of "where we are headed" and "what criteria will allow us to certify when we have arrived." Objectives should be related to results and target ends, never means.

Writing all objectives in terms of results is the fifth critical success factor:

Critical Success Factor #5: Prepare all objectives—including mission objectives—in terms of results. Never include methods, resources, how-to-do-its, or processes in any objective.

3. Identify Needs

Defining a need as a gap in results,[7] and employing both performance and perceptions data, the gaps between current results and desired results are identified (starting with gaps for the ideal vision). (In step 6, we will use this to identify needs in closer years, such as year 2010, 2000, 1998).

The importance of conducting a needs assessment—identifying and prioritizing needs—that defines "need" as a gap between current and desired results is fundamental. To do otherwise allows means and resources to be selected without justifying them on the basis of getting from current results, payoffs, and consequences to desired ones.[8]

This definition of "need" is so vital that it is the sixth critical success factor:

Critical Success Factor #6: Define "need" as a gap between current and desired results, never as a gap in inputs and/or processes.

Many so-called needs assessments are wish-lists or solutions assessments. For example, "training needs assessments" often assume that the solution will be training activities. This locks everyone into defining training requirements

---

[7] The importance of defining a need as a gap between current and desired results cannot be overemphasized. It can mean the difference between success and failure.

[8] Note that this is a variation of Critical Success Factor #4, which urges that ends and means not be blurred.

before defining gaps in results for associates, organization, clients, and society to which training could or could not be responsive.[9]

Needs are prioritized on the basis of "what you give as compared to what you get." A needs assessment allows a decision to be made on the basis of what it costs to meet a need versus what it costs to ignore it. For example, what were the economic and social costs of not desegregating in the United States after the Civil War? What does it cost the nation to continue to have very low birth-weight babies? What did it cost a major baby food company not to recall some defective products, rather than "toughing it out" with quality control data, which impressed very few mothers?

A bonus of using "need" as a gap in results is that it provides the basic criteria for evaluation. In comparing intentions with accomplishments, the "what should be" criteria are used for evaluation. Thus, one does not have to develop an independent evaluation process but uses the "what should be" criteria directly from the statement of need.

4. Identify the Primary Mission Objective

At this fourth step, the primary[10] mission objective (including detailed performance criteria) is derived. It is based on the part of the ideal vision the organization commits to deliver and to continuously move toward. The mission objective serves as

---

[9] The term "training requirements analysis" is more appropriate than "training needs assessment." If a need is a gap in results, and training is a means, not an end, the term "training needs assessment" is an oxymoron.

[10] I introduce the term "primary" mission objective for this initial and over-arching mission objective. The reason for the term "primary" is to distinguish it from derivative mission objectives, which identify organizational purposes between the closest-in mission to the primary one.

the basic direction in which the organization will head. It states the macro-level results (outputs) to be delivered.

The primary mission objective[11] is derived from the ideal vision and the needs identified and selected at that primary level and is stated in performance terms. When the needs have been identified at the ideal-vision level, the planning partners estimate the costs versus consequences for meeting and not meeting the needs. From that, the planners identify those elements of the ideal vision it commits to deliver.

Thus, the primary mission objective is based on (a) the selection of, and commitment to, the mega level for strategic planning, (b) the derivation of a results-referenced ideal vision (including reconciled beliefs and values), (c) identified needs, (d) costs/consequences estimations based on what it costs to meet and what it costs not to meet the needs (cost being financial and social), (e) the elements of the ideal vision the organization commits to deliver, and (f) the existing mission (which usually has been transformed into measurable performance terms).

If an organization selects a mission objective that is not derived from the mega/ideal-vision level, it severely risks the entire enterprise. If you do not intend to contribute to getting continually closer to the ideal vision, what are your intentions? Are you willing to risk the future of an entire organization that does not contribute to creating a better world?

The primary mission objective is based on a comparison of current intentions (the results-defined current mission) and desired results (based on the ideal vision and meeting priority needs) to define what it will take to get from "what is" to "what should be," or from current results to desired ones.

---

[11] The term "primary mission objective" is used only to emphasize that it is the basic one from which all other mission objectives (for years between now and this primary one) derive and relate.

A primary mission objective identifies the measurable destination on an interval or ratio scale.[12] A mission statement identifies destination intentions that are measurable only on a nominal or ordinal scale:

mission statement + interval/ratio scale criteria =
mission objective

The skills of preparing measurable performance indicators and writing mission objectives in terms of results at the appropriate (and selected) level are key (Mager, 1975; Kaufman, 1992, 1996; and Kaufman, Rojas, & Mayer, 1993).

Planning

The products from scoping provide the basis for building the strategic plan.

5. Identify Strengths, Weaknesses, Opportunities, and Threats (SWOTs)

Unearthing the organization's Strengths, Weaknesses, Opportunities, and Threats (SWOTs) is accomplished and analyzed, usually through internal and external scanning (Kaufman, Herman, & Watters, 1996; Kaufman, 1995a) of the inside- and the outside-organization environments. Scanning should include objective appraisals of the SWOTs. It is counterproductive to lie on your own analysis or fail to recognize that old ways and means—frames of reference and organizational

---

[12] S.S. Stevens (1951) identified four scales of measurement: Nominal (naming), Ordinal (greater than, less than, or equal to), Interval (equal scale distances with arbitrary zero point) and Ratio (equal scale distances with known zero point). Interval and Ratio measures are more reliable than Nominal or Ordinal. Under these definitions, *everything* is measurable (Kaufman, 1992 & 1996).

approaches and climates—might be antagonistic to current and future realities (Argyris, 1991; Barker, 1989, 1992, 1993; Martin, 1993). Future trends as well as opportunities are identified and documented at this step, such as those identified by Naisbitt and Aburdene (1990) and Toffler (1990). While many are tempted to only examine weaknesses and threats, this step allows the identification of possibilities that might otherwise remain obscured (Kaufman, 1992).

Even though some conventional strategic planning approaches start at this level, it seems difficult to understand how an organization can sensibly identify SWOTs without knowing what its mission is. The determination of SWOTs provides the "realism" to the strategic planning process.

6. Identify Long- and Short-Term Mission(s)

Based on the shared ideal vision, identified needs, the primary mission objective, and the SWOTS, select the "building-block" (long- and short-term destinations) mission objectives. These linked, en route mission objectives—from the year 2010 to 2005, from 2000 to next year—contain the measurable specifications for the organization in terms of its outputs— what skills, knowledge, attitudes, and abilities learners will have when they leave the system. These long- and short-term missions build a bridge between current results and the achievement of the primary mission objective.

These "building-block" mission objectives are based on trend data and what is currently known and possible. The SWOTs information provides a database for determining the long- and short-term missions. They are written in measurable performance terms, as are all objectives. The ideal vision and the related "results ladder," which defines intended accomplishments from today toward the ideal, provide the basis for the continuous improvement of the system and its components (Kaufman & Zahn, 1993).

The primary mission objective (derived in step 4), based on the ideal vision, and the building-block missions identify the results that the organization commits to deliver. Also, the mission objectives provide the criteria for en route missions, which will bridge from this year to that future. This step identifies a measurable objective, which is a clear statement of "where we are headed" plus "what criteria we will use to know when we have arrived," for close-in and distant destinations.

7. Develop the Strategic Plan

Based on the products from the strategic planning elements 1, 2, 3, 4, and 5, the product of this step is answering the key questions: What? How? Who? When? Why? Where? (Kaufman & Grise, 1995).

Reconciling differences among the planning partners might have to be done here once again. It is imperative that the strategic plan be based on the ideal vision, identified needs, the primary mission objective, and the associated long- and short-term missions. Every part of the plan must be selected on the basis of the contribution to the missions and ideal vision.

When disagreements occur, they are usually over means and not ends. The products of steps 1 to 5 provide the common ground: results to be achieved. Use the previous data and information to negotiate to do what is right, not just what is acceptable.

At this step, the planning partners might have to go back and collect new and different data from the statement of the ideal vision and needs, as compared with the existing mission. A continuous emphasis on the relationship between ends and means is vital. While it is tempting to be "politic" or "diplomatic" at this point and move ahead even with some means and resources instead of ends, doing so is an invitation to failure. Ends provide the only rational basis for identifying and selecting means. To allow any group to dictate a means, resource, or process before identifying and justifying the needs it will reduce or eliminate is to risk disenfranchising clients and stakeholders—those who deserve the most effective and efficient system possible.

Operational, or en route, milestone results—called functions—for implementation are set, along with the identification and subsequent selection (from alternatives) of the tactics and approaches (methods-means) to be used. The functions may be arrayed to form a management plan—called a mission profile—that identifies the results to be accomplished and the order in which they should be completed.

Strategic plans should not be long nor complex. No more that ten pages is a good length for most organizations. Tactics and operational plans, which should be based on the strategic plans, best form a separate document. These also usually contain budgets, personnel and resource requirements.

Implementation and Continuous Improvement (Evaluation)

8. Put the Strategic Plan to Work

The activities and results of this last step include:

- Developing a tactical plan: defining and selecting the best ways and means to deliver the results required in the strategic plan. The tactical plan includes the specifications for designing methods, means, and resources; justifying what is to be accomplished and how it will be done on a costs/results basis. During this step, you may identify what should be delivered through your organization as compared with other interventions and other delivery agencies (such as job aids, job redesign, assignment, hiring, training, a current competitor, etc.) as well as consider alternative tools and techniques.

- Developing an operational plan. The tactical plan identifies the steps for the how-to-do-its, including the development of timelines for accomplishing each product and delivering it where and when it has to be there. The operational plan (a) defines the details of getting all of the tactics (methods-means) delivered including the developing (or acquiring) of the resources, (b) implementing what has been planned, (c) conducting formative evaluation, and (d) revising as required while implementation is being carried out.

- Implementation: putting the plans to work and tracking progress to change what is not working and continue what is. Quality management (Deming, 1986; Dick & Johnson, 1993; Joiner, 1986; Juran, 1988; Kaufman, 1991; Kaufman & Zahn, 1993) provides the process for continuous improvement to deliver useful results. When used consistently and properly, exceptional results occur.

It takes commitment to get to these implementation and continuous improvement elements—completing all of the previous steps in this strategic planning framework—but now all of the requirements are justified on the basis of:

1. An ideal vision, which defines in measurable terms the world for tomorrow's children;

2. Gaps in results (needs);

3. Priority needs to be reduced or eliminated;

4. Mission objectives, which identify the results to be accomplished to get from current results to the achievement of the ideal vision;

5. Measurable performance specifications for functions (building-block results) against which alternative

methods-means (including curriculum and instruction) may be considered and selected on the basis of a costs/consequences analysis.

This last SP+ phase includes summative evaluation where purposes (objectives) are compared with results. Based on the evaluation—comparing results with intentions—decisions are made about what to continue and what requires revision. In addition, the evaluation/continuous improvement criteria are directly taken from the "what should be" portion of the needs assessment.

Strategic planning is a continual process. It is a way of thinking and a tool for deriving a formal plan. By taking a mega perspective, the linkages will be:

Current and Future Societal + Community Well-Being

↕

Strategic Plan Objectives

↕

Delivery Unit (e.g., Marketing, Health Services) Objectives

↕

Training, Methods, HRD Procedures: Interventions

↕

Resources

↕

Implementation

↕

Evaluation and Continuous Improvement

Implementing Strategic Planning Plus (Sp+)

Following are the steps for a proactive and holistic SP+ activity:

1. Obtain partner's commitment to mega-level strategic planning.

2. Obtain planning-team commitment.

3. Develop or ratify a shared ideal (mega-level) vision. The planning partners will have the opportunity to clarify values and might change their beliefs and values, including those related to change itself, one's self, and others.

4. Transform an existing mission statement to a mission objective (where the system is headed and how to measure success).

5. Identify needs (gaps in results) through comparing the ideal vision with current results and consequences.

6. Prepare a primary mission objective for the entire organization.

7. Identify SWOTs through internal and external scanning.

8. Prepare "building-block" mission objectives for distant and closer-in results to be achieved in specified years to move continuously closer to the primary mission and the ideal vision.

9. Derive functions and specific performance indicators required to meet the mission objective.

10. Identify roles for accomplishing the products of 6, 8, and 9.

11. Identify and select ways and means to accomplish 6, 8, and 9, including costs/results-costs-consequences analyses.

12. Manage implementation, including a serious and consistent continuous improvement process.

13. Determine met and unmet objectives based on the needs met, and those still unmet, and revise/continuously improve as required.

Linking Strategic Plans to Operations

Because everything an organization uses, does, produces, and delivers should be vertically integrated through the micro, macro, and mega levels, the following internal actions are suggested. These steps should be applied after the selection of an ideal vision along with an associated primary mission objective, which clearly details those parts of the ideal vision the system is willing to help achieve:

1. Conduct a needs assessment—identifying and prioritizing gaps between current results and desired ones— and place the needs in priority order. The needs assessment best begins at the mega level. A needs assessment may be completed, in turn, for the macro and micro levels.

2. Develop strategic objectives at the mega (societal) level and then for the macro (organizational) and micro (individual employee/learner) levels.

3. Devise and implement a continuous improvement monitoring procedure to maintain and improve the qualitative level desired by ensuring that what is to be

produced is what is actually produced, and what is assessed and continuously improved is data-based. The objectives are the "what should be" dimensions of the needs selected for closure, including the measurable performance standards that form the objectives.

4. Ensure vertical and horizontal articulation of what is planned, taught, and learned so that the mega, macro, and micro levels are achieved.

5. Institute a quality management process that ensures continuous improvement of the entire system as it moves constantly toward the mission objective and the ideal vision.

6. Design and develop processes, tools, procedures, and methods that will efficiently and effectively deliver quality results. The methods and techniques of systems design and development are invaluable for this. This is the step in which HRD, training, and development methods and means are produced based on the contributions each will make to the higher levels of results.

7. Consider the use of technologically driven methods to ensure efficient delivery and continuous improvement.

8. Model, with our methods and procedures, what we want our associates to master and apply.

9. Implement and conduct formative (en route) evaluation, changing what is not successful and continuing that which is. A "quality system," which includes useful and valid data for decision making, is imperative. Provide modified methods and means, where what is being used has not been effective.

10. Evaluate the effectiveness and efficiency of the methods, means, and processes and decide what to change and what to continue.

11. Revise as required; continuously improve as you move toward your mission objective and the ideal vision.

Mistakes Made by Strategic Planners

Here are the most frequent mistakes strategic planners commit. Avoiding them could mean the difference between just another document, which gathers dust, and a revitalized and continuously improving organization.

1. Plan at the department, section, or program level, not at the mega level. Increasingly, organizations are chartered to provide quality and cost-effective outputs, which will allow all to be successful in an ever-changing world. Our organizations will be responsive[13] and responsible, or they will cease to exist. If we don't define future societal success and realities, we are assuming that what we do will be useful. How successful is our current organization? Can it be patched and mended by adding a process here, tougher requirements there? All three levels of results (mega, macro, and micro) must be integrated.

2. Prepare objectives in terms of means, not results. Objectives tell us where to head and how to know when we have arrived. If we only set our sights on processes (hold quality meetings, buy new equipment) or resources (higher spending) we put the methods cart before the expected-results horse. Objectives must identify ends, not means and/or resources.

---

[13] It is important to realize that new opportunities may be identified and pursued.

3. Develop a plan without the contributions and cooperation of representative organizational and external partners. While a plan will be put together more quickly by a small group, the product likely will not be accepted by others who don't feel they contributed. Besides, partners who actually develop the plan will be able to contribute to it and make it better, more representative, and, thus, adoptable.

4. Select solutions before identifying destinations. Just about every group has a favorite solution or quick-fix. Resist picking a solution (or resource) until you know where you are headed and why. Often, ineffective HRD and training initiatives are selected without previous steps and relation to the mega-level strategic plan. Doing so risks interventions that are not successful.

5. Set objectives based solely on the perceptions of the planning partners, not also anchored in performance realities. While people know what they want, they don't often know what they should have. They also don't know much about gaps between current results and required ones. Provide planning partners with the realities of future trends, opportunities, and consequences. By starting with the collection of "core values," you risk being prematurely locked in to old frames of reference, which are not functional in today and tomorrow's world. By starting with the development of an ideal vision, you allow the partners to grow, develop, and change.

6. Define and identify needs as gaps in resources, methods, or techniques. When "need" is used as a verb (we "need more money," "we need less money," "we need more technology," "we need training," etc.), you select solutions that really aren't responsive to the basic problems. If you first identify gaps between current results and desired ones (needs), you are free to select the most efficient and effective ways to meet the needs.

7. Skip some of the steps of strategic planning. While there are a number of steps, leaving out even one will diminish the quality and usefulness of the plan. Review the model (Figure 1) and the questions (Table 1). Which steps and questions can really be omitted?

8. Assume that all strategic planning approaches are basically the same, and/or are nothing but common sense/intuition. All models are not the same. Most are reactive *and* start at too low a level; they attempt to improve efficiency or increase worker skills rather than turn out deliverables that will be useful and appropriate. If intuition were sufficient, your organization would be wonderful as it is.

9. Develop training programs on the basis of producing efficient delivery without questioning the validity and usefulness of the learning objectives. Many current organizational improvement initiatives assume that the current objectives are correct and useful, and go directly to improving the efficiency of delivery and production. Efficient is not the same as effective.

10. Fail to integrate strategic planning with other improvement initiatives such as quality management, needs assessment, benchmarking, and reengineering. While most organizations are appropriately moving into strategic planning and quality management (or total quality management), they are splintering efforts instead of integrating them. Quality management and strategic planning use the same databases and also must involve all partners in their pursuit and accomplishment.

Benchmarking and reengineering (Hammer & Champy 1993; Hammer & Stanton, 1995) can be powerful and also deceptive (Kaufman & Swart, 1995). If one is benchmarking another organization, it is vital to ensure first that the other organization has the right objectives (doing the right thing) and is doing things right; your organization cannot leap over the competition and create a new reality (Hamel & Prahalad,

1994). Too often, benchmarking and reengineering do not first link to the mega level and result in improving a process, operation, or an organization that is not a solution to a current or future problem or opportunity.

Summary

Strategic planning (and thinking) ensures that useful and justifiable missions, values, and needs are identified, reconciled, and used in selecting strategies and tactics. Built on societally useful (mega-level) objectives, an appropriate, useful, and valid strategic plan may be fashioned.

There are critical differences and relationships among mega, macro, and micro levels of planning. They differ in terms of the primary client and beneficiary of what is planned and delivered. We identify a generic process for strategic planning for any organization that intends to help fashion a better world and design the organizational and associated performance system that can help make it a reality.

Improvement should be based on the results of a valid and useful strategic plan. Strategic objectives should drive operational objectives, and these, in turn, should be used to develop detailed objectives and related methods and means for delivery. Using strategic thinking and planning, we can have strategy-driven budgets, not the conventional-wisdom budget-driven strategies.

Organizations and their partners can choose to both think and plan strategically. Much of our society's economic and physical health, survival, and future well-being depend on this conscious and conscientious choice.

References

Adams, S. (1996). *The Dilbert principle: A cubicle's-eye view of bosses, meetings, management fads & other workplace afflictions.* New York: HarperBusiness.

Argyris, C. (1991, May-June). Teaching smart people to learn. *Harvard Business Review.*

Barker, J.A. (1989). *The business of paradigms: Discovering the future* (videotape). Burnsville, MN: ChartHouse Learning.

Barker, J.A. (1992). *Future edge: Discovering the new paradigms of success.* New York: William Morrow.

Barker, J.A. (1993). *Paradigm pioneers: Discovering the future* (videotape). Burnsville, MN: ChartHouse Learning.

Block, P. (1993). *Stewardship.* San Francisco, CA: Berrett-Koehler.

Bryson, J.M. (1988). *Strategic planning for public and nonprofit organizations.* San Francisco, CA: Jossey-Bass.

Deming, W.E. (1986). *Out of the crisis.* Cambridge, MA: Massachusetts Institute of Technology, Center for Advanced Engineering Technology.

Dick, W., & Johnson, F.C. (Eds.). (1993). Special issue on quality systems in performance improvement. *Performance Improvement Quarterly, 6*(3).

Drucker, P.F. (1973). *Management: Tasks, responsibilities, practices.* New York: Harper & Row.

Drucker, P.F. (1992, September-October). The new society of organizations. *Harvard Business Review,* pp. 95-104.

Drucker, P.F. (1993). *Post-capitalist society.* New York: HarperBusiness.

Drucker, P.F. (1994, November). The age of social transformation. *The Atlantic Monthly,* pp. 53-80.

Drucker, P.F. (1995, February). Really reinventing government. *The Atlantic Monthly,* pp. 49-61.

Hamel, G., & Prahalad, C.K. (1994). *Competing for the future: Breakthrough strategies for seizing control of your industry and creating the markets of tomorrow.* Boston, MA: Harvard Business School Press.

Hammer, M., & Champy, J. (1993). *Reengineering the corporation: A manifesto for business revolution.* New York: HarperBusiness.

Hammer, M., & Stanton, S.A. (1995). *The reengineering revolution: A handbook.* New York: HarperCollins.

Joiner, B.L. (1986, May). Using statisticians to help transform industry in America. *Quality Progress,* pp. 46-50.

Juran, J.M. (1988). *Juran on planning for quality.* New York: The Free Press.

Kaufman, R.A. (1972). *Educational system planning.* Englewood Cliffs, NJ: Prentice-Hall.

Kaufman, R. (1988). *Planning educational systems: A results-based approach.* Lancaster, PA: Technomic.

Kaufman, R. (1991, December). Toward total quality "plus." *Training.*

Kaufman, R. (1992). *Strategic planning plus: An organizational guide* (rev.). Newbury Park, CA: Sage.

Kaufman, R. (1993, October). Mega planning: The argument is over. *Performance & Instruction.*

Kaufman, R. (1995a). *Mapping educational success* (rev.). Thousand Oaks, CA: Corwin Press.

Kaufman, R. (1995b, November-December). Mega planning: The changed realities. Part 1. *Performance & Instruction.*

Kaufman, R. (1996). *Strategic thinking: Identifying and solving problems.* Washington, DC: International Society for Performance Improvment / Alexandria, VA: American Society for Training and Development.

Kaufman, R., & Grise, P. (1995). *How to audit your strategic plan: Making good education better.* Thousand Oaks, CA: Corwin Press.

Kaufman, R., Herman, J., & Watters, K. (1996). *Educational planning: Strategic, operational, tactical.* Lancaster, PA: Technomic.

Kaufman, R., Rojas, A.M., & Mayer, H. (1993). *Needs assessment: A user's guide.* Englewood Cliffs, NJ: Educational Technology.

Kaufman, R., & Swart, W. (1995, May-June). Beyond conventional benchmarking: Integrating ideal visions, strategic planning, reengineering, and quality management. *Educational Technology.*

Kaufman, R., & Watkins, R. (1996). Mega planning: A framework for integrating strategic planning, needs assessment, quality management, benchmarking, and reengineering. In J.E. Jones & E. Biech (Eds.), *The HR handbook,* Vol. 1. Amherst, MA: HRD Press.

Kaufman, R., & Zahn, D. (1993). *Quality management plus: The continuous improvement of education.* Newbury Park, CA: Corwin Press.

Lloyd, B. (1992). Mintzberg on the rise and fall of strategic planning (interview). *Long Range Planning, 25*(4), 99-104.

Mager, R.F. (1975). *Preparing instructional objectives* (2nd ed.). Belmont, CA: Pitman Learning.

Marshall, R., & Tucker, M. (1992). *Thinking for a living: Education & the wealth of nations.* New York: Basic Books.

Martin, R. (1993, November-December). Changing the mind of the organization. *Harvard Business Review.*

Mintzberg, H. (1994). *The rise and fall of strategic planning.* New York: The Free Press.

Naisbitt, J., & Aburdene, P. (1990). *Megatrends 2000: Ten new directions for the 1990's.* New York: William Morrow.

Nanus, B. (1992). *Visionary leadership.* San Francisco, CA: Jossey-Bass.

Nolan, T.M., Goodstein, L.D., & Pfeiffer, J.W. (1993). *Shaping your organization's future: Frogs, dragons, bees, and turkey tails.* San Diego, CA: Pfeiffer & Company.

Popcorn, F. (1991). *The Popcorn report.* New York: Doubleday.

Senge, P.M. (1990). *The fifth discipline: The art & practice of the learning organization.* New York: Doubleday-Currency.

Stevens, S.S. (1951). Mathematics, measurement, and psychophysics. In S.S. Stevens, *Handbook of experimental psychology.* New York: John Wiley & Sons.

Toffler, A. (1990). *Powershift: Knowledge, wealth, and violence at the edge of the 21st century.* New York: Bantam Books.

Watkins, R. Triner, D., & Kaufman, R. (1996, July). The death and resurrection of strategic planning: A review of Mintzberg's "The rise and fall of strategic planning." *International Journal of Educational Reform.*

PREPARING PERFORMANCE INDICATORS AND OBJECTIVES

Roger Kaufman

Performance indicators, and objectives of which they are a part, specify the evidence required to prove that a planned effort has achieved a chosen result. They have two important uses, one proactive and the other reactive:

1. To identify what is to be accomplished, and

2. To provide criteria for judging success or failure.

Performance indicators may be used in several ways, ranging from providing personnel performance appraisal standards to supplying criteria for the evaluation of human resources development; identifying valid human resource or training interventions to defining new organizational destinations and purposes.

As a part of an objective, performance indicators provide the specific criteria required to confirm the attainment of results. They may also be used for planning the destinations for any organizational activity or intervention. Any objective, including its performance indicator, should include a statement of (a) where you are headed, and (b) how to tell when you have arrived, including:

• A clear, unambiguous statement of required results.

• Precise criteria to measure actual results.

- Specification of who or what will demonstrate the intended results.

- Statement of under what conditions the results or performance will be observed.

No matter what we do, or how we do it, organizations are only successful to the extent to which they get results. Useful performance indicators, therefore, best relate to valid *ends* (results, consequences, performance, payoffs). Indicators that target *means* (how something gets done, processes, methods, techniques) or resources (people, time, money, facilities) provide feedback on performance compliance, fidelity of implementation, or how faithfully or to what degree a specific job is being done: they deal with how, not what. How is only sensible in terms of what they deliver, so beware of writing objectives for means without relating them to ends and consequences.

There are two types of performance indicators:

Type R: Results-oriented indicators that identify measurable performance, consequences, payoffs, or ends. Results targeted may include individual contributions as well as organizational results and consequences.

Type I: Implementation-oriented indicators that identify fidelity of activity and compliance in the application of methods, means, resources, and/or approaches.

Although both types are widely used, Type R is strongly urged: if we do not intend to deliver useful results and their consequences, our efforts might be wasted. Therefore, this chapter will deal only with Type R performance—results-oriented—indicators because ends-based objectives provide the best assurance that selected means will deliver desired consequences.

During operations and implementation, however, a performance improvement professional might want to use a means- (or process-) oriented (Type I) set of criteria (McLagan, 1983) to provide employees with feedback on how well they are doing in a particular activity. This can be helpful *if* there is assurance that the activity, when done correctly and to specifications, will deliver important results. (By only examining means, however, the user risks begging the question of the *usefulness* of any results that flow from the means, or activities. One may be performing a task as specified, but the task may not be useful to the organization.)

Some Important Features of Performance Indicators

A useful performance indicator,[1] and its objective, target only ends. In addition, when clearly stated, it eliminates confusion concerning exactly what results are to be accomplished. Performance indicators provide criteria to be used in evaluation.

Not all results are equal. Individual accomplishments within an organization must combine with all others to provide a useful organizational contribution; some results are "building blocks" for larger, overall ones. These en-route results are only useful when they "add up," or combine, *within* the entire organization to properly serve *external* clients (Drucker, 1992, 1993, 1994, 1995; Kaufman, 1992, 1996; Kaufman, Herman, & Watters, 1996; Kaufman & Grise, 1995; Popcorn, 1991). This "contributing relationship" of all of the means and ends of an organization makes up a "results chain" (Kaufman, 1992) that spans from organizational resources and efforts to organizational results and finally to client and societal consequences. This is a big-picture perspective that

---

[1] For the balance of the chapter, "performance indicator" refers to the results-oriented, Type R variety.

encourages the formal consideration of the implications of what one's organization does, accomplishes, and delivers to the outside world.

Three Levels of Planning and Results

There are three levels of planning: mega, macro, and micro (see Introduction). *Mega-level* planning targets society as the primary client and beneficiary of what gets delivered. When the primary client and beneficiary is the organization itself, planning is *macro-level*. When the primary client and beneficiary is an individual or small group, the focus is *micro-level* planning. Table 1 in Chapter 4 shows the three levels of results and the questions they address, with two other organizational elements related to means and resources.

The means and ends of any organization can be described by five organizational elements (see Table 1, Chapter 4) that relate what organizations use, do, and deliver. The *means* include inputs and processes that are the available or required resources and the methods and means employed to get results. The means may include performing a job correctly or using the right tools in performing a task.

There are three *ends* (or results) to which the means contribute. Performance indicators may be written for each. The most basic and important level of results are *outcomes* that indicate the mega-level contributions of the internal results, processes, and resources to external clients and society (Kaufman, 1992, 1996). The other two types of *ends* are internal (within-the-organization) results: *products* are the building-blocks of organizational contributions at the micro level, and *outputs* are the macro-level results that can be or are delivered to clients.

Performance indicators, while relating to the three types of ends (products, outputs, outcomes), should have identifiable linkages among all five organizational elements. Means and ends should be related. Examples of objectives for each level of results (mega, macro, and micro) are presented in the Appendix.

Possible "Templates" for Improving Performance Indicators

Three major considerations for developing useful performance indicators include:

1. Differentiation among means and ends,

2. The rigor of measurability of the results,

3. Array and range of organizational elements covered: mega/outcomes; macro/outputs; micro/products.

When preparing (or reviewing) performance indicators, one, two, or three "templates" may be used to compare each with these three realms.

Template #1: Means and Ends

The single most important factor in deriving a useful performance indicator is whether it deals with results or means, with consequences, or resources. Determine if any would-be performance indicator relates to a means or an end:

MEANS

ENDS

Ends are *results* to be accomplished; *means* are the possible techniques, procedures, methods, and resources used to obtain ends. Means are selected best only on the basis of the results they are to accomplish. One clue for discriminating a means is if the indicator includes a word with an "ing" suffix (e.g., training, developing, learning, planning, using, showing, demonstrating, etc.). Such "ing" words usually identify a means, not an end. If a would-be performance indicator only identifies a means to an end, change it to target only the intended result.

To derive an ends-related indicator from means-related ones, ask "what would be the result if this means (or resource) were successfully implemented?" For example, an intent to "improve learning of basic performance indicator concepts" is better stated: "correctly list four characteristics of a valid objective, including its performance indicators and write one that will identify intended measurable results." (Note that "learning" is a process; mastery is an end.) Ends-oriented performance indicators are encouraged because, sooner or later, performance and results will be the basic test of whether or not any process, resource, or method is worthy.

Template #2: Measurability

Classify each of the performance indicators as to its level of measurement. There are four scales of measurement (Stevens, 1951):

    1. Nominal[2]

    2. Ordinal[3]

    3. Interval[4]

    4. Ratio[5]

---

[2] Naming
[3] Rank ordering
[4] Equal scale distances with arbitrary zero-point
[5] Equal scale distances with known zero-point

Objectives are measurable on an interval or ratio scale, while goals, aims, and purposes use nominal and ordinal scales (Kaufman, 1992, 1996). Performance indicators (and associated objectives) should be measurable on an interval or ratio scale to ensure their accuracy and reliability.

Template #3: Organizational Focus

To ensure that the accomplishment of a performance indicator yields individual performance improvement as well as organizational accomplishments and useful contributions, sort the performance indicator into one of the five organizational elements:

MEGA/ ⟨⟹⟩ MACRO/ ⟨⟹⟩ MICRO/ ⟨⟹⟩ PROCESSES ⟨⟹⟩ INPUTS
OUTCOMES   OUTPUTS   PRODUCTS

Make certain that a possible indicator falls in one of the results elements (mega/outcomes, macro/outputs, micro/products) unless compliance is the only intended consequence. In addition, link any performance indicator to the other organizational elements by identifying the interactions between the performance indicator and the total array of elements. This confirms that there will be a results chain, which links internal, organizational results with external, outside-of-the-organization consequences.

If there are no linkages for a performance indicator with all five of the organizational elements, this serves as a warning signal that the performance under consideration might not be useful within and/or outside the organization. Without such ties among the elements, there is little rationale for moving on with a planned effort.

Using the Templates

All, two, or one of the three templates may be useful. All three ensure the usefulness of the derived performance indicators. Figure 1 shows the flow of the use of all three templates.

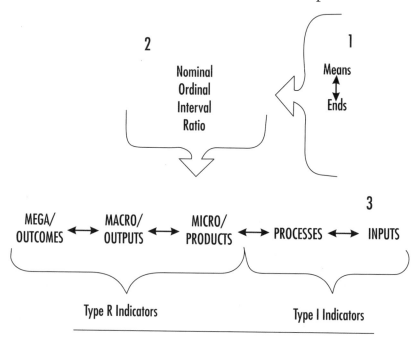

Figure 1. Template for Writing Useful Objectives and Related Performance Indicators

Beyond Simple Improvement of Efficiency: Optional Template #4

Often, performance indicators are used simply to improve current results without questioning their validity and utility. If one is confident of the validity and utility of current objectives, the three templates will suffice.

However, it might be useful to follow Drucker's advice (1973) and ask if the job to be done is worth doing in the first place. If one is willing to question whether or not the current objectives at the product, output, and/or outcome levels are correct and practical, template #3 may be expanded to have two dimensions, "What Should Be" and "What Is," to form template #4.

	MEGA/ OUTCOMES	MACRO/ OUTPUTS	MICRO/ PRODUCTS	PROCESSES	INPUTS
WHAT SHOULD BE (OR COULD BE)					
WHAT IS					

For a "holistic" or "strategic" frame of reference (viewing the total organization in a societal context) one should have performance indicators in each of the three "What Is" results cells (mega/outcomes, macro/outputs, micro/products) as well as ones in each of the three "What Should Be" results cells. (Recall that Type R performance indicators deal with results, not processes or resources). A "comprehensive" unit of analysis will have entries in each results cell except for ones in the outcomes category. A "middle-level" frame of reference only requires indicators for the products cells.

A bonus for using this additional template #4 surfaces when doing an evaluation for continuous improvement. By examining both "What Is" and "What Should Be," an evaluation and continuous improvement process may be planned to compare three types of results (or levels) and then two types of means (resources and processes). This allows contrasting "what was intended" with "what was delivered" for each of the organizational elements instead of lumping all means and ends together or confusing the different possible levels of evaluation.

The optional use of four templates provides another flow.

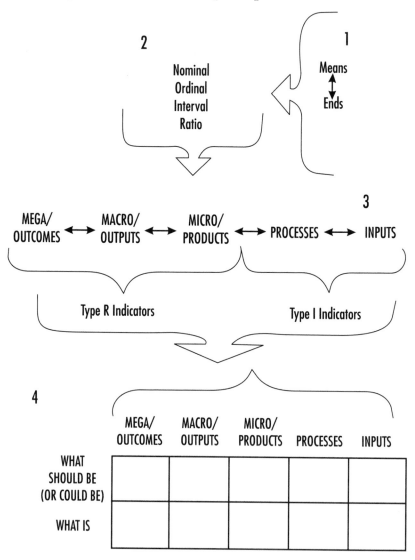

Figure 2. Holistic Template for Preparing Useful Performance Objectives and Indicators.

Summary

Two types of performance indicators are in use today. Type R deals with results, while Type I focuses on implementation and compliance. This chapter discussed the recommended results-oriented performance indicator (Type R).

Objectives and their performance indicators should

- Relate to ends, not means, processes, or resources in isolation from the results they should deliver,

- Be precise and measurable on an interval or ratio scale, and

- Be related and incorporated into a results chain that links all organizational efforts, organizational results, and client and societal payoffs and consequences.

If they do not have all of the these characteristics, it is possible that the performances for which one is devising indicators may not be productive.

Another option is available if performance indicators are desired for deriving new and useful purposes and objectives, not simply increasing the efficiency of achieving existing ones. By ensuring that there are indicators for the two dimensions, "What Should Be" and "What Is," one may shift from improved efficiency to improved effectiveness as well.

References

Drucker, P.F. (1973). *Management: Tasks, responsibilities, practices.* New York: Harper & Row.

Drucker, P.F. (1992, September-October). The new society of organizations. *Harvard Business Review,* pp.95-104.

Drucker, P.F. (1993). *Post-capitalist society.* New York: HarperBusiness.

Drucker, P.F. (1994, November). The age of social transformation. *The Atlantic Monthly,* pp. 53-80.

Drucker, P.F. (1995, February). Really reinventing government. *The Atlantic Monthly*, pp.49-61.

Kaufman, R. (1988, September). Preparing useful performance indicators. *Training & Development Journal*.

Kaufman, R. (1992). *Strategic planning plus: An organizational guide*. Newbury Park, CA: Sage Publications.

Kaufman, R. (1996). *Strategic thinking: Identifying and solving problems*. Washington, DC: International Society for Performance Improvement / Alexandria, VA: American Society for Training and Development.

Kaufman, R., & Grise, P. (1995). *How to audit your strategic plan: Making good education better*. Thousand Oaks, CA: Corwin Press.

Kaufman, R., Grise, P., & Watters, K. (1992). Preparing useful performance indicators. In K.L. Medsker & D.G. Roberts, (Eds.), *ASTD trainer's toolkit: Evaluating the results of training*. Arlington, VA: American Society for Training and Development.

Kaufman, R., Herman, J., & Watters, K. (1996). *Educational planning: Strategic, tactical, operational*. Lancaster, PA: Technomic Publishing.

McLagan, P.A. (1983). *Models for excellence: The conclusions and recommendations of the ASTD training and development competency study*. Washington, DC: American Society for Training and Development.

Popcorn, F. (1991). *The popcorn report*. New York: Doubleday.

Stevens, S. S. (1951). Mathematics, measurement and psychophysics. In S.S. Stevens, *Handbook of experimental psychology*. New York: John Wiley & Sons.

Appendix

Hypothetical Objectives/Performance Indicators for the Three Types of Results: Mega/Outcome, Macro/Outputs, and Micro/Products

Following are examples of objectives and performance indicators for each of the three types of results.

Mega/Outcome-Linked: All the sold and delivered automobiles turned out by the plant after June 4 will be safe and effective as indicated by no court-ordered changes, mandated modifications, or returns; no complaints under the "Lemon Law;" no upheld successful lawsuits attributed to manufacturing defects, or air pollution. There will be no loss of life attributed to defective design, development, or fabrication.

Macro/Outputs-Related: At least 99 percent of all parts manufactured by the Santo Placebo Plant after next month will meet all quality acceptance standards without remanufacturing and will be shipped to distribution points and/or to customers on or before the times contracted, as indicated by no client complaints about timeliness or quality, or returns for defects or dissatisfaction.

Micro/Products-Related: At least 99.8 percent of all computer monitors delivered after January 1 will meet all quality acceptance standards, as indicated by sign-off by the quality inspector on each shift and by no rejects from the quality assurance test laboratory.

NEEDS-ASSESSMENT BASICS[1]

Roger Kaufman

Introduction to Needs Assessment

Defining Needs Assessment

Needs and wants, results and processes, consequences and methods, competence and training, human resource development and performance. Although these pairs might be related, they are different. What they do have in common is that the first in each pair is an *end* and the second is a *means*. If you want to select a useful destination (an end), you best proceed by defining the gap in results, a *need*, between where you are now and where you want to be. The process of defining those gaps in results and selecting the most important ones for reduction or closure is called *needs assessment*.

---

[1] This chapter builds on the definitions and concepts in other chapters. For a discussion of the Organizational Elements Model (OEM) please refer to the chapter on strategic planning, especially Table 1 for the definitions of outcomes, outputs, products, processes, and inputs. It is assumed that the definitions of the three levels of planning [(1) mega: the primary client and beneficiary are the external clients and society, (2) macro: the primary client and beneficiary is the organization itself, and (3) micro: the primary client and beneficiary are individuals or small groups within the organization] are understood.

As noted in the chapter on strategic planning (Chapter 4), needs assessment is part of holistic strategic planning. When selecting the organizational destination and defining and relating what contributions must be delivered from within the organization, needs assessment provides the performance data for those decisions. Chapter 5 identifies how to prepare useful performance objectives and how to use those objectives in identifying needs. The chapter on client satisfaction (Chapter 28) notes that the data from a results-referenced needs assessment provide basic information for continuous improvement.

Selecting Where to Head

Most performance improvers start with a problem to resolve or a deficiency to fix. Identification of the problem to be resolved is usually left up to a client, or a subject-matter expert defines the purposes. Performance specialists (they have a variety of names, including instructional systems technologists, performance technologists, performance analyzers, educational psychologists, etc.) are experts in using "technology" for dealing with performance systems. Their tools include human resource development (HRD), organizational development (OD), performance technology (PT), training, systems analysis, performance analysis, job aids, needs assessment, needs analysis, front-end analysis, problem analysis, task analysis, and training requirements analysis. These specialists are primarily concerned with resolving problems.

As important as such "repair" efforts are, it is probably more important first to identify and justify the actual problem (and also to search for opportunities at the same time). While setting measurable objectives is usually the starting place for applying performance technology, it is usually vital first to make certain that the objectives are the right ones and that their accomplishment will lead to individual competence, organizational success, and usefulness to external clients.

Needs assessments provide the direction for useful problem resolution through identifying, documenting, and selecting appropriate problems.[2] By selecting important problems and deriving useful objectives before rushing off to resolve them, performance systems professionals may improve the effectiveness and efficiency of any organization and its individual operations.

Needs assessment may be either the starting place for HRD and organizational improvement or, better, it can be an integral part of strategic planning. We urge that needs assessment be conceived and accomplished as an integral part of strategic planning in general and relate to what HRD specialists select, do, and deliver. Regardless of whether or not you start with a needs assessment, it can provide the basic rationale for justifying where you are headed and why you should get there.

Need and Needs Assessment

Absolutely vital to needs assessment is the definition of a need.[3] For the purposes of planning, it is important to use the following definition: A need is the gap between current results and desired or required results.

A need is not a gap in resources, processes, methods, or how-to-do-its (such as training, HRD, supervising, etc.). A gap in a method, resource, or process is called a *quasi-need*. A

---

[2] Although this chapter refers to identifying and resolving *problems*, "problem" should be read as "problems and opportunities." Needs assessment can be used to identify both gaps between current and required results as well as the gaps between current and desired (but currently not included) results.

[3] There are differing views of what a "need" is (Sleezer, 1992; Witkin, 1984). It is strongly urged that problems of definition, statements of purpose, justifications for selection of methods and means, and evaluation are clarified and simplified by defining "need" as a gap in results.

needs assessment identifies gaps between current results and desired (or required) ones and places them in order of priority for resolution, based on the cost to meet the need as compared to the cost of ignoring it.

The Nine Steps of Needs Assessment

Following are nine recommended needs-assessment steps. Each employs different tools and techniques. The specific choice of tools and when to use each depend on the type of needs assessment you choose.

1. Decide to plan (and do human and organizational performance improvement) using data from a needs (not a "wants") assessment. Planning is a substitute for good luck. A properly completed needs assessment replaces luck in determining where you should be headed and justifying why you want to get there.

A plan is a blueprint for useful action. It identifies the functions—deliverable products—an organization must produce to get from where it is to where it wants to be. A management plan derives from determining where you want to go and justifying why you want to go there.

Using a needs assessment affords your gaining control over events. All the partners in planning (see step 3 below) must agree to such commitments. Critical partners include those who will be affected by the results and those who will have to implement any resultant plan.

2. Identify the three needs assessment (and planning) levels to be included—mega, macro, and micro—and commit to needs assessment (and planning) at the mega level as the starting place. How much of your operational world (and realities) should you consider and tackle? The following three levels or units of analysis are possible:

- Mega. This level combines the results—products and outputs—of the macro level with a consideration of how useful the organization's contributions (or *outcomes*) are to its clients and to the world in which its contributions must function. This level includes what an organization uses, does, produces, and delivers as well as the impact these have on both clients and on society. The results at this level contribute to moving ever-closer to the ideal vision (Kaufman, 1996).

A *manufacturing example:* Combining the contributions of trained and competent welders, manufacturing workers, supervisors, managers, and executives with quality management used by all associates, the deliverables of this company should be of sufficient quality and value to increase the number of new clients, retain the existing ones, and help clients become self-sufficient. They not only will be satisfied, but also the outputs will be safe, effective, and efficient. In addition, they must not pollute or bring harm to any living thing.

- Macro. This level combines the micro-level contributions (products) to form what an organization can or does deliver (*outputs*) to its external (outside of the organization) clients. The macro level's unit of analysis is the total organization. This level is made up of what an organization uses, does, and delivers to itself as well as to its external clients.

The manufacturing example continued: A welder's competence combined with the fabricated products of other workers, the contributions of a total quality management program that had been initiated, and the contributions of committed and productive coworkers will increase the price and attractiveness of the company's outputs to existing and potential buyers.

- Micro. This level of needs assessment and planning includes a concern for the cumulative contributions of (1) organizational resources (or *inputs*), plus (2) the procedures and methods (or *processes*) to be employed in organizational activities, plus (3) the immediate results (or *products*) accomplished.

This level of needs assessment, for example, might be directed toward improved competence of welders or addict counseling specialists. Improving employee proficiency may require finding resources (inputs and/or processes) such as money, trainees, and/or unique training methods that will deliver on the measurable performance objectives.

You may assess needs at any of these three levels. Choosing the micro or macro level, however, assumes that the contributions of those results will be responsive to client and societal requirements and realities at the mega level.

The Organizational Elements Model (OEM), shown in Table 1, provides a holistic framework for identifying needs, analyzing them, defining useful objectives, and then selecting effective and efficient interventions. Using this model will help you identify, define, and relate what organizations use, do, and deliver. The OEM links internal and external resources and processes with three kinds of results: products, outputs, and outcomes. Note the relationship among the organizational elements and the three levels of planning and needs assessment.

3. Identify the needs assessment and planning partners. Successful needs assessment and any resultant plans, procedures, and payoffs depend on choosing the correct planning partners to guide the process and to "own" it when it is completed. An otherwise good plan might fail simply because uninvolved or unrepresented people may not see that an imposed change, no matter how rational, might benefit them.

Derived from Kaufman, 1992. Copyright © R. Kaufman, 1992.

Table 1. The Organizational Elements Model and Its Relationship to Organizational Dimensions

	OUTCOMES (the contributions of outputs in and for society and the community)	OUTPUTS (the aggregated products of the system that are delivered or deliverable to society)	PRODUCTS (on-route—building-block—results)	PROCESSES (how-to's, means, methods, procedures)	INPUTS (resources, ingredients)
ORGANIZATIONAL LEVEL	OUTCOMES	OUTPUTS	PRODUCTS	PROCESSES	INPUTS
EXAMPLES	Self-sufficient, self-reliant, productive individual who is socially competent and effective, contributing to self and others; no addiction to others or to substances; financially independent; continued funding of agency, etc.	Graduates, completers, dropouts, job placements, certified licenses, etc.	Course completed, competency test passed, skill acquired, learner accomplishments, instructor accomplishments, etc.	Total quality management, continuous improvement, teaching, learning, in-service training, managing, accelerated learning, site-based managing, accountability, etc.	Existing personnel; identified needs, goals, objectives, policies, regulations, laws, money, values, and societal and community characteristics; current quality of life; learner entry characteristics; teacher competencies; buildings; equipment; etc.
CLUSTER	SOCIETAL RESULTS/IMPACT	RESULTS		EFFORTS	
SCOPE	EXTERNAL (Societal)	INTERNAL (Organizational)			
PLANNING LEVEL	MEGA	MACRO	MICRO		
PRIMARY CLIENT OR BENEFICIARY	SOCIETY/COMMUNITY	SCHOOL SYSTEM OR SCHOOL	INDIVIDUAL OR SMALL GROUP		
STRATEGIC-PLANNING QUESTION	Do you care about the success of learners after they leave your educational system?	Do you care about the quality and competence of the completers when they leave your educational system?	Do you care about the specific skills, knowledge, attitudes, and abilities of the learners as they move from course to course and level to level?		

You can usually aid in any plan's adoption and resultant changes by having people affected participate as partners in the planning or having them represented in the needs assessment and resultant plan's creation.

There are three human needs assessment and planning partner groups and one performance data-based one. The partners should include

- Those who will be affected by the results;

- Those who will implement the plan;

- Clients or society who will receive (and/or be affected by) the results.

The needs assessment (and planning) partners selected depend on the type of organization and who its clients are. Usually the planners and their operational unit (such as personnel, engineering, quality) will be the implementers and the planners' immediate clients—such as trainees, supervisors, or patients—will be the recipients.

"Society" is an inclusive term that encompasses those who will be affected by what an organization and its external clients deliver. For example, a community service for the handicapped might include paraplegics; ailing and infirm elderly; people who are blind, hard-of-hearing, physically disabled, or mentally diminished; and their neighbors. In computer software manufacturing, "society" would include wholesale and retail sales organizations and the end users.

When selecting the planning partners, ensure that they are typical representatives of their constituencies. If ethnic or age composition is important, secure a representative sample. If particular skills are critical, ensure that these are represented among the partners.

Usually, a stratified random sample of each partner group will provide representativeness. Do not create huge groups—just representative ones. The number of planning partners depends on what you are planning and who the planned changes are supposed to serve. Because the partner group should represent the actual operational world, it should not include "tokens" nor be packed with friends.

Again, the word "need" has, unfortunately for human and organizational performance purposes, several conventional and accepted meanings. Make sure that all the partner groups are working with the same definition (Kaufman, 1992, 1996). The importance of using need (as a noun, not a verb) to describe a gap in results cannot be overemphasized.[4]

The partners will offer judgments concerning perceived needs. Because these perceived needs are based on personal observations and feelings, they are termed "needs sensing" or "soft" data. Sensed needs often provide perceived reality and sensitivity to issues of values and preferences about current problems and consequences. They also may reveal observations about the methods and procedures that led to the currently undesired results. This type of data is often termed "soft" because of its attitudinal origins and because it is not independently verifiable.

You also require data concerning gaps in performance. These independently verifiable needs may be both in human and organizational performance. Such data are termed "hard" because they derive from actual, observed performance. Hard data might include external results (*outcomes*) such as profits, organizational image, death rates, numbers of people with positive credit ratings, returns to healthy functioning, and quality of community life. Hard data also might include internal organizational performance indicators (*outputs* and *products*) such as productivity, rejection rates, case completions,

---

[4] Sometimes this distinction is dismissed as trivial. It is not. Nor is the related distinction between ends and means. When "need" is used as a verb, there is a jumping from a situation to a solution, almost always prematurely.

absenteeism, morale, corporate climate, delivered services, and complaints.

You can look at the performance-based data as a nonhuman partner because they supply additional facts you should consider in identifying, documenting, and selecting needs. Together, the sensed needs from the implementers and recipients and external society/clients plus the performance-based data provide the needs assessment data. They are provided by the "partners for planning."

4. Obtain the participation of your needs assessment (and planning) partners. It is not enough to identify the partners. They must be active participators and contributors. Contact the selected partners and reveal to each your expectations, required time commitments, desired products, and level of contributions. Disclose how much you will support them—with funds, travel, data, materials, and support services. Be clear about how you will use and consider their inputs.

After getting commitments from the partners, design and schedule the first meeting. Meetings can be simply face-to-face or can include written surveys, the Delphi technique, teleconferencing, or computer interface. Replace partners who do not come or who do not contribute.

5. Obtain acceptance of the mega frame of reference for the needs assessment and planning. Share with the partners the three needs assessment and planning levels—mega, macro, and micro (see step 2). Get their commitment to mega. By familiarizing them with the optional levels and the advantages and disadvantages of each, you allow the partners to make an informed choice. It is important that all partners know the scope of the needs assessment and have a common set of expectations. If they select a level below mega, be sure they know and are wiling to assume the risks of doing so in terms of their accountability for not delivering societally useful results.

Explain to the partners the basic concepts of needs assessment. Needs assessment is the process for identifying, documenting, and justifying the gaps between "what is" and "what should be" concerning the three types of results: outcomes, outputs, and products.

Figure 1 illustrates that there may be three kinds of needs assessments—one relating to each of the three types of results. The open arrows show possible needs assessments, and the dark arrows are possible quasi-need assessments. The mega level (outcomes) of needs assessment is strongly recommended as the safest, most pragmatic, and most practical starting place (Drucker, 1993, 1994, 1995; Kaufman, 1992, 1995; Kaufman & Grise, 1995; Popcorn, 1991).

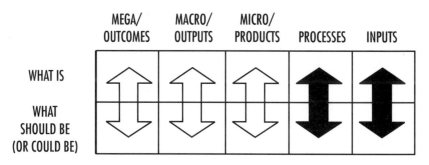

Figure 1. The Two-Tiered Organizational Elements Model

Needs analysis consists of taking the determined gaps between adjacent elements and finding the causes of the inability for one level (e.g., aggregate products) to deliver required outputs. Possible needs analyses are shown in Figure 1 as solid arrows.

Some confuse needs assessment and needs analysis, perhaps not realizing the basic functions required: to analyze anything, including needs, one has to identify what to analyze. Thus, needs analysis rationally only comes after identifying the need (gaps in results) to be analyzed.

A few practitioners even fail to distinguish among needs assessment, needs analysis, problem solving, troubleshooting, problem isolation, and problem diagnosis (e.g., Lewis & Bjork-quist, 1992). Regardless of what a needs analysis gets labeled, it rationally follows needs assessment and needs selection and is a part of identifying and solving problems.

6. Collect both internal and external needs data. Collect external (and internal) needs data. Internal needs data concern performance discrepancies within an organization, and external needs data concern performance discrepancies of your clients and their world.

When collecting data on internal performance, you should look at two information sources: the perceptions of the planning partners and the actual performance discrepancies collected from objective observations.

You can collect partners' perceptions about performance discrepancies—referred to earlier as needs sensing—by using a variety of tools, ranging from face-to-face meetings to remote data-collection methods, including rating scales, questionnaires, Delphi technique, nominal group technique, structured interviews, or some paper-and-pencil assessments. The sensed needs of the partners will supply data concerning performance discrepancies they feel are important. People's perceptions are their realities. Be sure to collect both hard and soft data; needs assessments are more than just questionnaires (which only harvest soft data).

In designing or selecting data-collection instruments for needs sensing, you must be sure they pose the correct questions without bias. Make certain the instrument and its questions focus responses on results, not on resources (inputs) or methods and techniques (processes). Also be sure the questions are comprehensive in order to cover the possible array of needs without afflicting respondents with overly complex and time-consuming issues. The data-collection instruments must be valid—measuring what they are really supposed to measure—and reliable—measuring the same thing consistently.

Collecting internal organizational performance data is usually simpler than it first appears. Most organizations have a lot of hard data; you only have to figure out what you want and then go find it. Useful data might include absenteeism, production rates, cases closed, audit exceptions, ethics violations, accidents, on-site fatalities, grievances, courses completed, certified competencies, sick leave, work samples, and rejection rates. Look for validity and reliability of these data, and use them only when they supply useful information concerning performance.

For the mega assessment level, collect external performance data. You frequently will find useful information within and external to the organization. Some examples are data concerning clients' perceptions and satisfaction, return rates, recidivism, complaints, profits, arrests and convictions, successful law suits, return on investment, and income.

Even though you will use hard and soft data, both should focus on results rather than on methods, means, processes, techniques, procedures, resources, or personnel. Targeting results in needs assessment is essential in relating means and ends.

A needs-assessment summary format (Table 2) allows the needs to be openly listed and ensures that all levels of needs— ega, macro, micro—are represented and linked.

Before setting priorities, deriving objectives, and selecting interventions, the partners must agree on a set of needs. When there are disagreements, you might have to help the partners come to an agreement. Tools for getting agreement are (1) technical, and (2) group-process oriented.

Technical resolution possibilities include the following:

- Reconcile the sensed needs with those based on the hard data.

Table 2. A Needs-Assessment Summary Format

Current Results	Possible Means	Required Results	Related Ideal Vision Element	Need Level		
				Mega	Macro	Micro

The Guidebook for Performance Improvement

- Derive a common set of needs supported by the hard and soft data, and request additional data if there are insurmountable differences.

- Translate the disputed perceived needs into results and ask the partners if the revision represents their concern. If it does not, ask them to revise it into a results-oriented statement that will address the concern. Most arguments over needs concern incorrectly (usually tenaciously) adhering to talking about gaps in methods and resources (quasi-needs) rather than actual gaps in results.

- Ask the disagreeing partners to define the result that will be obtained if a certain "need" were to be met. This encourages the partners to track the linkages from processes to results and then to a defined gap in results. Then, they can sensibly rank the needs, now gaps in results, for resolution.

Group-process oriented resolution possibilities include the following:

- Discourage special-interest groups from pushing a pet solution, such as computer-aided instruction or quality management training; a method, such as self-paced or multimedia instruction; or a resource, such as money or people, without first identifying and selecting the need their favorite solution is intended to address.

- Encourage all partners to define needs as gaps in results (and model the behavior yourself).

- Be certain that everyone knows that needs assessments are not public relations vehicles to favor one intervention over another.

- Be patient and open. Listen.

When Things Come to a Grinding Halt

Sometimes there are differences that seem to stall everything. Do not go ahead without substantial agreement, and don't cave in just to keep the peace. Most partners are honorable, concerned, and want to identify and meet the right needs. Often what is missing is additional data.

Frequently, the hard and soft data disagree, in which case you will have to get additional, more responsive data by using a revision of the techniques you selected in step 6. By merging opinion and empirical results data, you may find areas of common agreement on needs.

It is important that there be substantial agreement between sources of data. Otherwise, the partners, and the interests those partners represent, will not perceive the needs assessment database as useful and will not accept the results. Where there is no accord, initiate further fact-finding or reeducate the needs assessment and planning partners so they can agree. Figure 2 shows a flow process for merging the two types of data and deciding the areas for collecting additional information.

When disagreement still lingers, you often will have to revisit the historical context and the futures data to provide a frame of reference concerning "what was," "what is," "what will be," and "what could be" and finally selecting "what should be." Again, most disagreements stem from (a) confusing ends and means, (b) insisting on a favored means and not being open to first defining gaps in results (needs) before finding an appropriate means, or (c) people playing power games. Discuss these possibilities with the planning partners, and list the existing "needs." Make a simple chart with the "needs" in a first column and two other columns marked "ends" and "means." Have the group fill out the chart—they will usually notice that some premature "means" have slipped in.

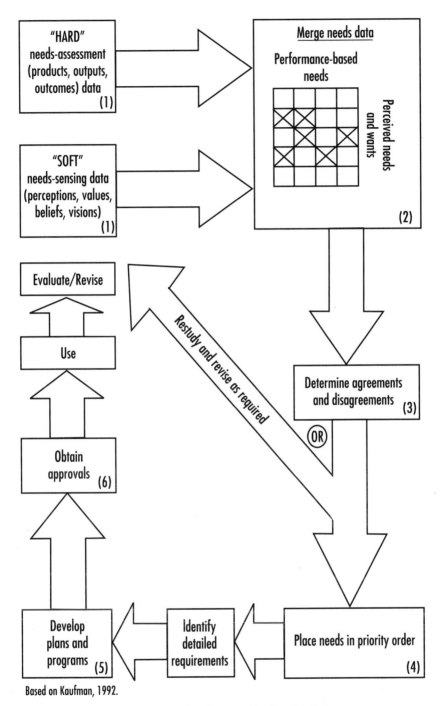

"HARD"
needs-assessment
(products, outputs,
outcomes) data
(1)

"SOFT"
needs-sensing data
(perceptions, values,
beliefs, visions)
(1)

Merge needs data

Performance-based
needs

Perceived needs
and wants

(2)

Evaluate/Revise

Use

Obtain
approvals (6)

Restudy and revise as required

Determine agreements
and disagreements (3)

(OR)

Develop
plans and
programs (5)

Identify
detailed
requirements

Place needs in priority order

(4)

Based on Kaufman, 1992.

Figure 2. A Process for Merging Hard and Soft Data

7. List identified, documented, and agreed-on needs. Using a needs-assessment summary format, as in Table 2, list the agreed-on needs. These will become basic information for the needs assessment findings and will provide basic data for strategic planning and for the later selection of HRD and organizational-improvement interventions.

Two variables, often assumed, are worth considering in a needs assessment: past history and the future. Time to perform is important for shaping the future because it provides the potential to manage forthcoming events. Responding to here-and-now problems and criteria requires us to react and provides the opportunity to design and deliver a more productive future. After needs have been identified, selected, and used for planning and implementation, patience (defined as time to have things happen) must be allocated. We should not be in such a hurry for a change to occur that we destroy the process by always questioning its effectiveness before an impact takes place.

History—former accomplishments and influences—helps us evaluate the past and make predictions about the future. Needs assessment and planning help us define the extent to which we will move toward a more productive and satisfying future.

8. Place needs in order of priority (based on the costs to meet and not meet the needs) and reconcile differences. Provide each of the partner groups with the list of needs they must prioritize plus the hard data from actual performance. From the listed needs in step 7, ask each partner and then partner group to set priorities among the needs.

To set priorities among the listed needs, you should select criteria for weighting them. One useful priority-setting method is asking the partners to assign a value, often in monetary terms, for each need in terms of what it will cost to reduce or eliminate the need and what it will cost to ignore the need. You can view "cost" in financial as well as in quality-of-life terms. This process of estimating a detailed return-on-investment analysis is termed a "costs-consequences" analysis. (Kaufman, 1996; Kaufman & Watkins, 1996). Based on these costs-consequences estimated, each group can meet with one of the others and derive a common set of rankings.

9. List problems (selected needs) to be resolved and obtain agreement of partners. Compare the needs selected for resolution to a projected budget and use the priorities to assign funds until you exhaust the anticipated total sum. Sometimes you can justify additions to the budget by asking decision makers to reconsider the previous budget allocation based on the solid needs assessment data and the partnership-derived priorities.

After the partners have selected the problems to be resolved and you have obtained the budget—but before work proceeds—make certain the partners agree with the final results. If they do not, have them recommend modifications and justify revisions to the decision makers.

Important-But-Subtle Payoffs from this Approach to Needs Assessment

The data provided from the multilevel needs assessment will allow you to make justifiable decisions regarding organizational and human performance improvement interventions. By identifying the gaps in results and associated consequences, you can justify what you propose to use, do, and deliver on the basis of "what it costs to meet the need as compared to what it costs to ignore the need." Such justification is virtually impossible to derive if one does not use the definition of "need" as a gap in results. Also, when using "need" as a noun—a gap in results—there are two more "bonus" consequences:

1. The "what should be" criteria provide the design and performance improvement criteria, and

2. The "what should be" criteria provide the bases for evaluation and continuous improvement—there is no requirement to develop a separate evaluation and continuous improvement plan or initiative.

Why Bother?

Act in haste and repent in leisure, the old adage tells us. If you are in a hurry to get going with needs assessments, you might be tempted to fall into some convenient (and conventional) traps. Here is a list of potentially hazardous shortcuts and reasons why you might want to avoid them:

1. Start with a problem analysis and just identify current performance discrepancies. While you will identify performance deficits, their resolution might not have any impact at the upper organizational levels, at the macro level, or at the mega level.

2. Start with a "training needs assessment." While it is tempting to apply training right away, if you already know training is the solution, why go to the trouble of doing a needs assessment? The term "training needs assessment" is better termed a "training requirements analysis" and is applied *after* a needs assessment has identified gaps in results, problems selected, and training selected in detailed planning. People who are very well trained may not be competent in areas important to organizational success.

3. Send out questionnaires and ask people "what they 'need.'" Involving others is important, but simply asking such a question will result in confusing means (preferred methods and solutions) with ends. Using "need"

as a verb encourages people to provide solutions to problems that they probably have not calibrated in terms of results and payoffs. Solutions are best considered after you have identified the needs—gaps in results to be closed—and selected the high-priority problems to resolve.

4. Use soft data only. Opinions are perceived reality. They can and should be tempered by performance, accomplishments, and consequences.

5. Use hard data only. We often collect performance data on what is easy to measure. Sometimes people's observations and perceptions can provide some additional clues to performance problems and opportunities. Combine both hard and soft data sources in your needs assessment.

6. Restrict your needs assessment to the micro/product level. When you do this, you assume that the individual elements of positive performance will integrate and add up to organizational efficiency and client/societal payoffs, which is a risky assumption.

7. Confuse needs and wants, ends and means; use the term "need" as a verb. Ends are not means. Means are most sensibly selected on the basis of ends to be accomplished.

8. See yourself as a powerless "victim" who cannot make changes or provide suggestions to upper management. If you see yourself as powerless, you will render yourself such. Modern leadership principles tell us that without each member of the organization working to define and achieve positive results, the organization will falter. Empower yourself and others to contribute. Be proactive, not just reactive.

9. Continue to work with others who confuse "public relations" and needs assessment. Some organizations, especially those which want to prove a point (or justify a mission) naively turn to "needs assessment" to show what they do is important. Be clear that a needs assessment is an impartial process for defining and prioritizing gaps in results, not gaps in services, demands, or desires.

Conducting a results-oriented needs assessment does not have to be expensive or time-consuming. Outcome (mega level) data are available readily, as are many forms of output and product data. You can collect needs-sensing information by using or modifying a number of instruments on the market or in the literature, or you can construct your own.

Deriving and using needs assessment and planning partner groups might seem bothersome, but modern management techniques increasingly promote such quality-type activities, and such partnership groups represent the growing trend toward involving significant others—your associates and partners—in organizational decisions and activities. Empowerment flows from working together, finding a common set of purposes, and trusting each person to make appropriate contributions.

Needs assessments provide cost-effective alternatives to designing interventions that, while meeting product-level objectives, often fail to contribute to the organization's value to its clients, communities, and employees. It seems less expensive to find out where your organization should be headed, why it should go there, and tailor interventions to accomplish this, than it is to fail and have to determine what went wrong and try again.

References

Drucker, P.F. (1993). *Post-capitalist society.* New York: HarperBusiness.

Drucker, P.F. (1994, November). The age of social transformation. *The Atlantic Monthly,* pp. 53-80.

Drucker, P.F. (1995, February). Really reinventing government. *The Atlantic Monthly,* pp. 49-61.

Kaufman, R. (1992). *Strategic planning plus: An organizational guide* (rev.). Newbury Park, CA: Sage.

Kaufman, R. (1995). *Mapping educational success* (rev.). Thousand Oaks, CA: Corwin Press.

Kaufman, R. (1996). *Strategic thinking: A guide to identifying and solving problems.* Washington DC: International Society of Performance Improvement/Alexandria, VA: American Society for Training and Development.

Kaufman, R., & Grise, P. (1995). *How to audit your strategic plan: Making good education better.* Thousand Oaks, CA: Corwin Press.

Kaufman, R., & Valentine, G. (1989, November/December). Relating needs assessment and needs analysis. *Performance & Instruction Journal.*

Kaufman, R. & Watkins, R. (1996, Spring). Costs-consequences analysis. *HRD Quarterly.*

Lewis, T., & Bjorkquist, D.C. (1992). Needs assessment: A critical reappraisal. *Performance Improvement Quarterly,* 5(4).

Popcorn, F. (1991). *The Popcorn report.* New York: Doubleday.

Sleezer, C.M. (1992). Needs assessment: Perspectives from the literature. *Performance Improvement Quarterly,* 5(2).

Witkin, B.R. (1984). *Assessing needs in educational and social programs.* San Francisco, CA: Jossey-Bass.

A Systems Schema

Frank W. Banghart

This chapter presents a schema for performing a systems study. The systems analyst is somewhat like the hunter who enjoys the chase more than the kill. Systems work is a searching, problem-solving type of activity. Consider the following definitions of system and systems:

- A system (the operand) is a set of components, interactive and interdependent, that work together as a functional entity to achieve some specific objective.

- Systems (the operator) is the set of techniques and procedures that make up the discipline, which we use to examine the system.

The term "systems" is generic (not plural), as in statistics, genetics, physics, and economics.

The tasks of the systems worker involve the following:

1. Define the boundaries of the system.

2. Identify the components of the system.

3. Examine the nature of the interactions and interdependencies.

4. Identify and study the effects of the forces impacting on the components.

The Systems Approach

Traditionally, the tools of operations research and systems analysis (ORSA) have been used. These tools have relied heavily on mathematics. The algorithms associated with linear programming, information theory, PERT/CPM, queuing theory, game theory, and various optimizing techniques are typical of the ORSA person's bag of tools.

The early reliance on mathematical techniques caused considerable discomfort for the user (as opposed to the analyst). One analyst, for example, when solving a transportation problem for a large national trucking company, came up with a solution that involved sending a delivery van from Seattle, Washington, to Bangor, Maine. This solution was offered in spite of the fact that the company had warehouses and trucks in New York City. Of course, this did not overly impress the owner who had come up through the ranks without a technical background.

In another study an analyst's solution recommended that a farmer allocate his crops by planting 125.37368 acres of corn. Such a solution is not likely to get the analyst invited for dinner by the farmer even though the solution might be mathematically correct.

There have also been reports that the U.S. Navy optimized the Navy meals by coming up with a solution of beans and fat bacon seven days a week. The sailors protested. The point is that although ORSA solutions, which are designed to optimize complex systems, might be mathematically sound, they might not always appeal to the nonexpert (e.g., sailors).

The systems approach is also markedly different from that of the statistician. In statistical work one typically:

1. Sets up a control and an experimental group,

2. Makes certain that both groups are representative,

3. Sterilizes the environment,

4. Prays for the experimental group,

5. Conducts the experiment,

6. Throws a statistical test at the two groups, and

7. Pronounces that the difference noted by the analysis is likely or unlikely to be due to chance (i.e., asserts that nothing had or did not have an impact on the control group and something did or did not influence the experimental group).

Statistical work sometimes lends itself to meaningless conclusions. For example, in a British statistical study on baby formulas, it was discovered that the difference between formula A and formula B was highly significant. Because the consumption gain was approximately .01 of an ounce, I'm not sure that the babies or their mothers were terribly impressed.

Also, there is a story of a drug company researcher who reported remarkable results with the company's new anti-seasickness drug. When asked about the study design, the researcher described the rigorous procedure in setting up the control and experimental groups, "I gave the experimental drug to the sailors and the placebo to the passengers." Unfortunately, I have lost the scientific references to these studies.

From the discussion above one might assume that the system in "systems" work is a live, dynamic entity. The world does not stop to let the analyst get on or off. One cannot control the variable involved in the process. Indeed, the challenge is to devise a plan that will let one analyze the living, changing dynamic system during its lifetime.

We propose an operational plan in the schematic shown in Figure 1. Space does not permit a presentation of the specific details of the techniques to be used for the analytical work (i.e., the study of the principal components—their interactions and interdependencies and the forces that have an impact on the components).

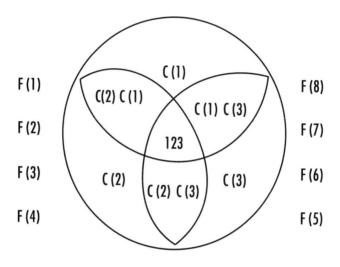

C = components of the system
F (1) = forces impacting on the system

Figure 1. Systems Schematic

We might illustrate the schema with a governmental system. One commonly thinks of these components as consisting of the executive, legislative, and judiciary. This breakout might be appropriate for governmental philosophers and/or theorists. However, for the systems person concerned with an operational understanding of the system, such a breakout is not very helpful. One may want, instead, a definition of the boundaries of the system, the operational components of the system, and the forces impacting on the theoretical schema. This system is depicted in Figure 2.

Let us apply a system to the executive branch, as shown in Figure 2. Consider component P, the elected official. Not only does the official have many factors impacting on the activities of the office (e.g., constituents, financial contributors, various special interest groups, PACs, lobbyists, etc.) but the official is also influenced by and influences the other two major components of the system (e.g., career staff and political appointees).

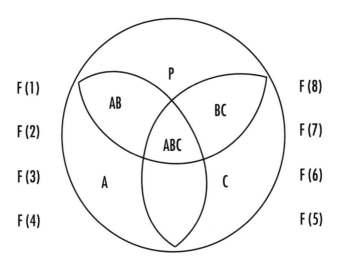

P = elected officials
C = career staff
A = political appointees
B = boundary of defined system
F (1) = natural constituencies
F (2) = financial contributors
F (3) = special-interest groups
F (4) = lobbyists
F (5) = television
F (6) = voters
F (7) = PACs
F (8) = entitlements

Figure 2. Theoretical Schema

In operational terms it is difficult to imagine how the political figure can do anything that will not be influenced by or have some influence on the political appointees and the career service staff. There have been suggestions to the contrary, of course. It is also difficult to imagine that the components of career service staff and political appointees can function in any way without having an influence on the others.

In our schema, we have diagrammed the impact of such factors as special interest groups, television, lobbyists, voters, PACs, and the vast number of recipients of U.S. Federal programs, such as Social Security, welfare, guarantees, etc. These diverse governmental programs ranging from education to prisons constitute powerful influence groups that have major impacts on government operations through their sophisticated lobbying efforts.

Like a giant ecological system, the governmental operations represent a complex, dynamic entity. This entity can only be understood via a systems approach. Looking at government as a tripartite entity gets us nowhere. The tripartite partition is for territory protection. It tells us nothing about the complex operational aspects of government. The role of the systems person, then, is to (1) define the scope (i.e., boundaries) of the governmental system, (2) specify the actors (i.e., politicians, political appointees, and career service staff), and (3) examine the forces impacting on the governmental agency under scrutiny.

Performing the Systems Work

Now comes the time for the systems person to go about the business of performing the analytical work relative to the scope, actors, and forces involved in the system.

The ORSA investigator has a bag of tricks. Of course, the statistical procedures are also available. The discipline called "systems" is essentially eclectic. That is, the systems person steals from any other discipline or source that seems appropriate. This may be anything from mathematical optimizing routines to regular garden variety statistics.

One of the most productive routines for the systems worker is that of sensitivity testing. An example of sensitivity testing might be drawn from the early days of the "cold war." In a test of wills the Soviets opted to "shut off" supplies to the West Berliners. A massive simulation model was built, and sensitivity tests were run. An example of the sensitivity test follows.

Assume that the supplies were prevented from reaching West Berlin. If that happened, what would be the probability that West Berlin would fall to the Soviets? If West Berlin fell, what would be the probability that West Germany would fall? If West Germany fell, what would be the probability that France would fall? If France fell, what would be the probability that Italy would fall? This was continued through Spain, Portugal, and England.

Once a decision was made to supply West Berlin, the next issue was *"how?"* Each of the various means of transportation were considered, (i.e., trucks, barges, trains, and finally planes). It would be easy for the Soviets to block waterways, trains, and trucks without a major international political uproar. Action on the part of the Allies called for something dramatic—an airlift.

It should be pointed out that the same sensitivity tests were used for each type of transportation. Obviously, governments do not make decisions solely on the basis of mathematical models. Neither do large corporations. But if used properly, such models are extremely helpful.

The life and death decisions regarding the Berlin airlift are not substantively different from those associated with getting a school bond passed. The components are similar: (1) the politically active groups, (2) the staff working on the project, and (3) the various voting blocks. The systems worker must determine how those three major components interact and the nature of their interdependencies. The systems analyst must also determine the nature of the forces impacting on those three major components. Developing a procedure for determining the impact of the forces that influence the components may turn out to be one of the most difficult tasks of the study.

We have seen that the task of the systems analyst is to devise the necessary analytical tools for (1) understanding the nature of the interactions and interdependencies and (2) determining the relative influence of the various factors that impact on the system in general and the components in particular. As indicated earlier, the analytical tools can be quantitative or qualitative. The procedure is eclectic. Hence, it borrows from many other disciplines.

Summary

In this chapter we have shown that "systems" as a discipline is both procedural and analytical. Carefully designed systems studies are eclectic and involve using mathematical and heuristic procedures. All systems studies are characterized by seeking practical solutions to real problems. As such, the studies place great emphasis not only on the technical aspects of the problem but also on the environment within which the study takes place.

The keys to any systems study are (1) the definition of the boundary of the system, (2) identification of the major components of the system, (3) the nature of the interactions and interdependencies of the components, and (4) identification and understanding of the forces that have an impact on the components. The contribution of "systems" lies in the fact that all of the above operate as a single entity that is striving to attain some specific goal.

One final word of caution. Systems work is essentially forecasting. Accordingly, unless one is projecting one hundred years into the future, one should be extremely aware of all the key factors involved.

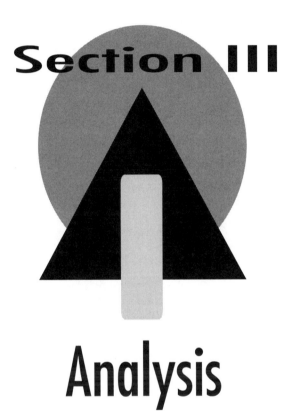

Section III

Analysis

BUSINESS UNIT PERFORMANCE ANALYSIS AND DEVELOPMENT

Danny G. Langdon

Business unit performance analysis and development (BUPAD) is a technique devised by this author in response to the requirement to integrate performance technology with the total quality management (TQM) process. BUPAD is one of four major levels of business improvement that are part of a "new language of work" (Langdon, 1995). The other three levels are process, work-group, and job-level performance analysis and development. This chapter describes only the business-unit level; the other levels of analysis and development are similar, and generalizations can be made from BUPAD to the other levels.

BUPAD was developed using a specific organization—a business unit—and, therefore, is a practical approach based on a real work environment. The business unit produced profit; had a number of clients; had a solid work force; had defined technologies and processes with both product and service orientations; operated within a larger corporate setting with all its support, layers of management, and constraints; and was in a business situation that required performance improvement, even though on the surface it was successful.

BUPAD is a macro approach to performance improvement in that it is used to effect change in a large performance environment. The macro level includes a whole corporation or any of its major divisions or field offices. Although BUPAD is a macro approach, its systematic components can easily be translated to micro work applications, such as problem solving, work planning, business planning, and performance review. The approach described here is a universal model for application throughout the organization, for everyone from worker to manager to executive.

The Structure of BUPAD

The eleven steps in BUPAD follow a systems approach, as reflected in performance technology. A definition of performance technology and TQM follows to help the reader understand why BUPAD is structured as it is and why the order of development must be followed to ensure its success in an organization.

> Performance technology is the systematic process of identifying that a need exists to establish, maintain, extinguish, and/or improve performance in an individual, team, and/or organization. The steps include analyzing the need, identifying, implementing, and networking appropriate interventions, and validating that the results are true improvements (Langdon, 1991; Langdon & Whiteside, 1991).

> Total quality management is the systematic process of identifying, selecting, defining, implementing, and measuring quality improvement points (QIPs) to continually improve individual and business performance to meet client expectations (Langdon, 1992).

On the surface, performance technology and TQM are synonymous. In actual practice, they complement each other. TQM can be the driving force an organization uses to propel and guide the individuals and organization as a unit toward achieving quality. Performance technology, on the other hand, can drive TQM to be the most effective and efficient means to achieve quality ends. Other means of driving TQM are either nonsystematic or, at best, only partly systematic. The "partly" systematic nature of these means is driven primarily by reliance on "measurement," which, although vital and systematic, is only part of a truly systematic process. Performance technology, while incorporating measurement in the form of evaluation/validation, also includes many other essential procedures and processes, such as emphasis on front-end analysis, definition of performance objectives, multi-intervention solutions, and evaluation. These factors "close the loop" of a comprehensive, systematic process. They are the "technology" aspects of performance technology.

The "performance" aspects of performance technology are equally important to TQM. The following are some aspects of performance that are worth noting:

- Performance involves inputs, conditions, processes, outputs, consequences, and feedback in an operational paradigm used to view and practice performance in ways that are meaningful to the organization, its processes, groups of workers, and individuals. Any attempt to define work with other than a complete view of "performance" will produce an inaccurate picture and paltry solutions to business requirements.

- Performance change includes not only how to "improve" performance, but also how to maintain, extinguish, and/or establish performance. The differences in these are significant in determining what interventions must be chosen to change performance. For example, the selection of training, an intervention that *establishes* performance, is not necessarily an appropriate intervention for *maintaining* performance.

- An important operational distinction exists between correcting and preventing performance problems. TQM seeks prevention as its end, rather than merely correction.

- Performance improvement involves the recognition that change brings conflict, and conflict should be viewed as constructive.

It is important for workers, managers, executives, and clients to fully understand, accept, and practice these aspects of performance as these individuals and groups relate with one another to make improvements. For example, authoritarian managers (who view change as a personal affront to their authority) usually will experience personal frustration in, and may not survive, a TQM process. On the other hand, managers who practice "influence," which Adizes (1991) defines as "the capability, not the right, to make another person do something without using authority or power," do survive and flourish. They flourish because the work force is flourishing by participation in the processes of work and, in particular, the improvement of work. Performance technology simply brings the more important systematic and useful procedures and processes to the application of TQM.

The Eleven Steps of BUPAD

The eleven steps of business unit performance analysis and development (BUPAD) that follow describe in detail how the process can be used. BUPAD incorporates both performance and technology to achieve quality ends for the organization.

1. Orientation to work-flow analysis

2. Finalization of work-flow diagram for the organization

3. Identification of performance questions

4. Discussion of performance questions

5. Prioritizing performance questions

6. Measuring quality with the performance questions

7. Meeting performance-improvement requirements and involving others

8. Farming out to division, corporate, and outside resources

9. Reporting on intervention solutions

10. Implementation

11. Evaluation of results and making of further improvements

Steps 1 and 2: Orientation to Work-Flow Analysis and Finalization of Work-Flow Diagram for the Organization

Rummler and Brache (1991) note that managers typically describe how work is accomplished by describing their organizational charts. Organizational charts only show how we are organized to do work, not how work is accomplished from a performance perspective. Work is most accurately described as involving outputs, inputs, conditions, consequences, process, and feedback. One way to portray work is by using "work diagrams." These graphic representations help everyone to discuss and arrive at consensus about what the "work" is with a minimum of emotional interference.

Figure 1 is a work diagram—a sophisticated "conceptual diagram" (Langdon, 1992). It is an actual example from an organization whose work is project-management oriented, as is often true of engineering and construction organizations. The following scenario describes how the work diagram is best formulated.

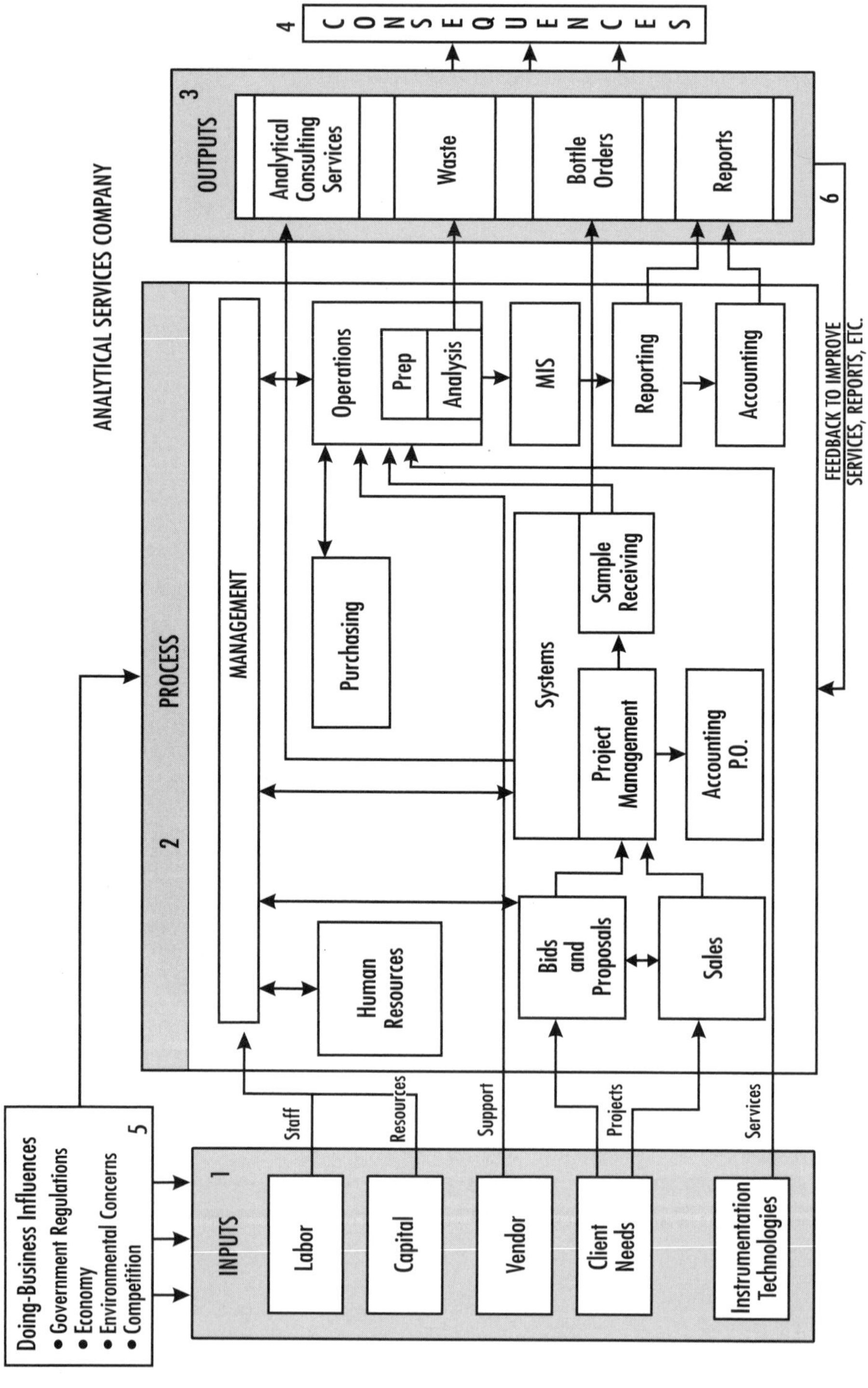

Figure 1. Business Unit Work Diagram

The business-unit manager (director, VP), his or her direct reports, and other personnel, as appropriate, are oriented to the six work elements of a typical work diagram. Within each element, the group is asked to define in proper position and sequence the work that reflects its business. There are six basic work components: first the output, then the inputs, conditions (internal and external), consequences, process, and feedback (i.e., from outputs, during processing, etc.). An initial draft of this map should be shared in a group discussion with others throughout the business to obtain clarity, completeness, and buy-in through involvement in refining the graphic representation depicted in the "work diagram."

Steps 3 and 4: Identification and Discussion of Performance Questions

Managers and other key employees are asked to formulate a series of performance questions for their own and other work groups that, when answered, will accurately and completely define how the various work groups should be measured to demonstrate that they are achieving quality results for their internal and external clients. Figure 2 is a list of performance questions designed to measure the human resources work group in Figure 1. The first question, "Are in-house resumes available/updated?" is certainly important in a project-management-oriented organization. Résumés are important for proposal writing and for finding the right people for the projects that have been approved. Thus, the human resources work element is both responsible for and partially measured by its success in meeting the requirements implied by this question.

The order in which the performance questions are determined is important. The following is a description of how management and other key personnel are asked to do this step of the BUPAD process.

Outputs	Performance Questions
	Human Resources
Résumés	1. Are in-house résumés available/updated?
Performance-Review Plans	2. Are workers provided meaningful performance reviews annually?
Training Program/ Performance-Improvement Programs	3. Are workers receiving needed training and other performance-improvement programs to establish and/or maintain skills and to obtain the knowledge to perform future jobs?
Career-Development Plans	4. Given growth plans, are workers provided career-development opportunities?
Compensation Package Salary Ranges Flexplan	5. Are compensation expectations clearly defined? 6. Are salary ranges in line with competition standards? 7. Is the "flexplan" meeting work needs for health care relative to business ability to provide?
Recruiting Program	8. Are we able to recruit skilled employees to meet general business and project contract requirements?
Employees Hired	9. Are skilled employees hired?

Figure 2. Performance Questions for HR Work Group

After being oriented to the nature and scope of the performance questions—a step that is vital—each individual (initially alone and later with others) is asked to first define the performance questions for his or her own work group. This is designed to get a personal perception of what each group sees as its specific responsibilities (accountabilities) *and how they are measured*. Then, the group is directed to define any performance questions about other work groups that provide input to its own. Next, group members develop performance questions for work groups to which they give their output. They produce performance questions for any other work group in the organization for which they think they can formulate questions. Finally, they are asked to write "general performance questions" that may cut across and between various work elements.

	INPUT	CONDITIONS	PROCESS	OUTPUT	CONSEQUENCES	FEEDBACK
WHAT EXISTS	1. Existing job descriptions 2. Job-task list of past performance 3. Interview with others who know of worker's performance	1. Schedule for reviews 2. Beginning of employment/ 6 months/ tied to salary review, etc. 3. Documentation	1. Worker and manager use Performance-Review form	1. Completed X Corp. "Employee Review Program" booklet 2. Review of past (6-12 month) performance	1. Worker understands past performance and why some opportunities were not feasible 2. Supervisor understands past performance achieved and reasons why opportunities for others were not possible	1. Provide past performance reviews on specific tasks related to each accountability from supervisor and others 2. Job satisfaction in general 3. Periodic progress discussions during the year on current performance
WHAT SHOULD EXIST	1. Projection of job-task needs 2. Career-development objectives	1. Career-development opportunities	1. Need to reflect "Performance Plan" for next 6 months 2. Need to tie job responsibilities to those in job description(s)	1. Performance plan for next 6-12 months 2. Career-development opportunities that are tied to specific job responsibilities of a new job (description)	1. Understand areas for future improvement in present job 2. Understand what job responsibilities to work on for career development 3. Understand relationship of job responsibilities to other jobs he/she works with, for, or might grow toward	1. Periodic progress discussion during the year on career development
SOLUTION(S)	1. Career day; "Somebody Else's Job" 2. Career book 3. Job lunch	None	1. Manager and associates discuss future performance plan for specific responsibilities tied to current job description 2. They list new job accountabilities and how to achieve them	1. Expansion of the existing form to include a plan for the next 6-12 months for current job responsibilities 2. A new section of the performance-review plan that incorporates (a) new job responsibilities to work on, (b) specification of what job the responsibility relates to, and (c) plan for achieving the responsibility over the next 6-12 months	1. Employees' sense that company is proactive in career development and job planning 2. Reduce turnover 3. Meet future job needs 4. Increase morale	1. Add career-development feedback discussions 2. Provide progress reports to human resources on career development for potential job vacancy needs

Having defined the performance questions for its own and others' work elements (it is best to consult with the others in their own work elements), the group meets to discuss each work group one by one and to formulate a set of questions that all members can agree on. This critical discussion serves many purposes, including (1) clarification of one's own and others' responsibilities; (2) establishment of ownership for what one is responsible for and will be measured by; (3) development of quality measurements; (4) the addition, subtraction, or realignment of responsibilities; and, in some instances, (5) the solution to some individual and group performance problems.

One of the more interesting aspects of this approach to defining performance questions (measures) is that it is a "safe" way for those in the organization to express how they would improve their own performance and that of others without appearing to be critical. Also, the approach helps shy people with good ideas to come forth. Nearly everyone in an organization has ideas about how others could work better. When couched in the form of performance questions, these opinions come out in the form of proposed measurements, rather than as criticisms. More important is the clarity of roles and ownership in the business that is established.

Step 5: Prioritizing Performance Questions

The performance questions that are typically formulated through the BUPAD process represent a large amount of information. Not every question can be worked on to improve quality immediately, although some improvement will occur because the topic has been raised. The organization should prioritize the questions to be worked on: first are those with the greatest impact on client satisfaction, the bottom line, and worker involvement. A number of analytical techniques are available, such as nominal grouping, but the best technique may be determined by the group that mapped the organization. Because there are situational factors that set priorities in any organization, asking the group to define these factors and then prioritize in light of them is a more sound and acceptable method than imposing a "sorting" method on the group. Listening to a group that is trying to prioritize soon reveals the criteria it is using, and these can be enumerated and expanded. In this manner, the group's criteria are used systematically to prioritize its performance questions.

Step 6: Measuring Quality with the Performance Questions

The initial principle in applying a performance-technology approach is the determination that a "need" truly exists. A "need" is the difference between "what is" and "what should be."[1] Answers to performance questions establish "what is." Try to answer the performance question in terms of "where on the scale of client satisfaction are we?" "What should be" already has been established by the performance question, although more details often are required for true clarity. Clarity is best defined as a list of desirable characteristics, never as solutions, since this is the mistake of many problem solvers who jump to conclusions.

Again, the clarification required is the degree of improvement that is required to achieve customer satisfaction. Generally, it is not that the work force doesn't know how to do quality work, but rather that something is standing in the way of doing it.

There are a number of measurement techniques (e.g., Pareto diagrams, benchmarking, control charts). Some measurements are as easy as numbers (e.g., work units/hour),

---

[1] According to Kaufman (1992), the gap between "what is" and "what should be" in terms of results of an organization at the micro, macro, and mega levels is a need. Gaps in inputs or processes of the organization are considered "quasi-needs."

while others are much more subjective (e.g., the quality of a proposal). The main objective to be achieved in this step of BUPAD is a measure of client satisfaction. A thorough description of measurement is not possible here. A general guideline is to make sure you measure each performance question in terms of the performance it specifies, avoiding indirect measurement. For example, asking for an opinion where a quantitative measurement is required would be inappropriate.

Steps 7 and 8: Meeting Performance-Improvement Requirements and Involving Others, and Farming Out to Division, Corporate, and Outside Resources

In the tradition of TQM, those who are in the best position to solve problems are the ones affected by the problem. They may want the help of some outside expertise, but those affected should take ongoing participative and leadership roles. Otherwise, ownership in the process is diminished and the process is doomed to failure. People must have the authority, power, and influence to solve the problems that affect their own operations. The next step in BUPAD is to improve those things that require improving.

There are several techniques available for meeting business-unit-improvement requirements. These include brainstorming, several versions of problem solving, some job aids, flowcharting, and force-field analysis. One of the more interesting techniques at the micro level that is similar to a work diagram (see Figure 1) is the ICPOCF (inputs, conditions, processes, outputs, consequences, and feedback) model of solving problems. Table 1 is a matrix diagram of the ICPOCF model. The following scenario describes how the model is used by a group.

During problem solving, the group is asked to list (starting with outputs) the various inputs, conditions, processes, outputs, consequences, and feedback related to the performance-improvement need under consideration. Both what exists currently and what should exist are to be specified. From the discrepancies between these—the difference between what exists and what should exist—the necessary interventions are identified as the solutions to business-improvement requirements.

No matter what process is used to meet business requirements, it is critical to involve others—particularly those who are affected by the change. This not only provides good input, it builds commitment to change in the organization as a whole.

Step 9: Reporting on Intervention Solutions

Group interaction in the analysis, problem solving, implementation, and evaluation stages is an important part of the ICPOCF process. This is particularly true when reporting on proposed intervention solutions because of the following:

- The group discussion is used to check on the group and individual development of analytical and problem-solving skills. Experience has shown that providing training and having group members practice analytical and development skills in the training environment does not ensure that members will apply the skills on the job. The facilitator should keep checking on and assisting the learning/application process when and where it is actually to be used.

- Reporting keeps the team on the BUPAD track—a road from which groups easily stray because it is much easier to concentrate on "getting work done."

- The group sessions provide an excellent opportunity to introduce and learn new techniques—particularly as they may relate to a current problem.

- The process often leads to the identification of other performance-improvement requirements. This encourages the view that BUPAD is an ongoing activity. For example, performance requirements discussed "in the halls" and in other meetings should be brought into the BUPAD analysis process. If they are not systematically incorporated, these needs simply fester because "nobody does anything about them." BUPAD can help ensure that this does not happen.

- BUPAD is merely the tip of the iceberg from which analyses and development of processes, work groups, and individual jobs are looked at for improvement. When BUPAD is done right, the other levels of analysis in the business are much easier to accomplish. This is a matter not only of gaining experience, but also of realizing that the improvement of processes, work groups, and job levels is directly dependent on the first stage of BUPAD.

Steps 10 and 11: Implementation and Evaluation of Results and Making of Further Improvements

Implementation and evaluation follow the usual conventions of either an instructional or a performance-technology approach. As described in step 6, there are a variety of evaluation techniques, including benchmarking, client surveys, control charts, histograms, and Pareto diagrams. However, the direct evaluation of the performance implicit in the performance-improvement requirement is paramount. One of the more immediate requirements (beside measuring client satisfaction) is to provide accurate data to improve the interventions that are being used to make an improvement. The intent is not just to prove that the intervention did or did not work! Evaluation often necessitates revisions to the intervention. Once the interventions are doing what they are designed to do, other evaluation techniques that typically demonstrate the effect of several related interventions should be implemented. This is particularly true of macro evaluations that measure internal and external client satisfaction and employee satisfaction.

Benefits of BUPAD

Business unit performance analysis and development is a systematic approach to improving the effectiveness and efficiency of an organization. Used by an organization dedicated to using TQM, it is particularly systematic. Combine this with the use of other performance-technology principles and procedures, and one can expect outstanding results.

For the managers and workers using BUPAD, one can expect:

- Clarification of expectations and responsibilities;
- Building of the kind of mutual respect and trust that is necessary to have a truly committed work force (Adizes, 1991);
- Clear understanding of how individuals and work groups will be measured in their performance and contribution;
- Systematic problem solving;
- Measurement against output to and from other internal and external clients.

For the organization itself, BUPAD provides the most systematic approach to identifying and interrelating required improvements. Large lists of quality-improvement requirements can be derived from "brainstorming" or simply asking workers and managers to make suggestions. These are useful techniques because employees feel that they are making a contribution. Only a systematic process like BUPAD ensures that all aspects of each work element are defined as outputs for a particular work group and inputs for other elements. Only BUPAD can help to show the *interrelationship* between these requirements. Because a solution in one work group of an organization affects other work groups, knowing the inter-relationships is important. One must remember that business-unit performance is made up of one group's output, which affects another group's input. An independent, one-department approach to solving "our own problem" is not valid if the organization is to improve as a whole. BUPAD ensures an interdependent view of the work elements that make up an organization.

References

Adizes, I. (1991). *Mastering change*. Santa Monica, CA: Adizes Institute.

Kaufman, R. (1992). *Strategic planning plus: An organizational guide*. Newbury Park, CA: Sage.

Langdon, D.G. (1991, August). Performance technology in three paradigms. *Performance & Instruction Journal*.

Langdon, D.G. (1992). *The total quality management orientation workshop*. Performance International, Santa Monica, CA.

Langdon, D.G. (1995). *The new language of work*. Amherst, MA: HRD Press.

Langdon, D.G. (1995). *The work technology series*. Performance International, Santa Monica, CA.

Langdon, D.G., & Whiteside, K. (1991). *The performance technology workshop*. Performance International, Santa Monica, CA.

Rummler, G., & Brache, A.P. (1991). *Improving performance: How to manage the white space on the organization chart*. San Francisco, CA: Jossey-Bass.

ORGANIZATIONAL MAPPING

*Randolph I. James
and Carol Panza*

The sales division manager of an organization that sells industrial gases has set some lofty expectations for its sales employees. "These goals are certainly realistic. We can achieve a 25 percent increase in sales just by concentrating on new customers within our existing regions," he explains at the annual sales retreat. "I have total buy-in from upper management and they have assured me that we will receive all the administrative support that we require."

The objective has been set (a 25 percent increase in sales) and the strategy has been developed (expand the customer base). The accounting and legal departments are primed and waiting to process the new contracts the minute that they close. The sales force has been increased substantially and descends on the region. New sales are found quickly, contracts are written and signed.

Three months later the sales manager learns that a mere 4 percent of the new contracts have actually resulted in new sales (and new revenues). Unfortunately, the tank installation function was not staffed at a level consistent with the customer development goals of the sales group. Since the company is unable to meet the criteria specified in the contract, many new customers are now turning to a competitor to meet their requirements.

Situations like this are quite common in many organizations. Goals are set and pursued in one part of the organization without any regard to what must be done to support the effort in other parts of the organization. Before you can manage or improve a process (or an organization), you have to understand how the functional pieces interact with and depend on one another. Detailed work flow diagrams are often used to look at a specific process. However, managers should first have a "big-picture" view of how that process fits in with other organizational processes (e.g., the sales function with *all* other organizational functions). This view can be accomplished by developing an *organization map*.

Standard Management View

The standard way that organizations are managed and organized is functional and vertical (as described by a typical organization chart). The chart in Figure 1 presents the sales function described in the previous example. It gives you a good idea of who reports to whom but does little to describe just how the business really operates.

Common Sense Management View

An organization should be viewed and managed the way it operates. This common sense (or operational) view gives management the ability to manage the critical functional interfaces (a frequent source of opportunities for improvement). The diagram in Figure 2 (an organizational map) describes an operational view of that same sales function yet identifies those critical functional interfaces and their valued inputs and results.

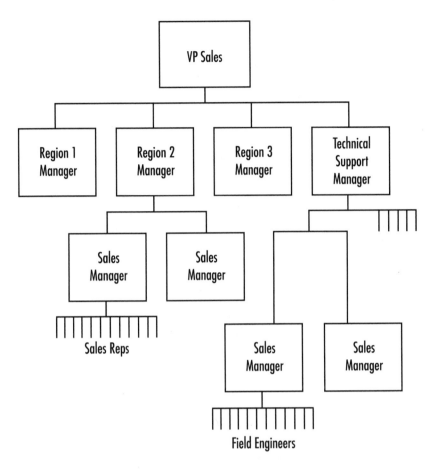

Figure 1. Organizational Chart

An organizational map is a graphic representation of how a process or an organization works. There are many areas that have an impact on performance (organizational) results (see Figure 3). Organizational mapping gives managers and/or analysts the ability to visually present a great deal of information about what is, and/or what should be happening within a process or organization. Suppliers, customers, inputs, and results, etc., are presented in a clear, concise, and easy-to-understand format. Figure 4 describes the features and benefits of using the organizational mapping tool.

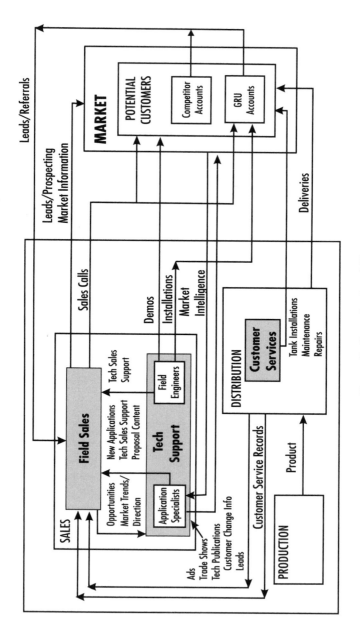

Figure 2. Organizational Map

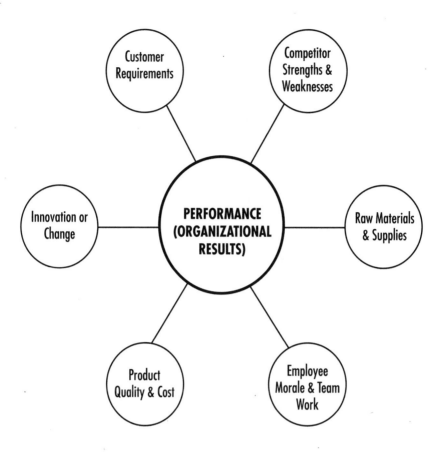

Figure 3. Ogranizational Results

Impact Area	Map Use/Features	Benefit(s)
Customer Requirements Competitor Strengths & Weaknesses	Describe the organization's performance (market) context and overlay objectives.	A logical and practical way to calibrate your own output measures to the marketplace to ensure management control directed to market success.

Figure 4. Benefits of Organizational Mapping

Impact Area	Map Use/Features	Benefit(s)
Raw Materials & Supplies	Describe all necessary inputs including when and where they are required, dependencies, and specific requirements.	A way to clearly and completely establish input requirements, specific vendor expectations, and tradeoffs or contingency-plan needs.
Employee Morale & Team Work	Show the interface between functions and/or work units and what the various components get from and provide to one another.	Supports a team orientation by highlighting operations and unique contributions to common/joint goals rather than focusing on hierarchy and reporting relationships.
Product Quality & Cost	Show the sequence of steps completed (accomplishments) or required to produce any valued product or service.	Facilitates the identification of gaps or overlaps of responsibility, highlighting of current or potential stress points, development of practical process-supportive measurement and, therefore, performer feed-back/management information.
Innovation or Change	Describe the interfaces and/or steps required to produce a new or modified product/service or to handle a new or modified input.	Allows the organization to anticipate supplies/supplier requirements, performer feedback, and management-information requirements as well as to develop useful implementation plans for required changes or innovations.

Figure 4 (continued). Benefits of Organizational Mapping

Levels of Vantage

Organizations and their component functions have no lives of their own. They are collections of performers. So, it is important to conduct any analysis or performance improvement effort at several organizational levels of vantage. Organizational mapping can be undertaken using the same mega, macro, and micro framework presented in the introductory chapter. Figures 5, 6, and 7 present organizational map examples at each of these levels for a public service agency (a retirement system) that provides investment and benefit payment services for a particular member population (teachers and their dependents).

Constructing an Organizational Map

Mapping requires analytical, communications, and even graphics skills. All these skills can be acquired and honed to a very useful level of competence. However, it does not happen overnight. True skill development requires a learning process that includes conceptual knowledge acquisition and opportunities to practice the critical skills. Organizational map construction can be summarized in four steps.

Step 1: Identify Primary Components

The primary components to identify are the supplier(s), input(s), customer(s), and valued results (outcomes, outputs, and products). Begin your map by placing these components in a *systems flow* format. The following example addresses a typical purchasing process. The primary supplier (a requesting department) and value outputs were identified and placed on the map.

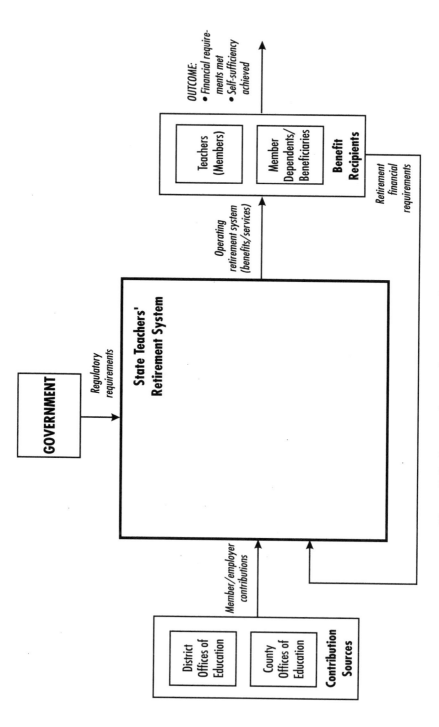

Figure 5. Retirement-System Organizational Map

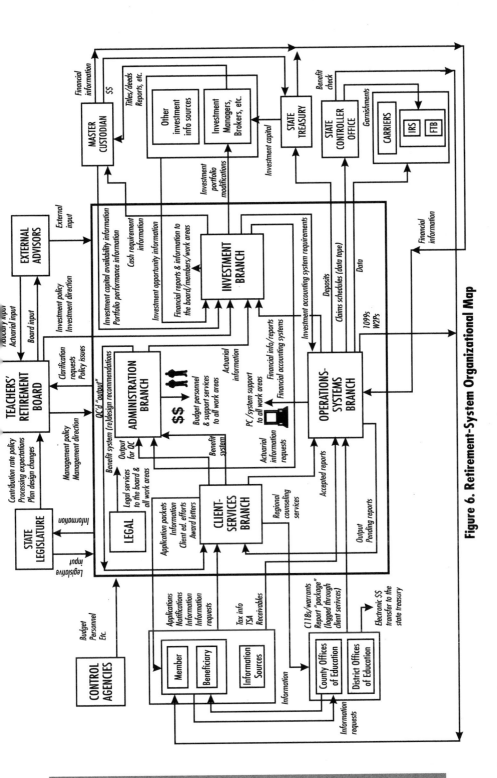

Figure 6. Retirement-System Organizational Map

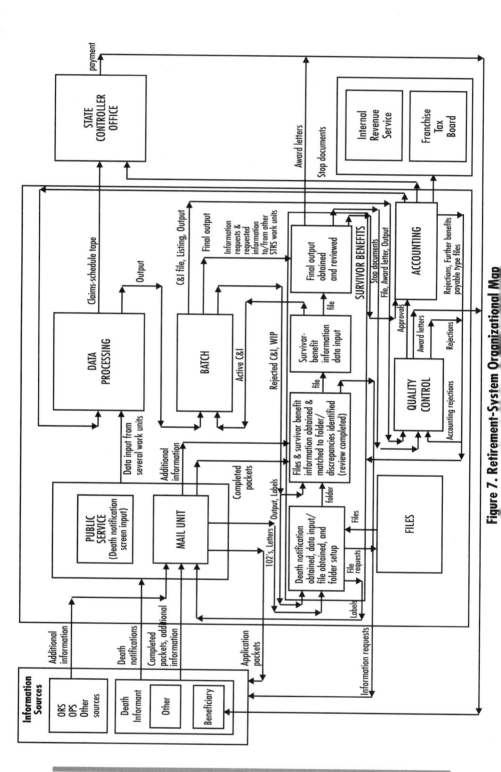

Figure 7. Retirement-System Organizational Map

The Guidebook for Performance Improvement

Level of Vantage	Valued Result
Mega	*Outcome:* old age security, well-being, and high quality of living of pensioner/dependents
Macro	*Output:* operating retirement system (benefits and servides)
Micro	*Products:* benefit checks (in this case for member survivors)

Figure 8. Levels of Vantage and Results

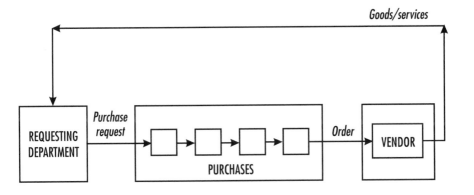

Figure 9. Primary Components

Step 2: Identify Other Related Subprocesses (or Functions)

An organization (or process) is wired together by the inputs and products that are received from or provided to other organizational entities (divisions, sections, work units, etc.) and/or related processes. In the example (Figure 10), two other organizational units are also involved in the purchasing process: stores (receives, logs, stores, and distributes the purchased product) and accounting (receives, secures approval, and pays the invoice).

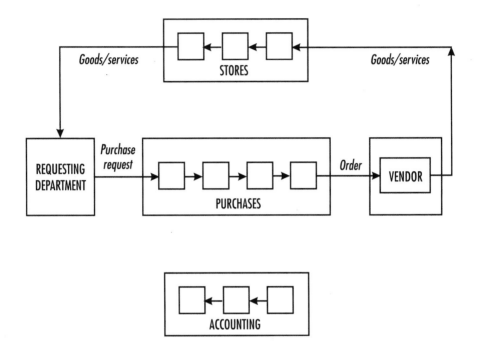

Figure 10. Related Subprocesses

Step 3: Identify and Label Subprocess (or Functional) Products

Each identified subprocess (or work unit) also has a defined and valued product. In the purchases example (Figure 11), products were defined for the accounting work area (the payment subprocess), the purchases work area (the bidding subprocess), and the stores work area (the reorder subprocess). All these products reconcile with the primary output of the purchases process. It is important to document the flow of these products on your map with lines and arrows.

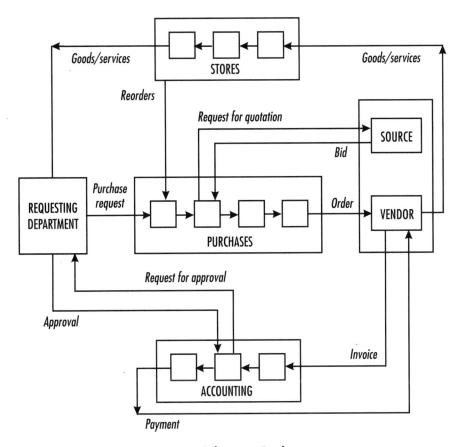

Figure 11. Subprocess Products

Step 4: Draw and Label the Major Boundary

The last step in developing an organizational map is to draw and label the major processing-system boundary. This gives the map a *systems perspective* and makes it easier to identify key feedback channels and important functional interfaces. The finished example in Figure 12 truly documents the process being examined. It is now possible to see how different work units (and subprocesses) interact with and depend on each other. This information is not available on the standard organizational chart.

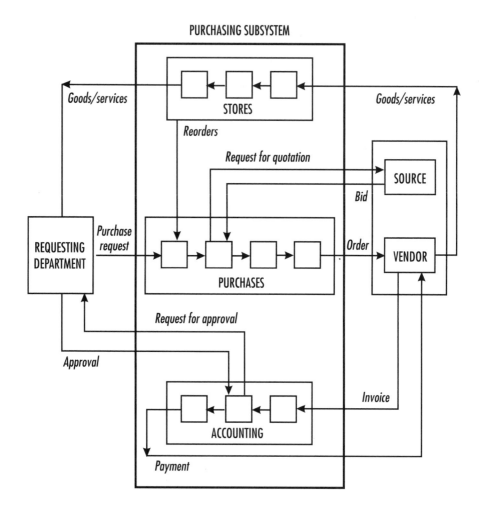

Figure 12. Major Processing-System Boundary

The mapping process is an excellent vehicle for converting large amounts of data (gathered through interviews, existing work-flow documentation, organizational charts, etc.) into information. However, the informative value really depends on the nature of the intended audience and how the information will be used. That means thinking about who is going to look at the map and what information they require before you begin to develop it. Before constructing a map, you should think through the following checklist of questions (Figure 13).

Being competent at converting data into information requires practice and skill. It also takes some artistic/graphics talent to package the information in a way to achieve its intended purpose. Figure 14 presents a simple checklist to be used to review the design or layout characteristics of an organizational map.

☐ **Who is the intended audience for this map?**

    ☐ How are they likely to react to a map? (Could they be intimidated or turned off by boxes and arrows, a complex graphic, a simple graphic, etc.?)

    ☐ Are there any politics that would lead you to position functions in any particular way within the map or cause you to consider size or highlighting?

    ☐ Are there any labels or jargon that should be included or excluded?

    ☐ Will the map be presented, or will the target audience be reviewing the map on its own? In other words, will the map have to stand alone?

    ☐ Is there any reason to believe that comprehension skills may be an issue?

☐ **How do I want the target audience to react or what do I want them to do as a result of reviewing this map?**

☐ **How will I know if I have achieved the desired results with this map?**

Figure 13. Checklist of Questions

DESIGN/LAYOUT CHECKLIST

☐ Are all labels legible (with the naked eye)?

☐ Is language style, jargon, and tense usage consistent?

☐ If there are labels (words) on both boxes and arrows, are they clearly differentiated?

☐ Would the additon of symbols like ℂ ✐ ✉ add to the communication effectiveness?

☐ Have shading or line weight/patterns been used to maximize the clarity of groupings of things or differentiation of things?

☐ Can arrows be followed?

☐ Is the language and direction of "yes" and "no" exits for flow decision-diamonds consistent?

☐ What can a non-subject-matter expert tell you about the organization mapped after an unguided review? After a guided walk-through? How about subject-matter experts?

☐ Have boxes been positioned to minimize the need for arrows to "jump over" each other?

☐ Is the overall appearance of the finished map professional or just "busy"?

☐ How do non-subject-matter experts react to the first sight of the map? What about management-level individuals?

☐ How do subject-matter experts react to the first sight of the map?

Figure 14. Design/Layout Checklist

Summary

Before you can manage or improve a process (or organization) you must understand how it works (or is going to work). Organizational mapping helps managers, analysts, and technicians understand how the functional pieces of a process (or organization) interact with and depend on each other. An organizational map also can be used to help

- Identify opportunities for performance improvement;

- Gain agreement on roles and/or interface requirements between functions;

- Design a way to produce a new or modified product/service;

- Describe the performance context for a given organization or specific functional component.

Organizational mapping is a valuable tool for practitioners undertaking performance management, improvement, and/or planning efforts.

JOB-TASK ANALYSIS

Wallace Hannum

Definition and Rationale

A fundamental assumption in performance technology, as well as in instructional systems development, is that the education and training a person receives should focus on enhancing his or her job performance. Thus, determining what a person must know and must do to carry out a specific job is one very important aspect of enhancing job performance. Task analysis serves this function. Task analysis is the process of identifying the various tasks a person must perform while completing a job, determining which of these tasks require training, and identifying the component knowledge and skill that a person must possess in order to perform each task acceptably.

In many respects, task analysis "drives" all of training by establishing the content of the training. Task analysis is the basis for development of the instructional objectives and assessment items; these follow directly from the job tasks. To the extent that instructional strategies are selected according to the objectives to be taught, task analysis is also a principal basis for the instructional strategy selection. Finally, since the evaluation is based on mastery of objectives and job performance and, since objectives follow directly from the task analysis and the evaluation of job performance assesses tasks identified in the task analysis, task analysis serves to guide the evaluation of the training. Thus, task analysis defines the starting point and focus for training (the objectives), contributes to selecting the methodology for training (the instructional strategies), and forms the basis for assessing the effectiveness of training (criterion tests and job tasks). In short, information collected in a task analysis is vital to all aspects of training (Kemp, Morrison, & Ross, 1994). It is hard to imagine how education and training could proceed effectively without attention to task analysis data.

Role of Task Analysis in Performance Technology

Before examining task analysis in depth, let's look at the relationship of task analysis to other aspects of performance technology. Since task analysis identifies the content for training, task analysis presupposes the existence of a performance problem that can be resolved through training. The only way to be certain this is the case is to conduct a thorough needs assessment. Needs assessment and task analysis serve a different purpose. Needs assessment is used to determine the overall direction by focusing on discrepancies between the ideal and the actual situation (Gentry, 1994, Kaufman, 1994). If there is no discrepancy—no need—then there is no reason to complete a task analysis or to provide training. It is when discrepancies are documented through a needs assessment that task analysis becomes necessary.

When discrepancies are found, most needs assessment models also rank order the discrepancies according to severity. Some discrepancies may be so minor that they are not worth addressing. Finally, through needs assessment or performance analysis the probable causes of the discrepancies are determined. Discrepancies between the ideal, or desired, state and the actual state may arise for many reasons. For example, inadequate tools or faulty equipment may cause performance discrepancies. Poor motivation due to a lack of any incentives for proper performance may lead to performance discrepancies.

In these cases, additional training is likely to be of little value in resolving the performance discrepancies because the problem is not a lack of knowledge or skill but rather a lack of proper tools and proper incentives. Training is a solution only when the performance discrepancies arise from a lack of knowledge or skill. So, before initiating a task analysis, you should complete a needs assessment to determine whether documentable needs exist and complete a performance analysis to determine whether they arise because of a lack of knowledge or skill (Hannum & Hansen, 1989). Then task analysis is appropriate, even essential, to continuing the performance improvement process.

Common Task Analysis Functions

There are many different task analysis models and procedures, but most share three common functions (Jonassen, Hannum, & Tessmer). First, task analysis models include procedures for deriving a list or inventory of tasks performed when conducting a specific job. Second, task analysis models include procedures for selecting, from among all the tasks performed when conducting a specific job, those tasks that require additional training. Third, task analysis models include procedures for analyzing or breaking down tasks performed into their subtasks and supporting tasks. Thus, most task analysis models contain the following three components:

- Task inventory
- Task selection
- Task analysis

A task inventory is simply a listing, or inventory, of all the specific tasks a person may perform when doing a certain job. For example, a task inventory for an automobile mechanic would include such tasks as remove and replace spark plugs, diagnose the cause for stalling, and adjust the timing.

Task selection occurs because most jobs include rather long task inventories listing what a job incumbent may do in that job. It is rarely possible, or necessary, to provide training for each task contained in a task listing. Rather, some tasks are more important or more critical than others; job incumbents should be trained to perform these tasks. Other tasks are less important to overall job performance or can be learned easily when on the job. Thus, it may not be necessary to develop or provide training for these tasks. Task selection is that aspect of task analysis that attempts to determine which tasks require training.

The actual task analysis occurs once a task inventory is completed and tasks are selected for training. Most task analysis models break these tasks into component subtasks that represent smaller tasks. In fact, some task analysis models break tasks down into very small, discrete motions, such as grasping the handle on a socket wrench to remove the spark plugs. Other task analysis models identify the underlying knowledge a person must possess to perform each specific task. This step is the very heart of task analysis since it identifies how a task is accomplished. Different task analysis models have different procedures for completing the analysis but the intent is essentially the same—to determine how a job task is, or should be, performed.

Task Inventory

The first aspect of overall task analysis is to complete a task inventory. There is considerable agreement among task analysis models regarding task inventories; the inventory lists the specific tasks that make up a job. The language that different task analysts use in task inventories differs somewhat. The differences are primarily in terms of the level of specificity in wording and the degree of observability of the tasks in the listing. Some task listings include rather broad tasks: edit documents; others include only very specific tasks: correct spelling errors. Some task listings include only tasks that are behaviorally stated and directly observable: check voltage of circuits; others include nonbehaviorally stated tasks: troubleshoot electrical problems. The intent among task analysts preparing task inventories is the same—to capture the tasks that make up a job. The differences that appear in task inventories are a matter of judgment in wording of the tasks, not a fundamental difference among task analysts.

Task analysts use several data sources and data-collection methods for gathering data when compiling a task inventory (Campbell, 1989). A common source for gathering information for task inventories are job incumbents. Task analysts ask people skilled and experienced in completing a particular job what they do in their job.

Several different data-collection methods can be used to gather data from job incumbents to construct task inventories. Task analysts can observe job incumbents as they perform their jobs and record what tasks they perform. Observing job incumbents is time-consuming and expensive but is based in the reality of actual job performance. The task analyst using observation for data collection may, however, not notice the job incumbents perform certain tasks. Plus, the task analyst cannot probe further about the tasks.

An alternative to observation for collecting task inventory data is to interview job incumbents. This allows the task analyst to gain the job incumbents' point of view regarding tasks they perform and allows the analyst to probe further about specific tasks performed. An interview can accommodate individual job incumbents and may in the process get better information than a survey, which by its very nature is the same for all job incumbents. A specific incumbent may not understand a survey question but could seek clarification in an interview. Of course, both observations and interviews are limited to a few job incumbents because of the time and expense of gathering data in this manner.

As an alternative to the observation and interview methods for completing task inventories, the task analyst may survey a larger number of job incumbents and have them indicate what tasks they perform in completing their jobs. Surveys are much less time-consuming and expensive than observation or interviews. Much data can be gathered quickly from more job incumbents. Thus, a survey may ensure a more adequate representation of job incumbents than observing or conducting interviews with a small number of job incumbents. Of course, in a survey the task analyst cannot probe further about a specific job task as in an interview.

Some task analysts may use a combination of observation, interviews, and surveys to create task inventories. This combination of data collection methods can alleviate the weaknesses of any one method used alone. Naturally, using a combination of data-collection methods is expensive.

Another source of task inventory data are supervisors or managers since they know how a job is to be performed. Data from supervisors and managers are usually collected through interviews or surveys rather than observation, since these people do not perform the job tasks routinely. The advantages and disadvantages of interviews and surveys as data-collection methods, mentioned in the context of job incumbents, remain the same when collecting data from supervisors and managers.

When a job requires the use of some specialized equipment, the equipment manufacturer may supply a listing of the tasks to be followed when using their equipment. This information may be used when preparing a task inventory. This is particularly true if the job involves using newly invented or developed equipment. In this case, there are no existing job incumbents since no one has used the equipment before. In this circumstance the task analyst must rely on the manufacturer to identify the tasks. Experts in a particular field are another source of information for developing task inventories. Some task analysts rely on experts to describe how a job should be done rather than on incumbents who may not be performing a job optimally.

There are advantages and disadvantages of using each group of people to capture the reality of doing the job and describe the tasks they complete. Some job incumbents may "shortcut" the recommended procedures for completing certain aspects of their jobs and, thus, make their job easier or quicker to do. Their task inventory represents their way of doing the job, which may be less than ideal. Supervisors and managers may be able to give a better idea of how the job should be done devoid of "shortcuts." However, the supervisors and managers may be too far removed from the actual work itself to provide a reasonable task inventory. Their task inventory may be either outdated, reflecting how the job was done years ago when they did the job, or too idealized, reflecting only a "textbook" knowledge of the job devoid of the essential day-to-day reality.

Equipment manufacturers can provide information about the tasks that must be completed when using one of their products. However, their view of the job may be at variance with the actual job; they may describe how to use the equipment under ideal circumstances. The care and use of the equipment on the job may be at considerable variance from a manufacturer's suggested use.

Experts in the job can supply information about the steps in doing a job well. Experts, likewise, may give flawed task inventories. They may describe an idealized way to complete the job, consistent with the theory and textbook, but at odds with reality. Or, they may describe a method that works for them based on a characteristic they have, such as superior hand-eye coordination. When the majority of workers attempt the same task, they may fail since they lack the superior hand-eye coordination.

Some task analysts maintain that job incumbents may describe how they do a job without representing how the job can best be done or should be done. In short, these task analysts do not want information about how a job is done by average or below-average performers to be the basis for training new people how top performers do the job. Experts, on the other hand, can describe how the job should be done, not just how most people do it. The experts may be selected from among top-performing job incumbents, supervisors, or those who have studied the particular job.

Some task analysts prefer to use a combination of data sources and data-collection methods when compiling a task inventory. This combination can overcome the limitations encountered by relying totally on one data source and collection method. The task analyst can compare data from multiple sources collected in multiple ways to corroborate tasks in a task listing. If a task was mentioned in interviews with incumbents and supervisors and reported by large numbers of incumbents and supervisors in a survey, and the task analyst observed incumbents performing the task on their job, the analyst can be reasonably certain that task is an inherent part of doing the job. Thus, that task belongs on the task inventory. Of course, this comprehensive approach to compiling a task inventory is often impossible because of budget and time constraints.

Task Selection

The second aspect of overall task analysis is task selection. When task analysts complete task inventories, they identify numerous specific tasks that make up a job. Since training budgets as well as the time available for completing training are limited, few organizations provide training on all of the tasks in the task inventories. Thus, most task analysis models provide procedures for selecting tasks for which training should be provided from among all the tasks in the task inventories.

The common task selection procedure is to collect information about each specific task in the task inventory. This information is used to determine whether to provide training on that task. For example, if a particular task is very critical to overall job performance, then training would be provided on that task instead of another task that was less critical to overall job performance.

Different task analysis models employ different criteria for task selection. Tracey, Flynn, and Legere (1966) specified several criteria for use in task selection in a model developed for the U.S. Army. Prior to their work, most of the decisions about task selection were subjective, not based on any tangible criteria. The task selection procedure developed by Tracey, Flynn, and Legere included the following task selection criteria:

- Universality
- Difficulty
- Criticality
- Frequency
- Practicability
- Achievability
- Quality
- Deficiency
- Retainability
- Follow-on training

They suggest that each task in the task inventory be rated either yes or no on each of these criteria. The final task selection would be based on the results from several people who evaluated the tasks. The other military services and private companies adopted similar task selection methods but altered the ten criteria to meet their requirements. The most common set of task selection criteria include only four of the original ten criteria: universality, criticality, difficulty, and frequency (Jonassen, Hannum, & Tessmer, 1989). One common approach to task selection is termed the D-I-F model because it uses difficulty, importance, and frequency as the task selection criteria.

Many users of a task selection process use a scale for rating each task on each criterion rather than a simple yes/no. Thus, the difficulty of completing a task, or the importance of a task, may be rated from 1 to 9 rather than the binary difficult/not difficult, important/not important.

The data collected for task selection are typically placed in a matrix with individual tasks as one dimension and the selection criteria as the other. Each cell contains the score for that task on that criterion. These scores may be the sum across all raters or the average of these because the task selection process is so quantitative. Many organizations have straightforward procedures for making decisions about which tasks to include in the training. Some simply rank each task according to its total score and select for training as many tasks as time and budget allow. Others use a differential weighing scheme, which places greater value on certain criteria, such as criticality. Users of this differential weighing scheme use a formula multiplying the score of each task on each criterion by a weight reflecting the importance of that criterion.

Expert systems have been developed for task selection as a way to automate the task selection process. The expert systems are based on rules for sorting and ranking tasks based on a data matrix that includes the score for each task on each of several criteria. This is the same data that task analysts would use when making similar decisions. The expert systems automate the process and make appropriate task selection decisions when no task analysts are available.

Task Analysis

The third aspect in overall task analysis is also termed "task analysis." This creates some unfortunate confusion in terminology, but the term "task analysis" is descriptive of the third part of the overall approach to task analysis. This aspect involves the actual breaking down, or analysis, of tasks into subtasks or component tasks and the identification of the knowledge and skill necessary for successful task performance. In many ways, this task analysis step is the very core of overall task analysis.

While the procedures for conducting a task inventory and task selection are fairly straightforward and agreed on at least in a general sense, appropriate procedures for task analysis are debated. The many models describing how to do task analysis differ considerably in their approach. In a comprehensive review of task analysis models, Jonassen, Hannum, and Tessmer (1989) described twenty-seven task analysis models that differ primarily in terms of how they analyze tasks. They grouped the task analysis models in three categories: learning analysis, behavioral job analysis, and content or subject-matter analysis. Learning analysis models are appropriate for identifying the requirements for learning how to perform a certain task.

Behavioral job analysis models include the traditional task analysis models that start with a job and seek to determine the various tasks one must do to perform that job. Models for content or subject-matter analysis include procedures for defining a traditional school curriculum of math, English, or sciences. The learning analysis and behavioral job analysis models are more appropriate for performance technology. These two types of models differ primarily in their focus. The learning analysis models are focused more on instruction rather than on the job. The behavioral job analysis models are focused more on the job rather than on instruction. The learning analysis models seek to identify what one must learn in order to achieve a certain instructional outcome. Behavioral job analysis models seek to identify the various tasks and subtasks one must perform to accomplish the job.

The difference among the various task analysis models can also be understood by noting the distinction between job tasks and learning tasks. Job tasks are those tasks, and subtasks, that one does as a part of his or her job. Learning tasks are those outcomes sought during instruction.

Of course, the learning tasks may be based on the job tasks; in a training environment one hopes this is the case. But there is a fundamental difference in job tasks and learning tasks: job tasks reflect what is done in a job; learning tasks reflect what is to be learned in school. Some task analysis models are appropriate for analyzing job tasks (the behavioral job analysis models); other task analysis models are more appropriate for analyzing learning tasks (the learning analysis models). In an overall approach to performance improvement, you may first use a behavioral job analysis model to analyze job performance and establish direction for the training. Then, when the job performance has been translated into the training environment and training goals and objectives have been established, a learning analysis model may be used to analyze these instructional outcomes to identify the prerequisite knowledge and skill that must be taught. The focus in this chapter is on task analysis for job tasks rather than the analysis of learning tasks. For a more exhaustive description of task analysis models, the reader should consult the volume by Jonassen, Hannum, and Tessmer (1989).

Behavioral Job Analysis

The most common task analysis method for analyzing job tasks requires a decomposition of job tasks into simpler subtasks, component tasks, or steps. Often a task analyst will begin with a job, then identify separate duties that make up that job, and finally identify the tasks that make up each separate duty (Hannum and Hansen, 1989). Task analysis models that proceed in such a fashion are usually behaviorally based. Years ago Miller (1962) described a model for task analysis, termed "task description," in which the task analyst described exactly what a person would do in his job. Based on systems analysis, this task description approach seeks to define how a worker interacts within an overall system to enhance its effectiveness. This approach seeks to maximize the interface between people and equipment for effective job performance by indicating exactly what a worker should do when using a piece of equipment. A task description is considerably detailed and includes the cue that initiates the action, the cue that calls for a response from the worker, the equipment or object to be controlled, the specific action of the worker, and the feedback indicating a satisfactory response.

Several other task analysis models have a behavioral orientation and, thus, are very similar to Miller's task description model. McCormick (1979) developed a behaviorally based task analysis model he termed "methods analysis." Methods analysis begins with broad job categories and processes to identify small discrete motions by the workers. As with other behavioral task analysis models, methods analysis assumes one can break complex job performances into very simple, discrete units of motion. This model takes an industrial engineering approach to task analysis, seeking to describe an optimal job performance composed of these small, elemental motions identified by a trained analyst.

Fine and his colleagues (1973, 1974) used a precise vocabulary and classification system to identify the functions a person performed when completing a job. They believe that any job may be described in terms of the relation among people, data, and things. Each task can be rated on their standardized worker function scales. Their people scale includes mentoring, negotiating, supervising, consulting, etc. Their data scale includes synthesizing, analyzing, compiling, etc. Their things scale includes setting up, handling, controlling, etc. By including a precise statement of what a worker did in terms of people, data, and things, they sought to develop standardized task descriptions that cut across jobs.

The task analysis model developed by Mager and Beach (1967) is an example of a behavioral approach to task analysis. Their model breaks a job down into specific tasks and then steps performed when executing the task. Another behavioral task analysis model is the training situation analysis model developed for the U.S. Navy. This task analysis model organizes related tasks into blocks, indicates the time spent by workers on each block, describes activities of a single task, and specifies training requirements.

Process and Task Analysis

Some task analysis models seek to identify the procedures a job incumbent must complete in his or her job. These models extend beyond just breaking an overall task down into its component subtasks. They seek to identify the step-by-step procedures a job incumbent follows when completing a task (Merrill, 1980). These models result in flowcharts depicting what is done in a particular job. These procedural task analysis models are appropriate when incumbents follow algorithms in completing their jobs. In completing a procedural task analysis, the task analyst would observe the performance of a job incumbent and represent this performance in a flowchart. Naturally, the task analyst would observe more than one job incumbent to establish the flowchart. The task analyst would also review the flowchart with job incumbents to verify the steps in the flow- chart, particularly any decision points. Some procedural task analysis models attempt to identify what knowledge a person must possess to perform the procedures. The extended task analysis procedure model developed by Reigeluth and Merrill (1984) is an example of such a model.

While there are some distinctions among these models, the similarities are more striking. These task analysis models are all behaviorally based—they begin, and end, with descriptions stated in terms of observable behaviors. All these models assume that an overall job can be broken down into a series of simpler behaviors. They differ in terms of the degree of specificity of the behavioral specifications of tasks. Some have a very exacting vocabulary; others allow more flexibility. These task analysis models represent slight variation on a common theme—breaking work down into simpler steps.

The behaviorally based task analysis models grew from work initiated fifty years ago, and they blossomed in the 1950s and 1960s. There is little quarrel with their intent: to identify what people do in a specific job and use that information as the basis for their training. That concept is a fundamental principal of performance technology. But are these task analysis models appropriate for much of the work performed in the 1990s?

Recent Developments

Two developments in the past two decades should cause us to rethink how we conduct task analysis.

More and more, the "work" performed by people in completing their jobs is not a series of observable behaviors leading to task completion. We are no longer a nation of assembly-line workers who install this part on that object all day. In a manufacturing economy, most of the work done was observable. It involved the movements people executed when manipulating some piece of equipment in making some object. In an information economy, the work happens internally, in the workers' heads, not with the workers' hands. Thus, this work is not directly observable.

Consider two jobs: a textile worker and an insurance adjustor. A textile worker stitches a seam to join the sleeve to the body of a shirt. This work is directly observable. The essence of the work is what the textile workers do with their hands and sewing machines. Observe and describe that, and you have captured their job. On the other hand, insurance adjustors do little with their hands other than write on forms. Their work is done in their heads when they make a variety of decisions and resolve problems before they complete the forms. This decision making and problem solving are not directly observable and are not amenable to traditional behavioral task analysis approaches.

Consider the job of a neurologist. If one used behavioral task analysis to describe the work of a neurologist, one would miss the very essence of the job (Evans & Patel, 1989). While observing a neurologist, the task analyst would record that the neurologist shined a light into the patient's eye, hit the patient's knee with a rubber hammer, had the patient close his eyes and point to his nose with either hand, and, last, the neurologist stuck the patient in several places with a small pin. If that was a complete task analysis for the job of a neurologist, their training could be completed in a few hours instead of several years! Of course, although that task inventory does describe what you see a neurologist do, it does not adequately encompass their work. The problem for the traditional, behaviorally oriented task analyst is that the work the neurologist was doing during the examination was not directly observable by the task analyst. The work was completed in the neurologist's head. The neurologist was using the information gathered from the examination of the patient to determine what, if any, neurological problems existed by comparing this information with a great store of data about normal and abnormal findings. A variety of hypotheses were considered by the neurologist and accepted or rejected based on the findings from the physical examination. When the work is not directly observable, traditional task analysis methods are insufficient.

The second development beginning to change task analysis is the advances in understanding human thought being made in cognitive science (Gardner, 1985). Research in human problem solving, for example, has extended beyond the study of observable behaviors to the examination of thought processes. Research on the differences between experts and novices in several domains of knowledge can serve as a basis for identifying what an expert does. This is, in essence, a task analysis of an expert. Researchers in cognitive science have pioneered various procedures for representing what a person knows and how he/she uses this knowledge in solving a problem. Research in artificial intelligence has included techniques for knowledge extraction and representation so that the knowledge of experts could be placed in computer programs, called expert systems. These expert systems perform various tasks, such as locating potential oil deposits, conducting medical diagnoses, or selecting profitable stocks, that previously required human experts. Work in metacognition has sought to determine how individuals monitor and control their own thought processes while learning. This work explores the inner workings of the mind. Research on mathematical problem solving has studied mental processes while a person is attempting to solve mathematical problems. This research has lead to fruitful discoveries regarding how to solve mathematical problems. Research on medical diagnosis has proceeded similarly to determine how skilled physicians solve medical problems.

The implications for task analysis from this research are not the specific findings from individual studies but rather the methodologies used in the studies to understand human thought. These methods are ripe for use by task analysts who are analyzing jobs in which the work happens internally in the incumbents' heads, not with their hands. Procedures cognitive scientists use to understand how a physician diagnoses ailments can also be used to identify the tasks and accompanying knowledge a physician must master to perform well.

Cognitive Task Analysis

Analyzing tasks that are completed in one's head requires a cognitive approach to task analysis, not a behavioral approach. Traditional task analysis methods fail because they rely on behavioral observation or reports of behaviors. This is not adequate when the task is completed internally. Cognitive task analysis methods would seek to determine what information an individual used in completing a task and how he or she used, or processed, the information. For example, insurance adjustors have to determine if the insurance company is liable for any portion of a loss. To make this determination, they must acquire and process considerable information. Adjustors must relate information gained about the specific claim to their knowledge of claims in general and to their knowledge of the specific insurance policy. A task analysis of an insurance adjustor's job must determine what an adjustor thinks about and how he or she must think when completing the job. The job of the task analyst is not unlike the job of a developer of an expert system for insurance adjustors. Both have to determine the facts and concepts an insurance adjustor must possess as well as the rules an insurance adjustor uses to manipulate the facts and concepts to resolve a specific case.

Several methods can be used to collect data for cognitive task analysis. Simple observation of an incumbent completing a task is not sufficient since it does not reveal internal thought processes. Getting information about an incumbent's thoughts while he or she is completing a task is more fruitful since this reflects the "work" done in completing the task.

One method for doing this is to have task performers describe what they are doing in a running dialog as they are completing some tasks. This is often called the "talk through" approach since the task performers talk their way through doing a task. As she is performing a task, the task performer tells the task analyst what she is thinking, what she is doing, and why. The analyst records this information as the basis for the task analysis. This talk-through method captures the actual behavior of the task performer but, more importantly, it also captures what is going on in her mind—her thought processes.

The talk-through method has been criticized by some as obtrusive and altering the way tasks are routinely performed. That is, the information gained in this talk-through approach may reflect a more idealized way of performing job tasks rather than the actual way. This approach makes three assumptions: (1) that we perform tasks in a completely rational fashion, (2) that we are totally aware of what we are doing and why, and (3) that the process of talking about performing a task as we are performing it does not modify what we normally do when performing that task.

An alternative method for completing a cognitive task analysis is termed the "think-aloud" method. When using a think-aloud method, the job incumbent vocalizes his thoughts as he completes a task to reveal his thought process. For example, a physician may indicate that since some finding in a physical examination is in the normal range, she will check the possibility for some other potential cause of the patient's complaints. The vocalized thoughts reveal the rules that the physician is using during the diagnostic process. The task analyst focuses on the physician's thought processes revealed through the vocalized thoughts rather than the observable behavior. It is these thoughts that best reflect the work.

In contrast to the talk-through cognitive task analysis approach, proponents of the think-aloud approach argue that it exerts less influence on routine task performance. They state that in this approach task performers do not have to consider or even think about what they are saying; they just utter thoughts as they occur. In the talk-through approach to cognitive task analysis, they must think about what to say to describe their performance as they are performing the task. Proponents of the think-aloud approach argue that it is not obtrusive since task performers are not carrying on a conversation, describing, or justifying what they are doing. Rather, they are just vocalizing their thoughts instead of keeping the thoughts to themselves.

A less obtrusive technique for cognitive task analysis is to have the task performer recall his thoughts while completing a task in an interview after he has completed the task. The task performer neither talks through nor thinks aloud during the task performance. After completing the task performance, the task performer describes what he did and what he thought about while completing the task. This method exerts no influence on the task performance itself because it does not modify anything during the task performance. It addresses the limitations of both the talk-through and think-aloud approaches to cognitive task analysis. This method is criticized as giving too idealized a view of task performance.

When task performers recall what they were thinking about while completing a task, they may describe what they think they should have thought about when completing the task, not what they actually thought about. They may give a standard, textbook view of how others describe how the tasks should be performed. They may describe rationalized thoughts about task performance, not actual thoughts. There is a question about our ability to be aware of our mental processes while performing tasks. We may not really know how we do some tasks, even simple tasks. Have you ever tried to describe how you identify your grandmother? This is a very easy task, something you learned to do at an early age, and perhaps something you have done often. Yet it is difficult to describe how to do it. There is also a question about the extent of our ability to recall completely our thoughts. Even if task performers are aware of how they complete some task, they may not recall all that they think about while completing a task. These are some of the limitations of having task performers describe, after completing a task, their thoughts during the task performance.

A similar approach to the cognitive task analysis method of recall is to record people's task performance on videotape and then have them describe their thoughts while viewing the tape later. This does not interfere with or modify the task performance as may occur with the talk-through and think-aloud methods. This method also has an advantage over the recall method: Using a videotape to stimulate the recall may result in more complete recall when compared with unaided recall. This method requires that the task performers remember exactly what they were thinking and that they give the task analyst an unedited recollection of those thoughts. This method is criticized as being susceptible to influence, or editing, by the task performers. They may have made some instinctual decisions during task performance or just guessed. During the viewing of the tape, they may justify their decisions by referring to some rational model of decision making. This after-the-fact justification does not reflect the actual thought process during task performance. The stimulated recall may be at variance with actual thoughts during task performance.

There are striking differences among the cognitive task analysis methods of talk through, think aloud, unaided interview, and interview while viewing a videotape. Yet, all have the same purpose: to identify the internal thoughts of a person while he or she completes some task that is a part of the job. The task analyst must identify the knowledge a person uses while completing a task and how this knowledge is processed.

Cognitive task analysis is more speculative and less certain than traditional, behaviorally based task analysis. However, cognitive task analysis is more appropriate for jobs that involve processing information rather than making things. Cognitive task analysis also builds on work in cognitive science that seeks to establish what experts know and do—how they represent and use their knowledge. Cognitive task analysis will continue to be a fruitful approach to capturing the tasks done when performing a job.

We have described three approaches to task analysis: behavioral, procedural, and cognitive. Behavioral task analysis focuses on the observable behavior of job incumbents in discrete units. Behavioral approaches to task analysis break jobs down into very small, independent motions and describe each motion in depth. The data are gathered through observation, interview, and survey. The general steps in doing a behavioral task analysis are as follows:

- Identify the job to be analyzed;
- Identify the tasks that make up that job;
- Describe each task initially;
- Describe each task in depth, including the cue that initiates the task, the cue that calls for an action, the object of the action, the specific action, and feedback resulting from the action.

Procedural task analysis focuses on the behavior of job incumbents when they are completing algorithmic tasks as part of their jobs. Procedural task analysis identifies the sequence of steps performed while completing a task. The primary source of data when completing a procedural task analysis is observation of task performers. The general steps in doing a procedural task analysis are as follows:

- Identify the task to be done;
- Select a skilled task performer;
- Observe the task performer completing the task;
- Record for each task the operations performed, the results, and decision points;
- Develop a flowchart representing the operations, results, and decision points;
- Verify and revise the flowchart.

Cognitive task analysis focuses on the mental processes of job incumbents as they perform their jobs. Cognitive task analysis identifies the thought processes and knowledge job incumbents use while completing a task. The primary source of data when completing a cognitive task analysis is interviews with task performers, either as they complete tasks or after. The general steps in doing a cognitive task analysis are:

- Identify the task to be done;
- Select a skilled task performer;
- Determine the data-gathering procedure: talk through, think aloud, subsequent interview, videotape and interview;
- Observe the task performer completing the task;
- Record for each task operations performed, knowledge used, rules applied to the knowledge base, result;
- Develop a representation of the operations, knowledge, rules and results;

- Verify and revise the representation.

These three approaches to task analysis are appropriate for different situations. The task analyst does not have to attempt to determine which approach is best overall, but rather which approach is appropriate for the situation—for the job task analysis. If the job is composed of tasks that are observable and nonalgorithmic, the task analyst should use behavioral task analysis methods. If the job is composed of tasks that are observable and algorithmic, the analyst should use procedural task analysis methods. If the job is composed of tasks that are not observable, the analyst should use cognitive task analysis methods. A skilled task analyst must be able to use these different task analysis methods.

Summary

Task analysis continues to be a main part of performance technology. Task analysis is fundamental to developing effective and efficient education/training programs. There are a large number of different task analysis models, but there are three general approaches to task analysis of jobs: behavioral task analysis, procedural task analysis, and cognitive task analysis. These different approaches are not competing task analysis approaches so much as they are different approaches that are appropriate for analyzing different jobs.

References

Campbell, C. (1989). Job analysis for industrial training. *Journal of European Industrial Training, 13*(2), 1-58.

Evans, D.A., & Patel, V.L. (1989). *Cognitive science in medicine.* Cambridge, MA: The MIT Press.

Fine, S.A. (1973). *Functional job analysis scales: A desk aid.* Kalamazoo, MI: W.E. Upjohn Institute for Employment Research.

Fine, S.A., Holt, A.M., & Hutchinson, M.F. (1974). *Functional job analysis: How to standardize task statements.* Kalamazoo, MI: W.E. Upjohn Institute for Employment Research.

Gardner, H. (1985). *The mind's new science.* New York: Basic Books.

Gentry, C.G. (1994). *Introduction to instructional development.* Belmont, CA: Wadsworth.

Hannum, W.H., & Hansen, C.D. (1989). *Instructional systems development in large organizations.* Englewood Cliffs, NJ: Educational Technology.

Jonassen, D.H., Hannum, W.H., & Tessmer, M. (1989). *Handbook of task analysis procedures,* New York: Praeger.

Kaufman, R. (1994). A needs assessment audit. *Performance and Instruction, 33*(2), 14-16.

Kemp, J.E., Morrison, G.R., & Ross, S.M. (1994). *Designing effective instruction.* New York: Merrill.

Mager, R.F., & Beach, K.M. (1967). *Developing vocational instruction.* Belmont, CA: Fearon.

McCormick, E.J. (1979). *Job analysis: Methods and applications.* New York: AMACOM.

Merrill, P.F. (1980). Analysis of a procedural task. *NSPI Journal, 19*(2), 11-15, 26.

Miller, R.B. (1962). Task description and analysis. In R.M. Gagne (Ed.), *Psychological principles in systems development.* New York: Holt, Rinehart and Winston.

Reigeluth, C., & Merrill, M.D. (1984). *Extended task analysis procedures (ETAP), User's manual.* Lanham, MD: University Press of America.

Tracey, W.R., Flynn, E.B., & Legere, C.L. (1966). *The development of instructional systems.* Ft. Devens, MA: U.S. Army Security Agency Training Center.

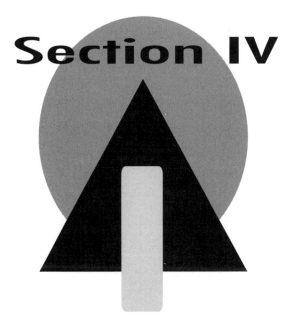

Section IV

Design and Development

THE HIERARCHY OF INTERVENTIONS

Judith A. Hale

Performance technology requires needs assessment models that are not predisposed to certain solutions. It requires models that are "proactive," in Kaufman's terms, by design; that is, a model that is open to the whole array of possible interventions. The term "intervention" is used to mean conscious, planned processes. It means interventions designed to affect human and organizational performance.

The Hale Hierarchy Model is a proactive needs assessment model in that it determines

1. What is working successfully;

2. What new should be added;

3. What old should be deleted or modified for the total organization (Kaufman, 1983).

Each level of the hierarchy represents a different arena of inquiry (see Figure 1).

The model considers problems and opportunities within all ten arenas. The model, "...assumes nothing about the existence, validity, utility, and correctness of the current organization, including its goals, objectives, and the assignment of personnel and their duties" (Kaufman, 1983). The model is designed to help performance technologists align an intervention with a need.

```
 1.  Mission and Policies
 2.  Goals and Objectives
 3.  Organizational and Job Structures
 4.  Procedures and Practices
 5.  Documentation and Standards
 6.  Physical Work Place
 7.  Environmental Working Conditions
 8.  Job Aids, Signage, and Labels
 9.  Training and Development
10.  Resource Capacity and Sufficiency
```

Figure 1. Hierarchy Model

The term "hierarchy" refers to the priority of the arenas of inquiry. It infers that problems and opportunities at the top of the hierarchy (mission and policies) should be resolved before addressing those identified at lower levels. Hierarchy does not refer to the power, preference, or importance of one intervention over another except to the degree it is aligned with the need. Therefore, the model supports addressing needs at the level where they are identified.

Interventions address what people, individually and collectively, do to accomplish desired outcomes. People have been intervening in others' lives since the beginning of time. However, organizations, as they are known today, are a phenomena of the 20th Century. The growth of industry, labor unions, government agencies, agricultural enterprises, and professional associations brought with it ideas about how these organizations should function. Similarly, the complexity of the organizations triggered the search for new ideas about how to improve operations and the quality of life. The search for solutions to inefficiency and ineffectiveness encouraged the development of theories and models about how to improve organizational performance. The theories reflected the disciplines of the people doing the inquiry, for example:

- Management

- Engineering

- Communications

- Psychology

Management experts developed organizational models for how to group and define functions. They studied the roles managers play and at what levels decisions are made. They looked for deficiencies in performance due to violations of management and organizational principles. Engineers looked at job design and job processes. Communication experts developed models of how information is gathered and distributed. They focused on the role of management as one of persuasion and influence. Industrial psychologists studied incentives and disincentives to performance.

Such discipline-dependent assessment models are still with us today. Instructional technologists apply assessment processes to identify problems attributable to deficiencies in skills and knowledge. People trained in ergonomics and interior design apply processes to identify inadequate and inappropriate use of environmental elements (space, light, ventilation, furniture, fixtures, finishes, and equipment).

The challenge to the performance technologist is to apply an assessment process that is not predisposed to a solution, but is open to the possibility of diverse causes and solutions.

What seems to be missing, according to Kaufman, is a frame of reference and a model that helps would-be organizational improvers to:

1. Define and relate available tools, techniques, models, and approaches.

2. Determine what each is capable of providing.

3. Determine which, if any, and in what possible combinations individual models and approaches are useful

for meeting the requirements for useful and measurable organizational improvements and impact.

4. Relate the roles and responsibilities for application of each useful approach, tool, technique, and model at the various levels within any organization (Kaufman, 1983).

The Hierarchy Model, developed by Odin Westgaard and Judith Hale, provides that frame of reference (Hale, 1986). They wanted a needs assessment model that (1) identified factors that enhance and impede individual and organizational performance, (2) was not predisposed to a solution (e.g., training), (3) did not focus on a narrow range of interventions (e.g., job aids, incentives, or training), and (4) helped them better select an intervention that would accomplish the desired outcome.

Questions and hypotheses, developed for each level, guide the scope and design of the inquiry and the choice of methods, such as:

- Who to involve and when to involve them;

- How to involve them: for example, observe, interview, survey, test;

- How to validate the findings.

The questions and hypotheses in Figure 2 illustrate the thought process.

What is discovered at each level further directs the human performance technologist to the appropriate intervention and measures for evaluation. The challenge is to take the results of the assessment based on the Hierarchy Model and decide if an intervention is appropriate and what type of intervention might be used. The model is open to the possibility that some solutions may require more than one intervention at more than one level.

Hierarchy Model and Questions	Working Hypotheses
Mission and Policies A. Is there a mission statement? B. Does the mission reflect current requirements, desires, and the environment in which it (the organization) operates? C. Is there a consensus on what the mission is? D. Is the mission a part of long-range planning? E. Do policies support the mission? F. Is there agreement on the policies?	1. Leadership lacks direction or is not in consensus about what the direction is. 2. The mission is out of sync with the environment. 3. The mission is not aligned with the structure, policies, practices, etc.
Goals and Objectives A. Are the goals congruent with the mission? B. Do they reflect the resources and operating specifics required to progress as a whole? C. Do they exist for each operating unit? D. Do people know what they are? E. Are they followed?	1. Interim goals and objectives do not support the mission. 2. People do not have sufficient resources to accomplish the interim goals and objectives. 3. Cross-functional goals are not aligned, not clear, etc. 4. People are unclear about what is expected. 5. Consequences do not support the goals.

Figure 2. Hierarchy Model Questions and Hypotheses

Hierarchy Model and Questions	Working Hypotheses
Organizational and Job Structures A. Are jobs clearly defined? B. Are positions given appropriate responsibility? C. Are positions, responsibilities, and reporting relationships effective and efficient? D. Does the structure facilitate communication, decision making, and accountability? E. Are tasks grouped effectively and efficiently? F. Is the span of control effective? G. Is each unit of command appropriate?	1. Task, jobs, and functions are not defined and/or grouped to support efficiency or effectiveness. 2. People lack the responsibility, authority, and access to information and resources they require to accomplish what is expected.
Procedures and Practices A. Who does what levels of planning? B. How are staffing decisions made? C. Are duties assigned in ways that are effective and efficient? D. Do procedures exist and are they followed consistently? E. Who assigns resources and how? F. How do people get feedback? G. Are there consequences to performance? H. Are those consequences carried out?	1. Planning and decision making are not being done at the right levels. 2. Staffing procedures do not support the requirements of the task. 3. Tasks, duties, and jobs are designed inefficiently. 4. What people do is not what they say they do or what others think they do. 5. People do not have control over the resources they require. 6. Consequences do not support desired behaviors, outputs, or outcomes.

Figure 2 (continued). Hierarchy Model Questions and Hypotheses

The Guidebook for Performance Improvement

Hierarchy Model and Questions	Working Hypotheses
Documentation and Standards A. Are procedures and practices documented? B. Are they accessible and usable? C. Do they reflect desired practice? D. Are there standards? E. Does standardization support innovation, compliance, commitment, etc.?	1. Documentation does not support actual practice. 2. Documentation does not support the transfer of intelligence within and across units. 3. Standards are insufficient. 4. Standards and communication systems are not in place to support timely feedback or evaluation. 5. Standards thwart innovation.
Physical Work Place A. Is space adequate and used well? B. Do the space and layout facilitate work flow? C. Do the space and layout facilitate communications? D. Do the technology and systems support the required work processes?	1. Use of space, layout, traffic patterns, placement of supplies (equipment, etc.) does not support efficiency, goals, or objectives. 2. Configuration of work stations, space assignment of work units, etc., does not support collaboration or the required work processes.
Environmental Work Conditions A. Are work conditions safe? B. Do environmental conditions (temperature, light, noise) support the required work processes? C. Do environmental conditions support health? D. Do conditions support commitment, innovation, compliance?	1. The design of work stations, poor ventitlation, and noise level contribute to fatigue. 2. The work environment does not support satisfaction, growth, or productivity.

Figure 2 (continued). Hierarchy Model Questions and Hypotheses

Hierarchy Model and Questions	Working Hypotheses
Job Aids, Signage, and Labels A. Do job aids, signs, and labels exist? B. Are they used? C. Is intelligent, exemplary performance captured in a usable form? D. Do the job aids, signs, and labeling support the desired and required performance?	1. Visual, tactical, and auditory cues are inappropriate, missing, or confusing. 2. Procedures are not documented in a form that is easily usable. 3. Performance is inefficient because of a lack of or poorly designed job aids, labels, or signs.
Training and Development A. Are skills maintained? B. Are skills developed? C. Are skills and knowledge adequate for required and desired processes? D. Are innovation and self-empowerment supported? E. What methods are used for development (coaching, cross-training, etc.) and do those methods support the desired and required performance?	1. People lack the skills, knowledge, or information they require to perform as desired or required. 2. Current skills and knowledge will not support innovation. 3. Current training and development content, methods, and delivery mechanisms are inadequate, not accessible, inappropriate, etc.
Resource Capacity and Sufficiency A. Do people have the emotional, physical, intellectual, and economic capacity to achieve the desired and required performance? B. Are there support systems and processes in place to either offset, reduce, or remove deficiencies in capacity? C. Are support systems sufficient for the desired and required performance? D. Do values conflict with the requirements of the job or the desired outcomes?	1. The demands (requirements) of the job exceed the capability and capacity of the people. 2. Skills and knowledge alone are not adequate for required or desired performance. 3. There has been a change in capacity. 4. Support systems (job aids, job design, environmental conditions, space, layout) are not adequate for the required performance. 5. Beliefs and values conflict with what is required to perform the task.

Figure 2 (continued). Hierarchy Model Questions and Hypotheses

The Guidebook for Performance Improvement

The interventions used to improve or support human performance have been categorized by family and listed in Figure 3.

---

1. *Define*

    Acts to specify or clarify the mission, vision, purpose, processes, products/services, and outcomes.

2. *Inform*

    Acts to communicate goals, objectives, expectations, results, and discrepancies.

3. *Document*

    Acts to codify information; that is, to preserve it and make it accessible.

4. *Structure*

    Acts to organize or (re)arrange business units, reporting structures, work processes, jobs, and tasks.

5. *Standardize*

    Acts to systematize or automate processes and standardize tasks, tools, equipment, materials, or measures.

6. *Redesign*

    Acts to produce a safe and ergonomically designed environment, workplace, equipment, and tools.

7. *Motivate*

    Acts to induce and maintain desired behaviors, eliminate undesirable behaviors, and reward desired outcomes.

8. *Counsel*

    Acts to assist individuals either singularly or collectively to deal with work, personal, career, or financial issues (e.g., employee assistance programs).

9. *Instruct*

    Acts to expand skills, knowledge, and confidence through the use of instructional and developmental strategies, tactics, and delivery mechanisms.

10. *Align*

    Acts to achieve congruence between purpose and practice.

11. *Reframe*

    Acts to generate new paradigms so people can experience new perspectives, find creative solutions, integrate new concepts in their behavior, and manage change.

12. *Enforce*

    Acts to actualize consequences and achieve compliance.

Figure 3. Families of Interventions

Figure 4 shows each level of the Hierarchy Model and interventions typically applied to problems and opportunities identified.

Level of Inquiry	Family of Intervention
1. Mission and Policies	Define, Reframe, Inform
2. Goals and Objectives	Define, Reframe, Inform
3. Organizational and Job Structure	Structure, Align
4. Procedures and Practices	Define, Align, Motivate
5. Documentation and Standards	Document, Standardize, Enforce
6. Physical Work Environment	Redesign, Motivate, Align
7. Environmental Work Conditions	Redesign, Align, Motivate
8. Job Aids, Signage, and Labels	Document, Standardize, Inform
9. Training and Development	Instruct, Inform
10. Resource Capacity and Sufficiency	Counsel, Structure, Redesign

Figure 4. Hierarchy Model and Typical Interventions

Interventions are created in response to social, political, and economic pressures. Therefore, they can be applied at the mega, macro, and micro level, that is, society and communities, families, and individuals. Performance technology discusses them in terms of organizations, departments and work groups, and individual performers. At whatever level they are applied, the intent is to accomplish a desired outcome. For example:

- The adoption of international symbols (e.g., hazardous materials) illustrates an integrated implementation of interventions (standardization, dissemination, and enforcement) at the mega level.

- Color coding pipes and adding procedures about the use and placement of intake valves for pharmaceutical manufacturing plants illustrate the same interventions (standardization, dissemination, and enforcement) at the macro level.

- Creating job aids with standard symbols for data input uses documentation, standardization, and informs on the micro level.

- Designing switches on an instrument panel in a nuclear power plant so it takes four hands (two people) to manipulate them is an example of combining job tasks (structure) with the design of the instrument panel (redesign) on the micro level.

- Implementing self-managed teams (structural) is an intervention on the macro level.

- Implementing a national health insurance system would require a structural intervention on the mega level.

- Having managers go through a group process (develop or instruct) to challenge their assumptions, think creatively, and come up with new paradigms (reframe) is an application on the micro level.

- Redefining the mission to take advantage of changes in the marketplace could involve define, reframe, inform, and align on the macro level.

- Adopting and enforcing laws protecting endangered species is at the mega level because preservation affects national and international commerce. It calls for interventions from define (multiple stakeholders have to define what species are endangered), inform (the public and industry have to be told), document (what constitutes a violation has to be consistently communicated), and enforce (consequences must be carried out).

- AIDS is worldwide. It is, however, one leading cause of death that can be prevented by changing behavior. Distributing literature about AIDS to every household uses interventions from inform (disseminate) and document on the mega level because it is an effort to change behavior on a national scale.

- Distributing an employee handbook that describes behaviors that will result in termination (and following through when those behaviors occur) makes use of documentation, dissemination, and enforcement applied to the macro level.

- Making counselors available when coworkers are killed on the job or when members of a community suffer losses from a tornado is an intervention applied to all three levels (mega, macro, and micro).

- Rewarding performers who meet their goals is to motivate on the micro level.

- Redesigning jobs to use new technologies and then training people to use the technologies are interventions from the structure and develop on the macro level.

If performance technology is to distinguish itself as bringing value to human endeavor, it must apply models that are systematic and integrated. Its assessment processes, by design, must surface problems and opportunities. They must diagnose causes. They must prescribe appropriate interventions to improve individual and organizational performance. Assessment models that are discipline specific (engineering, training, management) narrow the discovery process. They present organizations with a limited number of choices. They offer fewer possibilities for action. The Hierarchy Model was developed because performance technologists require a discovery (assessment) process that is not biased by design. The Hierarchy Model draws on the theories of the other disciplines. It guides the performance technologist through a discovery process that recognizes the breadth of factors that influence individual and organizational performance. It requires the performance technologist to consider a broader array of possible solutions. It helps the performance technologist stay "needs" driven, not intervention driven. The model supports the premise that performance technology is a systematic integrated process.

References

Hale, J. (1986). *Capability document.* Western Springs, IL: Hale Associates.

Kaufman, R. (1983a). *Planning for organizational success: A practical guide.* New York: John Wiley.

Kaufman, R. (1983b, October). A holistic planning model: A system approach for improving organizational effectiveness and impact. *Performance & Instruction Journal.*

Applications of Total Quality Concepts to Organizational Effectiveness

Ahmad K. Elshennawy
and William W. Swart

Introduction

In today's increasingly competitive markets, quality has assumed a much larger role than its traditional meaning. Quality has been adopted as an organizational or corporate philosophy where it can no longer be the sole responsibility of the production floor worker to produce acceptable items. The meaning of quality must stretch to include all employees from the top management through the entire organization as well as vendors.

Quality assurance has assumed a role far beyond its traditional meaning as "all those planned or systematic actions necessary to provide adequate confidence that a product or service will satisfy given needs" (American Society for Quality Control, 1983). It has become a tool for providing continuous feedback to the organizational production and business systems with the objective of producing products with high quality at minimum cost, and thus increasing the organizational performance. Customer's continuous demand for superior quality products and an increasing competition in the world market have imposed an even more important role for quality in the effectiveness of organizational performance.

Implementing a quality assurance program is a task involving human relations and employee participation. Hence, implementing a quality assurance program is both a channel of communication and a means of participation. Product quality information must be communicated to all concerned employees throughout the organization. There is a requirement for the employees to feel like they are "part of it."

Achieving high levels of organizational performance can be realized through the achievement of:

- Customer satisfaction through an improved product/ service quality;

- Providing a means for continuous improvement of the organizational processes;

- Implementing a total quality concept throughout the organization.

These tenets can be presented best through the implementation of total quality management. This chapter focuses on the presentation of a total quality management approach for improving organizational performance.

Total Quality Management and Organizational Performance

The purpose of total quality management (TQM) is to implement a process that is long-term and to provide continuous improvement initiatives throughout the organization. TQM integrates the fundamental techniques and principles of "quality function deployment," Taguchi methods, "statistical process control," "just-in-time," and existing management tools into a structured approach. The primary objective of this approach is to incorporate quality and integrity into all functions at all levels of the organization.

TQM makes the improvement process part of the company's everyday operating system. It is also important that before embarking on TQM, a company take some preparatory actions that will make the transition period easier and more likely to succeed. Harrington (1987) indicates that beginning the process of TQM implementation requires the following actions:

1. Become aware of the principles, practices, techniques, and tools associated with TQM.

2. Provide key personnel with TQM training.

3. Begin a dialogue with suppliers to encourage self-initiation of TQM.

4. Examine the processes and identify ways in which to improve their using TQM principles.

5. Establish process improvement teams to pursue improvements aimed at increasing customer satisfaction, improving performance, reducing cyclic time, and reducing cost.

6. Begin TQM organizational planning.

7. Identify those suppliers who are qualified and receptive to the intensive applications of TQM principles.

There are many tools that are used in TQM for the improvement of organizational performance. They range from customer surveys to just-in-time and process-improvement education. An overview of some of the concepts for the improvement of quality and organizational performance is briefly presented in this chapter. Each of these concepts addresses different areas of quality management. It is neces-

---

sary, however, to modify the concept to the given situation. This is where TQM takes over by educating and providing a nurturing environment so that these concepts can be modified and used as building blocks. The improvement process has a beginning, but there is no end to it. Figure 1 represents Shewhart's Cycle for the process of continuous improvement (Deming, 1986).

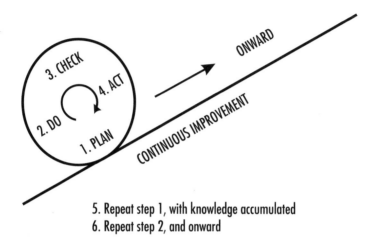

5. Repeat step 1, with knowledge accumulated
6. Repeat step 2, and onward

Figure 1. Shewhart's Cycle

Deming's Philosophy

Deming's chain reaction (Deming, 1986) is a good example of how good quality practices lead to an effective organizational performance. This chain reaction (shown in Figure 2) became engraved in Japan as a way of life.

Deming's fourteen points describe a system for organizational performance. Adoption of the fourteen points is a signal that management intends to stay in business and aims to protect

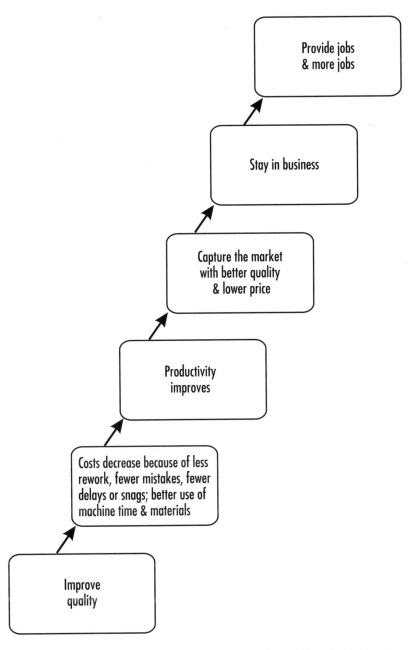

Reprinted from *Out of the Crisis* by W. Edwards Deming, by permission of MIT and The W. Edwards Deming Institute. Published by MIT, Center for Advanced Educational Services, Cambridge, MA 02139. Copyright 1986 by The W. Edwards Deming Institute.

Figure 2. Deming's Chain Reaction

investors and jobs (Deming, 1986). Deming's fourteen points are as follows:[1]

1. Create constancy of purpose toward improvement of product and service, with the aim to become competitive and to stay in business, and to provide jobs.

2. Adopt the new philosophy. We are in a new economic age. Western management must awaken to the challenge, must learn their responsibilities, and take on leadership for change.

3. Cease dependence on inspection to achieve quality. Eliminate the need for inspection on a mass basis by building quality into the product in the first place.

4. End the practice of awarding business on the basis of price tag. Instead, minimize total cost. Move toward a single supplier for any one item, based on a long-term relationship of loyalty and trust.

5. Improve constantly and forever the system of production and service, to improve quality and productivity, and thus constantly decrease costs.

6. Institute training on the job.

7. Institute leadership. The aim of supervision should be to help people and machines and gadgets to do a better job. Supervision of management is in need of overhaul, as well as supervision of production workers.

8. Drive out fear, so that everyone may work effectively for the company.

---

[1] Reprinted from *Out of the Crisis*, by W. Edwards Deming, by permission of MIT Press. Published by MIT, Center for Advanced Engineering Study, Cambridge, MA 02139. Copyright 1986 by W. Edwards Deming.

9. Break down barriers between departments. People in research, design, sales, and production must work as a team to foresee problems of production and in use that may be encountered with the product or service.

10. Eliminate slogans, exhortations, and targets for the work force asking for zero defects and new levels of productivity. Such exhortations only create adversarial relationships, as the bulk of the causes of low quality and low productivity belong to the system and thus lie beyond the power of the work force.

11. a. Eliminate work standards (quotas) on the factory floor. Substitute leadership.
    b. Eliminate management by objective. Eliminate management by numbers, numerical goals. Substitute leadership.

12. a. Remove barriers that rob the hourly worker of his right to pride of workmanship. The responsibility of supervisors must be changed from sheer numbers to quality.
    b. Remove barriers that rob people in management and in engineering of their right to pride of workmanship. This means, *inter alia*, abolishment of the annual or merit rating and of management by objective.

13. Institute a vigorous program of education and self-improvement.

14. Put everybody in the company to work to accomplish the transformation. The transformation is everybody's job.

Deming's fourteen-point philosophy underlies many of the present quality systems that are now being implemented. They provide the guidelines for creating an environment for a TQM system.

Juran's Trilogy

Juran believes that there are three basic managerial processes through which we manage quality. The three processes (the Juran Trilogy) are quality planning, quality control, and quality improvement (Juran, 1988a). Quality planning provides the operating forces with the means of producing products to meet customers' requirements. The planning process attempts to reduce the amount of waste that has become chronic because the process was designed that way. Quality control inspects the quality within the process to get rid of this chronic waste. Quality improvement rids the process of the chronic waste by designing a system that addresses the problem.

The Juran system has many of the same criteria of the other systems. It requires being in touch with customers' requirements, having a system for measuring quality, designing products that meet customers' requirements, optimizing product design, and utilizing process development to increase quality.

Total Quality Control

In 1951, Armand V. Feigenbaum's book, *Total Quality Control*, was released, advancing the concept of quality control in all areas of business, ranging from product design to sales. It was one of the first books to address prevention and not detection of defective products. Feigenbaum defined total quality control (TQC) as an effective system for integrating the quality-development, quality-maintenance, and quality-improvement efforts of the various groups in an organization so as to enable marketing, engineering, production, and service at the most economical levels that allow for full customer satisfaction (Feigenbaum, 1991). As can be seen from this definition of TQC, it is the beginning of modern TQM. Feigenbaum emphasizes the importance of statistical quality control through control charts and sampling methods. He also emphasizes the importance of incoming-material control and new-design control. These are all seen as important parts of the TQM philosophy.

Off-Line Quality Control—The Taguchi Way

Genichi Taguchi, a Japanese statistician and Deming Prize winner, has extended quality improvement activities to include product and process design; this is called off-line quality control. Taguchi methods provide a system to develop specifications, design those specifications into a product and/ or process, and produce products that continuously surpass said specifications. There are seven aspects to off-line quality control (Kacker, 1986):

1. The quality of the product is measured by the total loss created by that product to society.

2. Continuous quality as well as cost improvement are a necessity.

3. Quality improvement requires reduction of variability around nominal values.

4. Society's loss due to performance variation is frequently proportional to the square of the deviation of the performance characteristic from its nominal value.

5. Product and process design have great impact on a product's quality and cost.

6. Performance variation can be reduced by exploiting the nonlinear effects between a product's and/or process's parameters and the product's desired performance characteristic.

7. Product and/or process parameter settings that reduce performance variation can be identified with statistically designed experiments.

These aspects describe Taguchi's views on how to improve quality through design and statistical analysis of products or processes.

Just-In-Time

The goal of implementing just-in-time (JIT) is twofold. The short-term goal is to reduce the total cost of manufacturing by improving productivity. The long-term goal is to develop (1) the manufacturing flexibility to shorten the lead time a company gives its customers and (2) the ability to support more product changes in a given time (Lubben, 1988). As a result, cycle time and inventory levels will be reduced so that slack will be taken out of the system. Slack is denoted by excess inventories, excess capacity, overtime costs, long lead times, and poor vendor performance. By making the system more repetitive, the company is able to reduce the number of disturbances that bring slack into the organization. Keys to JIT are reducing setup times and lot sizes. The concept of JIT plays a major role in any quality assurance management system.

TQM Attributes

TQM integrates fundamental management techniques, existing improvement efforts, and technical tools into a disciplined approach focused on continuous process improvement. There are many attributes for successful TQM implementation. Some of the key attributes of TQM are discussed here.

Continuous improvement is essential in increasing customer satisfaction and alleviating waste of employee time and company resources and should extend to the mega level (Kaufman, 1991). It challenges everyone in an organization to remove the mind set of "if it works, don't fix it," and replace it with thoughts of "what can I do to improve it?" A crusade of this type not only will increase internal and external customer satisfaction, but also will result in a cultural change. This cultural change will be realized in customer relations, the quality and reliability of the product offered, and increased employee morale.

Multifunctional team formation is intended to break down the organizational barriers that exist in an organization. The team's function is to constantly search for opportunities to improve. The team aims to better meet customers' requirements by analyzing critical product characteristics through a technique called "quality function deployment." Product design teams, whose objective is to reduce product design and process variation using Taguchi methods, are formed in the design phase of the product development life cycle. And, in production, "tiger teams" are formed to collectively solve problems faced during the production phase of the product development life cycle.

Variability reduction can be achieved through manufacturing work standardization and simplification, as well as through statistical thinking. This can be attained by a combined effort of Taguchi methods and the JIT methodology.

Education and training are principal ingredients in motivating an organization toward the TQM philosophy. Education is required on the concept itself, and training is necessary for those in an organization to use the various techniques available to support the TQM process. Senior management down to the shop floor personnel must partake in the education and training provided.

Supplier integration is twofold. It involves not only selecting those suppliers who can deliver a (quality) product on schedule, but also encouraging their adopting TQM, if not already adopted.

Invoking these attributes will position a company to grow as a TQM-based organization.

Tools for Process Improvement

Although there are many techniques for describing and evaluating product quality, statistical process control has proved to be a powerful technique for updating product quality information through the use of statistical tools. Process control describes the use of information about the quality of products or services to achieve an acceptable quality level of a given process. Process control techniques are statistical by definition where their key benefit is to provide immediate feedback to identify causes for out-of-control processes. An implementation procedure for statistical process control is presented.

Statistical Process Control

Statistical process control (SPC) is a scientific system to build quality in products and services through process control. Facts and data are collected and analyzed using statistical techniques to control and improve quality. A variety of statistical tools are used in SPC from histograms and Pareto, bar and control charts to regression analysis, tests of hypotheses, analysis of variance, and design of experiments. These statistical techniques enable the decision maker to take appropriate actions at the right time based on facts and data. Causes for quality problems are discovered. Consequently, defects, rejects, and rework are reduced or even eliminated; quality is improved and productivity is increased (Aly & Murti, 1991).

Even though SPC was first introduced over sixty years ago, its strength in improving quality was rediscovered

　　　　The Guidebook for Performance Improvement

recently by many companies and it has been expanding rapidly since. It is important, though, to recognize that SPC implementation is not an objective in itself, but SPC is a very important tool to gain a competitive edge through quality and productivity improvements.

Successful implementation of SPC as a tool for total quality control is a key step toward achieving continuous quality and productivity improvement systems in an organization. Aly and Murti (1991) describe a model for a systematic implementation of SPC, discuss the basic elements necessary for its success, and also provide a feasible schedule for all required activities.

SPC Implementation Program

Statistical process control is a management philosophy for doing things right the first time. This requires many changes in the organization: from dealing with suppliers to workers' responsibilities in collecting and analyzing data. Hence, many elements have to converge smoothly for SPC implementation to be successful. These elements are discussed below. They constitute the SPC implementation program, although the order and importance of these elements may vary from one organization to another.

Management Commitment

This includes the following tasks:

1. *Involve top management (top-down directive).* Implementing SPC should start at the top. Without full and continuous top management support, the program may not survive. Corporate management should be involved as early as possible. They also should model the program themselves.

2. *Solicit top management commitment and understanding for the requirement to change.* The commitment of top management of all departments (marketing, accounting, production, purchasing) and their cooperation should be solicited. Efforts should be made to explain the demands for change and the emphasis on quality, customer satisfaction, and continual improvements as means for gaining a competitive edge.

3. *Make quality goals an integral part of strategic planning and management processes.* After soliciting top management understanding and commitment, their commitment should be solidified by making quality goals an integral part of the company's strategic planning and performance review process.

4. *Motivate via company-wide communication.* Prepare the ground for the coming changes by communicating the quality goals through the appropriate channels at all levels of the company. All of the company's employees as well as suppliers have to understand and implement the company's commitment to quality.

Quality and Productivity Steering Team

This includes the following tasks:

1. *Select a steering team of key managers.* A team of dedicated managers should be selected to lead the program. These managers should be true believers in quality and have the energy, knowledge, and patience to make the program succeed. The tasks ahead of this team are great; therefore, a full-time quality manager should be assigned to lead the program.

2. *Make quality job number 1.* The major task of the team is to make quality job number 1 and make the necessary efforts to successfully implement the program. Some of the preliminary activities are:

- Promote a philosophy of quality and make everyone in the company aware of and responsible for it.

- Conduct a company-wide quality audit, where all quality activities in the company are surveyed, analyzed, and documented including customers' requirements and complaints.

- Flowchart all processes.

- Plan and schedule training.

- Supervise and follow up implementation.

Management Training and Education

Training at the managerial level should start as early as possible. Management's understanding of statistical techniques used in quality and productivity improvement tools is essential to the success and continuity of the program. Training should include topics such as total quality control concepts, productivity, and quality improvement techniques.

Quality Awareness

Once the top management training is completed, management becomes responsible for spreading quality awareness at all other levels of the company. This may be achieved through:

1. *Creating an environment favorable for a statistical approach to quality.* This environment can be achieved gradually, focusing on using facts, data, and statistical tools in the daily decision-making process.

2. *Soliciting union and supervisor support and commitment.* Early communication with the labor union and supervisors and soliciting their understanding and support will facilitate the implementation of the program.

3. *Motivating workers and employees.* Communications should be extended to every worker and employee in the company. Meetings should be held. Discussions should be encouraged so that everyone will know why the company is going in this direction and the effect it will have on every worker, as well as on the company's future.

4. *Initiating the program.* It is helpful to "officially" initiate the start of the program. However, it is equally important to emphasize that this program will become a continuous and never-ending process of quality and productivity improvement.

Suppliers' and Vendors' Involvement

The involvement and communication with suppliers should start very early. It could take suppliers a long time to implement SPC or even to provide statistical data with their products. A continuing effort should be made to seek their cooperation because without their help the successful implementation of SPC will be incomplete. Communication with suppliers can follow the following steps:

1. Explain your new philosophy of quality.

2. Offer brief SPC training for suppliers.

3. Certify suppliers and reduce their number based on their quality, long-term commitment, and reliable cooperation.

SPC and Problem-Solving Training

Supervisor, worker, and employee training in SPC and problem solving should be scheduled. Eventually, everyone working in production should be trained. The training level and time may vary according to tasks performed.

Quality and Productivity Improvement Teams

The heart of SPC implementation are the quality and productivity improvement teams formed in every workplace to tackle quality and productivity problems at their workplace. Quality circles, if in existence, could be integrated into these teams.

1. Select a leader for every team. Additional training for team leaders may be necessary.

2. Define quality and productivity problems to be addressed by every team.

Unlike in Japan, productivity teams in the United States work effectively if management-initiated problems are presented to them.

Establishing SPC

Process control builds quality in products and helps improve the product's quality of conformance and eliminate waste. The following are the basic steps required to establish SPC for every process and product. Quality and productivity teams can play a major role in accomplishing some of these steps under the supervision of the steering team:

1. Start with a simple part of the system (product, production line, or process) where there is a known quality or productivity problem and the potential for improvement is present.

2. Identify areas and locations where quality and productivity problems exist. Analyze these problems; define the standard processes, procedures, and important quality characteristics that must be controlled.

3. Start data collection, analysis, and display.

4. Select appropriate types of control charts to be used and construct, monitor, and update them.

5. Tackle and eliminate causes of "out-of-control" processes. Establish process capability when control is achieved.

6. A continuous process of improvement and problem solving should follow to improve the system in a more advanced stage. The use of regression analysis, correlation, design of experiments, and multivariate techniques may be necessary to identify problem causes and to find the optimal operational settings to improve quality and productivity.

7. Be patient! The process of finding the causes of quality and productivity problems takes time.

Total Involvement

Because quality is everyone's responsibility, efforts should be made to get everyone at every level in every department involved. That includes marketing, design, purchasing, production, accounting, and sales. Appropriate training for every department should be planned and scheduled to prepare everyone to help in the process of continuous improvement.

Constant Improvement

The main objective of quality programs is to establish a system that constantly improves products, processes, procedures, equipment, and techniques. Also, programs for quality measurement, evaluation, and improvement should be established. This may be achieved by considering the following:

1. Set goals that are measurable and attainable.

2. Provide ways and schedules to achieve these goals.

3. Establish a quality information system, where quality records and data are readily available for anyone.

Recognizing Achievements

Teamwork achievements should be encouraged and quality performance should be made an integral part of employee annual evaluations.

Evaluation Procedure

Finally, an evaluation procedure should be established to guarantee that the program is on the right track. This procedure should take into consideration:

- Customer reactions and feedback.

- Quality cost and improvement records.

SPC Implementation Schedule

One of the main problems many companies encounter when trying to implement SPC is scheduling all the required activities and carrying them out in the proper time and order. Many times, an activity is missing, forgotten, or not done on time, which is often discovered very late. Figure 3 depicts a detailed SPC implementation schedule (Aly & Murti, 1991). It also shows the sequence of its implementation relative to other departmental activities and how the program can lead to ongoing improvements in quality and productivity.

Figure 3. SPC Implementation Schedule

CORPORATE HQ & TOP MANAGEMENT	Commitment	Plan & Set up	Training	Provide continuous motivation, support, leadership, and participation
STEERING COMMITTEE		Promotion & Motivation	Quality audit & Flow charting	Monitor & follow-up implementation & progress
MIDDLE MANAGEMENT		Promote / Training	Training	Direct & facilitate implementation
PRODUCTION WORKERS			Motivate / Training	Quality teams — Data collection / Process capability / Process control — Problem solving & continuous improvement
SUPPORT DEPT. MANAGEMENT & EMPLOYEES			Promote / Training	Improving design, equipment, process, & procedures
SUPPLIERS			Communicate	Prepare to match quality standards & certification

Reproduced by permission from "Statistical Process Control (SPC) Implementation: A Step-by-Step Program," by N.A. Aly and G. Murti, International Journal of Materials and Product Technology, 6(1), 1-8, 1991. Copyright 1991 by N.A. Aly and G. Murti.

Conclusion

In this chapter we have shown how the once narrow concept of "quality" has evolved from being product-oriented to being a pervasive description/prescription of how an organization should conduct its business. Key in that prescription is the realization that quality consists of meeting or exceeding customer expectations. On the surface, defining who the customer is seems almost a trivial exercise. In reality, that is the most critical aspect of implementing a total quality program. In making the determination of who the customer is, it is critical to look beyond the immediate recipient of services and to recognize that almost all fields of endeavor have an impact on our society and the world that we and our children will live in. Hence, as Kaufman (1991) emphasizes, the implicit recognition of society as a customer is key in ensuring that a total quality program enhances long-term organizational effectiveness.

References

Aly, N.A., & Murti, G. (1991). Statistical process control (SPC) implementation: A step-by-step program. *International Journal of Materials and Product Technology, 6*(1), 1-8.

American Society for Quality Control. (1983). *Glossary & tables for statistical quality control.* Milwaukee, WI: ASQC Quality Press.

Deming, W.E. (1986). *Out of the crisis.* Cambridge, MA: MIT Center for Advanced Engineering Study.

Feigenbaum, A.V. (1991). *Total quality control* (3rd ed.). Milwaukee, WI: ASQC Quality Press.

Harrington, H.J. (1987). *The improvement process.* New York: McGraw-Hill.

Juran, J.M. (1988a). *Juran on planning for quality.* New York: The Free Press.

Juran, J.M. (1988b). *Quality control handbook* (4th ed.). New York: McGraw-Hill.

Kacker, R. (1986, December). Taguchi's quality philosophy: Analysis and commentry. *Quality Progress*, pp. 21-29.

Kaufman, R. (1991, December). Toward total quality "plus." *Training*, pp. 50-54.

Lubben, R.T. (1988). *Just-in-time manufacturing: An aggressive manufacturing strategy.* New York: McGraw-Hill.

Taguchi, G. (1986). *Introduction to quality engineering: Designing quality into products and processes.* New York: Unibub/Quality Resources and Dearborn, MI: American Supplier Institute, Asian Productivity Organization.

DEVELOPING FRONT-LINE EMPLOYEES: A NEW CHALLENGE FOR ACHIEVING ORGANIZATIONAL EFFECTIVENESS

Michael J. Jones
and Ronald L. Jacobs

Until recently, organization leaders focused most of their efforts on developing supervisors and managers. The prevailing argument was that because these individuals, especially at the senior levels, influence organizational effectiveness more than any other group, greater benefits can be expected when making human resource development (HRD) investments on their behalf. Today, an increasing number of authors, such as Tom Peters (1987), doubt this argument and point out that separating employees who "think" from those who "do" as the major part of their jobs is no longer practical. Organization leaders must now call on all the capabilities of their employees, regardless of employment level.

Increasingly, this alternative view has focused greater attention on the requirements of employees who are closest to the actual production of goods or the delivery of services— that is, front-line employees. In fact, front-line employees can do as much, or more, to influence organizational effectiveness as can supervisors and managers. Organization leaders are faced with the new challenge of meeting the development requirements of front-line employees, which must be addressed if the benefits of quality and productivity improvement efforts are to be fully realized.

The purposes of this chapter are to first, discuss front-line employees in greater depth; second, describe an emerging goal among many organizations—to have front-line employees become more multiskilled within their work areas; third, propose an employee development system designed specifically for front-line employees; and finally, describe some on-the-job and off-the-job approaches for developing front-line employees.

Front-Line Employees

Front-line employees are those who are closest to the actual production of goods or delivery of services in organizations; they are the individuals who do the work of the organization. Front-line employee describes a unique category of individual in organizations that transcends other commonly used categories, such as blue-collar, managerial, or professional. Of importance here is describing employees in relationship to their contributions, instead of their location on organizational charts or educational levels. Front-line employees most often make use of inputs, frequently from other front-line employees, to produce things or deliver services and then supply them to both internal and external customers. Many organizations have workflows that are composed of strings of front-line employees who have direct supplier-customer relationships with each other.

Given this definition, front-line employees may include semiskilled and skilled workers such as assemblers, operators, and technicians. They also may include service employees such as customer service representatives, salespersons, and office workers. And, they may include professional workers such as production engineers, purchasing agents, and health-care specialists. Some supervisors and managers have responsibilities that may seem similar to front-line employees. All front-line employees share the common feature of making things or providing services, as opposed to supervising people, as the major part of their work.

In the past few years, front-line employees have experienced several noticeable changes in their workplaces. Toffler (1990) suggests that individuals at the lowest levels of organizations have been among the first to experience technological change. He states that the demands of a changing marketplace have increased the requirement to provide real-time, continuous flows of information back and forth between all levels of the organization. Making information available instantly is feasible only by using advanced technology. From the hand-held computer used to maintain inventory, to the display panel on the industrial robot, to the patient's monitor at the nurses' station, these are among the many technological advancements that are now being used by front-line employees.

Another change affecting front-line employees involves the ongoing transformation of their expected roles in organizations. Historically, front-line employees are at the lowest rungs of organizational hierarchies and, because of their lessor status, were expected only to carry out policies formulated by others. Thus, it was considered appropriate that front-line employees maintain a more passive role when considering the affairs of the organization. In contrast, front-line employees are now being solicited to become more actively involved in solving problems and making decisions.

Given efforts to improve quality and productivity, especially in view of the demands of meeting ISO 9000 requirements in many organizations, this role transformation seems logical. After all, as the term implies, front-line employees are on the leading edge of the organization and should have the most accurate perspective about how best to improve critical work procedures and processes. In many respects, front-line employees have become partners with managers in their common concern for the health and well-being of the enterprise.

Multiskilled Front-Line Employees

An emerging goal among many organizations is to have front-line employees become more multiskilled. Multiskilled front-line employees are those individuals who can perform a wide range of the tasks required to produce products or deliver services. Multiskilling has emerged as a major part of many quality-improvement programs. While the specific features of quality programs typically differ across organizations, one constant has been that front-line employees must know more and do more on their jobs. For example, it is common knowledge that front-line employees in companies such as Procter and Gamble, General Electric, and General Motors are now ordering parts, scheduling production, helping design new products, improving workflows, participating in the selection of new employees, and contributing in many other meaningful ways that affect their work areas.

Figure 1 contrasts the features of traditional front-line employees having more narrow responsibilities with those of multiskilled front-line employees having more inclusive responsibilities. Multiskilling leads to greater workforce flexibility by reducing the barriers that commonly exist when using narrow job boundaries. In practice, greater flexibility occurs when front-line employees can rotate jobs among themselves, often to reduce boredom, and assist one another during peak production or service-delivery times.

Multiskilling usually results in having just a few or even one job title. For instance, a manufacturing company recently implemented self-managed work groups with the goal that all front-line employees would be multiskilled. The result was that sixteen job classifications were collapsed into one broad

Traditional	Multiskilled
• Perform a limited range of tasks	• Perform a variety of tasks; development plan determines scope
• Have many distinct job classifications	• Have a single or just a few job classifications
• Have responsibility for a small part of the work	• Share responsibility with others for completing the entire product or service
• Have a "we, they" attitude with management; limited ownership and pride requirements	• Recognize that a partnership exists among all employees and that each has a stake in the enterprise
• Believe that managers should solve problems and make decisions	• Believe that problem solving and decision making must be a shared activity
• Unwilling to share expertise, thinking that this will increase job security	• Willing to share expertise so that greater flexibility can be achieved, increasing job security through competitiveness
• Expect supervisors to direct the work at all times	• Expect supervisors to support and facilitate the work
• Regard proposed changes with reluctance and suspicion because of limited involvement with the process	• Regard proposed changes as part of a new way of doing business using continuous-improvement process
• Expect recognition and rewards to be linked to seniority, job classification, and individual performance	• Expect recognition and rewards to be linked to group performance as well as individual performance

Figure 1. Features of Traditional and Multiskilled Front-Line Employees

job classification, called "all-purpose operator." Figure 2 is the company's statement about the APO function.

All-purpose operators (APOs) work together to perform all operations to produce a completed product. APOs are responsible and accountable for all aspects of the process including safety, quality, and maintenance. APOs conduct and participate in meetings to improve the product, process, and quality of work life.

APOs rotate and assist one another in performing the following:

- Operating all equipment in the work area
- Assembling component parts
- Conducting part inspections
- Ordering production materials and supplies
- Scheduling production operations
- Maintaining statistical-quality-control charts
- Moving materials and completing subassemblies
- Troubleshooting safety, quality, and production problems
- Performing planned maintenance
- Participating in team meetings
- Training new APOs
- Preparing production reports

Figure 2. All-Purpose Operators

To a large extent, multiskilling, a notion originally from the past, is now being revisited with a slightly different twist. Carnevale (1991) chronicles how skill requirements have changed using different production and service-delivery systems. These systems roughly follow the major economic trends from the past century until today. Under the preindustrial craft system, artisans were autonomous and possessed deep occupational knowledge about their crafts. In a sense, artisans can be considered multiskilled since they do most of the tasks required to complete their products. In differentiated mass production and traditional service-delivery systems, production employees and nonsupervisory employees have the most narrow skill requirements and the least discretion on the job because many of their tasks are repetitive in nature. On the other hand, managers and service professionals have more abstract skill requirements and enjoy greater discretion on the job since exceptions are generally the rule.

The new economy represents a complex interaction of the previous two systems. There is at once a requirement to provide greater independence and autonomy among production and nonsupervisory employees so that they can reclaim ownership of their efforts. Networks of people, teams, and organizations must be more fully integrated, increasing the interdependence of employees with each other. Not unexpectedly, skill requirements for all employees, especially front-line employees, in the new economy are a mixture of abstract reasoning abilities and specific task-oriented skills, enabling everyone to handle repetitions and exceptions when they should occur (Carnevale, 1991).

Front-Line Employee Development System

How to develop front-line employees has become a new challenge for achieving organizational effectiveness. In general, employee development is the process of enhancing capabilities through a variety of experiences. Because of today's changing economy, employee development has evolved from being considered a perquisite to that of a strategic part of organizational change (Vaught, Hoy, & Buchanan, 1985). Employee development as a perquisite is characterized by having individuals merely select from optional training programs or self-awareness courses provided though the HRD department. In contrast, as part of organizational change, employee development is characterized by being articulated with the change effort to help ensure its success.

Employee development systems for front-line employees seemingly must accommodate the requirements of society, organizations, and individuals. For organizations, employee development systems must be job-related to prepare individuals to perform their present and future jobs. This goal benefits organizations in three ways. It eases the transition when front-line employees enter new work areas. It increases the flexibility of how they can be used within those work areas. Finally, it reduces the adjustment time required when organizational changes occur. Organizations must view employee development systems as the primary means to unleash expertise to all front-line employees.

For individuals, employee development systems must promote greater personal growth and enrichment. This goal benefits individuals by encouraging them to become more proficient in areas other than those explicitly required for their present jobs. Personal goals are undertaken with the assumption that what is good for individuals will, in the long run, be good for organizations as well. In this sense, besides promoting growth and enrichment for individuals, personal goals also may serve organizations in the long run. For instance, individuals who have developed new areas of expertise, such as computer-programming skills, might be asked to perform specific tasks for the organization apart from their job expectations, in turn, providing the individuals with a renewed sense of self-value and esteem.

Figure 3 describes each of the five parts of the front-line employee development system (FEDS). The parts can be implemented in the sequence suggested or each part can be used as required.

Part	Activities	Products
1. Define the Process	• Document all workflows • Document tasks within workflows • Identify prerequisite knowledge and skills • Identify safety precautions and potential hazards • Define customer requirements	• Completed capability studies of all workflows • Completed analyses of all workflows and tasks • Posted performance aids describing critical steps, safety information, potential hazards
2. Conduct Work-Area Orientation	• Explain work rules • Identify customers and their requirements • Describe relevant workflows • Describe critical tasks within relevant workflows • Explain safety precautions and potential hazards • Point out performance aids	• Informed front-line employee who can -identify relevant workflows -describe critical tasks -recognize safety precautions and potential hazards -explain the purpose and content of performance aids
3. Prepare Development Plan	• Identify present capabilities of front-line employee • Describe required knowledge and skills of work area • Identify personal goals of front-line employee • Establish job-related and personal goals	• Mutually identified job-related and personal-developmental goals

Figure 3. Front-Line Employee Development System

Part	Activities	Products
4. Identify Developmental Approaches	• Select on-the-job approaches • Select off-the-job approaches	• Identified matches between goals and developmental approaches • Assigned schedule for achieving goals
5. Management of Performance	• Provide scheduled feedback about job performance • Evaluate progress toward stated developmental goals • Revise developmental goals based on anticipated needs of organization and emergent interests of individual • Solicit suggestions from front-line employees about improving work flows and tasks, using continuous-improvement process	• Informed front-line employee who has knowledge of job performance and progress toward developmental goals • Revised development plan • Improved work flows and tasks • Involved front-line employee who assumes ownership of the goods being produced or services being delivered

Figure 3 (continued). Front-Line Employee Development System

More importantly, as shown in Figure 4, the five parts of the FEDS should be viewed as links of a chain. When all links are secure and adequate, there is greater likelihood that front-line employees will make more valuable contributions to achieve organizational effectiveness. If any of the links are weak or inadequate, then unpredictable results will likely occur.

The first part, "define the process," identifies the activities that must be completed before the remaining four parts.

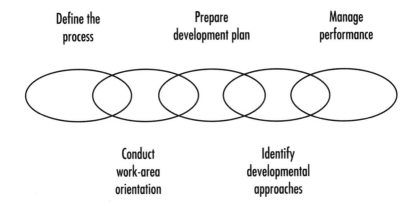

Figure 4. Front-Line Employee Development System

During this first part, process capability is determined and the "best" ways to organize the workflows and perform the tasks safely and efficiently are documented. Quality and statistical measures are built into capable processes. Critical steps are posted near where the tasks are performed for easy reference. Process definition activities are usually performed by a team composed of expert front-line employees, engineers, quality specialists, supervisors, and HRD professionals.

"Conduct work-area orientation" identifies the information that managers and supervisors must present to front-line employees when entering new work areas or when organizational changes occur. This information can be presented one-on-one or in small groups. This part does not replace the broader orientation to the organization that front-line employees typically receive as new hires. Instead, this part focuses on information specific to the work area in which front-line employees will be employed. Describing workflows, identifying customer requirements, explaining safety and quality practices, and stating customer requirements are some activities of this part.

"Prepare development plan" requires supervisors to identify in a collaborative manner the present abilities of front-line employees and compare them with the knowledge

---

and skill requirements of the work area. Knowledge and skill requirements can be separated into three areas: (1) technical; (2) troubleshooting; and, (3) interpersonal. As discussed, supervisors also must help front-line employees identify their personal goals. Goal selection is a critical aspect of the entire system. In all instances, goals must be explicit and reconciled with work-area and organizational accomplishments (Jacobs, 1988; Rummler & Brache, 1990).

"Identify developmental approaches" identifies how the job-related and personal goals will be achieved. Developmental approaches should be matched with each goal and made explicit on the development plan. As presented in Figure 5, developmental approaches can be distinguished by those that occur on-the-job or off-the-job. These developmental approaches will be discussed in greater depth in the next section. Obviously, certain developmental approaches are better suited for some situations than others, depending on the needs of the front-line employee, the nature of the task, and time and cost constraints.

The final part of the FEDS, "management of performance," gives the manager and supervisor the tools to ensure that job-related and personal goals will be achieved. In addition, this part helps ensure that the development plan will be viewed as a dynamic document, changing as new ideas are introduced by the organization and new interests emerge among front-line employees. The FEDS also has been instrumental when used as part of the continuous-improvement process. Feedback of this nature redefines what is the "best" way of sequencing workflow operations and performing specific tasks.

On-the-Job Developmental Approaches

Developmental approaches can be separated by the two basic locations in which they occur. When the approaches occur mostly in the actual work setting, they can be categorized as on-the-job training (OJT) approaches. These include the following methods.

On-the-Job Training Approaches	Off-the-Job Training Approaches
• Structured OJT • Apprenticeship training • Mentoring • Coaching • Job rotation • Self-paced materials	• Classroom training • Laboratory training • Off-site technical and educational courses • Basic skills remedies • Field trips

Figure 5. Acquiring New Knowledge and Skills

On-the-Job Training

Arguably, some form of OJT is the most frequently used method for most front-line employees. Unfortunately, most instances of OJT are unstructured, such as a situation in which an inexperienced employee informally "picks up" job information from one or more experienced employees. Experienced employees pass on what they know, or think they know, about aspects of the job. Structured OJT differs in that work behaviors are separated into manageable units and documented in modules. Experienced employees then use a specific delivery process to deliver the job information under more controlled conditions with more predictable results (Jacobs, 1991; Jacobs & Jones, 1995). If OJT is the most frequently used employee development method, then it must be used in a structured form to ensure greater reliability and predictability of its results.

Apprenticeship Training

Usually associated with the preparation of skilled trades persons, this method follows an established curriculum leading to a certification that is approved by a governing body. Apprenticeship training combines OJT that is delivered by journeymen and formal classroom instruction, usually conducted in a technical school or on-site classroom. Certain aspects of apprenticeship training, such as independent certification and restricted entry, make it unique from other OJT training approaches.

Mentoring

This method matches employees who are at different points in their careers to provide information useful for career planning and management. Mentors meet with persons of lessor status and share their insights about understanding the company culture, selecting different work assignments, and navigating through the formal and informal power structures. Mentoring programs occur on-the-job but do not involve imparting specific job information. In fact, many successful mentoring relationships are established between people from different work areas. The key aspects are the mentor's willingness to share and the mutual respect that may develop between the individuals. Mentoring programs have been used for sales, managerial, and professional employees. Mentoring programs for front-line employees can help pass along cultural aspects such as customer-service orientation and reliance on continuous improvement to assist problem solving.

Coaching

Coaching occurs when some specific aspect of an employee's behavior is deficient and must be modified by one-on-one instruction. Coaching does not encompass an entire task as does OJT, but only a small part of a task. In addition, coaching differs from OJT in that it focuses more on refining already known skills. In this way, coaching sessions are useful in transferring the special techniques and shortcuts that distinguish expert employees from beginning employees. Coaching occurs on an almost continuous basis within most work areas, among employees and between supervisors and employees.

Job Rotation

Used when the company wishes to move employees temporarily from their present jobs and work areas, job rotation can last from several days to several months or years. Initially, this method was used as part of the career development of managerial and professional employees. More recently, job rotation has taken on new meaning among front-line employees. Job rotation among front-line employees means assisting others when there is a backlog of work or sharing repetitious or monotonous tasks. In addition, job rotation provides a broader view of the workflow, increasing the probability that employees will have more ownership about the outcomes of the workflow.

Self-Paced Materials

This method is considered an off-the-job development approach. However, self-paced materials, which do not require special delivery systems, can be used directly in the job setting. Self-paced materials allow front-line employees to obtain training during convenient times at their desks or work stations. In the past, self-paced materials were assumed mostly to be programmed instruction. Structured writing formats have allowed more flexible ways of presenting the information. Self-paced materials often use a combination of media, such as printed booklets, printed booklets with audio tape, or computer-based instruction.

Off-the-Job Developmental Approaches

When the approaches occur outside of the actual work setting, they can be categorized as off-the-job developmental approaches. These include the following.

Classroom Training

Historically, most training programs have been presented in a classroom setting. The training classroom provides a separate environment for making presentations, facilitating discussions, and conducting role plays. In most training classrooms, employees are away from their jobs, but not too far away so that they might be contacted in case of a question or an emergency. In many organizations, front-line employees have had fewer opportunities to leave the work area and attend classroom-based training, compared with most other employees.

Laboratory Training

Not all off-the-job training can be conducted in a classroom setting. The presentation and practice of technical information are often conducted in special training laboratories, which often are made to resemble actual work settings. For example, experienced tool-and-die makers might use a lab setting, with all necessary tools and equipment, to practice a new technique and to receive individual feedback. In another example, one section of an assembly line might be set up to allow new employees the opportunity to practice an operation without the pressure of a moving assembly line.

Off-Site Technical Education Courses

Increasingly, companies and vocational schools and two-year technical schools have linked together to help meet the needs of front-line employees. Companies contract with these educational institutions to provide specific courses that are not available through the company. The courses are taught by faculty who have considerable experience in their technical or educational specialties. Many courses are generic and include topics such as shop math, blueprint reading, business writing, statistical process control, and computer basics. Linkages with educational institutions can provide a cost-efficient way of achieving certain types of job-related and personal development goals.

Basic-Skills Remediation

Increasing skill demands for most jobs have increased the need for offering basic-skills remediation for some front-line employees. Workplace basics include understanding technical information, written business communications, and basic arithmetic. Greater awareness of these deficiencies has resulted in programs to address the issue. In many instances, there is little systematic analysis of the basic skills required and the diagnosis of present skills to determine whether a problem, in fact, exists among front-line employees. Basic-skills remediation services are provided through many adult services departments of public school systems and post-secondary technical education institutions.

Field Trips

Often regarded cynically as a way to get away from the facility for the day, field trips have become important for two reasons. First, they provide a means for front-line employees from supplier companies to visit their counterparts in customer companies. Establishing a close supplier-customer relationship is important for meeting customer requirements. Second, field trips provide a means to visit companies undergoing similar types of organizational changes. For example, while bank clerks might seem at first to have little in common with production employees, a closer examination might reveal that both sets of front-line employees are becoming multiskilled, and sharing the challenges associated with this change could have benefits for each.

Conclusion

There can be no doubt that front-line employees have experienced dramatic changes in their workplaces. The front-line employee development system presented in this chapter is intended to help address those changes for the benefit of organizations and individuals. But, organization leaders must decide what results they want to achieve beforehand through a planned process that involves all planning partners. Otherwise, the system might well achieve unintended outcomes, which could be counterproductive in the long run. Without direction, front-line employees will undoubtedly experience frustration and retreat to their traditional feelings of mistrust and cynicism about the sincerity of managers to institute organizational change (Kaufman & Jones, 1990). Other chapters in this text present excellent ways to plan large-scale organizational change efforts.

Emphasis in this chapter has been on balancing the needs of organizations with those of individual front-line employees. It may not always be desirable to equally balance needs between the two, since the needs of the organization usually predominate. However, this does not necessarily relegate individual-development needs to a lower status or to being expendable during times of organizational stress. To the contrary, societal, organizational, and individual needs link together, such that a win-win situation can result for all.

References

Carnevale, A. (1991). *America and the new economy.* Alexandria, VA: American Society for Training and Development.

Jacobs, R. (1988). A proposed domain of human performance technology: Implications for theory and practice. *Performance Improvement Quarterly, 1*(2), 2-12.

Jacobs, R. (1991). Structured on-the-job training. In Stolovitch, H., & Keeps, E.J. (Eds.), *Handbook of Human Performance Technology.* San Francisco, CA: Jossey-Bass.

Jacobs, R., & Jones, M. (1995). *Structured on-the-job training: Unleashing employee expertise in the workforce.* San Francisco, CA: Berrett-Koehler.

Kaufman, R., & Jones, M. (1990). The industrial survival of the nation: Union-management cooperation. *Human Resource Development Quarterly, 1*(1), 87-91.

Peters, T. (1987). *Thriving on chaos.* New York: Harper & Row.

Rummler, G., & Brache, A. (1990). *Improving performance: How to manage the white space on the organization chart.* San Francisco, CA: Jossey-Bass.

Toffler, A. (1990). *Powershift: Knowledge, wealth, and violence at the edge of the 21st century.* New York: Bantam.

Vaught, B., Hoy, F., & Buchanan, W. (1985). *Employee development programs: An organizational approach.* Westport, CT: Quorum Books.

JOB AIDS

Jeff Nelson

Introduction

There are many challenges facing organizations today:

- Rapidly changing technology
- A changing workforce
- Competition
- Innovations in products and services

All these challenges place a continual burden on human resource professionals to, among other things, find ways to train that are less expensive, faster, and better. This implies several things:

- *Quick development and implementation.* Training programs have cycles just as products do. The less time it takes from inception until the product is distributed, the more responsive the organization will be to consumers and the more competitive. If training programs are to keep pace with the changing requirements of the workplace, they must have shorter "training-cycle time."

- *Easy modification.* Training programs must be packaged in ways that are easy and inexpensive to modify. If training is tied up in media that are difficult or expensive to change, the training programs will not be able to keep pace with organizational requirements.

- *Reduced time away from the job.* Trainee salaries during training are the greatest cost in any training program. The more quickly the training is done, the less time the trainees will spend away from their jobs.

- *Enabling people to produce quality goods and services.* Training *must* enable people to accomplish their job requirements. What people learn during training must be directly related to their job performance.

Job aids can help to meet these requirements. They are key components of any performance system. Before discussing what job aids are and how to use them, we will look at the bigger picture.

Performance, Accomplishments, and Influences

People perform tasks on the job in order to produce accomplishments—that is, outputs that have worth to the organization.

Job Title	Tasks	Accomplishments
Insurance sales person	Identify potential customers	List of customers
	Write a policy	A policy in force

To do their jobs and produce accomplishments, people require the following:

- *Skills and knowledge.* People have to know how to do their jobs, what the standards are, and when to do the tasks.

- *Motivation.* People must want to perform. They require the proper incentives and consequences.

- *Environment.* "Environment" refers to anything outside the employee, such as heat, light, work space, tools, equipment, and supervision.

The diagram below shows a simple performance system.

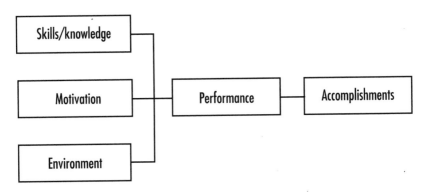

If *all* these influences are present in the workplace, people will be able to do their jobs and produce quality goods and services. If one or more is deficient, people will *not* be able to produce to the desired standards.

Job aids are a way to provide people with the skills and knowledge that they require to do their jobs.

What Job Aids Are

Job aids are checklists, standard operating procedures, technical manuals, and "how-to" guides that explain how to do a task. People use job aids while actually performing tasks. For example

- A preflight checklist used by a pilot

- A troubleshooting guide used in a manufacturing plant

- A one-page guide for "where to direct customer inquiries" used in the order-taking department of a catalog-sales company

Job aids can reduce errors, especially for tasks that contain a lot of steps, require complex decisions, or are not done very often.

Job aids can be written on paper, shown on a computer screen, recorded on audiotape or voice chips, or stamped on equipment, on packet cards, and on posters.

A job aid puts the how-to information in the worker's hands instead of in his or her head. When the time comes to do the task, instead of trying to do the task from memory, the person simply reads what to do and how to do it. The following (on the next page) is an example of a typical job aid.

What Job Aids Are Not

Job aids tell the user how to *do* something on the job. As such, job aids are not intended to provide motivational information, general information, or theory about a subject. If background concepts or information are required to effectively use a particular job aid, it is better to present that type of information during training sessions as handout materials. If that information *is* put into the job aid, it will slow down access to the relevant, how-to information.

Tools are not job aids. A tool is something a person uses when doing a task. Information about how to use a particular tool (or piece of equipment) is a job aid.

Where How-To Information Should Be Stored

A key decision when developing training is where the information essential to doing a task will be stored. There are three options:

- Option 1: Store all the information in people's heads: Make them memorize what to do and how to do it. When the time comes to do the task, they must be able to do it from memory.

- Option 2: Store all the information in people's hands: Write a job aid that explains in detail what to do and

The name of the task is at the top.	
If required, there is a brief context statement.	**Calculate Final Cost** Use this procedure to adjust the price on key items. You will have to use a calculator and the Final Cost Worksheet.
The steps are numbered or lettered.	**Do this:** **1. Calculate the Basic Discount** • Turn the calculator on. • Enter the cost of the item. • Subtract 14%.
Examples are given as required. "White space" separates the steps.	Example: Item cost = $34.85 Basic discount price = $34.95 – 14% = $30.05
Decision tables explain any decisions.	**2. Calculate the Bonus Discount**
Bold, italics, etc., highlight important information.	
Steps are written using "action verb + object."	Example: Cost after Basic Discount = $30.95 Item is from Group A. Bonus Discount = $30.05 – 8% = $27.65

If item is from group	Then subtract an additional
A	8% (–8%)
B	5% (–5%)
C	3% (–3%)

how to do it. Provide no other training. When the time comes to do the task, they refer to the job aid and do the task.

- Option 3: Store the information in *both*. Write a job aid *and* provide training to go along with the job aid.

Storing all the skills and knowledge in a person's memory has the advantage of quick access when it is required (as opposed to getting and reading a job aid). The disadvantage is that human memory is not very reliable for tasks that are not done often or for tasks that contain a lot of steps.

Of course, there are ways to help people remember how to do tasks. One can provide lots of practice and repetition or use memory joggers (mnemonics) to help people remember key items. One can provide refresher training at various intervals or simply do the training just before the task is to be performed.

Storing the information in a job aid allows a person not to have to rely solely on memory when doing a task. The advantage is that people will make fewer errors because the job aid, not memory, is the source of the information. Training time also can be reduced because people will not be expected to remember everything. The disadvantage is that it takes time to read the how-to information. For some tasks (e.g., emergency tasks), it may take too long to get the information from a job aid. So, the information *must* be stored in memory.

When to Write a Job Aid

The following factors indicate that a job aid should be written:

- The task is not done very often. The person will forget how to do it. What "often" and "not often" mean depends on the task.

- Something bad will result if a step is missed or done incorrectly. (For example, preflight check of an aircraft.)

- There are a lot of steps and/or complex decisions in the task. (For example, troubleshooting the panel instruments of an aircraft.)

- The procedures change often or there is a high personnel turnover.

- Training must get on the line quickly. (For example, a new manufacturing line must be up and operating within three months.)

- Training must be exported to several locations.

- Existing job aids are written at too high a level, or information is missing or inaccurate. (For example, a technical manual is confusing and hard to follow.)

There may be additional factors, depending on the particular situation. For example, company policy may require that job aids be written.

When Not to Write a Job Aid

The following factors indicate that a job aid should not be written:

- Using a job aid would slow down a person too much. (For example, giving first aid.)

- Physical conditions do not permit the use of a job aid. (For example, the task is done in darkness.)

- Using the job aid would embarrass the person. (For example, supervisors would be embarrassed to use a troubleshooting checklist because it would make them look as if they do not know how to do the task.)

- The task is done so often or is so simple that the person will easily remember how to do it.

An example of something done often is a daily start-up procedure. Something done not often might be a weekly sales analysis. A task that is simple is making copies on the copier machine. Something that is complex is troubleshooting problems with the copier.

It is possible to overcome some of the reasons for not using a job aid. For example, if the work environment is damp, you could laminate the job aid. If a person must have both hands free to do the work, you could have someone else read the job aid to the person doing the work.

The following may help you to decide whether or not to write a job aid:

1. Draw a form like this on scratch paper:

Task	Factors *for a* job aid	Factors *against* a job aid	Job aid? (Y/N)	Notes

2. List the tasks that will require some sort of skills/knowledge intervention (based on a front-end analysis).

3. For each task, list the factors for and against writing a job aid.

4. Consider the factors and decide whether or not to write a job aid. (Write "Y" or "N" under the "Job aid?" column.)

5. Write notes or explanation about your decision under the "Notes" column.

The following is a sample form for the job of payroll auditor:

Task	Factors *for a* job aid	Factors *against* a job aid	Job aid? (Y/N)	Notes
Examine time cards	Complex Infrequent		Yes	
Review night-pay calculation	Complex Infrequent		Yes	
Brief pay clerk on the findings		Too slow Impractical to use a job aid in front of clerk	No	

Guidelines For Writing A Job Aid

Information must be technically correct. Because we expect people to do what the job aid says to do, the job aid must have the correct procedure. This means that anyone using the job aid and following the steps should be able to achieve the desired result. Incomplete, missing, or inaccurate information is one of the quickest ways to sabotage the use of a job aid. The best source for technically correct information is an accomplished performer—somebody who does the task the way everyone should do it. Existing documentation and job aids are another source, but unless you know how the information was developed, be wary.

The format must be easy to follow. Once we have technically correct information, we must put that information into a format that people can follow. To illustrate how the format makes a difference, read the paragraph in the example that follows. See if you can determine what to do if a customer orders Model Z. The information is technically correct.

Example:

Orders for Model K should be sent to the marketing department. Refer to the supervisor any orders for Model L or Model M. Customer service should be given any requests for Model Y or Model Z. Speed and courtesy are important when processing any orders.

Because of the way the information is formatted, you have to read the entire paragraph to find out what to do. Here is the same information presented as a decision table:

If the customer orders model:	Then send the request to:
K	Marketing department
L	Department supervisor
M	
Y	Customer service
Z	

With a decision table, you read down the left-hand column until you find the situation that applies and then look to the right to find out what to do.

Apply the look-away rule. Write the job aid so that the user can read what to do, look away to do it, look back at the job aid, and easily find his or her place. To accomplish this, use white space (blank space) between steps, number or letter the steps, and keep the sentences short and specific.

Allow one-stop shopping. Put all the information that the user must have on the same page or on opposing pages. That way, the user will not have to continually be turning pages back and forth to get the information he or she requires.

Emphasize key information. Use **bold** type, *italics*, or ALL CAPS to call the reader's attention to key information. But, DON'T overdo it. FOR EXAMPLE, A SENTENCE OF ALL CAPS SOON LOSES ITS EFFECTIVENESS BECAUSE <u>ALL</u> THE WORDS ARE "EMPHASIZED."

Use two columns. There may be times when you want to provide additional explanation or background information about each step in the job aid. If you use two columns, you can do that without cluttering up the how-to information. Label the left-hand column "Steps" and the right-hand column "Notes," "Guidelines," or "Examples." The following is an example:

Steps	Notes
1. Enter the amount of the deposit	Remember to include the service fee Use the "Amounts Table" on page 4 in the company policy manual
2. Calculate the bonus amount	**Always** round **up** to the nearest dollar. Be sure to double check the result.

Write decision tables. If a particular step requires a decision, write a decision table. Put the "If" on the left and the "Then" on the right. If there are intermediate conditions, write an "And" column. Use an arrow to show that a particular situation doesn't matter. For example:

If payment code is	And credit code is	Then mark the form
Immediate	Good	A
	Marginal	B
Delayed		C

Use an "action verb + object" format. When explaining what to do, use an action verb plus object. For example:

Action Verb	Object
Operate	the calibration machine
Decide	whether or not to increase production
Interview	new customers

Don't use the passive voice, e.g., "the calibration machine should be operated."
Don't use "fuzzy" verbs, e.g., "be familiar with how to interview new customers"; "understand how to calibrate the machine."

Try Out the Job Aid

The best way to be sure that a job aid works is to try it out on the job. Give a copy of the job aid to the person who will actually be using it. Have him or her use the job aid to do the task. Use the following checklist to review the job aid:

- Has a front-end analysis been done that supports the development of training and job aids?

- Ask the job-aid writer for evidence that the job aid works. Can a person actually use the job aid to do the task on the job?

- Read the job aid. Does it tell what to do and how to do it (action verb plus object)?

- Is the step-by-step information in sufficient detail so that the intended user will be able to do the task?

- Is the information technically correct? Has it been reviewed and approved by a technical expert?

- Read one of the steps. Can you read what to do, look away, look back, and find your place?

- Is all the information you must use to do a step on the same page or opposing pages?

- Is there an implementation plan—a detailed plan for how the job aid will be implemented and evaluated?

- Can the job-aid writer give you good reasons why a job aid was written for the task (infrequency of task, complexity of task, bad consequence if errors occur, etc.)?

- Is the job aid packaged in a way that is easy to use and that people are likely to use?

- Are drawings or pictures used when these will make the steps clearer?

- If the job aid is to stand alone (there will be no training or explanation other than the job aid itself), can the job-aid writer justify that decision?

- Is there plenty of white space or do the words and pictures appear crowded?

Provide Training and the Job Aid

In the workplace, a person receives a job aid and reads step-by-step how to perform a task. If written in enough detail and thoroughly tested, a job aid might "stand alone," that is, the user might be able to use the job aid without any further training. In most situations, however, both the job aid and training will be necessary.

Following are some of the reasons to provide training:

- There are definitions, concepts, background information, or theory that the user must know to do the task.

- There are fine motor skills involved in doing the task that the user will have to practice.

- The task is dangerous and must be supervised.

- The task must be practiced before doing it on the job because there are standards that the user will not be able to achieve the first few times the task is performed.

- The use of job aids is new to the organization, and users will require an orientation—what job aids are, why to use them, and how to use them in the workplace.

The Overall Flow

Job aids are an integral part of any performance system. On the next page is the job-aid development process overlaid on a performance-system model.

Summary

When used as parts of a performance system, job aids offer a practical and effective technique for helping people to produce quality goods and services. Job aids can reduce training costs, reduce on-the-job errors, and improve human performance. Job aids offer a way to make training more responsive, timely, and flexible to meet the training demands of the workplace.

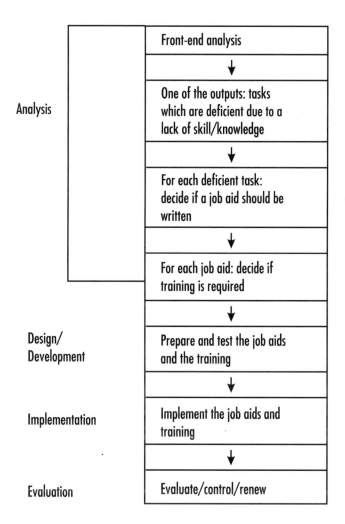

Analysis	Front-end analysis
	↓
	One of the outputs: tasks which are deficient due to a lack of skill/knowledge
	↓
	For each deficient task: decide if a job aid should be written
	↓
	For each job aid: decide if training is required
	↓
Design/ Development	Prepare and test the job aids and the training
	↓
Implementation	Implement the job aids and training
	↓
Evaluation	Evaluate/control/renew

Job-Aid Development Process

ORGANIZATIONAL DEVELOPMENT FOR HUMAN PERFORMANCE TECHNOLOGISTS

Richard Pearlstein

This chapter examines the field of organization development (OD) today and suggests that it has much to offer practitioners of human performance technology (HPT). The bulk of the chapter suggests some basic principles for practicing OD within an HPT context.

Although OD is now widely accepted in corporate circles, it only became recognized as a field in the early 1960s (Burke, 1982). Practitioners of OD make a distinction between organization development and organizational development. For example, Vaill (1971) notes that organizational development refers to

> ...development that occurs in organizations. The phrase says nothing about *what* is being developed...[but] does imply...that the organization itself, as a totality, *is not* the object of development. [The] focus [of organization development] is clear; it means "development of organizations."

In other words, OD traditionally focuses on developing the entire organization, as opposed to some aspects of the organization. This distinction underscores both a great strength of OD and its Achilles' heel, as leaders of organizations often claim to want to develop the entire organization, when, in fact, they are interested only in changing a few well-circumscribed aspects. OD, in its "classical" sense, then, is best applied in those few circumstances when top management does want to develop the entire organization and is prepared to pay the price. HPT practitioners would also favor such a system-wide approach but, like most OD practitioners, usually have to settle for effecting change within a smaller sphere of influence.

Defining OD Within the Context of HPT

This chapter promotes a nonclassical definition of OD, referring to it as "organizational development" in accordance with Vaill's connotation: "Development that occurs in organizations." I would add to Vaill's statement as follows: Organizational development aims to facilitate development within organizations, *with the ultimate goal of helping members of the organization bring their best talents to serve the organization's mission, helping to align it with the broader needs of the society in which the organization exists and the world.*

By this definition, ordinary organizational problem solving or capitalizing on opportunities would not necessarily qualify as OD, even if the problems or opportunities affected the entire organization. Instead, an OD endeavor not only would have to develop some aspect of the organization but also would have to clearly enhance the ability of some employees to use their talents more fully and/or align organizational functioning to better serve societal needs. This focus on what Kaufman (1989) calls the "mega" level of planning—planning with the understanding that society (even global society) is the ultimate client—is central.

In fact, OD as a field has traditionally recognized the importance of societal impacts. According to Gellermann,

Frankel, and Ladenson (1990), an ethical policy statement for practitioners of OD should prohibit acting against the social good. But, in the midst of organizational life, it is easy for human-performance consultants to lose sight of the many ways in which organizational changes can impact the society in which the organization functions. In order for HPT or OD consultants to avoid this blind spot, every project should examine potential mega-level impacts.

Even worse from the point of view of the OD purist is my assertion that OD can affect some aspects of the organization, as opposed to the entire organization. For example, Gallessich (1982) notes that OD is "...a broad spectrum of human process and structural interventions that are, *by definition, system wide*" (pp. 200-201)[italics mine]. Nonetheless, I maintain that if we were to limit it to system-wide interventions, most OD practitioners would be out of work.

Although this perspective of OD is not the conception of the field that many OD practitioners have, I believe that it is much more aligned with organizational realities. Attempting to develop some aspects of an organization is a much more achievable goal than attempting to develop the entire organization and it more clearly reflects what most consultants are able to accomplish.

OD and HPT Would Benefit from Cross-Pollenization

The approach I suggest to OD also has the value of promoting experimentation within a field that had its origins in experimentation (industrial psychology, sensitivity training), but which is often surprisingly fixed in current practice. OD practitioners use an approach called "action research," which, in principle, includes the following steps:

1. Contract with the client.

2. Help the client diagnose the situation.

3. Feed back diagnostic findings to the organization.

4. Plan a change strategy with the client.

5. Apply and evaluate the change strategy.

Although action research is, in theory, an excellent approach, many practitioners use a more fixed form, as follows:

1. Conduct a survey.

2. Tell the client what the survey found.

3. Help organize groups to discuss and suggest a strategy for dealing with survey results.

4. Help the client to implement the strategy.

5. Conduct a new survey.

The real potential for genius within OD lies in the research that precedes the action and in planning change accordingly. Many classical OD studies reflect this genius (Argyris, 1970; Lippitt, Watson, & Westley, 1958). Unfortunately, where OD is weakest in current practice is in collecting data and planning the change strategy.

Many OD practitioners rely too much on survey data—as opposed to more direct modes of data collection, such as observation—and let the client lead the way in developing interventions. In fact, OD practitioners often are reluctant to suggest interventions because to do so substitutes a directive role for a facilitative one and may interfere with "letting the client own the problem." Burke (1982) notes that most OD professionals take a facilitative role but argues that they should begin as facilitators and become more directive as the situation warrants (pp. 98-103). I recommend Burke's approach for HPT practitioners as well.

The overreliance on survey data means that many OD practitioners refer to anything that people in the organization say as "data." From my behavioral perspective, data may include what people say but certainly must include what they do. Too often, survey respondents are "helpful," offering opinions when they are uncertain of the facts. Although a tabulation of opinions may reflect how people feel about the organization, it is less likely to describe organizational behavior accurately. OD practice would benefit from the "harder" data collected by HPT practitioners.

The fields of OD, HPT, and total quality management (TQM) can all benefit from cross-pollenization. Each of these fields excels in terms of having a large array of interventions to suggest for effecting change. Although both HPT and OD are strongly influenced by behavioral science, their emphases are different, probably because HPT draws much more from behaviorism (having strong roots in operant conditioning applied to instructional issues), whereas OD draws much more from social psychology (having its strongest roots in the work of Kurt Lewin). TQM has its roots in statistical process control and industrial engineering; it shares an emphasis on precision in measurement with HPT. And TQM and OD share strong value orientations toward participative management. But, although TQM places most value on reducing variability in an organization's products or services, OD places most value on creating a more humanistic environment in an organization.

Each of the three approaches can draw from the others to improve its practice (Pearlstein, 1991). For example, HPT can benefit from OD's research and refinement of the consulting process, teaming to involve clients much more in analysis, implementation, and evaluation, thereby increasing buy-in and effectiveness. HPT can also benefit from many of Deming's (TQM) fourteen principles, especially teaming to apply concepts of statistical process control in performance analysis and evaluation. OD can learn lessons of precision from both HPT and TQM: The more clearly you draw your targets, the easier it is to tell when you hit them. And TQM can benefit from applied behavioral science, learning from both HPT and OD how to analyze performance problems (HPT) and how to build organizational support for the long-term effort required by a TQM program (OD).

Although HPT practitioners generally take an expert role in designing, maintaining, or modifying human-performance systems, OD and TQM practitioners usually take a facilitative role, stressing that design/maintenance/modification functions be planned and implemented by workers in the affected organizational units. Many HPT practitioners try to be facilitative and promote involvement and buy-in when working with organizational units, but they also try to apply their particular HPT expertise. For example, if analysis were to suggest that a skill/knowledge deficiency did not underlie a performance problem, we would recommend against a training solution, whereas an OD or TQM practitioner would be likely to support the group's solution, even if it were training.

A Disclaimer

I have intentionally left out one important area of OD. This area is called by a variety of names, including group dynamics, sensitivity training, T-groups, and group process. In their work, OD consultants often use group-process skills for a wide range of purposes, including the following:

- Helping to resolve organizational conflicts between individuals and between groups,

- Helping to build individual and group awareness of and sensitivity to issues important to the organization,

- Promoting buy-in to new projects,

- Surfacing hidden agendas, and

- Providing difficult feedback within a caring forum.

Group-process skills are beyond the focus of this chapter for two reasons. First, group-process skills are best learned through experiential means. Group-process cornerstones include understanding how others see you and becoming more aware of your own motivations. These are not communicated well in writing. To build group-process skills, I recommend attending experiential training courses. Second, because this chapter is relatively brief, it must address those aspects of OD most easily adapted by the HPT practitioner.

Nine OD Principles for HPT Practitioners

How can HPT practitioners develop organizations? I believe that we can draw some basic principles from OD and TQM, in addition to using our HPT expertise. Rather than being doctrinaire, we can apply these principles creatively, always falling back on the basic general system theory (GST) used by HPT:

Define desired outcomes, determine how to measure success in achieving them, apply an appropriate intervention, measure what has been achieved, and recycle as necessary until success occurs.

The remainder of this chapter discusses and provides tools for applying nine basic principles to develop organizations effectively. Most are not new or innovative principles, and some are currently used by practitioners in OD, HPT, or TQM. Taken together, these nine principles represent a good beginning for HPT practitioners who wish to help organizations develop.

Principle 1: You can develop a work unit, rather than having to develop an entire organization. Often it is preferable to practice OD with a work unit—a department, division, or section—because you are likely to have freer access to the key decision makers than if you were attempting to develop the entire organization. What's more, if successful, you can export your approach to other work units, eventually helping the entire organization to develop.

This principle is contrary to conventional wisdom, which says that OD requires a commitment at the highest organizational levels. Although the higher your support in the organization, the more solid your foundation for facilitating change, developing organizational units is feasible so long as you focus on processes that are internal to those units. In other words, for work to be effective at the unit level, you at first have to act as if the unit's inputs and outputs are "givens." You may be able to work with these inputs and outputs later in the developmental process, but the minute you do, you are involving additional organizational units.

Principle 2: Make sure that your client includes the chief decision maker for the work unit with which you are working, as well as other important decision makers in that unit. Although this principle applies equally to external and internal consultants, internal consultants are more likely to know who the real decision makers are. In any case, this principle is critical because, if your client does not include the chief decision maker, your project can be derailed at any time. Many consultants have designed and successfully implemented appropriate projects, only to find later that their product or service is discontinued before bearing fruit. The chief decision maker has only to ask, "Why wasn't I consulted?"

What makes this principle easier said than done is that chief decision makers often delegate to someone lower in the organization. The acting project manager may claim that he or she is in charge, and external consultants might have no idea that is not the case, especially when the acting project manager has arranged for the consultation. Internal consultants, who are familiar with the organizational structure, can more easily see through these claims, but they often have difficulty surfacing their concerns. Internal and external consultants can ask questions such as the following to determine the identity of the chief decision maker:

1. To whom do you report? Does he or she fully support this project? What about his or her boss?

2. Who has the final say in whether or not we proceed?

3. Does the overall manager of the organization or sub-unit know about this project? Does he or she have particular ideas about how it should be conducted or what outcomes are required?

4. Who will be most affected if this project succeeds or doesn't succeed?

5. Who other than you has a say in whether or not the results of this project will be used?

If these questions yield the names of people other than the person to whom you are directly reporting, arrange to meet those people. Include them in any meetings that you schedule in accordance with principles three, four, and five. If they are at the executive level, or so high in the organization that your contact is reluctant to help you to arrange a meeting, at least try to include them in a summary meeting or phone call. For example, you might call the chief decision maker and say something like:

"Charlie and I agreed to...by such-and-such a date.
If we achieved those results, would you be satisfied
with the project outcomes?"

Use a similar process to include other important decision makers. Sometimes an important decision maker is someone relatively low in the organization, so you might have to check your understanding of the situation with a question such as, "Who else has to agree with our work before it can be used?" When you are working with a unit that truly practices participative management, all decisions should be consensual. This is especially important at the time of project initiation.

Principle 3: Start by reaching agreement with the client as to what desired outcomes will look like, how you will know when to stop, what you will do, what he or she will do, and what others in the organization will do. As HPT practitioners, we know that desired outcomes should be specified in terms of what will be different in the organization's outputs. For example, if the client were to say, "I want everyone trained in word processing," we would recognize that as an improper specification. To clarify, we would ask something like, "What would be different if everyone were trained in word processing?" The client then might say, "Reports would be submitted in time." Soon, you would be conducting a full-fledged performance analysis (Gilbert, 1978; Harless, 1970; Mager & Pipe, 1984) and you would arrive at the real desired outcomes for the organization.

The determination of when you should stop—when the project is done—depends on the consulting relationship you have with the client. I advocate setting clear objectives for projects, with clear review and end points, as well as a plan for summative evaluation that will show the client what the project achieved in terms of organizational impacts. Then, when you have met objectives for a given project, you have the opportunity to renegotiate for additional projects. This consulting approach assumes that you will work by the project, rather than having an open-ended relationship, even if you are an internal consultant. It does not suggest that you leave the client "high and dry" at the end of a project. In fact, principle nine suggests ways of closing a project effectively.

One basic tenet of OD is to never do the same project twice for a client; in effect, you should teach the client to fish rather than just providing the fish. In other words, good OD consulting includes educating clients so that they can repeat the project without your help. You may have some HPT or TQM expertise that took years to develop and that would be impossible to develop in the client during the course of a typical project. Nonetheless, when you have concluded a project, you should leave the client prepared to conduct a similar project with only minimal input from you. At the least, you should leave the client better able to recognize the qualifications of professionals who can help with that kind of project.

For example, if you helped the client to reduce errors by developing job aids, the next time the client wants to develop job aids, he or she should be able to collect and analyze data and draft, test, and revise job aids. The client might call on you to check his or her data-collection plan and analysis, suggest designs, and review the drafted job aids. Or the client might decide to have another consultant develop job aids, in which case he or she would know how to "shop" for an effective consultant.

The final part of good consulting is specifying who will do what. Take care to do this in sufficient detail so that any two people in the organization could agree on what was to be completed, by whom, and by when. Table 1 suggests a format for this type of specification.

Principle 4: Insist on behavioral measurement, but first listen carefully to statements of the client's values, visions, and dreams. As HPT practitioners, we know that behavioral measurement is essential to our craft. Naturally, when doing OD consulting, we render clients' goals and objectives in behavioral terms. That way, we can measure to determine how well we have helped clients to achieve their desired results. Behavioral specification and measurement is a major way in which HPT practitioners can contribute to OD consulting.

Table 1. Sample Form for Recording Agreements with Client and Example Agreements

WHO	WHAT	WHEN	EXAMPLE
Self	Description of project deliverables	Review dates and due dates	Prepare all project deliverables noted in attached contract: data-collection forms, data-analysis report, draft job aids, test results, final job aids—to specified standards by dates shown for each.
Client	Description of client duties	Dates for receiving/ completing reviews	Review all project deliverables and provide written feedback of required changes within the review periods shown on contract.
Client's staff	Description of client/staff duties	Dates for inputs to and outputs from staff	Staff given data-collection form on 1/17; collect and present tabulated data by 3/13; staff to begin testing job aids by 4/2; deliver test results by 6/5.

The Guidebook for Performance Improvement

However, many clients ask for OD consulting when they have ambiguous ideas, "big pictures," or only vague notions of how they want their organizations to change. They know that they want change but articulate their goals in broad, nonspecific terms. If you try prematurely to help clients specify their desired changes behaviorally, they may decide that you do not understand them.

To help clients who present problems vaguely, you first have to understand what they really want. Start by using their language—especially their metaphors—to draw them out. If they talk about dreams, say, for example, "I'm unclear about that last image," or "Tell me more about your dream," or "What is the most useful outcome you can imagine?" If clients talk about values, ask, for example, "What's most important to you?" or "What do you really value about...?" If clients talk about visions, say, "Tell me more about what you see happening," or "That sounds like a real revelation...would you expand on it?"

Once you have helped clients to flesh out their ideas, check that you both agree before proceeding. Ask something like "Do you think I have the big picture?," "Am I sharing your dream in what we are discussing?," or "Do I seem to hold the same values as you on this project?" When you have assent, you can begin moving toward behavioral specification.

Move slowly. Start by saying something like "Well, it would be helpful if we had some checkpoints in this project. Let me suggest some subgoals and see if they seem on target." Then offer a behavioral objective as an example of a checkpoint. For example, "How about if I give you a written report in a month that describes the major obstacles to higher morale?" If the client agrees, you might add more detail, such as, "I'm thinking of describing at least three things that management does or doesn't do that make workers feel as if their efforts are unappreciated. I won't name names; I'll just list items about which there is consensus. Would a report on that be a worthwhile first step? "

After agreeing on a first, data-gathering step, begin specifying outcomes. You might ask, for example, "If a survey were to show that more than 80 percent of your employees agreed that you provided a good work environment, would you be satisfied that morale was good?" If the client disagrees, help modify the statement to his or her satisfaction, while retaining behavioral specificity. If the client says, "Yes, but there's more...," keep adding statements until the client says something like "That should do it."

Proceeding in this way, move from the general and vague to the specific and measurable. When you have sketched out all desired outcomes, check again with the client by asking, "If we accomplish all I've set down here, will you be satisfied that we've accomplished what you want in this project?" If you get any answer other than "yes," go back to modifying and adding items.

Principle 5: Make sure that the client considers the mega level in addition to the micro and macro levels. Typically, clients focus on the micro or the macro level, depending on whether they are interested in improving outcomes within organizational units or outcomes related to external clients. If the client seems to be interested solely in the micro level, you should point out macro-level considerations. For example, if the client is interested in improving teamwork in the sales department, ask him or her how that might affect work in the production department, perhaps by saying something like "If we improved teamwork so that sales increase by 20 percent next quarter, would production be able to meet the demand?" You may want to "prime the pump" with a few more questions, but your client should soon begin discussing macro-level issues on his or her own.

When you have clarified the impacts of the planned micro-level intervention on other work units and on the organization's clients, you have considered the macro level adequately. Your client may find that other work units should become involved in the intervention, or even that a higher level of management should sponsor the project. Proceed cautiously, and you may be able to benefit the client and the entire organization more than originally planned. Don't push for greater macro-level impact lest you lose your original client. Instead, make sure your client owns the macro-level change, or, at least, can take credit for initiating it.

Helping clients to consider the mega level is even more difficult than helping them to explore the macro level. Traditionally, OD's domain is the macro level, so clients who have asked for OD consultation should not be surprised if you begin exploring impacts throughout the organization. But when you raise mega-level concerns—impacts on society of which the organization is a part—your client may perceive you as intruding. Move slowly and relate macro-level considerations to the organization's bottom line.

For example, if asked to help an organization to deal with downsizing, you would want to help your client consider the impacts on the communities in which jobs would be lost. What would these changes do to the communities' economies? Are there ways in which the organization can help these communities? If the organization fails to help these communities, what would be the impact on the public's perception of the organization? Asking such questions should help "prime the pump." Your intent should be to help the client see the big picture, not to make the client a morally better individual. (If the client suspects that the latter is your intent, you will have one less client.)

Usually, simply understanding potential mega-level outcomes will encourage the client to pursue a course of action that will achieve the most social good. Acting in such a way is a matter of enlightened self-interest. Those companies that are seen as acting responsibly in the face of adversity almost always do better in the marketplace than those who are seen as acting to cover up their wrongs.

Principle 6: Meet with all key players individually and as a group. During these meetings, work to make sure that everyone is clear about (a) who the client is; (b) what micro-, macro-, and mega-level outcomes are planned; and (c) what roles you, they, and others in the organization are expected to play. Your goal is to ensure that everyone shares the same expectations about the project outcomes. I recommend scheduling the meetings something like the following:

Meeting	Objectives
1. Initial meeting(s) with client.	Identifying the chief decision maker and other key decision makers. Specifying desired outcomes for the intervention in measurable terms. Considering the micro, macro, and mega levels of outcomes. Determining roles.
2. Meeting with the chief decision maker (if not the same as the client).	Checking that the client's desired outcomes are consistent with the chief decision makers'. Making sure that project roles are acceptable. Reviewing micro-, macro-, and mega-level impacts. Determining if there are other key decision makers.
3. Individual meetings with other key decision makers.	Checking that they agree with the desired outcomes expressed by the client and chief decision makers and that impacts at various levels are acceptable to them. Discussing roles.

Meeting	Objectives
4. Individual meetings with others who have important roles in the intervention.	Discussing outcomes, roles, and impacts. Determining if any of these appear to be "show stoppers" (or even "show slowers").
5. Follow-up meetings with client and chief decision maker. (You may have to intersperse these meetings with the preceding ones.)	Surfacing any conflicts concerning expected outcomes, impacts, or roles that became clear in the course of the preceding meetings. When there are conflicts, you should have the client resolve them before you continue with the project. If the client is not the chief decision maker for the project, the situation is trickier. Ask the client to get the chief decision maker to resolve the conflicts or, at least, to support the client's attempts at resolution. Try to keep the chief decision maker in the loop through the planning stage so that you can be sure that the planned intervention will meet his or her approval.
6. Group meeting with all those who have roles in the project.	During this "kickoff" meeting, you and the client will describe the project, present planned outcomes, and review everyone's roles. Also, resolve any conflicts that may remain.

Although this schedule of meetings seems daunting, you may be able to accomplish the specified objectives in less than a week. The most time-consuming work lies in resolving conflicts, which—unless you are appointed to the role of conflict resolver—you are better off leaving to the chief decision maker. Whether you are appointed to the role or not, encourage parties to work out all conflicts consensually, even if the chief decision maker could just say "do it." Obviously, if all parties concur with the plan, they will carry it out much more energetically.

If there is a lot of conflict in planning the project, dealing with the conflict may be even more important than the planned intervention. If you find so much conflict that you cannot complete initial planning within a couple of weeks, you may want to refocus the effort with the chief decision maker, saying something like, "Maybe we'd accomplish more for the organization if we were to find what underlies this conflict than if we proceed as scheduled. Do you think it might be worth the effort to explore this option further?"

Remember, your overall goal is to see that all parties share the same expectations about the project's outcomes. As long as everyone is clear about what is to be done, who is to do it, and what is to result, the project can proceed. If there are serious disputes, do not proceed.

Principle 7. Seek consensus; share, don't force, your expertise. Stand by your expertise instead of collapsing or undermining your principles. This is a real divergence from the majority OD opinion, according to which your role would remain facilitative, not prescriptive. As a practitioner of HPT, you have the obligation to share your expertise; as an OD consultant, you also have the duty to help the client's organization own the change process.

I think we should try to reconcile the two obligations. If we succeed in promoting an intervention that performance analysis suggests, although the client resists, we run two risks. First, the client may undermine the change effort. Second, we may miss the chance to help develop the organization, which, given analogous problems or opportunities in the future, would probably not use a similar process.

Conversely, if we implement an intervention that the client requests, despite a performance analysis that suggests that such an intervention is inappropriate, we encounter two other risks. First, although the client will work hard to support the intervention, if it is inappropriate, it will not be effective. Thus, the client will fail to solve the problem or make use of the opportunity that presented itself. Second, we again miss the chance to help the organization develop. If it encounters analogous problems or opportunities in the future, it will not have had the benefit of your intervention on which to base similar interventions.

Your recourse is to reconcile your OD obligations with your HPT obligations. You may be able to do this by persuading your client. If you conduct a careful performance analysis and lay out the results convincingly, the client may support your approach, even though he or she had a "pet" intervention in mind. By logically laying out matches between desired outcomes and interventions that will overcome the obstacles to achieving those outcomes, you may help the client to "see the light."

More often than not, though, the client or the chief decision maker will demand a specific intervention, saying something like, "Look, the results of that analysis are interesting, and we'll certainly consider them, but we hired you to write documentation...." or "If you don't want to develop the training in-house, maybe we should look at outside vendors." In cases like these, your best chance for reconciling the dual obligations is to do a little of what the client suggests while implementing the interventions suggested by the performance analysis.

For example, suppose an organization's reports have become sloppy and riddled with grammatical errors. The client suggests that the sloppiness is a result of decreased morale and asks you to conduct some team building to improve morale. The client also tells you that he or she wouldn't mind if you were to arrange some training in grammar. You say you would like to conduct a performance analysis and begin to sketch out the approach, but the client interrupts with "We don't have much time here. Once the new quarter begins, we'll be swamped, and I want us to take advantage of the window of opportunity now."

You say, "Sure, I'd be glad to help you with the sloppy writing problem, and I'll schedule those team-building sessions now." And you do. Only, you use the team-building sessions to collect performance data on the sloppy report problem. You discover that the primary reasons that reports have become sloppy are (1) staffers have stopped proofreading their work because the pace of production has become more hurried, and (2) reviewers correct reports without showing the errors to the authors. You also learn that staffers are embarrassed to see examples of sloppy reports—they are highly motivated and only slightly rusty on grammatical rules. In fact, they would prefer to turn in higher-quality reports but are certain that the reports are a low priority to the boss. Their morale does appear to have slipped; they feel that it is much more difficult to take pride in their work when they cannot take the time to ensure its quality.

You explain your findings to the client, who grasps their import but has already promised his or her boss that training in grammar will be supplied. You work out a compromise: You will arrange a morning of "grammar-review" training. As the closing part of the training, your client will address the staff members and explain that reports should be neat and accurate and that they are an important source of information for corporate executives. The client also will state that to underscore the importance of the reports, he or she will lower production targets five percent and that employees are to use the time freed up to proofread their reports. Further, reviewers will be required to return reports to their authors to make suggested corrections to grammatical errors and sloppy writing.

Follow-up three months later shows that reports have become much neater, more accurate, and grammatically correct. Further, productivity has risen beyond preintervention levels because staffers are spending less time correcting mistakes. And morale has improved, because staffers once more are taking pride in their work. Your client saw the light. When you reviewed the evaluation data together, the client realized that the grammar-review training had little to do with the improvements. What had the most impact was conveying expectations clearly and modifying the work process so that staffers would proofread and then correct their own errors.

In summary, you can reconcile the dual obligations of OD facilitator and HPT consultant by acting in accord with the client's requests while implementing interventions suggested by performance analysis. Your client may not buy in to your approach at first. By feeding back to the client what you discover and acting with professional integrity, you help to develop your client. Be sure to explain to your client all the elements of your interventions, after they have taken effect, so that he or she can learn from your efforts.

Of course, never deceive your client. If, in good conscience, you cannot implement the desired intervention even a little, you have to decline. This can cost you money as an external consultant and be difficult to do as an internal consultant. However, if you decline respectfully and your reasons are clear, your client is not likely to act vituperatively.

Principle 8: Give interventions time to work. Remember TQM's principle: "No instant pudding" (Scherkenbach, 1988). TQMers estimate that TQM interventions typically take five to seven years before they begin bearing fruit in large organizations. So do not be pushed into abandoning an intervention that requires more time to take effect. Instead, remind the client of your original estimates of the project's timetable, as well as of the benefits to be achieved.

If there has been a change of administration, a reorganization, or some other event that jars organizational memory, you have to inform the new clients of the original intents of the project and the timetable. Help them buy in on their own terms, if possible, by relating project outcomes to what is important on their agendas.

Finally, to avoid "ratio strain," divide longer projects into briefer components, each of which has some useful results of its own. A good rule of thumb is to divide projects that will take more than six months into phases of about two months, each of which ends with a milestone that is a measurable product or service with some independent value to the organization. For example, if the overall project involves automating a major function that formerly was done manually, a couple of the milestones might include:

- Completing a preliminary design document. By sharing highlights of the proposed design, you can inform employees that "help is on the way," promote buy-in, and even surface some additional design requirements that might have been overlooked.

- Preparing training for using subcomponents of the new system. Employees can be trained in using each subcomponent if the system is to be introduced in phases. By dividing training into manageable components, you can reduce the fear that is prevalent when a new system is introduced.

Regardless of the specific milestones, review the progress of the project with all key players, using the milestones as interim goals. Also encourage the key players to share these interim results with other staffers, perhaps in a special project newsletter or bulletin.

Principle 9: Close well with your client. How you end your consulting relationships is as important as how you begin them. Taken together, your beginning and ending activities generally contribute an inordinate amount to an entire project's value—probably more than half. Because planning and follow-up activities are so often neglected, organizations spend a lot of time conducting projects that should not be conducted and fail to make use of good results when they do achieve them. So, as an OD practitioner, you add value two ways by concentrating on good beginnings and endings. First, you ensure that effective outcomes are achieved and used. Second, you give the client a model for conducting good planning and follow-up activities.

Closing well with your client consists of three steps:

1. Help collect and disseminate summative-evaluation data.

2. Help the organization to celebrate its victories.

3. Help the organization to plan its next steps.

Each of these three steps is guided by one rule: *Don't just leave it to the client.* If you do, the client will not do it in most cases, because none of the steps is typical organizational behavior.

Summative evaluation is the first thing to go when schedules get busy, which they usually do. If you want it to happen, you must address summative evaluation—especially the steps for collecting the necessary data—in your initial meetings with the client. (Formative evaluation is easier to ensure; you do this by building in appropriate pilot tests.) Also, you have to monitor data collection well after completing the intervention-implementation phase of the project, lest it be dropped at some point.

When you have the results of your summative evaluation, you should help the client to disseminate it. This is harder than it sounds. First, you may have to help the client overcome the feeling that to share good news is somehow distasteful, like bragging. You can do this by pointing out that disseminating results is helpful to the organization and not at all like bragging. Disseminating results helps the organization several ways: by improving morale; by sharing a model for achieving results; and by informing others of new opportunities, methods, products, or services.

Second, you must couch the results in terms that will be meaningful to different factions in the organization; you must let them know what the project has done for them as an organizational division. You should also point out how various organizational entities contributed to positive project results. Help the client to prepare attractive "one-pagers" targeting different groups within the organization. These brief summaries should quantify benefits when possible and should always be simple and in the language of the particular organizational group.

Third, you should help the client to plan a strategy for physically distributing the information. Who should have copies? Are supervisors likely to distribute copies to their employees, or should copies be addressed directly? Who will actually have the information printed, folded or collated, addressed, and mailed? By preparing a specific plan, you can ensure that the word gets out. Also, by focusing on details such as those mentioned, you may help your client to overcome the resistance he or she may feel about "bragging."

The second step of closing is to help the organization celebrate its victory. Celebrating a victory, like disseminating results, is unusual in many organizations but provides a number of benefits. Celebrating victories calls attention to accomplishments, builds morale, and demonstrates that the organization values good outcomes. It also provides another forum for sharing information about what worked.

Work with your client to find a form of celebration appropriate to the organizational culture. In some organizations, an informal "beer bash" might be appropriate, while in others a more formal awards banquet might be more suitable. You can explore many creative forms of celebration, but check out ideas with individuals in different organizational divisions to avoid embarrassment.

The key to an effective celebration is *inclusivity*. If the celebration honors only a few individuals or pays tribute to only one or two work units, it may punish more than reward. Instead, be sure that the celebration includes all participants, even those with tangential roles. Be sure to give special recognition to those who played key roles. Otherwise, the celebration becomes just an excuse for a party.

A good victory celebration should be well-publicized and well-planned. Organizational leaders should attend and give recognition to as many project participants as possible. If numerous awards are planned, some of them should be given to groups so that the ceremony does not become tedious. The celebration should include fun activities. People should leave feeling that they are glad they attended even if they did not personally receive an award.

The final step of a good closing is to plan the next steps with your client. Planning probably will follow naturally from the results of the summative evaluation. If some desired outcomes were not achieved, help the client to determine why. If those outcomes are still desirable, help the client to understand the evaluation data in order to determine what obstacles should be overcome. Then work with the client to develop a plan to do so as a follow-up to the original project.

Planning next steps should not result in a plan that includes a role for you. In fact, if a project follow-up will involve the same sorts of processes that you just helped the client to complete, you should encourage the client to phase you out. Suggest that you consult at a few points, and only to review progress with the client. Of course, you also will let the client know that you would be delighted to work on other projects when these arise and that you are phasing out because you are confident that the client can achieve good results in similar situations on his or her own.

Sometimes, conducting a project will surface new problems or opportunities. You can use these results to work with the client to plan entirely new projects. Because such projects are not really follow-ups, you can legitimately use a current project's ending as a new beginning. Evaluation data from the current project become needs-analysis data for a new project.

Whether your closing activities result in new work or not, take the time to summarize the project with the client, in terms both of what the organization achieved and what the organization learned. So, for example, instead of just pointing out how the project reduced rejection rates in production, also review how the process achieved that reduction. Suggest circumstances that are likely to arise in which the client can apply a similar process.

In this chapter, we have reviewed a model for conducting OD while practicing HPT. This model, of course, is just a shell. What will give it substance is your own competence in practicing HPT, TQM, or other systematic approaches to improving human performance to achieve specified outcomes. OD is a powerful approach and it lends itself well to borrowing analytical processes and tools from many disciplines.

References

Argyris, C. (1970). *Intervention theory and method: A behavioral science view.* Reading, MA: Addison-Wesley.

Burke, W.W. (1982). *Organization development: Principles and practices.* Boston, MA: Little, Brown and Company.

Gallessich, J. (1982). *The profession and practice of consultation.* San Francisco, CA: Jossey-Bass.

Gellermann, W., Frankel, M.S., & Ladenson, R.F. (1990). *Values and ethics in organization and human systems development.* San Francisco, CA: Jossey-Bass.

Gilbert, T.F. (1978). *Human competence: Engineering worthy performance.* New York: McGraw-Hill.

Harless, J. (1970). *An ounce of analysis*. Newman, GA: Harless Performance Guild.

Kaufman, R. (1989). Selecting a planning mode: Who is the client? Who benefits? *Performance & Instruction, 28*(2), 6-8.

Lippitt, R., Watson, J., & Westley, B. (1958). *The dynamics of planned chance*. New York: Harcourt, Brace & World.

Mager, R.F., & Pipe, P. (1984). *Analyzing performance problems* (2nd ed.). Belmont, CA: Fearon.

Pearlstein, R.B. (1991). Who empowers leaders? *Performance Improvement Quarterly, 4*(4), 12-20.

Scherkenbach, W.W. (1988). *The Deming route to quality and productivity: Road maps and road blocks*. Washington, DC: CEEPress Books.

Vaill, P.B. (1971). OD: A grammatical footnote. *Journal of Applied Behavioral Science, 2*(2), 264.

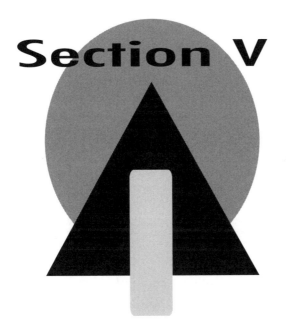

Section V

Implementation

PERSONNEL SELECTION AND ASSIGNMENT

Seth N. Leibler and Ann W. Parkman

The most rapid and cost-effective advances any organization can make toward becoming more competitive in today's global economy will come from what the organization does to reexamine and improve its workforce performance. Filling a vacant position presents an opportunity to integrate the functions of the job (micro level) with the requirements of the organization (macro level) and the heightened expectations of the organization's clients (mega level). This integration then creates the opportunity to fill every available position with individuals who are able to meet or exceed the expectations of both the organization and its clients.

This chapter leads the reader through each step of a human-performance system designed to meet this challenge of selecting and assigning the right person to do the right job. The proactive application of human-performance systems minimizes performance deficits that result from inappropriate selection and assignment. Some managers may resist implementing such a comprehensive performance system for filling a position, saying that it is too time consuming and that the individuals hired in the past have "worked out all right." In such a situation, it is important for the manager to estimate the consequences of performance problems that result from selection error. Preventing performance problems will almost always be more cost effective than fixing performance problems once they occur.

Selecting individuals who do not possess appropriate entry-level skills, knowledge, or other required characteristics can be very costly to the organization, not only in dollars but in time, effort, and frustration. Once a performance problem is suspected, supervisors spend a great deal of time observing and analyzing job performance and searching for a way to raise performance to the required level. The individual may require more extensive training than had been anticipated. In some cases, other employees must take time from their assigned functions to fulfill the nonperformer's responsibilities.

If supervisors are not skilled in performance analysis, or if they are too busy or frustrated to fix such performance problems quickly, they may want to have the nonperformer fired or transferred, a process that requires laborious, time-consuming documentation. This solution is, predictably, punishing to the supervisor, the employee, and other employees who are aware of the situation (Leibler & Parkman, 1992, p. 260).

In addition, an employee who is fired (or unwillingly shunted to another job or location) may formally complain through a legal grievance process. Management must then divert substantial time and legal expertise to respond.

In many cases, supervisors fail to recognize and weigh the costs of removing an individual from his or her position against the costs of raising performance to an acceptable level. Usually, the costs of performance improvement are far less than the costs of removal and replacement. But, because the costs are not overt, organizations tend to remove employees from positions far more frequently than is beneficial.

Employing the performance system we suggest for the selection of personnel (see Figure 1) will greatly reduce the occurrence of selection errors and the resultant costs. This system is designed to eliminate selection errors by ensuring that job-performance objectives are relevant to the organization and its customers; selection criteria are derived from these objectives; procedures are designed to assess whether candidates meet these criteria; and job performance is monitored after selection. If there has been an error in selection, each step of the selection process is reexamined for appropriate improvements. This self-corrective feedback allows for the continuous improvement of the performance system until virtually all errors of selection are prevented.

A Performance System for Selection

Step 1: Defining Job-Performance Objectives

The first step of a performance system for selection is to define the job-performance objectives for the position to be filled. This requires a thorough and accurate analysis of the job. Each major task that the job holder will be expected to perform must be identified, as well as the sequence in which these tasks should be performed, and any special conditions or constraints under which the tasks are to be carried out. All important decisions for which the individual is responsible must be included. The objectives should also include how someone will know when each task has been successfully performed (Leibler & Parkman, 1992, p. 261).

At this point, managers may benefit by turning to their training or human resources department to obtain the services of a skilled performance technologist. Such individuals are experienced in conducting the kinds of job and task analyses required for selection purposes and for writing precise, measurable job-performance objectives.

Selection officials should obtain the information necessary to complete the job analysis from all major levels of the organization (Kaufman, 1992, p. 4): the individual performing

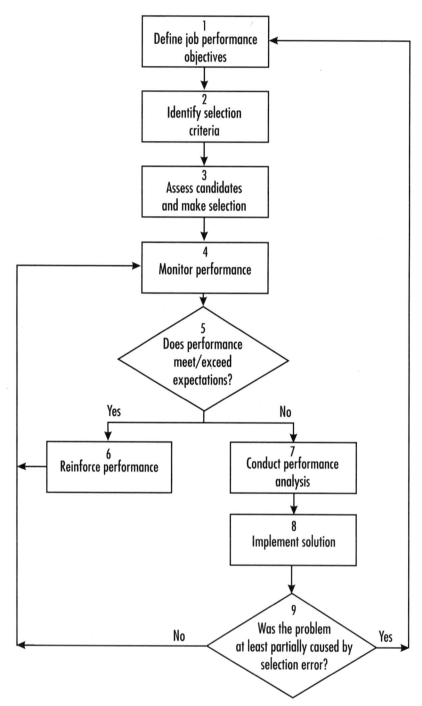

Figure 1. A Performance System for Selection

The Guidebook for Performance Improvement

the job (micro), the organization as a whole (macro), and the organization's customers (mega). Specific, measurable job-performance objectives give those individuals being considered for the position (micro) a clear understanding of what they will be expected to do, under what conditions, and to what level of proficiency. At the mega level, the objectives ensure that supervisors, internal clients, and others involved in the selection process will have the same expectations for desired job performance. Because the customers' (mega) expectations of success shape the position's job-performance objectives, this planning process allows the organization to continually improve its capacity to meet or exceed clients' expectations.

At the micro level, data should be obtained primarily from competent individuals already occupying the position. Observation of their actual performance is one essential source of information. These observations should be supplemented by interviews in which the incumbents explain why certain tasks are being done and why they are done in a particular sequence. Such interviews should also reveal how an incumbent knows when he or she is performing competently.

Since even a competent individual's perception of his or her job rarely is identical to the organization's perception, data must be obtained at the macro level as well. Interviews with the incumbents' supervisor and that individual's supervisor will provide insights into the organization's expectations for the job. Although written documentation of the organization's expectations may exist (e.g., job descriptions, performance expectations), such records are usually out of date and ignored in day-to-day management practice. They may be useful, however, as a stimulus in drafting questions for interviews with management.

Internal clients (those within the organization who depend on or benefit from the work of the incumbent) are another valuable source of information. These individuals rarely have an opportunity to express their expectations for positions that serve them (except in times of organizational crisis). Their participation in defining job-performance objectives, however, can significantly improve the quality of the organization's performance.

Similarly, if the position provides outputs to external clients, directly or indirectly, an opportunity exists to involve individuals at the mega level in the development of job-performance objectives. Customers' expectations form a crucial element of the analysis of such a job, and their inclusion will allow planning of desired job performance that is in harmony at all three levels. As a result, individuals (micro) will be hired to perform functions that are consistent with the organization's (macro) expectations and with the expectations of (and payoffs for) those whom the organization serves (mega).

During the analysis, it is not surprising to find disparities in expectations between the three levels. Such results should be brought to the attention of management. This data will enable the organization to consider these differences in determining what job-performance expectations will best serve all levels and, consequently, best contribute to organizational success.

Once the analysis has been completed, the major tasks should be expressed as performance objectives: precise (that is, not open to variations in interpretation), measurable statements of desired job performance. Such performance objectives consist of the expected performance, the conditions under which that performance is to take place, and the criteria that will be used to assess whether performance meets expectations (Leibler & Parkman, 1992, p. 262).

Step 2: Identifying Selection Criteria

The first step in identifying the criteria that a candidate must meet for selection is to list all the skills and knowledge that are required to perform the job according to the job-performance objectives. Most of this information will come from observing and interviewing competent performers and interviewing those performers' supervisors. If there is no incumbent for the position, look for someone in a similar job in another department or company. As with the previous step, the assistance of a skilled performance technologist will improve the accuracy and speed with which this step is completed.

The second step in identifying selection criteria is to decide which skills and knowledge are essential for selection and which could be added later through training or job aids. There are two issues to consider in making this decision: what level of skill and knowledge can realistically be expected from the pool of candidates; and what are the costs associated with providing further training to the candidate lacking necessary skills and/or knowledge?

It is important to set the standards for selection so that there are a sufficient number of candidates from which to make a decision. On the other hand, it is important to make an accurate assessment of the costs associated with providing a new employee with additional training. Many of these costs are not readily apparent. Such covert costs would include the trainee's time away from the job, the materials and equipment used during training, the cost of the job not being performed at the desired level of proficiency until training is complete, and the cost of having other personnel "cover" for the trainee at the expense of their work load.

A performance technologist can help by creating a skills hierarchy (Mager & Pipe, 1991). The skills hierarchy, a tool used in instructional design, maps out what skills and knowledge must be acquired before other, dependent skills can be added. This depiction makes it easier to differentiate between entry-level and subsequent skills. Using the skills hierarchy will make the identification of entry-level skills more accurate and objective.

The third step in identifying selection criteria is to list all physical and personal characteristics required for competent performance of the job. The sources who identified necessary skills and knowledge for competent performance will also be helpful in listing required personal and physical characteristics. Observing and interviewing competent performers and speaking with their supervisors is essential. It is also worthwhile to talk with the internal clients of the position to be filled.

Sometimes interviewees have difficulty in specifying personal characteristics necessary for competent job performance. They will tend to describe characteristics in general terms: "The candidate should be a team player." Here again, a skilled performance technologist can be helpful by using a procedure called goal analysis to translate abstractions into precise, observable performances (Mager, 1984). This will prevent confusion during assessment about whether a candidate possesses the characteristic in question.

The fourth step in identifying selection criteria is deciding which physical and personal characteristics are essential for hire. If a candidate is found to be lacking in important skills after hire, the organization can always provide those skills through training or other performance interventions (though at some cost). If, however, a candidate does not have the personal (e.g., integrity, flexibility) or physical characteristics the position demands, it may be more difficult for the organization to accommodate the individual.

To determine which characteristics are essential for hire, ask these questions for each characteristic on your list:

- Is it true that an individual could not perform the job at the required level of proficiency without this characteristic?

- Is this a characteristic that could feasibly be acquired or enhanced after hiring?

- If a candidate met every other criterion for selection, could the organization compensate for the lack of this characteristic (e.g., restructuring the job, assigning certain tasks to another employee)?

The Americans with Disabilities Act, which went into effect in July, 1992, for organizations with twenty-five or more employees and in July, 1994, for organizations with fifteen or more employees, imposes significant new legal restrictions and obligations on employers with respect to hiring, job applications, and all other terms and conditions of employment. Organizations should seek legal counsel to determine how this Act will impact their personnel selection process.

Step 3: Assessing Candidates and Making the Selection

Every assessment procedure must be valid (i.e., it measures what it's supposed to measure) and reliable (it consistently measures what it's supposed to measure, time after time). Although there are several types of validity, the most useful for selection purposes is predictive validity (how accurately the assessment procedure predicts future performance).

It is important to maintain data on the validity and reliability of the assessment procedures used for selection purposes. These data indicate the usefulness of each assessment procedure in comparison to others, thus allowing for continuing improvement of the performance system. In addition, the organization may be required to produce the data if a disgruntled candidate feels that his or her assessment was inaccurate or biased in some way.

There are several methods for assessing the extent to which candidates meet the selection criteria, each with its strengths and weaknesses. These methods include interviews, reference checks, paper-and-pencil tests, biographical data, academic achievement, work samples, peer judgments, expert judgments, and assessment centers.

Interviewing is by far the most popular procedure for assessing a candidate's suitability for a position. The subjective nature of the traditional interview, however, has caused this procedure to score very low in reliability and validity.

The structured interview ranks higher on the validity scale because the interviewer is less likely to act on snap judgments than in a traditional interview. A structured interview involves asking preplanned, targeted questions to assess how well the candidate meets the selection criteria; scoring the candidate's responses to these questions; and applying the same structure (in questions and interview length) for all candidates for the position.

A third kind of interview, the structured behavior interview, scores high in both reliability and validity. In this type of interview, candidates are asked to describe a recent situation (which parallels the position to be filled) in which they feel they performed well. They are encouraged to be very detailed in discussing what they did and said. The interviewer then scores how closely the described behavior meets the selection criteria.

A performance technologist may be helpful in framing questions that will elicit the desired information and in creating a job aid to ensure that the interviewer asks each candidate the same questions.

The reference check is another traditionally popular assessment method. Its validity is low, however, because candidates are likely to list as references only those persons who can be counted on to give a good report of them. Furthermore, a fear of legal repercussion has made many individuals wary of answering any questions about the performance of their former employees.

The selecting official may increase the validity of the reference check by speaking only to those people who have directly observed the candidate's work; asking specific, focused questions about the candidate's ability to perform critical tasks or about the candidate's areas of weakness; asking open-ended questions that cannot be answered with yes or no; and paying attention to verbal cues. Even if the former employer refuses to answer a question, an abrupt change in tone, a sudden silence, or a "no comment" may imply an unfavorable response.

The paper-and-pencil test is a favored assessment procedure because it is simple to implement and score. A study by Schmidt and Hunter (1981) found that results from paper-and-pencil tests designed to measure intellectual ability are valid predictors of job performance.

Collecting biographical data is a very simple assessment procedure and can be done for minimal cost. This information, gleaned from applications or interviews, usually includes educational background, former employment, personal interests, and health. All questions, particularly those of a more personal nature, must relate directly to the candidate's ability to perform the job according to the specified objectives. Otherwise, the organization leaves itself open to discrimination charges filed by rejected candidates. Although biographical data can be very useful and easily obtainable, there have been many instances in which candidates have falsified information that could not be quickly or easily verified.

Although academic achievement is often used as an assessment procedure, many feel that its validity is exaggerated. Scholastic records are difficult to compare, since the quality of institutions and the difficulty of courses vary from school to school. "Motivation plays a crucial part in human achievement and this is not always reflected in academic records...Evaluate the grades in light of other questions...did grades improve over the school years? Were reasonable grades maintained while the candidate worked to finance his or her education?" (Gery, 1974, p. 907).

In work sampling, a highly predictive assessment procedure, candidates are asked to complete, under controlled conditions, a sample of work that would be a normal part of the job. "Some examples of work samples include a driving course for forklift operators, a typing test for secretarial positions, and an 'in-basket test' that requires management candidates to react to memos typically found in a manager's mailbox.... Work samples typically possess high job-relatedness...[and] are valid for predicting job performance for both non-supervisory and managerial positions. In fact, a review showed that the results of work samples are more valid than the results from intelligence and aptitude paper-and-pencil tests" (Friedman & Mann, 1981, pp. 71-72).

A variation of this assessment procedure is to review samples of similar work the candidate has completed. This second method is less predictive, however, as selecting officials have no way of knowing under what conditions such "uncontrolled" work was performed or even if it represents the sole efforts of the candidate.

If candidates are not expected to possess the skills necessary to perform the job, a lesser-known approach called "miniature job training" or "miniaturized training tests" (MTT) may be employed (Siegel, 1983, p. 42). During this procedure, the candidate actually learns to perform a task that would normally be part of the job. The candidate's performance of the task is considered representative of future performance. This assessment procedure has high predictive validity.

Peer judgments, in which the peers of the applicants are interviewed, have proven worthwhile for assessing candidates for job promotion (Reilly & Chao, 1982, pp. 19-20). This procedure is not feasible for new hires, however, because of the difficulty of obtaining the cooperation of candidates' previous employers. Studies showing a strong predictive validity for this method have been limited to supervisory or sales positions.

Expert judges assist in evaluating how well candidates meet selection criteria by sitting in on interviews and reviewing data obtained through a variety of procedures. These judges may be (or may have been) superior performers in the position to be filled or they may have some expertise in matching candidates with selection criteria (e.g., consulting psychologists). Expert judgments are most often used in filling executive positions. This assessment method may be very cost-efficient if the judges are already employed by the organization in some capacity. It is advisable to use a job aid with this procedure to ensure that the judges are using the same criteria for each evaluation.

Assessment centers are sites where standardized selection procedures are applied, most often to identify management and executive candidates. Candidates participate in simulations of situations they would typically encounter on the job and their behavior is observed and assessed. The cost of using an assessment center to gauge applicants' suitability ranges from several hundred to several thousand dollars per participant. Although these figures may seem overwhelming, they should be weighed against the high costs of replacing nonperforming managers. The assessment center is most appropriate for large organizations with enough vacant managerial positions to justify the cost of establishing and maintaining a center.

No assessment method is infallible. Each has its weaknesses as well as its strengths (charismatic applicants may dazzle interviewers; competent performers may freeze on paper-and-pencil tests). Consequently, it is best to rely on several different assessment procedures and to interpret the results of each with caution. Assessment procedures that require candidates to demonstrate the skills they will be expected to use on the job generally prove to be the most predictive and reliable.

Such procedures may, however, be difficult and time-consuming to create. It is usually more cost-effective to rely on the less time- and effort-consuming assessment procedures to screen out unqualified applicants for the position. Use the more elaborate procedures to assess remaining candidates.

Keeping accurate records is crucial. The results of each candidate's assessment should be documented. Not only do these records act as a legal safeguard, but these data also allow the organization to evaluate the predictive validity, reliability, and cost-effectiveness of each assessment procedure.

When making the selection from the final candidates, perform a potential problem analysis for each of the remaining candidates (Leibler & Parkman, 1989). Involve several people from your organization in this process: their insight and perceptions will contribute to the accuracy and objectivity of the analysis. Using the data obtained from the assessment procedures, ask the following questions.

If this candidate were selected and subsequently did not perform the job at the level of proficiency required:

- Which tasks would the candidate be most likely to perform below expectations?

- If such a performance problem occurred, what would be the cost to the organization?

- What would be the most likely causes for this problem?

- Would the problem exist because he or she did not meet a selection criterion? Which one?

- Could this problem be prevented? In what way? What would be the cost of preventing the problem?

- What would be the cost to the organization if the problem were not solved?

Steps 4 to 10: Continuous Improvement of the Performance System

After the candidate has been selected and has assumed the duties of the position, the individual's supervisor should monitor (observe and analyze) job performance to determine whether it meets or exceeds expectations at all levels. A formal evaluation should only be made after the performer has had the opportunity to acquire and demonstrate mastery of all the skills/knowledge required for the position.

One reason for this evaluation is to catch any existing performance problems early, before they have a chance to grow. If the individual's performance meets or exceeds expectations, positive feedback should be provided. The results of the evaluation, whether positive or negative, should be added to the documentation of the effectiveness of the selection process.

If the individual is not performing at the level of proficiency required, enlist the help of a performance technologist in conducting a performance analysis (Mager & Pipe, 1984). This analysis will uncover why the individual is not meeting the criteria and will be useful in planning actions to remove the causes of the problem.

The performance analysis will also reveal whether an error was made during the selection process. Perhaps the job-performance objectives were not comprehensive: tasks were overlooked or conditions omitted. It may be that the selection criteria were not appropriate or that the assessment procedure was not accurately predictive. If such an error has been made, go back to the beginning of the system and examine each step. Because every subsequent action in the selection process is dependent on the job-performance objectives, the search for any error in the system must begin with the formation of the objectives, even when the supervisor's suspicions point elsewhere. Again, both the error and the steps taken to correct it should be documented to improve the selection system.

The performance system we have described calls for a heavy investment in the initial steps of the process. The analysis for creating job-performance objectives, identifying selection criteria, and choosing assessment procedures is a crucial and cost-effective factor in hiring individuals who can perform the tasks of the job at the proficiency required. Managers who claim that such analysis is not worth the time and money fail to consider the heavy cost of hiring the wrong individual, trying to remedy performance problems, and possibly even replacing the employee.

Every error in selection costs the organization at all three levels. At the micro level, the individual who cannot meet performance expectations will be frustrated and may lose confidence in his or her abilities and worth. The individual's performance problems, in turn, impact the efficiency and effectiveness of the organization at the macro level. When performance problems become visible at the mega level as well, there may be more at stake than the loss of repeat customers or a narrower profit margin. Imagine the cost to society of a selection error in personnel within a hospital, a law enforcement agency, a nuclear power plant, or a factory for automobile safety equipment.

Each step of the process may be simplified by making full use of the performance technology tools that should be available from the organization's training specialists. *Job and task analysis* will help in identifying all the skills and knowledge required for competent performance. Establishing *job-performance objectives* based on these analyses will ensure that individuals at the micro, macro, and mega levels all have the same expectations for performance. *Goal analysis* will transform vague statements of personal and physical characteristics required for selection into behavior that can be observed and assessed objectively. *Skills hierarchies* will be useful in determining which skills candidates should possess on entry. Using *job aids* will ensure that all relevant information is obtained in interviews, reference checks, and peer and expert judgments. *Potential problem analysis* enables management to anticipate possible performance problems and prevent them from occurring. Where performance problems do exist, *performance problem analysis* will uncover the causes and find solutions to remove those causes.

Using this self-corrective performance system, with careful analysis and use of the appropriate performance technology tools, will ensure that the organization will select candidates who are able to perform their jobs at the level of proficiency expected and required by micro, macro, and mega levels of the organization.

Acknowledgment

The author wishes to thank April Nixon for significant contributions to this chapter.

References

Americans with Disabilities Act, 42 United States Constitution, section 12101 et seq.

Friedman, B.A., & Mann, R.W. (1981). Employee assessment methods assessed. *Personnel, 58*(6), 69-74.

Gery, G.J. (1974). Hiring minorities and women: The selection process. *Personnel Journal, 53*(12), 906-909.

Kaufman, R. (1992). *Strategic planning plus: An organizational guide.* Newbury Park, CA: Sage.

Leibler, S.N., & Parkman, A.W. (1989). *Influencing the performance of others.* Atlanta, GA: The Center for Effective Performance, Inc.

Leibler, S.N., & Parkman, A.W. (1992). Personnel selection. In H.D. Stolovitch & E.J. Keeps (Eds.), *The handbook of human performance technology.* San Francisco, CA: Jossey-Bass.

Mager, R.F. (1984). *Goal analysis* (2nd ed.). Atlanta, GA: The Center for Effective Performance, Inc.

Mager, R.F., & Pipe, P. (1984). *Analyzing performance problems* (2nd ed.). Atlanta, GA: The Center for Effective Performance, Inc.

Mager, R.F., & Pipe, P. (1994). *Criterion-referenced instruction: Practical skills for designing instruction that works* (4th ed.). Atlanta, GA: The Center for Effective Performance, Inc.

Reilly, R.R., & Chao, G.T. (1982). Validity and fairness of some alternative employee selection procedures. *Personnel Psychology, 15,* 1-62.

Schmidt, F.L., & Hunter, J.E. (1981). Employment testing: Old theories and new research findings. *American Psychologist, 36*(10), 1128-1137.

Siegel, A. (1983). The miniature job training and evaluation approach: Additional findings. *Personnel Psychology, 16,* 41-56.

RECRUITMENT AND TURNOVER

Margie Bluett

Recruitment and Retention

Recruitment and retention practices in the majority of organizations around the world remind me of Bob Garratt's (1990) rhinoceros with exceedingly poor eyesight, which blunders along on a hit-and-miss basis. Many organizations use ineffective recruitment practices that they rarely analyze or assess the cost of; thus, they remain ignorant of their successes or failures and are unable to learn from their mistakes. Yet, it is critically important for organizations to know what they are doing right and what they are doing wrong. Peter Drucker's (1986) observation about "picking people" is an accurate reflection of today's hiring practices.

> Executives spend more time on managing people and making people decisions than on anything else. And yet, by and large, they make poor promotion and staffing decisions. By all accounts their batting average is no better than .333. In no other area of management would we put up with such miserable performance. Indeed, we should not, because in no other area of management do we know so much.

New employees (with their fresh approaches and new ideas) are critically important to all organizations. However, it is exceedingly expensive and inefficient to acquire new blood when the talent is already available within, and fresh approaches and new ideas can easily be encouraged with appropriate training, reinforcement, and reward.

Larger organizations, with turnover as low as 2 to 3 percent, can still gain fresh perspectives by transferring individuals to different divisions or different locations. For smaller organizations without these opportunities, turnover above 10 percent is wastefully expensive and disruptive.

It might help to start off by examining some of the problems caused by poor recruitment and retention practices.

Mega: A society heavily burdened with increased:

- Health costs (job stress, unemployment stress, and associated illnesses)

- Welfare costs (unemployment benefits, family support)

- Government support/initiatives to bolster both public and private sector organizations burdened with large turnover costs

- Hardship for shareholders of struggling or bankrupt organizations due, in part, to large turnover costs

- Difficulty in placement of employees who have been fired after unsuccessful recruitment

Macro: An organization burdened with:

- Adverse public relations in the marketplace
- Inability to attract the best employees
- Loss of business that departs with the unhappy employee

- Customers irritated by personnel changes and business lost as a result

- Loss of company secrets/expertise to the competition

- Huge waste of resources (time, money) recruiting people who do not stay

- Loss of managers' confidence and credibility

- Increased sick leave

- Disruption of work flow, corners cut, reduced quality

- Overload on other team members, extra overtime

Micro: An individual or team burdened with

- Damage to the self-esteem of departing employees after a recruitment mistake

- Adverse effects on the employees' family lives

- Increased stress-related illness and substance abuse

- Increase in number of job-related breakdowns and suicides

- Extra team overtime that disrupts team members' personal lives

Causes of Poor Recruitment and Retention

Although many organizations try hard to recruit well, there is still wide evidence of poor practice. Causes may include the following:

1. Little or largely ineffective checking into applicants' past histories (which can be highly informative when done correctly).

2. Scant attention to the matching of vision, ethics, integrity, values, and operating styles, which is a common cause of placement failure.

3. Use of highly unreliable interviewing methods. (The unstructured interview has a reliability of only 20 percent in predicting future job performance [Van Clieaf, 1991].)

4. Appointment of the applicant most closely matching the job description. This widely held practice ensures a quickly bored employee. The result is resignation, poor performance, or promotion, any one of which means that the organization is likely to experience the cost of another turnover. Herzberg, Mausner, and Snyderman's (1959) theory of work motivators seems to be largely ignored when it comes to recruitment practice.

5. Wide use of panel interviews, even though they are intimidating and counterproductive to open discussion. Paradoxically, those applicants who fare better in front of a panel are often those more experienced with the procedure, i.e., they have been in and out of jobs more often.

It is only through correctly identifying recruitment mistakes and realistically assessing their cost that organizations will realize the extent of waste and the millions that could be recovered with the use of enlightened recruitment practices. A look at the research reveals the following.

As a general rule, each white-collar employee turnover costs an organization two and one-half times the person's annual salary (Bluett, 1996). Although there are many articles and books that suggest a figure much lower than this, my research over the last six years suggests a figure much higher than what is generally quoted. For marketing positions for which a large number of training dollars have been expended or a sales territory has been left vacant or under-serviced, the cost is far higher. (Several years ago, a major computer company came up with a figure of $129,000 in direct costs only for the loss of one of their marketing trainees who had been with the company for two and one-half years.)

This may be difficult to accept, particularly if a conflicting figure has been prepared by your organization. As validation, look closely at the detailed breakdown of turnover costs on pages 351-354. Better still, take a recent turnover and give some approximate costs to all applicable items on the list. The costs will soon add up to the level I have suggested.

Measurable Objectives

To quote Roger Kaufman (1991), "Now where are we going and how will we know when we've arrived?"

Let us suppose that the majority of organizations are using the best recruitment and retention practices ten years from now. What would change for society, the organization, and the individual?

Mega

The benefits to society might be:

1. A 20-percent reduction of health dollars spent in the treatment of job-stress-related illnesses (strokes, heart attacks, asthma, high blood pressure, mental breakdowns, etc.). (Future Health Department statistics could show these reductions.)

2. A 10-percent reduction in the number of marriage breakdowns, with fewer families stressed by the high personal cost of job failure. (Future Divorce Court statistics could show these reductions.)

3. A 10-percent reduction in unemployment-benefit payouts to those employees who are fired without another job to go to. (Future Welfare Department statistics could show these reductions.)

4. An 80-percent reduction in the number of job-related suicides. (Future Police Department statistics could show these reductions.)

Macro

Within organizations, following the introduction of enlightened recruitment and retention practices, we could expect the following within the first five years:

1. A reduction in white-collar annual employee-turnover figures from about 30 percent to 10 percent. (The figure saved may be measured by showing the number of placements lost at 30-percent turnover, less the number lost at 10 percent, and multiplying the difference by the conservative white-collar turnover figure of $50,000 for each turnover [Bluett, 1996]. Blue-collar organizations should use the chart of turnover costs on pages 351-354 to compile their own average turnover costs, because little research has been conducted in this area.)

2. 80 percent of placements lasting for five years or more. (To be measured against personnel's annual departure figures. All departures not due to transfer of employee/ spouse, retirement, maternity, study/compassionate leave, retrenchment due to new technology, or illness/ death are considered avoidable turnover.)

3. A 20-percent advantage in turnover savings between an organization and its competition. (This may be measured more accurately if you know the competition's

approximate turnover level in comparison with your own.)

4. A 20-percent advantage in the organization's ability to attract and retain better employees. (This could be measured each year by the increase in the number of new employees displaying the top success competencies and the numbers of these employees retained over time [Saul, 1992]).

5. A 20-percent reduction in turnover could lead to an 80-percent reduction in management time spent interviewing, allowing more time for management activities such as reflection, visioning, planning, and mentoring, which should result in a better-run organization. (This could be measured through time sheets kept over a set period.)

6. A 50-percent reduction in sick leave—including less sick leave taken for job searches. (Sick-leave figures could be compared on an annual basis.)

7. A 10-percent increase in competitive ability. (This could be measured annually by identifying turnover savings as a percentage of overhead.)

Micro

The benefits to employees and teams that we could expect to see within five years are:

1. A 20-percent improvement in employee self-esteem. (This could be measured via attitudinal surveys.)

2. An 80-percent reduction in managerial time and trauma involved in employee terminations, exit interviews, counseling, etc. (This could be assessed annu-

ally via time sheets and personnel records regarding turnovers.)

3. Greater growth and learning through mentoring and on-the-job training. It is more important to choose an applicant who can grow into the job than to give it to the applicant who provides the best fit right away but subsequently leaves due to boredom or lack of growth. This could lead to a 50-percent improvement in multi-skilling and 50 percent of workers gaining two-plus days of additional training. (Personnel records could provide the means to measure these goals.)

There are significant benefits for society, for the organization, and for the individual from using enlightened recruitment and retention practices.

Rationale

If yours is a white-collar organization with one thousand staff members, that has an average turnover level of 30 percent, you are losing $15 million each year (300 staff members times $50,000 each turnover equals $15 million). Many fields traditionally have these high turnover levels: banking, nursing, retailing, insurance, etc.

However, if your organization were to reduce turnover over the next five years from 30 percent to 10 percent (some have done it in three years), you would save $10 million each year that you maintained the lower level of turnover (200 staff members times $50,000 each turnover equals $10 million).

Surely, this is the way we must look at our recruitment and retention policies. In dollar terms, we can see the costs of not improving our selection and retention practices. The way to ensure quality in recruitment and retention is outlined next.

Structured Recruitment and Retention

As with scientific experimentation, so with any form of evaluation: a consistent, structured approach and measurement of results must be applied to reach a valid conclusion.

In the future, it is likely that more evaluation will be conducted on computer. Regardless of who or what scores and assesses interview responses, a consistent, structured format must be applied, or validity is forfeited.

Figure 1 presents the steps required for structured recruitment and retention. The process is in five stages, shown as dashed-line boxes. The first of these is the job brief.

The Job Brief

List qualifications, experience, and skills required; plus hours, salary range, location, perks, etc.

Job Functions and Required Job Behaviors

These are drawn from the existing job description and what the incumbent has since added. If no job description exists, list all the functions required in the job and then all the skills and behaviors required to perform those functions. Prioritize and give estimated weightings as you proceed.

Once the behaviors are listed, add the extra skills or behaviors that you must allow for from the elements below.

Team Goals

What are the team's goals now and what will the team require, short- and long-term, to fulfill organizational and societal objectives? What can the applicant contribute?

STRUCTURED

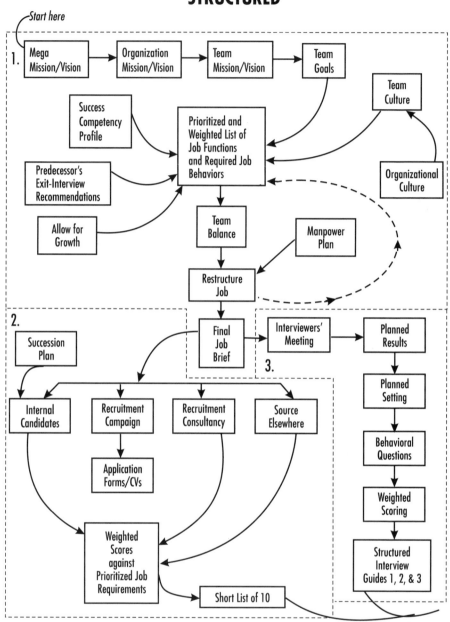

Figure 1. Flowchart of Structured Recruitment

RECRUITMENT

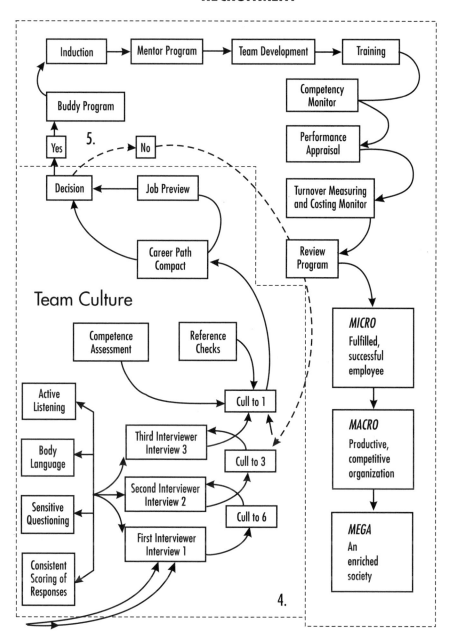

Figure 1 (continued). Flowchart of Structured Recruitment

Team Culture

List the team's values, ethics, and operating styles. These must be matched to avoid clashes.

Success Profile

What behavioral competencies have proved to be most successful in this role in the past? The *Management Competencies Development Program* (Saul, 1992) or a similar instrument will provide you with these data over time.

Exit Recommendations

What recommendations have been made by previous incumbents? They often have valuable suggestions and, as they are leaving and have little to lose, they are less fearful about making recommendations. Make sure the exit interview is conducted in a nonthreatening and friendly environment by an impartial manager with excellent listening skills.

Allowing for Growth

From the list you have just compiled, determine where you can slightly reduce the level of competence required on the job. Do this to allow room for the new job holder's growth and challenge. The required growth becomes part of the "career path compact" (see page 343) reached with the new job holder.

When all six areas have been examined, consider the balance of the team wheel.

Team Balance

Use of a suitable instrument or feedback mechanism will show a team's operational deficiencies. Reorganize team roles so that those with particular traits and interests are in the right jobs. If there are still deficiencies, try to compensate by choosing an applicant with the missing attributes.

Manpower Plan

The manpower plan for a particular area may show a drastic shortage in the skills and behaviors you have listed. At this point you must decide whether to proceed along this difficult path. If so, how difficult and time consuming will it be to attract the type of person you are looking for? If it looks too hard, consider restructuring the job before precious resources are wasted.

Restructure Job

Look at other options: Share the job among the team members (saving one salary may cover the cost of any extra hours). Borrow employees from a less-busy area. Retrain an existing employee. Employ some retirees one to two days per week. Subcontract. Introduce a job-share program.

If you decide to restructure the job, you may have to revise your original job function and behavioral data as a result.

Once all this is listed, prioritized, and given a weighted score, you have your final job brief. This will be used to measure applications, so care must be taken to give realistic weightings.

Reaching the List of Applicants

Succession plan

Your succession plan locks into your career-path compact. Grooming several candidates and giving them the opportunity to act as understudy on occasion is a sensible approach. Is one of these candidates sufficiently trained to be given a trial, perhaps under the current incumbent before he or she leaves?

Internal Candidates

Have you advertised the job internally? Is there another employee with sufficient training to take over? Can that person be given more training and support? Is someone available to do some hand-holding until he or she is proficient?

Recruitment Campaign

Who is available in the marketplace? Looking is very expensive and time consuming. Are you sure you want to spend the time and resources? Certainly new blood is important in building responsiveness in a fast-changing marketplace; however, existing employees are a great source of ideas and innovation if given the opportunity and encouragement.

Application Forms and Questionnaires

Use of a mailed or computerized application form or, better still, a job-specific questionnaire, can be highly valuable as an inexpensive weeding tool prior to interviewing. Its use can ensure that the questions you want answered are asked, thus giving you a cost-effective and reliable means of culling the list of applicants. A correctly designed questionnaire will identify the level of skills and competencies critical for the job and any gaps in the applicant's experience that may not otherwise be noted. Perusing applications for what is not said is important. Highlight anomalies as you proceed, in case a more detailed examination is warranted later on.

Recruitment Consultants

Using consultants is an expensive way to recruit, but it reduces hassles and usually comes with a free replacement guarantee. Develop an exclusive arrangement with a reputable consultant, who will get to know your organization and its mega vision well. Negotiate a reduced rate in exchange for an exclusive search contract and a six-month guarantee. (Three months are usually insufficient to test the success of a placement.)

Source Elsewhere

Don't neglect the more unusual ways of searching for new talent: ask employees, use posters or billboards, track down talent from business closures, try information seminars, ask real estate agencies for a list of families that are relocating to your area, do a mailbox drop, head hunt on the phone, try community or institute bulletin boards. Being innovative can save considerable expense.

Weighted Scores

From the twenty best applications, decide on a list of ten by scoring each against the weighted scores you have given the prioritized job requirements. Ensure consistency by recording the criteria for assessing all applications. Decision making is then easy, objective, and reliable.

Preparing for Interviews

Interviewers' Meeting

Where possible, use three interviewers to ensure objectivity. All three interviewers should meet beforehand to discuss the job description, look through the list of candidates, and decide on the consistent approach they will take.

Planned Results

Deciding on desirable interview results is important. Is there likely to be a surplus of good talent? Can it be directed elsewhere in the organization? When is it convenient to start someone? What training, equipment, and resources must be ready? Who will be the mentor? Will he or she have the time? Who should do the first, second, and third interviews, and who is best qualified to tackle which questions?

A Planned Setting

Where can you meet with the applicant to ensure privacy, no noise or interruptions, access to refreshments, and a congenial, relaxed atmosphere? If you want to encourage honesty, never interview from behind your desk or use a panel. The setting you choose should put the interviewee at ease.

Behavioral Questions

Since past behavior is the best predictor of future behavior, carefully write behavioral questions that seek specific past examples of competencies listed in the job brief. This form of interviewing is both reliable and objective. With a high predictive validity (70 percent), behavioral interviewing, coupled with the competency and team role preference tools, is replacing the use of psychological appraisal techniques, which are considerably less reliable (53 percent), and the use of assessment centers, which are even less reliable (36 percent) (Van Clieaf, 1991).

Weighted Scoring

Work out a weighted scoring for responses that tally with the weightings in the prioritized job description. Complete this section with structured interview guides for three sets of interviews, one for each interviewer.

Interviewing

Active Listening

Active listening calls for full concentration. If done well, it lets an interview quickly progress to a deeper level of trust and openness.

Body Language

Being receptive to the other 93 percent of communication that is conveyed through body language and voice qualities is a valuable ability. It not only expands the interviewer's awareness of the applicant, it also can break down barriers.

Sensitive Questioning

The interviewer must be alert to the ramifications of what is being said and recognize and probe issues that may impact decisions. It is important to be sensitive to what is not said. Be sure to meet all nondiscrimination requirements. Detailed discussion of your reference-checking procedures at the start of the first interview encourages the open, honest discussion you want.

Consistent Scoring of Responses

For any method of evaluation to be effective, consistent measurement must be made. The structured interview guide assigns score ranges to be used by each interviewer. Using the same interviewer for each interview series is also an important means of providing that consistency. It is essential that scoring occur immediately after each response. Scoring done after the interview is unreliable.

Culling

Each interviewer culls at the end of each interview series. Normally the first ten candidates would be reduced to six and then to three, from which the finalist is selected. The results of the interview and other scores form an objective basis for decision making, one which is easily defended if challenged.

Reference Checks

Done correctly, reference checks give valuable, candid information about the applicant that cannot be gained any other way. Explain to the referee that you will be checking with other referees in detail and that the applicant will not see what you are writing. Seek opinions regarding the applicant's suitability for the position being offered, ask about strengths and weaknesses and successes and failures, and be scrupulous about confidentiality. Make sure checking is done by someone who has clout, objectivity, sensitivity, and—above all—tact.

Competency Assessment

For consistency, use the same instrument that gave you the success profile for this position. Ideally, the instrument should measure desired behaviors via the applicant's response and that of five or six other different-level respondents who have worked closely with the applicant. This tool also identifies training needs, which feed into the career path compact.

Team Balance

Once again, the same tool should be used that established team balance deficiencies. Results will clearly indicate whether the candidate's preferred operating style will complement the team's styles and result in a more efficient, balanced, and productive team.

Career Path Compact

This document, which both parties sign, is a precursor to the first performance appraisal. It replaces the letter of employment and becomes ratified with the acceptance of the job. It covers objectives, skill and competence development, a proposed career path, resources to be made available, rewards for the reaching of objectives and competence levels, and time frames for these actions, as well as the usual employment information.

Job Preview

Where appropriate, the finalist takes a day of leave from his or her current job to work on a project with the new team. This is done prior to acceptance so that both parties can back down if there are doubts. The team works on a productive, nonconfidential project to test its compatibility with the finalist. This also gives the finalist a closer look at the organization's culture, systems, layout, facilities, and equipment. If the team gives a thumbs-down at this point, the employment should end.

Making the Placement Work

Buddy Program

The faster that assimilation into the new team occurs, the quicker the new employee is productive (Garratt, 1990). Ask the buddy to meet the new employee for coffee prior to his or her beginning the new job. The buddy or boss should meet the new employee at the front door on the first day. Have the team meet over lunch on that first day and have team members take turns eating lunch with the new employee for the first two weeks.

Induction

If the organization is not currently using an induction program, introduce one. It does not have to be complicated. The main ingredients are the type of organization it is, what it does (here and in other places), its vision, its goals, its structure, its people, its products, what performance counts, where to find people and things, where to get help, and who the buddies and mentors are.

Mentor Program

A structured mentor program is effective in encouraging top performance from new employees. Each new employee is assigned a mentor, who regularly guides his or her performance. The best mentors are those who hold high expectations for their charges and enjoy the mentor role. It can also be a means of using the skill and experience of retirees on a part-time basis.

Team Development

More and more organizations are using self-managing and cross-functional teams. To hone their effectiveness, members must acquire team skills as quickly as possible. Good training in these skills will help create and maintain synergy and empowerment.

Training

Training requirements for the first year of employment—which were identified by the competence tool and interview and listed in the career path compact—are reviewed in each performance appraisal. Training must proceed at a faster pace than change for the organization to go forward. Sharing what has been learned across the whole organization and having a management committed to learning and growth are essential prerequisites for success.

Competence Monitor

Behavioral training requirements have been identified. By using an appropriate instrument on a regular basis prior to major performance appraisals, acquisition of the most successful behaviors may be monitored over time.

Performance Appraisal

Frequent feedback, good and bad, is critically important for improving performance. The secret is to do it often and well and to focus on internal and external customer requirements. Additionally, reinforcing desired behaviors with recognition and rewards will reinforce skills. Ensure that the messages given during appraisals are reinforced by other organizational actions and communications. If you are sending conflicting messages, performance-appraisal efforts will be negated.

Measuring Turnover

The health of an organization can be measured by identifying where turnover problems are originating and where overspending is occurring. Line managers can monitor their own turnover performance, thereby creating a drive to eliminate the causes of employee turnover.

Reward Programs

Rewarded behaviors persist. Unrewarded behaviors die out. It is, therefore, very important to reward and to publicize the rewarding of the behaviors the organization requires to be successful. Most rewards do not have to be financial. Other rewards include time off, the opportunity to work with top management, a tee-shirt, mention in the company newsletter, a choice of projects, a special training opportunity, and so on.

Conclusion

Organizations are working hard to restructure themselves and to give more responsibility, autonomy, and variety to individuals and teams. They must identify the forms of recognition that motivate employees. This can be done, in part, during performance appraisals. Employees are highly motivated to reach the goals and gain the rewards that they have had a hand in selecting.

If an organization is run in a participative manner, if conflicting messages are eradicated, if policies are sensible and even-handed, if the basis for advancement is performance and not politics, and if unnecessary red tape is eliminated, the organization is likely to attract and retain top-performing employees. The individual, the organization, and society as a whole stand to benefit as a result.

The following is a checklist to help improve the quality of recruitment and retention techniques.

- Extend total quality management to include recruitment and retention practices.

- Have top management set a highly visible best recruitment practice and low turnover example.
- Give all managers the means to measure their own turnover rates and costs.
- Regularly monitor turnover levels and costs throughout the organization.
- Eradicate any conflicting messages occurring within the organization.
- Do not promote managers who have high turnover in their areas.
- When appropriate, introduce success profiles, competence measurement, succession planning, a team balance index, buddy and mentor programs, job previews, and career development compacts.
- Train line managers in how to recruit using reliable, structured techniques.
- Make appraisal of recruitment and retention practices more effective.
- Reward and publicize best recruitment and retention practices.
- Ensure that all recruitment mistakes are clearly identified as avoidable turnover and take steps to ensure that the mistake is not repeated.
- Make managers accountable for their turnover levels.
- When recruiting in large numbers, use a computerized project-management tool.
- Always ask departing employees for their recommendations during exit interviews.
- Use job-specific questionnaires prior to interviewing.
- Leave room for growth for new employees.

- Interview one-to-one; don't use a panel and don't sit behind a desk.

- Encourage top performers by removing red tape, rewarding successful innovation, and encouraging risk taking.

- Promote according to performance, not politics.

- Restructure jobs so that responsibility and accountability are passed down to the lowest levels possible.

- Ensure that the organization operates participatively and with fairness.

- Regularly measure employees' perceptions and morale.

References

Bluett, M. (1996). *Staff turnover costing and accountability.* Sydney: Keipat Pty. Ltd.

Drucker, P. (1986). *The frontiers of management.* New York: Harper & Row.

Garratt, B. (1990). *Creating a learning organisation.* London: Learning to Lead.

Herzberg, F., Mausner, B., & Snyderman, B. (1959). *The motivation to work.* New York: John Wiley.

Kaufman, R. (1991). *Strategic planning plus.* Newbury Park, CA: Sage.

Saul, P. (1992). *Management competency development.* Sydney: McGraw-Hill.

Van Clieaf, M. (1991, March/April). In search of competence: Structured behavior interviews. *Business Horizons*, p. 9

ACCOUNTABILITY FOR STAFF TURNOVER

Margie Bluett

Introduction

In a majority of organizations, managers are held accountable for the loss of financial resources, yet seldom are they held accountable for the loss of the organization's most precious resource, its people. This chapter describes how the gradual introduction of staff-turnover-accountability policies and practices and the use of a standard turnover costing methodology can save large organizations hundreds of millions of dollars each year (and smaller organizations a proportional amount). Staff turnover accountability means that the cost of the avoidable loss of an individual from a department is deducted from the operating budget of that department.

In 1988, a computer firm's Sydney offices established that losing a marketing trainee after two and one-half years' intensive training cost them $129,000 (Australian). In 1990, a large Australian retail group valued the loss of one of its first line managers conservatively at $20,000, and researchers at the Center for Industrial Relations Studies at the University of Melbourne estimated that the cost of turnover for a white-collar worker was up to $15,000 (Bluett, 1996).

A comprehensive survey of 450 managers in America prior to September 1987 gives an average turnover cost of

$75,000 (U.S), while a restaurant chain gave a figure of $70,000 for the loss of one of its managers.

McGill University, in Montreal, reported in 1990 a study in which each departing sales employee cost a large pharmaceutical company $51,000 (Canadian).

The fluctuation in the figures is not only due to staff being at different levels, but also because organizations use different methods to reach their total costs. More to the point, the leaner organization of today has a greater output per person than it did a decade ago. To achieve this, companies have increased their investment in employees' training and skills acquisition. When someone leaves an organization today, it costs the organization far more than it did a decade ago; this escalation of costs is unlikely to slow down.

> If you look at the 100 largest corporations (in the USA), the turnover rate at the division or subdivision level is about 25 percent per year. The primary reason for this high turnover rate is that companies are doing a poor job of developing their managers and executives.... Furthermore, companies have had a tendency to misuse their talented people and not have the proper perspective with less talented ones (Jennings, 1985).

Turnover Accountability

It appears that most organizations simply do not know what staff turnover costs them. Without these data, accountability is impossible.

Costs of Avoidable Turnover

The author believes that avoidable turnover should include all attrition that is not the result of death, retirement, leave (maternity, paternity, illness, or sabbatical), layoffs resulting from new technology, or transfer of employee or spouse. The departure of unsatisfactory employees must be included, as their recruitment was a mistake for which there should be accountability. Without direct accountability, recruitment mistakes have a tendency to be repeated.

Table 1. Legitimate Turnover Costs

SEPARATION COSTS
1. Redundancy/severance pay excluding superannuation and holiday pay.
2. Value of lost business that leaves with departing employee or is caused by disgruntled employee prior to departure.
3. Extra work required of others to retrieve lost business: numbers x salaries involved.
4. Legal costs (disputes, termination arrangements, breaking of contracts, etc.).
5. Equipment retained by the employee after departure (home computer, printer, software, modem, fax, etc.).
6. Gripe sessions: preresignation discussions x number of employees x time x salaries involved.
7. Exit interview: number of employees x time x salaries involved.
8. Outplacement fee.
9. Time off used by employee while searching for another job. Compare attendance with normal period prior to dissatisfaction and cost in difference.
10. Time spent writing reference and responding to phone/fax reference checks.
11. Administrative time spent calculating and organizing separation package.
12. Balance of company-paid fees, publication subscriptions, tuition fees, etc., written off after departure.

VACANT POSITION COSTS
13. Idle equipment x time x costs involved.
14. If sales position, sales lost while sales territory is vacant or until new employee can produce previous sales levels. Compare with normal sales levels and cost in difference.
15. If income-producing position, income lost due to vacancy or until new employee can produce previous income levels. Compare with normal income level for the position and cost in difference — where not duplicated in numbers 14, 16, or 17.
16. If measurable-output position, lowered position output while inexperienced or temporary person is manning position/equipment. Compare with normal output levels and cost in loss of output below normal levels — where not duplicated in numbers 14, 15, and 17.
17. If value-added position, for the period the position is vacant or underperforming until fully operational at previous incumbent's level, cost in the lost value on the following basis: Calculate value added by subtracting purchased goods and services from sales.
18. Lowering of team's efficiency/productivity caused by lower morale, operating one person short, or operating with inexperienced temporary/contract staff. Compare with normal team output and cost is loss of team output below normal level less the amount already costed in numbers 14, 15, 16, or 17.
19. Increased overtime required of others while position is vacant or underperforming x numbers x salaries involved.
20. Increased scrap. Compare with normal scrap levels and cost in the increased amount of waste.
21. Temporary/contract/freelance surcharges until replacement is found.
22. Administrative time spent deciding solutions and reorganizing workloads x salaries involved.
REPLACEMENT COSTS
23. Recruitment consultancy fees.
24. Recruitment advertising costs.

25.	Interviews x numbers employees x time x salaries involved.
26.	One-day job preview: time x salaries of those involved in the preview and any preliminary or resultant action (preparation of job preview program and preview report).
27.	Recruitment reward if existing employee recruits new employee.
28.	Medical/psychological testing.
29.	Legal fees (contracts/agreements with new appointee).
30.	Travel/accommodation/meals during recruitment process.
31.	Proportion of campus recruitment-program costs (campus recruiters' salaries, literature, cost of booth, meals, travel, etc.).
32.	Administrative time spent x salaries involved: - preparing/altering job specifications - briefing/writing/approving ads - discussing job with personnel and consultants - screening mail/phone applications - arranging appointments - preparing for interviews - preparing and matching success profile - checking references - writing letters to unsuccessful candidates - preparing employee agreements, if not covered in number 29
33.	Printed company material sent to interviewees and new recruits (excluding induction kit costed below).

INDUCTION/TRAINING COSTS

34.	Employee's salary while attending induction and internal and external training until fully productive.
35.	All external training costs (training fees, meals, travel, parking, accommodation) for new employee until fully productive.
36.	Percentage of salaries of trainers and other employees involved in induction and internal training x numbers and time involved plus proportion of fee if external trainer is used.

37.	A percentage of all internal training costs based on the amount of internal training provided to the applicant until fully productive (teaching aids, training room, proportion of total office rental, furniture, equipment, power, refreshments, course materials, etc.).
38.	Time spent mentoring/training on the job until employee is fully productive (excluding internal training courses costed above) x salaries involved.
39.	Time spent showing employee around and introducing him or her and/or time spent with buddy system x salaries involved.
40.	Cost of each induction kit.

LIKELY INDIRECT COSTS

1.	Use of company time and office equipment and stationery to apply for jobs, prepare and send CVs/letters, make appointments, and follow up (give best estimate). Use of: - company computer
	              - company stationery
	              - company photocopier
	              - company phone (sometimes interstate/overseas)
	              - company postage (sometimes interstate/overseas)
	              - company fax (sometimes interstate/overseas)
	              - loss of employee's time while thus engaged

2.	Current/future business lost due to work backlog/delays in department.
3.	Adverse publicity from dissatisfied previous employee that affects the organization's business/sales efforts/recruitment of new employees.
4.	Loss of highly specialized skills.
5.	Loss of company secrets/specialized methodologies/inside knowledge to a competitor.
6.	Loss of high-potential employee to competitor.

All these areas have a price tag attached to them. Putting a value on as many of them as possible is important if the full extent of turnover costs is to be recognized and put into proper perspective. The loss of any employee is likely to be much higher than previously thought.

Advantages and Benefits of Reducing Turnover

Those organizations that significantly reduce their turnover rate have a distinct market advantage over their competitors. This market advantage includes the following:

1. A distinct financial advantage over competitors, which, for large organizations, can add hundreds of millions of dollars each year to the bottom line.

2. The creation of an excellent public image, which will attract the best employees.

3. A reputation in the marketplace that attracts and keeps new business.

Other benefits include the following:

1. Strong board support and swift allocation of resources for projects to improve the workplace and cut avoidable turnover.

2. Ability, perhaps for the first time, to place turnover accountability with those people responsible for recruitment decisions and retention policies.

3. Identification of attrition hot spots and related management problems.

4. Value placed on previously uncalculated waste and causes identified and resolved.

5. Establishment of reward, appraisal, training, and other systems that will improve and support good recruitment and retention practices.

6. Having the figures on hand to establish:

   - when, in a recession, it is more cost-effective to retain than to lay people off,

- when it is wiser to offer generous relocation bonuses rather than to lose valuable employees,

- when it makes sense to use succession planning.

7. Fostering an organizational culture that emphasizes the welfare and interests of individual employees.

8. Creation of a happy, motivated, and highly productive work force.

Arguments Against Turnover Accountability

1. Accountability Will Encourage Managers to Retain Nonperformers

Organizations are right to be wary that turnover accountability is likely to encourage managers to retain nonperformers. Obviously, the ideal solution is to keep the employee, save the turnover costs, and redirect some of those savings toward reversing the poor performance, i.e., to train and to investigate and solve the problems that are contributing to the poor performance.

You can spend quite a few dollars in training and problem solving and still not spend what it would cost you to rehire someone. Additionally, by listening to and trying to correct the problems and by training the employee, you are likely to increase the employee's enthusiasm and loyalty and improve his or her productivity.

2. Turnover Activities Are Part of Managers' Normal Functions

If you can cut down the amount of time spent on turnover activities, you can save money by employing fewer staff in personnel or by having personnel/line managers more productively employed.

3. The Need for New Blood

An optimum level of attrition, which may be somewhere between 2 and 10 percent, depending on the industry and the size of the organization, allows for some injection of new blood and internal promotions. Having each department decide its own optimum turnover level, and the dates by which it will gradually be met, is one of the prerequisites for turnover accountability.

4. Managers May Feel Penalized If Organizational Decisions Create Turnover

Properly conducted exit interviews should determine reasons for employee departures. If any of the reasons given are related to overall organizational decisions or policy, then an appropriate proportion of that particular turnover cost (as suggested by the exit interviewer) should be borne by the organization, not by the department. This procedure will promote careful analysis of any organizational decisions or actions that could create turnover.

4. Accountability Is Threatening to Managers of High Turnover Areas

In the long run, sweeping turnover under the carpet will not benefit the manager or the organization. The best approach is to work very closely with the manager concerned and provide maximum support, training, and resources to remedy as many identified problems as possible prior to accountability being introduced.

With constant, strong support and cooperation from top management, the threatening nature of turnover accountability should diminish, particularly as departmental problems are solved, morale is improved, and turnover levels are reduced.

Overcoming Ingrained Attitudes

Many jobs are boring, repetitive, poorly paid, dirty, dangerous, involve shift work, and so on. These positions typically have a high turnover rate. However, many aspects of these positions can be improved and turnover reduced. Innovative approaches to the workplace can produce amazing results. Using employee participation, attitudinal surveys, team briefings, employee suggestions, and total quality management, many workplaces and organizational cultures have been improved dramatically.

Having the incentive of tangible rewards, managers are likely to be highly motivated to experiment, to seek counsel, and to find solutions. However, they will not do these things without continued support from top management. Of course, certain departments will still have higher turnover rates than others. The lowering of turnover in these departments may take a great deal longer. However, lowering of turnover rates in previously high turnover areas is certainly possible, as the following examples show.

Example 1: In previously high turnover areas (seasonal and full-time sales assistants), Cole National, in Cleveland, Ohio, was able to reduce turnover of seasonal staff by 50 percent and full-time staff by 33 percent simply by introducing employee-attitude surveys and acting on the results (Jennings, 1985).

Example 2: Marriott Corporation had a "shocking labor turnover rate" until it decided to use an attitude survey and then set to work to remedy employees' grievances and to act on their suggestions (Jennings, 1985).

Example 3: Rosenbluth Travel, Inc., U.S. winner of the Tom Peters Award as Service Company of the Year, uses employee-attitude surveys extensively and enjoys a turnover rate of only 6 percent, compared with industry turnover figures of 45 or 50 percent. Says Rosenbluth, "We look at human resources the way others look at financial assets."

Estimates of Savings

Figure 2 illustrates the cost savings from reduced turnover for an organization with five thousand, ten thousand, or fifty thousand staff members. The savings for these large organizations would be $37.5 million, $75 million, and $375 million, respectively. These savings can occur every year that the lower turnover levels are maintained.

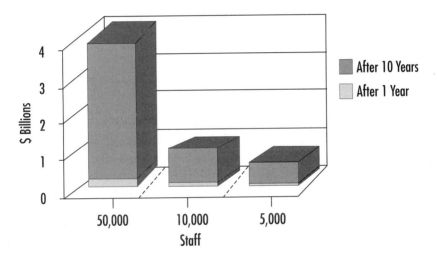

Figure 2. Large-Company Savings After Reducing Turnover by 15 Percent Below Industry

Strategies for Maintaining the Work Force

Retain Rather Than Lay Off

Another point that requires consideration is layoffs resulting from economic downturns. If a position eliminated today is reinstated later, the organization will have to go through the expense of rehiring and retraining.

If, however, the job incumbent is put in a temporary position until his or her old job is reinstated, the cost of training that employee for the temporary position is far less than the cost of training a new employee. Furthermore, severance pay does not have to be paid to the employee. It therefore makes sense to retrain the employee for other work until such time as his or her old position is reactivated. In most cases, an organization is better off retaining long-term employees whose positions will be reactivated with the upturn of the economy. This applies even if they earn less for the company in temporary positions for which they require considerable training.

Offer Relocation Inducements

By identifying how much each turnover costs, management can calculate exactly what incentives to offer highly qualified staff to relocate to new company premises. If an employee can be induced to make the move to the company's new location (with relocation expenses, such as legal fees, real estate commissions, movers, moving insurance, etc., paid for by the company), the company saves a great deal of money. If replacing the employee has an average turnover cost of $50,000 and the company spends $5,000 to $10,000 on relocation expenses to keep that employee, the company has saved $40,000 or more in the process. Savings of this order occur with the relocation of each individual to the new premises.

It helps if the organization works closely with staff members to win them over to the move. Paid trips to the new location, social functions there, and regular discussions with staff regarding the relocation all serve this purpose.

On the other hand, if staff members are not told of the impending move in time to adjust to the idea and make arrangements, they are likely to seek new work in their old location. The costs of replacing these staff members in a short period of time, both financial and organizational, are massive (Bluett, 1996).

Recruit in Advance

The costs of a vacant or underperforming sales territory can be tremendous. Other jobs that have the same effect when understaffed or underperformed include income-producing positions (consultants, lawyers, systems analysts, architects, project managers, trainers, film producers, artists, etc.), measurable-output positions, and value-added positions. These losses are valid turnover costs when they result from avoidable staff departures or underperformance. When lost sales figures or other lost revenue is added to additional turnover costs, the total climbs dramatically. Organizations can avoid such losses by having comprehensive succession plans. Having trained individuals "waiting in the wings" is, in most cases, far less expensive than leaving a territory or important job vacant or underperforming.

Prerequisites for Accountability

The following conditions need to exist before an accountability program can be installed effectively in an organization.

1. Turnover costs, attrition levels, optimum turnover levels, and exit interviews have to be established and methods of analysis set up, for individual departments and for the whole organization.

2. Managers must be trained in recruitment and retention skills before accountability is introduced.

3. Decisions must be made about the sharing of accountability between the personnel/human resources department and other departments.

4. The appraisal system must be adjusted to evaluate both the acquisition and the application of recruitment- and retention-skills training and the turnover levels reached.

5. The reward system must be adjusted to reward the gradual acquisition of optimum turnover figures.

Encouraging Cooperation and Fostering Accountability

The following are suggested policies for encouraging cooperation with the accountability program by managers.

1. Ensure that the accountability project is seen to be actively supported by *all* senior managers. The CEO must be seen as monitoring the whole process and should report on turnover progress to all staff members every six months.

2. Personnel, unions, and line managers must be involved in the design of the project from start to finish.

3. Give the project plenty of lead time. Encourage internal publicity and open debate.

4. Include optimum turnover goals in the organization's business plan and the vision statement.

5. Negotiate gradual turnover accountability, phased in over an agreed term and after initial training is completed and showing results. Share accountability in direct proportion to the level of responsibility held.

6. Provide departments with a wide choice of recruitment and retention training. Conduct periodic refresh-

ers to keep skill levels as high as possible. Train new employees as they arrive.

7. Encourage full participation by top management in the training and application of the skills learned; then have them lead by example.

8. Ensure that turnover figures and exit-interview results are covered in departmental reporting and pass this information to the CEO to keep him or her fully informed of progress on a monthly basis.

9. Relocate or replace those managers who consistently fail to reduce turnover figures. Before doing this, make sure that every effort has been made to train and support that manager over a reasonable time.

10. Create a culture that:

   • encourages participation, involvement, and commitment and rewards lateral thinking and creative problem solving. (Do not allow any manager to squash early employee attempts to offer suggestions or solutions.)

   • reminds all managers of the sources of employee motivation and satisfaction. (Enlarge the list and hang it in conspicuous places.)

Possible Initiatives

Some organizational initiatives that contribute to the success of an accountability program are described in the following sections.

Exit Interviews. Conduct exit interviews using impartial, top-ranking executives to show the project's importance to employees. The interviewer must establish, where possible, true reasons for departure and other contributors to dissatisfaction. An exit-interview report should be issued to each department for review prior to managers' performance appraisals.

The exit interviewer must have the authority to decide when overall company policy has contributed to the departure and the proportion of turnover cost the organization will assume.

Turnover Committee. A special turnover committee should be set up, with full authority to tackle all aspects of the accountability project and to ensure there is consistency of approach between departments. Invite those with the most at stake to serve on the committee. Make sure that all members of the committee receive training on "how to run successful meetings," and give this training to new committee members as they join. The committee should report directly to the CEO, thus ensuring swift and full cooperation.

Standard Turnover-Costing Methodology. Use a standard costing methodology so that individual departments can establish turnover costs and optimum turnover levels that not only are consistent across the whole organization, but also are consistent with those used elsewhere (Bluett, 1996).

Employee Attitude Survey. Conduct a full and confidential attitude survey of employees every two years, and conduct smaller spot surveys when required. Publish results and act on those results without delay. Keep employees informed.

Employee Suggestions. Introduce an employee-suggestion box. Suggestion boxes allow employees who are reluctant to speak up to voice their concerns anonymously. Use employees' suggestions to improve the work place and make the work more efficient. This will encourage retention and be attractive to new employees. Offer rewards based on a percentage of the money generated as a result of employees' suggestions.

Employee Referrals. Employees whose referrals lead to the hiring of new staff members receive a bonus or prize for each referral that proves successful over a designated time frame. This gives referring employees a stake in ensuring that the placement works out.

Succession Planning. Ensure that a succession plan is in place and working effectively for all high-level, sales, income-producing, or critical positions within each department.

Top-Performers Management. Develop a policy for the management of the organization's top performers or prospective top performers. Identify who they are, nurture them, reward them, and give them clear career paths and succession plans.

Pay for Performance. Use a well thought-out incentive program to pay employees for performance so that those who contribute most to the organization's success are rewarded accordingly and retained. Many no-cost recognitions can acheive the same result (Bluett, 1996).

Turnover Performance Bonus. Offer a significant and escalating turnover bonus to eligible managers as part of the incentive program. Base it directly on the percentage of turnover-reduction achieved against turnover objectives. Review it during each manager's performance appraisal.

Mentoring Program. Introduce a mentoring program, using motivated high-level managers or possibly retirees (part time). Mentoring has been identified as the most effective way to foster high performance (Collins, 1988). It maximizes employees' potential and is, therefore, highly attractive to existing and new employees as well as to the organization.

Turnover Competitions Between Departments. Informal competitions can be aimed at rewarding turnover performance between departments. Let the winning department decide on the reward of its choice from the budget allocated (movie tickets, lunch brought in, etc.).

Job Previews. Give a one-day job preview to the top applicant for a job, prior to his or her final acceptance of the position. Provide an accurate picture of the position, the department, and the organization.

Success Profiles. As appropriate, use a success profile compiled from input from present and previous successful employees in a position to map the particular competencies necessary for the position (Saul, 1992).

Buddy System/New-Employee Induction. Use the buddy system as part of the induction program. Arrange for the buddy and the new employee to meet before the new employee comes on board. Have them meet at the front door on the new employee's first day. Make sure everything is fully prepared for the new arrival. Impressions of the organization made in the first few days tend to be critical to the success or failure of a placement.

Departmental Brainstorming Sessions. For the first six to twelve months, conduct departmental brainstorming sessions for identifying and solving turnover problems. Invite suggestions across departments. Share the results with the total organization so that everyone can benefit from ideas and discoveries. Before beginning, provide training in the brainstorming technique. Review the success of this process during performance appraisals.

Ongoing Turnover Meetings. After six to twelve months of brainstorming, introduce and/or expand existing team briefings, quality circles, or other suitable monthly meetings. These meetings can provide a forum for discussing turnover-reduction tactics and for planning future strategies. Discuss the meetings during performance appraisals. Confirm major points in a one-page summary and action plan, and hang the list in a conspicuous spot.

Employee/Manager Appraisals. Extend the appraisal system so that employees give a confidential appraisal of their manager's recruiting, retention, and meeting skills and offer suggestions for improvements.

Organization/Employee Agreements. Give the top applicant for each job written confirmation of the functions and performance levels required by the position, together with an outline of all agreed discussion points prior to the one-day job preview and prior to the candidate's resignation from his or her current job.

For management roles, include turnover objectives in the agreements, discuss them fully, and agree on rewards during appraisals.

Implementing Turnover Costing

Stage 1. Establish Turnover Levels. To measure annual avoidable turnover, establish the number of employees who have left the organization for reasons other than death, retirement, transfer, leave, or layoffs due to new technology. (Include those who have left because of unsatisfactory performance. Also, include layoffs that will be rescinded when the economy revives.) Calculate your final number as a percentage of your total number of employees for the year, to arrive at your annual avoidable turnover rate.

Stage 2. Identify All Steps in the Recruitment Process. Isolate a typical job placement and follow the process step-by-step to identify all the steps and the costs of each step.

Stage 3. Establish a Cost for Each Step. Some turnover costs are direct, some indirect. Time sheets can be used to identify all the different turnover activities for the costing procedure. For the purposes of accountability, only direct costs are used. If your organization has additional direct turnover costs, these can be added to the turnover costing.

We generally use three turnovers from each of three salary tiers to give an averaged result. By dividing the whole organization into matching salary tiers, it is possible to make comparisons throughout the organization and with other organizations that use the same methodology. The program gives an average turnover cost for each salary tier in each department and calculates the cost of avoidable turnover per department for the current year to date. It also shows exactly where turnover money has been spent and thereby highlights imbalances and problem areas (Bluett, 1996).

Conclusion

Making managers and departments accountable for turnover is well worth the effort it takes. It also helps to ensure that the best managers are used to manage people. It identifies the losses that can result from using managers who may be highly qualified technically, but who have not developed their interpersonal skills sufficiently to manage people well. The turnover policies and practices suggested in this article focus attention on the building and rewarding of managers' interpersonal skills. It also makes everyone aware of the financial losses suffered by the organization through avoidable staff turnover.

Moreover, the policies and practices espoused here will help to streamline the whole organization. They will greatly improve the bottom line and give organizations significant market advantages.

References

Bergsweek, J. (1989). Recruitment and selection for company culture. *Journal of Managerial Psychology* (UK).

Bluett, M. (1995). *A recognition and reward smorgasbord.* Sydney: Keipat Pty. Ltd.

Bluett, M. (1996). *Staff turnover costing and accountability.* Sydney: Keipat Pty. Ltd.

Collins, R. (1988). Motivating staff. *Australian Managers' Audio Journal.*

Dahl, H. (1988, July). Four by four: What should human resource accounting systems count? *Training and Development Journal* (USA).

Darmon, R. (1990, April). Identifying sources of turnover costs: A segmental approach. *Journal of Marketing, 54.*

Dawson, C. (1988). Costing labor turnover through simulation processes: A tool for management. *Personnel Review* (UK) *17, 4.*

Fits-Enz, J. (1984). The hidden costs of lost time. In *Measuring employee relations activities.* New York: McGraw-Hill.

Godden, D. (1991, February 11-14). *Government public servants, interest groups and the public.* Paper presented at the 35th Annual Conference, Australian Agricultural Economics Society, University of New England, Armidale, Australia.

Halcrow, A. (1987, October). Employees are your best recruiters. *Personnel Journal* (USA).

Have a nice day; employee loyalty in service films. (1991, March 2). *The Economist* (Australia), p. 70.

Hendrickson, J. (1987, November). Hiring the "right stuff." *Personnel Administrator* (USA).

Jenkins, S. (1988, December). Turnover, correcting the causes. *Personnel* (USA).

Jennings, E. (1985, April). How to develop your management talent internally. *Personnel Administrator* (USA).

Kovach, K.A. (1987, October). What motivates employees? Workers and supervisors give different answers. *Business Horizons* (USA).

Many happy returns. (1987, October). *Face to Face, Inc.* (USA).

Mercer, M.W. (1988, December). Turnover: Reducing the costs. *Personnel* (USA).

Nankervis, A. (1990, May). Increasing productivity through participation. *Personnel Today* (Australia).

Patrickson, M., & Haydon, D. (1988, November). Management selection practices in South Australia. *Human Resource Management Australia.*

Saul, P. (1989, August). Using management competencies to improve management performance and stimulate self development. *Asia Pacific Human Resources Management* (Australia).

Smart, B.D. (1987, September). Progressive approaches for hiring the best people. *Training and Development Journal* (USA).

Smith, B. (1989, October). Make yourself a manager (Part I); Room at the top. *Personnel Today* (Australia).

Steffy, B., & Maurer, S. (1989). Conceptualizing and measuring the economic effectiveness of human resource activities. *Academy of Management Review, 13*, 2.

PERFORMANCE MANAGEMENT

Adrian Bell and Ron Forbes

Appraisal or Management?

Many organizations have performance-appraisal systems that do not deliver the expected results—not for lack of time and effort invested. Some of the various conditions that render performance appraisal ineffective or counterproductive are as follows:

- Focusing on inputs (functions and tasks), not results;

- Overseeing *how* people work rather than measuring their achievements;

- Concentration on prescribed standards of work and behavior;

- Controlling rather than encouraging;

- Conveying conflicting messages and lack of trust;

- Offering individual rewards that conflict with team-work and group recognition;

- Having a short-term view of profitability and productivity; and

- Having organizational values that do not support or conflict with personal values.

The concentration is on micro, and sometimes macro, goals with rarely more than token attention to the mega level (Kaufman, 1992). Some of the resultant problems follow.

Prescribed standards of work and behavior. These may be established either to satisfy managers' personal values and views of what is desirable conduct or to provide some measure of uniform behavior (for the convenience of the manager).

Short-term productivity. Performance appraisal is ostensibly directed toward productivity, but rarely does it allow employees to enter into the decision-making or policy-formulation processes or involve them in the consequences and payoffs. The achievements of staff members, their rewards, and their pay increases are not always linked to the business objectives of the organization. As a result, the appraisal aims at performance standards that are supposed to cut costs, save waste, and reduce customer complaints, while overlooking the critical part played by individual initiative, risk taking, and contributions on the front line.

Short-term profitability. Profitability is often a short-term objective (1 year to 5 years at most) and is derived either from projections from previous years or from projected sales, production, or cost budgets.

Setting objectives. However carefully objectives may be crafted (specific, measurable...), they still fail if they are set in isolation, probably to meet the requirements of the next appraisal, promotion, or salary review. They are then regarded as a useless imposition on a manager's time and become perfunctory and indefinitely postponable.

Culture and risk. All appraisal of performance takes place within a hierarchy and a corporate culture that may never be openly defined, and that often carries a high level of risk. The higher the threat for employees, the greater the likelihood of their playing "I'm doing a good job" or "play it safe" games rather than raising real issues. Systems of this kind *reduce* performance, especially around appraisal time.

Managing Performance

Most organizations are now in a state of rapid and continuous change. Performance management must operate in a way that combines direction and values for employees with what Peters (1992) calls "fashion"—responding rapidly to market opportunities.

Managing performance (rather than judging or appraising it) is the key way in which managers can be successful through delegating effectively, gaining support, and building synergy with their team members. It is the route to survival of the organization in times of change.

Effective performance management is based on several conditions:

- Encouragement of enthusiasm;
- Positive attitude (Hawley, 1992);
- Mutual planning;
- Increased delegation;
- Customer focus;
- Overall defined results linked to the mega plan;
- Challenge;
- Well-defined objectives linked to the business plan;
- Regular honest feedback and evaluation;
- Trust, participation, and involvement;
- Encouragement of innovative and creative behavior;
- Support in the form of counseling, training, etc.; and
- Room to grow.

These conditions fall within Herzberg's (1959) category of *motivators*. However, what he defines as *satisfiers* also must be present. Emery (1959) and Trist (1963) list them as (1) fair and adequate pay, (2) job security, (3) benefits, (4) safety, (5) health, and (6) due process.

Members of management frequently overlook the impact of missing satisfiers on motivation. They regard themselves as above "paper towels and toilet paper" disputes so long as *they* are well-provided for. Their motivators often do not exist on the shop floor or the front line.

Working Together

Anything in performance management that dampens enthusiasm is likely to be counterproductive. Increasing enthusiasm is the goal. This is best done by involving employees in planning (including the means of evaluation), aiming for a win-win outcome, and passing down as much responsibility as possible. It is critically important that commitment is not nominal but total and that the accountability to which team members are held is matched by equal responsibility.

An area that especially requires responsibility and trust is innovation. Drucker (1992) says that "the greatest change of all is probably that in the last 40 years purposeful innovation—both technical and social—has itself become an organized discipline that is both teachable and learnable" (p. 97) Even if learned, this skill will not be practiced without an atmosphere of trust.

Spirit in Work

Hawley (1992) says that for an organization to be successful, it must develop spirit. When people start reflecting deeply on their work, they talk about this. He says that organizations must develop from "uncivilized" (in the worst case) to caring, to respectful, and, finally, to reverent. For this to happen, there must be leadership as well as management.

Means Versus Ends

Drucker (1973) observed that "Management is doing things right. Leadership is doing the right thing." If we want to lead others effectively rather than just control processes, we must distinguish between the following:

Inputs and Processes and **Products, Outputs, and Outcomes**[1]
(the how of the job)   (the what and why of the job).

Concentration on products or outputs ensures that work efforts, systems, and resources are directed to doing the right "things" and jobs. Gilbert (1991) offers an account of how these approaches conflict in the Australian Public Service. Employees, when asked, "What do you do here?" responded most often with job titles, rather than naming the product or service they provided. To determine what a job is supposed to produce, employees must first ask themselves, "Who are my customers and what do they rely on me to provide—what are their expectations?"

A customer is anyone who depends on an employee's performance (product/output) to be able to do his or her job effectively. By identifying customers' expectations, employees can:

- Do the right jobs,

- Establish priorities,

- Use resources more efficiently,

- Ensure that efforts (functions/processes) add value,

---

[1] Based on the Organizational Elements Model, Kaufman et al., 1984.

- Establish relevant needs and objectives,
- Make customer satisfaction a top priority, and
- Be available as problem solvers and resources to others.

Internal customers include colleagues, supervisors, staff members, and related departments. Having a customer focus helps an organization become integrated and coordinated rather than operating as a collection of isolated, uncoordinated islands or even warring tribes.

It is more than twenty years since Drucker demonstrated the necessity of turning the traditional organizational pyramid on its head.

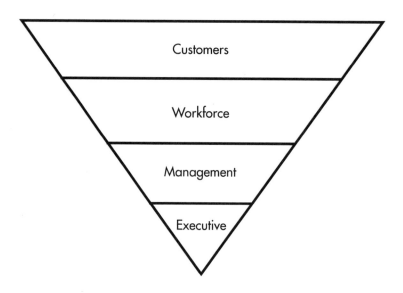

Figure 1. Traditional Organizational Structure "Turned on Its Head" (Drucker, 1974)

Not enough managers followed Drucker's advice. In the late 1980s his concept was rediscovered, and many organizations succeeded in improving their performance by becoming "customer driven."

Once the customer's requirements are translated into outputs, products, and services, we can determine tasks, functions, and processes. We must continually question why a task is performed and what requirement is being fulfilled. If there is no specific output directed toward a customer (internal or external), it is probably irrelevant.[2]

In the world today, the activities of governments and industrial and commercial enterprises are inextricably linked. Employees who are unaware of the full implications of their actions can bring a heavy cost in terms of legal infringements, lost public image, lost opportunities, and even the demise of the company.

Upward Feedback

The advice to put the customer at the top of the hierarchical pyramid was not followed until recently, when feedback to managers ("up" the pyramid) from their reports started to become fashionable (Forbes, 1995a). Farey (1993) instituted the system of upward feedback in the U.K. His Leader/Manager Map draws from fifty years of research to define the behaviors that most fully characterize managers and leaders. He finds that the impact on a manager of feedback from direct reports is far more powerful than that of feedback from peers or a boss. His upward feedback involves facilitated feedback between team and manager, leading to action plans.

---

[2] Concentrating on results alone also can cause problems. Issues such as safety, innovation, and flexibility can be overlooked. Garratt (1990), in his research into disasters in the U.K., tells how a memo from the captain describing dangerous conditions on a cross-Channel ferry was returned with the word "Wimp!" scrawled across it. More than two hundred people died as a result.

Thinking in Systems

The generalization of the feedback process is the systems thinking now popularized by Senge (1990). Even the simplest systems soon fail when treated as static. Wheatley (1992) takes the metaphor further and links organizations with quantum mechanics and chaos. Waldrop (1992) seeks order in chaos more broadly, showing that humans can never be "outside" a system they influence (can never ultimately "win" if someone or something "loses") and finds innovation at "the edge of chaos." Patterns and systems self-organize. This kind of thinking is increasingly a requirement in managing performance. Jacques and Clement (1991) insist that the level of an individual's cognitive power must match the level of complexity he or she has to manage.

Work, Life, and Motivation

In our society, life without work is generally very difficult (even those in retirement can suffer from the lack of work). Work is an essential part of our relationship to society and our adjustment to life, the manifestation of our basic drive to create, and the predominant way in which we acquire personal and financial security and recreation.[3] This is a major theme of the great social philosopher Rousseau (1712-1778), currently restated in the writings of Handy (1989).

What we work at ultimately creates the society in which we live. Therefore, we must ensure that in meeting our requirement to work, there can be both social and personal

---

[3] The people who shirk on the job are often found working hard at home or socially, at anything from home renovation or community activity to playing the horses. That work is a human requirement in our society has been recognized by the Australian Medical Association, which recently identified unemployment as a contributing factor to untimely death.

value. Selye (1974) summarized forty years of research in which he established the proposition that work is as natural as play for humans. McGregor (1960) pointed out that it is only the context in which the effort takes place and the reward systems that vary. There is a source of energy available for organizations that know how to make work meaningful to their people.

What Workers Want

Larkin (1992) has examined worker-supervisor relationships and demonstrated that the effective way to raise productivity and safety is to have the supervisors "talk performance," not statistics, directly to their workers, in their language. This agrees with the research of Herzberg (1959) and Maslow (1943), in that people at work like to be successful and part of a winning team.

Repeated research in first-world countries (Kovach, 1987) indicates that the top ten rewards employees seek are as follows:

1. interesting work,

2. full appreciation of work done,

3. a feeling of being in on things,

4. job security,

5. good wages,

6. promotion and growth in the organization,

7. good working conditions,

8. management's personal loyalty to employees,

9. tactful discipline, and

10. sympathetic help with personal problems.

Managers surveyed, on the other hand, think that "good wages" come first. Real motivation requires collaboration on job design to ensure that the task is matched to what people want.

All performance management must be part of "continuous improvement" (Drucker, 1992) and, therefore, the goals must constantly be reevaluated and changed. Retaining high performers in particular requires an environment of challenge, appreciation, removal of red tape, and career opportunities (Gray, 1988). This likely can be said of most employees.

In summary, because people want to work, it makes sense to design a job to make it as exciting, interesting, and fulfilling as possible (this may require some creative thinking). In any case, managers should talk to people honestly about how they are performing. Everyone in the organization must understand the mega approach.

Requirement for the Mega Level

Many managers pay lip service to the motto: "Our people are our greatest asset." Few organizations, public or private, show staff members in the assets section of the balance sheet. Likert argued for human-asset accounting in 1967. Knowles (1973) states that the human resource development budget should be handled as a capital investment, and Handy (1989) says that labor is an asset. Yet, staff members are still shown as an expense (cost) in the income and expenditure statements of almost all organizations. There are no "maintenance agreements" or "investment management portfolios" allocated to ensure maximum utilization of, and return from, the workforce. One result of this is that professionals tend to be loyal to themselves, or to an industry, rather than to an organization, while workers lack a sense of mutual obligation.

In helping to harness full human potential, the mega approach to performance management provides opportunities to:

- Develop individuals in the workforce;

- Release, encourage, and nurture creativity, talents, and skills;

- Increase concepts of responsibility to colleagues, clients, and customers;

- Contribute to society's well-being;

- Optimize resource utilization and preservation by those responsible for their use; and

- Create a global viewpoint in terms of the full spectrum of human enterprise.

The mega level adds society to the top of Drucker's inverted pyramid. Drucker (1992) states that "each organization has a value system that is determined by its task." An integrated approach to benefiting from diverse possibilities while also responding to other pressures and impositions has been provided by Kaufman (1992), with extensions by Humphries and Forbes (1993).

Self-Management

Our culture today is moving toward self-management. Patients in hospitals are allowed to administer their own levels of pain medication (and, as a result, take less); people are increasingly expected to manage their own careers and their own jobs. This brings out abilities that have previously been stifled in authoritarian structures.

Self-Managing Teams

Industries of all kinds are adopting the use of self-managing teams (SMTs). Each task group assumes its own supervisory role and inspects its own outputs. SMT members agree on ways to achieve targets, have high expectations of one another, are rewarded as a team, and hold themselves accountable for the tasks they take on. Although there is still some opposition to such groups because of past failures, there are many successes to report. SMTs in a Yorkshire coal mine were described in 1949 by an associate of Trist at the Tavistock Institute in London. Emery (1959) has pioneered the use of SMTs in Australia and Norway. Emery also introduced "open systems" thinking to Tavistock. The importance of systems thinking becomes obvious when designing the work of a self-managing group; soon the whole organization must be involved. The problem becomes one of ecology.

Emery clearly distinguishes between forms of "participation," "consultation," etc., and "democratization of work." The overriding aim is to get teams fully contributing and participating in the achievement of agreed goals. In this scenario, both managers and teams have rights and responsibilities, with teams having optimal (not maximum) freedom. Leadership is not static; multiskilling makes jobs interchangeable; and mutual training and learning are a natural consequence. Former supervisors take on roles as coaches, linkpeople, and boundary riders. They set or guard the goals and values and work on the team from the outside, providing feedback and avoiding task involvement. Although management traditionally has accepted the suboptimal solution of optimizing the technical or, on occasion, the social system, Emery's design leads to joint optimization of "sociotechnical" systems.

Emery's "six human requirements" for SMTs are:

- elbow room (be your own boss),

- a chance to learn on the job,

- optimal variety (avoid boredom, allow work rhythms),

- conditions of mutual help and respect,

- contributing meaningful work (societal context), and

- a desirable future (not a dead-end job).

Among the factors that have sometimes caused SMTs to fail are laissez-faire policies, structures that look like SMTs but are not truly participative, and the lack of trust in management support. Weisbord developed self-managing teams in the United States beginning in the 1960s, and his book, *Productive Workplaces* (1987), is a key resource in this area.

Levels of self-management are linked to leadership style and success in Australian organizations by Stace and Dunphy (1994). A structure involving high-level self-management is described by Mills (1991) as the "cluster group"—pulling together managers or specialists (or workers) from different areas, around a common goal. Semler (1993) in Brazil takes self-management so seriously that managers are rated by their teams, and some set their own pay.

Most of what is discussed here about performance management actually applies as much to self-managing groups as to individuals.

Self-management ultimately depends on human interactions, the organizational culture, and a general feeling of empowerment.

The Impact of Managerial Behavior on Performance

What benefit is it to the organization if short-term goals are met but the manager's behavior leads to industrial unrest, sabotage, or high staff turnover with loss of skills and knowledge?

Team Building

In the long run, successful enterprises are made up of successful teams. The ability of the manager to act as team builder is critical to the overall performance of the members of the group. Ultimately, good teamwork results from a facilitative leader who can encourage the team to work at its best without close supervision—a step toward self-management.

Regressing

Garratt (1990) describes newly promoted U.K. directors who, unsure of what they are supposed to do, revert to doing their old jobs. This affects the managers below as each, in turn, is pushed back into a lower role.

Team Role Preference

Several instruments are available to measure the roles that people prefer to take in teams (e.g., the *Margerison-McCann Team Management Index*, 1990; the *Belbin Team-Roles Inventory*, 1994). Aligning people's preferences with the roles required by the team leads to high team performance.

The Self-Fulfilling Prophecy

How we expect others to behave determines how we ourselves act toward them. If we have negative expectations (beliefs) about someone, our behavior will reflect how we feel, and we are likely to get the behavior we expect. This, of course, can severely impact appraisal.

Stereotypical beliefs are at work when organizations are divided into three performance levels: top, middle, and bottom. Often the employees at top levels receive favored treatment, encouragement, and support; efforts are made to retain them; and their mistakes are tolerated more frequently. The lower levels stagnate or leave—justifying the original beliefs (Livingstone, 1974).

Hawley (1992) describes how beliefs are built up and how they can suddenly be altered in individuals or in an entire organization. This gives a way to open the path to change. Peters (1992) picks trust as the missing "X-factor" in high-performing organizations. Trust grows from belief plus risk.

Performance Danger Signals

Performance danger signals include the following:

- Missing days, sickness, the "long weekend";

- Arriving late and leaving early;

- Indications of liquor or drug use;

- Unusual emotional states (may indicate personal stress or drug abuse);

- Poor health or poor health habits;

- Personal problems; and

- Unusual or erratic performance or behavior.

Although anyone can notice that a person frequently is missing on Monday, some manifestations require an observer trained in reading body language, facial expression, eye contact, and voice qualities. This suggests that managers should be well-trained in advanced communication skills. Managers' reluctance to recognize and deal with such problems increases when they have to act on the more subtle clues. However, when performance is affected, managers have the right to test out their impressions. Self-managing teams are generally quicker to confront the real issues, hence indicators such as absenteeism regularly decline with SMTs (Emery, 1989).

Counseling

Conducting a counseling interview with an employee requires that the manager have strong interpersonal skills. The manager must create a nonthreatening environment and encourage and willingly receive ideas and criticisms that may otherwise be held back. The point is not to judge, criticize, and challenge, but to open up dialogue, negotiate solutions, and hold individuals accountable for mutually agreed-on results.

Larkin (1992) states that most employees say that their failings are not pointed out to them and that there is too much tolerance of poor-quality work. Benchmarking performance against other organizations can tap in to the basic human qualities of pride, shame, and ultimately, our tribal sense. At the same time, Beer, Eisenstat, and Spector (1990) find "pay-for-performance" to be ineffective.

Gratton and Pearson (1993) show that bosses do not value subordinate managers for their empowering characteristics as much as do the manager's direct reports (this is reinforced by the research of Farey, 1995a).

Differences of Style

Differences in interpersonal relating styles and styles of communication can frequently create various issues among team members and between a team leader and team members. For example, some people use "big picture/bottom line" talk (they talk in telegrams and conclusions and expect you to interpret them) while others talk "detail." Managers and team members who have been trained to recognize and deal with different styles have a better chance of working effectively with others.

Competence Modeling

Modeling provides a framework in which managers can assess themselves and others against behavior and skill norms in their own or similar organizations. The results then provide a basis for professional development. Such required management competencies vary widely between industries, sometimes even in the same organization. A comparison between industries and a system for generating competencies is offered by Farey (1995b).

Corporate Culture and Risk

If we look to traditional techniques of organizational change, then any policy, philosophy, or change of practice must start at the top of the organization and filter down. Senior management must set the example and continually follow up and reinforce the processes. They do so within the corporate culture—"the way we do things around here." Commitment to the corporate mega plan within that culture has to be encouraged at all levels and in all functions.

However, research (Beer, Eisenstat, & Spector, 1990) shows that real change in the way things are done generally begins at some other point in the organization, where enough momentum can be generated. The role of senior management then becomes one of facilitating—fostering champions. In our own work, we have trained teams made up largely of staff members as change facilitators. Their job is to find problems and encourage others to fix them. They have become highly respected for their abilities. Their success depends ultimately on management support. Wherever change may start, the organization will ultimately have to achieve some kind of consensus, framed in strategic terms.

Critical to an organization's health is the right of employees to speak their minds without fear. Two key elements in performance management are upward feedback and an open door policy—the right to take a problem higher if a direct manager will not respond satisfactorily.

Implementing the Mega Plan

Performance management requires commitment, consultation, discussion, participation, and contribution from all levels. Understanding of the organization's mega plan makes possible:

- Commitment to the mega plan;

- Opportunity to contribute;

- A common vision, value system, and focal point for the whole organization;

- Incentive for initiative;

- A mind-set for a customer and community orientation;

- Anticipation of changing social values, market forces, community requirements; and, therefore,

- The likelihood of creative and innovative thinking and behavior patterns.

The following help to make the mega plan operative:

- Information given to prospective employees through recruitment advertising, literature, and face to face meetings;

- Induction and orientation programs to emphasize performance management and the mega-plan concept;

- Performance-appraisal sessions to encourage setting of objectives relevant to macro and mega plans, directed to customer satisfaction, community well-being, and social responsibility;

- Participative sessions on problem-identification-and-resolution;

- Participative sessions on work-improvement-and-innovation;

- Training and development programs based on skills acquisition and development of knowledge and attitudes conducive to the corporate mega plan;

- Counseling facilities; and

- Suggestion, reward, and incentive schemes.

On-the-Job Training

Employees at all levels should be encouraged to attend workshops, seminars, and in-house training programs that link job performance to the organization's micro, macro, and mega plans. The focus on the customer and on society and the environment should be present in all organizational activities and training.

References

Beer, M., Eisenstat, R.A., & Spector, B. (1990). *The critical path to corporate renewal*. Cambridge, MA: Harvard Business School Press.

Belbin, M. (1994). *The Belbin Team-Roles Package*. San Diego, CA: Pfeiffer & Company.

Drucker, P. (1974). *Management: Tasks, responsibilities, practices*. New York: Harper & Row.

Drucker, P. (1992, September-October). The new society of organizations. *Harvard Business Review*.

Emery, F.E. (1959). *Characteristics of socio-technical systems*. London: Tavistock. Also in *The emergence of a new paradigm at work*. Canberra: Australian National University, Centre for Continuing Education.

Emery, M. (Ed.) (1989). *Participative design for participative democracy.* Canberra: Australian National University, Centre for Continuing Education.

Farey, P. (1993). Mapping the leader/manager. In *Management education and development* (Vol. 24, Part 2). Lancaster, UK: Lancaster University.

Farey, P. (1995a). *The leader/manager framework in practice.* Unpublished monograph. [Peter Farey Training & Development, 21 Warren Wood Drive, High Wycombe, Bucks, HP11 1EA, UK.]

Farey, P. (1995b). *Competency studies: Some concerns.* Unpublished monograph. [Peter Farey Training & Development, 21 Warren Wood Drive, High Wycombe, Bucks, HP11 1EA, UK.]

Forbes, R. (1995a, August). What Karpin forgot. *The Company Director.*

Forbes, R. (1995b, October). Upward feedback: The neglected wisdom. *Management.*

Garratt, B. (1990). *Learning to lead.* London: Fontana.

Gilbert, R. (1991). *Reglomania. The curse of organisational reform and how to cure it.* Sydney: Australian Institute of Management & Prentice Hall, Australia.

Gray, R. (1988). *Proven strategies for retaining top performers.* Sydney: IIR Conference.

Gratton, L., & Pearson, J. (1993, January). *Empowering leaders: Are they being developed?* Paper presented at the UK Conference of Occupational Psychology, London.

Handy, C. (1989). *The age of unreason.* London: Basic Books.

Hawley, J. (1992). *Reawakening the spirit in work: The power of dharmic management.* San Francisco, CA: Berrett-Koehler.

Herzberg, F. (1959). *The motivation to work.* New York: John Wiley.

Humphries, E., & Forbes, R. (1993). The challenge of mandated organisational change. *Proceedings of Qualcon '93.* Brisbane: Australian Organization for Quality.

Jacques, E., & Clement, D. (1991). *Executive leadership: A practical guide to managing complexity.* Oxford: Blackwell.

Kaufman, R. (1992). *Strategic planning plus.* Newbury Park, CA: Sage.

Kaufman, R., Mayer, H., & Butz, R. (1984). *Defining and classifying the organizational elements.*

Knowles, M. (1973). *The adult learner: A neglected species.* Houston, TX: Gulf.

Kovach, K.A. (1987, September-October). What motivates employees? Workers and supervisors give different answers. *Business Horizons* (US).

Larkin, T.J. (1992). *Communicating change to employees.* Melbourne: Australian Human Resources Institute.

Likert, R. (1967). *The human organization: Its management and value.* New York: McGraw-Hill.

Livingstone, J.S. (1974). *Productivity and the self-fulfilling prophesy.* New York: McGraw-Hill/CRM Video.

Maslow, A.H. (1943). A theory of human motivation. *Psychological Review, 50.*

Margerison, C., & McCann, D. (1990). *Team management: Practical new approaches.* London: W.H. Allen.

McGregor, D. (1960). *The human side of enterprise.* New York: McGraw-Hill.

Mills, D.Q. (1991). *Rebirth of the corporation.* New York: John Wiley.

Peters, T. (1992). *Liberation management: Necessary disorganization for the nanosecond nineties.* New York: Knopf.

Selye, H. (1974). *Stress without distress.* New York: Harper & Row.

Semler, R. (1993). *Maverick.* London: Century Business.

Senge, P. (1990). *The fifth discipline.* New York: Doubleday.

Stace, D., & Dunphy, D. (1994). *Beyond the boundaries.* Sydney: McGraw Hill.

Trist, E.L., Higgin, G.W., Murray, H., & Pollock, A.B. (1963). *Organizational choice: The loss, re-discovery, and transformation of a work tradition.* London: Tavistock.

Waldrop, M. (1992). *Complexity, the emerging science at the edge of order.* New York: Simon & Schuster.

Weisbord, M. (1987). *Productive workplaces.* San Francisco, CA: Jossey-Bass.

Wheatley, M. (1992). *Leadership and the new science: Learning about organization from an orderly universe.* San Francisco, CA: Berrett-Koehler.

PROGRAM MANAGEMENT: ITS RELATIONSHIP TO THE PROJECT

Richard A. Cornell

Cheops gathered together his administrative team saying to all, "I want you to build an edifice, one dedicated to my name and one so massive that even our worst enemies will revere it. But first, you must organize this project in such a way that it will be completed before my passing...it must come in on schedule, no matter the cost (for we are indeed laden with gold!) nor the lives of those taken in its building. Go now forth and listen to your project director, for he acts as me."

Cheops's vision held, notwithstanding innumerable cost overruns, delays in materials shipped, and countless lives lost to industrial accidents. Scholars remain mystified as to how the Great Pyramid was engineered, let alone constructed. Beginning with a single pyramid (project), numerous others arose from Egypt's burning sands (a program). Missteps aside, they remain as mute testimony to history's earliest project management efforts (Dean, 1985).

When we have been tasked by our organization to manage a project, a need/want exists. Although our efforts do not include pyramid building, the desire to achieve exists.

Management involves innumerable elements. This article deals with five: people, time, money, the evolution of product, and the evolution of process, as the latter two relate to the former three. Within this context we delineate between the three basic, yet critical, levels: micro, macro, and mega. The aim is to make clear in what stage of a given process a particular category falls.

The individual project falls within the micro level of planning and delivery. Put a number of projects together and the result becomes a program that, if sufficiently encompassing and of high quality, may well transcend the macro level into that of the mega. Isn't that the "ideal" toward which all of us strive—to have done so well on a project that it is emulated well beyond our immediate corporate environment?

Although this chapter contains "program" within its title, it is the individual "project" level that forms the basis of achievement. King addresses generic strategic-choice elements to be made in any strategic planning process, one of which is designated "Programs/Projects" and defined as being "resource-consuming sets of activities through which strategies are implemented and goals are pursued" (Dean, 1985, p. 5).

Within the context of his overall strategic planning model, he depicts the diverse elements, one of which is "programs." He contends that it is the requisite interaction between and among that element and the others that ultimately contributes to the success (or lack of success) of the corporate mission (see Figure 1).

It is the project that forms the stepping stone to the program. That is why the material covered in this chapter stresses the importance of both project and program; one begets the other.

A number of practitioners were consulted in an effort to differentiate between conflict and agreement over problems of project/program management. Each consultant was asked,

"What are the major problems you face, start to finish, in managing a project for your organization?"

The practitioners were from private contractors to the Department of Defense (DOD), a large banking organization, and a leading entertainment/resort conglomerate. The DOD contractors have increasingly taken steps to diversify through the inclusion of nonmilitary clients.

Their answers tended to reflect their work environments and corporate objectives. Those organizations immersed in high-technology-dependent systems (and philosophies) reflected technological concerns. Service-oriented organizations highlighted problems related more to people than to things.

In the DOD-related sector, two micro-level problems were identified, both of which had macro and mega significance. As might be expected, the first major problem posed was that of continually changing technologies, occurring in the midst of a project.

(From William King, in Dean, 1985.)

Figure 1. Relationship Between Strategic Choice Elements

The schism between software and hardware development was said to be the cause of the changes. Specifically, "within long-term training and development cycles, the training platforms keep changing" (Fisher, 1992). An example of such changes was the development of the "Windows environment" now being used in the design and development of computer-based instruction. The impact of this software was that, literally overnight, earlier software became incompatible. The result was software obsolescence in the midst of a project.

It is not unusual for a project to last from three to five years from the time it is bid to the time of final delivery. It is reasonable to expect that the customer wants the completed project to reflect the latest software rather than a software program that has been replaced.

The solution to this problem, one defined in a micro sense, can rapidly take on macro or even mega proportions when the parties involved attempt resolution.

Limited alternatives may be employed. All require finesse in negotiation. You may (a) opt not to use the new software; (b) revise and compromise using the emerged product; or (c) capitulate to the client and use the new platform. Numerous factors will determine which option is chosen, but none favor the developer.

A second problem cited by the technology-based organizations was the need for good, ongoing communication between all parties involved in the design and development of a project. "People" issues aside, the problem once again traces its origins to the continually changing technologies that instructional developers must face.

The challenge lies in learning how to manage the creative process with so many options available. For example, one may now, with digital video processing cards (IBM in-Motion, Eliminator 16, DVA 4000, and others), manipulate images at the computer rather than only in the video suite.

To be successful, the instructional systems designer must know the specific system capabilities, be intimately familiar with the specific platform being used to both design and operate the system, and continually communicate with the programmer and video personnel.

Typically, however, there has been a tendency to compartmentalize rather than to communicate. Each "expert" does his or her own thing, often to the detriment of the overall project.

In addition, project managers have had to develop their own computer-based project-management software packages. Although commercially available products (e.g., McProject, Keyplan) were outstanding tools for the specific project purposes for which they were developed, they have proved to be unsuitable for other project-design tasks. Altering such software frequently proved difficult because of copyright limitations or because the specific product was so tightly designed (Fisher, 1992).

Some developers have experienced success through the use of software packages such as "Excel" and others that are adaptable to IBM and Macintosh platforms and can be modified without copyright violations. A new computer-based project-management program, soon to be delivered to the U.S. Navy, permits increased levels of excellence in the management function (Spears, 1992).

When the question of problems associated with program and project management was posed to Robert Spears of Simms Industries, he raised five major concerns:

1. There is inadequate definition of what is desired by the customer. Both the instructional systems designer (ISD) working "in the trenches" and the customer must agree completely on this issue. If miscommunication occurs, the ISD group will produce the wrong product or the customer will constantly change his or

her mind as to what is wanted, with a resultant increase in both time and effort, as well as increased costs for all.

2. Communication channels between line personnel working in both contractor and customer facilities ought to be continually open. Each of the concerned parties should clearly understand when decisions may be made at lower levels and when they must be made by higher authorities.

3. Accurate estimates of the level of effort required to complete a product or deliverable must be the norm, not the exception. If accuracy in forecasting is lacking, expect major problems between client and customer. Frequently, management estimates are in error, in part because hour actuals are dependent on the competency and efficiency of those tasked with completing the work. Good managers understand the capabilities of project personnel sufficiently to make accurate estimates.

4. Milestones established for design and development are often unrealistic, often because the project schedules have been so from the beginning. If these unrealistic milestones cannot be readjusted, late deliveries and missed production dates result. This, in turn, may give rise to negative contractual implications.

5. Finally, improper utilization of personnel and inadequately trained personnel were cited as being problematic (Spears, 1992).

Another DOD contractor traced similar sets of problems. Thomas Terrell of Regency Systems, Inc., began his analysis of problems associated with program/project management by beginning with the following assumptions:

1. There exists a product/deliverable orientation within the company.

2. Hardware is viewed with the current task order in mind and deliverable products are designed and produced around the capabilities and constraints dictated by the current hardware.

3. Project management starts from the position that there is an ideal project design that is immediately modified to accommodate extant skills of personnel and capabilities of available hardware.

4. Project management tries to produce what the marketing department sells.

Problems connected to these assumptions include:

1. The project manager never has enough time, personnel, or hardware.

2. Next year's product is being produced with last year's hardware.

3. All programmers want to design instruction, and most designers want to program—until the going gets rough!

4. Everyone wants to produce video.

5. Nobody wants to stay within budget.

Terrell cited the following program-management assumptions:

1. Products are viewed as components of an overall business plan.

2. Personnel consideration is given to allow mentoring and tracking of individual opportunities required to acquire sets of skills.

3. Long-term issues, such as developing project managers, must be planned for in advance.

4. Hardware is acquired to develop capabilities within a market niche.

5. Program management tries to direct what the marketing department should be selling.

Aspects associated with these assumptions included:

1. Project managers always want more money/hardware/people/time.

2. Other options must be encouraged to maximize available assets. Listening to the project manager will alert one to how feasible a given option might be, as he or she is tasked with actual implementation and knows both people and projects better than does the program manager.

3. Micro-managing projects by the program manager is often the cause of much frustration, loss of motivation, and just plain bad product.

4. Often a program manager's knowledge of production is outdated, content knowledge is superficial, and attention is distracted by multiple projects. Because the program manager signs the time sheets, however, his or her whims are followed to the letter.

5. Shift scheduling can maximize hardware productivity and reduce calendar time expended. With luck, productivity can actually be increased by aligning workers with their natural energy cycles.

6. The program manager's role is to provide direction and support, including constraints, to project managers. The program manager must delegate authority com-

mensurate with responsibility and provide information without constraint. The smallest detail omitted can bankrupt a company if left undetected until the last minute.

Terrell concluded that if the customer and client are to come together successfully, they must bridge the gaps in their knowledge. The customer knows the desired outcome and has content knowledge, while the production team knows how best to achieve the goal. The project manager is in constant contact with both parties and facilitates their communication; thus, he or she becomes the communications bridge. The program manager supports this bridge and everyone on it. When the program manager forgets this support role and tries to walk on the bridge, support vanishes and everything falls apart (Terrell, 1992).

The final interviewee, Bickel, comes from a major entertainment and resort organization. Bickel cited twelve major concerns:

1. Sufficient support and commitment from operations to implement a given program.

2. Communicating of project components and benefits to all involved.

3. Getting all involved in the program development by means of focus groups, input, and implementation so that employees develop a true commitment to and buyoff of the project/program.

4. Communicating overall guidelines, quality standards, program guidelines, and mission or goal of the project to employees.

5. Having sufficient time and money to properly carry out the project and ensure its effectiveness.

6. Dealing with apprehension induced through change; overcoming initial defensiveness to the program by the employees.

7. Maintaining momentum of the program after initial implementation; avoiding falling into the "old ways."

8. Troubleshooting—thinking of all possible details, obstacles, problems, or alternatives that may arise prior to implementation, thus ensuring a "snag-free" program.

9. Daily follow-through or follow-up by all involved to ensure long-term impact of the program.

10. Delegating responsibilities of a project and verifying that everyone is working toward the common goal and maintaining consistency.

11. Upper management support, understanding, and buyoff on the importance and potential impact of the program.

12. Taking concepts, themes, ideas, and program components and translating them into practical applications in the work environment (Bickel, 1992).

The respondents addressed emerging issues with which project and program managers must contend in addition to their continual attention to the basics of project management. To some of our readers, requisite steps in project and program management are akin to an automatic response system—they have been doing it so long, it has become second nature, even to the point of short-cutting certain steps or greatly reducing the time spent on some elements of the process.

There are others for whom the task of managing either project or program has become an elusive target, either because they have never had to do it or because, even if asked, they would decline, lest they fail.

Project and program management do not have to be laden with mystery; they rely heavily on common sense. Being able to plan ahead and to anticipate wants all along the line is a vital key to success.

Over the years we have created a great deal of jargon related to how projects and programs should be managed. Many terms evolved during the 1960s. It was during those years that PERT (project evaluation and review technique) became a managerial household word, as did Gantt Chart, PPBS (program planning budget system), CPM (critical path management), and a host of other acronyms. All of these depend on one basic strategy for success—the ability to plan ahead! Pertinent authors include Badiru (1988), Badiru and Whitehouse (1989), Bergen (1986), Dinsmore (1990), Frame (1987), and House (1988). These, while far from being all-inclusive, are major sources of some of the ideas presented in this chapter. For further scholarly work, see Cleland (1990), Goodman (1988), Hannum & Hansen (1989), Kerzner (1982), Roman (1986), Silverman (1988), and Tompkins (1985).

Perusal of most of these will reveal the following generic categories, each of which holds significance for the manager of projects and programs:

- Overview of basic management principles

- Organization and human resources requirements for projects

- Selection and planning requisites

- Availability of networks to assist in analysis

- Scheduling and cost-control elements

- Implementation of the project

- Evaluation of the project—formative and summative

- Lessons learned

Although volumes related to management exist, only a few have relevance for project and program managers. Taking each of the above categories and applying performance-based common sense, we will try to bring clarity to the arena of program and project management.

Basic Management Principles

Basic management principles mean a return to some fundamental truths and a heightened awareness that, within each of our organizations, there exists a "mission," a corporate raison d'étre. Corporate mission statements vary according to a number of elements, among them the product or process delivered, the geographic and product niche being served, the influence of executive officers and/or stockholders, and the wherewithal to deliver.

For example, an organization might have lofty ambitions and state them boldly in an annual report, yet be unable to deliver when challenged to do so. An organization, anticipating (or fearing) takeover, may "inflate" both its mission and its capability statements, thus making its holdings appear more attractive.

Regardless of how the mission statement is posited, basic management principles dictate that all within the organization know the goals of their employer and, more importantly, that they buy into them from the outset. There are numerous instances wherein a clear and universally accepted mission statement was not in evidence, and employee performance from the line to front office suffered drastically. The proverbial right and left hands did not know what was expected of the other.

In project and program management, if you don't know where it is you are headed, expect the trip to be long, torturous, and unfulfilled.

All must know the organizational mission and adopt it fully. If people do not feel positive about the organization, they will be continually looking for the next opportunity—outside their work site.

The project/program director should know that the team not only knows where it is going, but also that it is enthusiastically looking forward to the trip! Implicit in this basic management concept is clear, concise, and accurate communication at every level within the organization. It does little good if the employees can reiterate the organization's primary goals if they run adrift trying to analyze how the process will occur. It is in this realm that the role of project management within the context of team is vital, especially in view of contemporary technology-based work environments, in which change occurs with increasing rapidity.

Organization and Human Resources Requirements

The role of organizational "expert" is, at best, dubious when considering continual changes in process or product dictated by market shifts, technological updates, or sociopolitical forces that lie beyond the control of the organization. Although the concept of teamwork has waxed and waned over the past fifty years, the drive for organizational excellence and quality control mandates its resurgence as never before.

Increasingly, the face of business, industry, education, and government is changing from an autocratic, top-down management style to that of participative management. This change is a two-edged blade in that, while top and middle management may have had previous experience with alternative management paradigms, those "on the line" frequently have not. In short, they are unused to being asked what they think should be done, and how, when, and why.

A similar scenario is being played out in much of Eastern Europe and presents itself as an appropriate analogy. For the past forty or more years, entire nations have been subjected to dogma from birth to death. Essential skills were taught devoid of Western democratic values; only the "basics" requisite to laborer survival were stressed. Like their analogous counterparts in Western organizations, many will require "unlearning" and many more will want to acquire new competencies. No longer will Eastern bloc workforces rely on close adherence to the "party line" as a prerequisite to being hired and retained. No longer will Western workforces rely solely on the "word from above" as they supply product or process. Indeed, for both groups there will be massive realignments in how the organization is perceived and in how projects and programs are planned, implemented, and evaluated.

Selection and Planning Requisites

Determination of what projects and programs are selected by an organization has historically been a top-down process. As participatory management increases, such selection and identification of priorities will be spread among the workforce, and shared decision making will become the norm. Governing boards and officers of the organization will continue to impact decisions but, in many cases, the concept of shared responsibility will emerge more frequently.

Decisions will be made on the basis of diverse variables, i.e., environmental impact, social and/or political consequences, availability of resources, fragility of resources when available, market demand based on real versus perceived need, and above all, organizational accountability.

Like other aspects of organizational behavior, projects and programs will reach well beyond just the organization and into the community. The decision as to which projects and programs to undertake will less frequently be solely the organization's decision.

Availability of Analysis Networks

In the past, much of the analysis required during and at the conclusion of a project or program was conducted by only a few—often the chief operating officers of the organization. Such analyses were, at best, speculative and based on intuition, as opposed to hard data. It was reasoned that, if the analyzer possessed sufficient experience within the given situation, and all salient facts relevant to the production of product or process were available, either the analyst and/or a representative team could debrief the result and learn how to improve performance the next time.

In a simple manufacturing organization devoted to the production of a single product, such might have been the case. In today's organizational environment, however, the preponderance of technology-based systems, for either product or process, mitigates against this, and simplistic analytical methodologies will not suffice. "...high technology projects require more innovative approaches. Necessity may be the mother of invention, but need is going to be the father of innovation" (Badiru, 1988, p. vii). Indeed, the requirement for innovative approaches becomes foremost when high technology enters the picture. Not only does the speed at which such technology changes have an impact on analyses, but the available methodologies for performance measurement also do.

Key among the concepts that direct how analyses are conducted is the capability to go "on-line" between various members of the project team throughout the duration of a task. Formative evaluations occur, sometimes within milliseconds, thus saving the organization costly overruns, specification errors, or judgment errors. Numerous other process-related steps along the way can be caught, almost as they happen.

Computer-based "shareware" allows team members to participate simultaneously via local area networks (LANs) in analysis, design, development, implementation, and evaluation, thus using the congregate best to produce the end result.

Additionally, when network-based communication linkages are employed, there is a concomitant reduction in the number of interpersonal conflicts, if for no other reason than the avoidance of face-to-face disagreements between team members.

There has been a major move away from hand-created PERT and Gantt Charts. In their place have come the computer and a systems approach to program/project development and implementation. Badiru and Whitehouse (1989) provide an excellent overview of where project management is going via the computer and a multitude of valuable how-to chapters covering this relatively new development.

As a critical "high touch" balance to this emergent pattern of technology-based project planning and implementation, both House (1988) and Dinsmore (1990) concern themselves primarily with the quality of the person-machine interaction. It is interesting to compare earlier management books with the emphasis taken by both House and Dinsmore.

Inclusion of the "high touch" element is not accidental in this chapter. Given the direction of organizations and how they are and will be managed, discussion of high touch should be considered *de rigueur* in all future technology-based works.

Scheduling and Cost Control

No matter how sophisticated or unsophisticated the project manager might be, the bottom line revolves around cost. Prudent administrators rarely let such concerns slip beyond their grasp, because it is to their and the organization's advantage to bring in the project within budget. Those who lose sight of this fiscal fact of life will have a short-lived tenure within the organization.

Numerous mathematical formulae are designed to address cost control and scheduling, including a variety of spreadsheets (LOTUS 1-2-3, D-Base I, II, etc.).

In cost analyses and product/materials/process scheduling, being penny-wise can sometimes be pound-foolish. The "need" for immediate results can be costly, as can insufficient advance planning to ensure that the unexpected can be dealt with in the most expedient manner.

The thought of being overly expedient can send shivers up and down the back of even a careful project manager, not just the one who, working solely from an intuitive base, directs the team along a course destined toward defeat.

Everything discussed in this chapter has advance planning as its foundation for success.

Purchasing and scheduling policies and procedures should take their cue from historical necessity blended with anticipatory vision as to what the next hour, day, week, year, or decade will hold. The variables with which the project/program manager must contend become increasingly complex with both internal and external factors impinging on what decisions are to be made.

Although there is a wealth of sophisticated planning and implementation technology available to the planner, a strong sense of self, common sense, and the ability to share information with the team as the decision process occurs are the manager's best assets.

Implementation of the Project

Finally, there comes that time when all the facts, the projections, and forecasting are in, the manpower and materials assessments completed, and the assembly process readied. If you and your team have developed a list of performance indicators, factored in all the variables you could anticipate, and all else is in readiness, you and the organization are ready to implement.

Conditional in all the next steps is the fact that you and your team have conducted ongoing evaluation, that you have projected possible anomalies, and made allowances for them. The implementation process is analogous to a 747 pilot readying the aircraft for takeoff. The pilot does not conduct this process alone. Before the aircraft left the maintenance hanger after its last flight, it had been checked from one end to the other, inside and out. Before the captain ever climbed into the seat, the first or second officer conducted a walk-around of the aircraft, consulted the aircraft log, and noted any potential indicators that the latest inspection might predict an in-flight problem. Fuel calculations were computed on the basis of passenger, baggage, and cargo weights as well as distance to be flown, weather en route, time of day or night, and season of the year at both ends of the trip.

Similarly, before beginning implementation of any project or program, checklists must be devised that measure outputs and the tolerances acceptable at each stage of the process. If all the requisite data accumulated from the planning phase to implementation are available for final checkout, why delay?

Evaluation of the Project—Formative and Summative

Evaluation left to the end of a project spells disaster! If done on an ongoing (formative) basis, it increases the chances for success. Evaluation, if done honestly and shared by all team members, can be both a painful and a joyful process.

If, in your analyses and cost-projecting, you have been both fair and wise, you have insisted that the evaluation be conducted in-process as well as at the conclusion of the task. There are organizations that, seeking to maximize profit and lessen overhead, cut short the evaluation, sometimes hardly conducting any at all. They think, "Let's get this product out to the client as quickly as we can—they're really hurting for it and want it at any cost." Unfortunately, "at any cost" often cuts out anything but a cursory evaluation process—something destined to eventually return to haunt the contractor.

The project manager working from the autocratic model will most typically be the one to negate the value of ongoing and summative evaluation. The team-based project will most likely insist on it!

Lessons Learned

There is a strong linkage between the evaluation function and lessons learned, because one typically is an outgrowth of the other. Simply put, if your organization was asked back (to produce more product, conduct more seminars, create more programs, etc.), you were successful.

Success that breeds complacency is a pitfall that can be avoided by generous doses of honesty. Get your team together and debrief every aspect of the process, beginning to end. Identify what went right and, more importantly, what did not. Put all egos aside throughout the lessons-learned process. Share with your client how the next set of tasks will be even better than those previously accomplished, thus instilling greater confidence in your team by the client. Communicate to the team and others in the organization at every level that, because all worked together, success was achieved.

We have covered numerous aspects of project and program management within the matrix of micro, macro, and mega planning. We indicated that there are variables associated with project and program management that have an impact on people, time, money, product, and process. A symbiosis is present to the degree that if one is manipulated, all are affected. We have addressed organizational "wants" as opposed to needs in a proactive rather than reactive context. Finally, we have placed the role of project management within the larger context of program management and subjected both to organizational mission.

The role of technology in the management of both project and program has been emphasized because it is destined to remain with us. Our challenge is to capitalize on the best of what technology has to offer as well as to retain the respect and caring for each other within the rubric of humankind.

References

Badiru, A.B. (1988). *Project management in manufacturing and high technology operations.* New York: John Wiley and Sons.

Badiru, A.B., & Whitehouse, G.E. (1989). *Computer tools, models and techniques for project management.* Blue Ridge Summit, PA: TAB Professional and Reference Books.

Bergen, S.A. (1986). *Project management: An introduction to issues in industrial research and development.* Oxford, UK: Basil Blackwell.

Bickel, J. (1992, January 9). Personal communication. The Walt Disney World Company.

Cleland, D.L. (1990). *Project management: Strategic design and implementation.* Blue Ridge Summit, PA: TAB Professional and Reference Books.

Dean, B.V. (ed.). (1985). *Project management.* New York: Elsevier Science.

Dinsmore, P.C. (1990). *Human factors in project management.* New York: American Management Association.

Fisher, H. (1992, January 2). Personal Communication. Analysis and Technology, Inc.

Frame, J.D. (1987). *Managing projects in organizations.* San Francisco, CA: Jossey-Bass.

Goodman, L.J. (1988). *Project planning and management: An integrated system for improving productivity.* New York: Van Nostrand Reinhold.

Hannum, W.H., & Hansen, C. (1989). *Instructional systems development in large organizations.* Englewood Cliffs, NJ: Educational Technology Publications.

House, R.S. (1988). *The human side of project management.* Reading, MA: Addison-Wesley.

Kerzner, H. (1982). *Project management for executives.* New York: Van Nostrand Reinhold.

Roman, D.D. (1986). *Managing projects: A systems approach.* New York: Elsevier.

Silverman, M. (1988). *Project management: A short course for professionals* (2nd ed.). New York: John Wiley and Sons.

Spears, R. (1992, January 2). Personal communication. Simms Industries.

Terrell, T. (1992, January 7). Personal communication. Regency Systems, Inc.

Tompkins, B.G. (1985). *Project cost control for managers.* Houston, TX: Gulf Publications.

REWARDS AND PERFORMANCE INCENTIVES

Jack Zigon

Introduction

Have you ever done something especially well in your job, but your boss never said or did anything to acknowledge it? Or, have you done an outstanding job and then been *recognized* for it? How was your work affected by either of these experiences? If you are like most people, the reward probably fed your motivation, and the lack of attention removed some desire. Employees tend to repeat what they are rewarded for. And you, as a manager, can influence employees to perform better if you reward their good performance.

We cover three topics in this chapter: types of rewards, how to find rewards that fit your employees, and how to deliver rewards effectively.

What Is a Reward and Why Use It?

Something that increases the frequency of an employee action is a reward. Whether something is a reward or not depends *entirely* on its effect on employee behavior. If an employee's performance is followed by something, and the performance happens more frequently in the future, that something is a reward. If the performance happens as frequently or less often, that something is not a reward.

A reward increases the chances that a performance will be repeated. For example, a computer operator supervisor wanted to reduce the number of forms misprinted per day in the department. The supervisor complimented each operator when the number of misprints was lower than the day before. The number of misprints gradually decreased from fifty to twenty-three.

The supervisor's reaction (compliments) *followed* a decrease in forms misprinted each day. The number of misprints decreased from fifty to twenty-three after the supervisor began complimenting each operator whose performance improved. Therefore, compliments served as a reward for the performance.

You will want to use rewards when an employee's performance meets or exceeds your expectations or when the employee's performance has improved and you want those improvements to continue.

Rewards help you manage by

- *Improving* an employee's performance to what you expect.

- Getting an employee to *repeat* a performance that met or exceeded your expectations.

- Helping good performances to happen *more often.*

- Helping to create a more pleasant work environment, one where rewards are used more frequently than discipline to manage employee behavior.

Dysfunctional Rewards

As we said, rewards increase the chance that a performance will be repeated. Sometimes the rewards that naturally exist influence the employee in the wrong way. Part of rewarding employees effectively is removing those rewards that are not doing what they should be doing. Two common types of dysfunctional rewards are those that

- Reward undesirable behavior: The behavior you do not want to see is more strongly rewarded than the behavior you *do* want to see.

- Punish good behavior: Instead of rewarding a behavior, something exists that punishes the employee for doing the right thing.

When your investigation of a performance problem reveals either of these two dysfunctional rewards, correct them by using a combination of the following fixes. Here are two examples of dysfunctional rewards and how to fix them.

Let's assume that Michael is doing a poor job of completing a very difficult and tedious report. You ask Sherry, whom you can trust to do the job well, to redo the report. Sherry does the job so well you assign it to her on a permanent basis. Unfortunately, Michael has been accidentally rewarded for making errors and Sherry has been punished for doing a good job.

Dysfunctional Reward	How To Fix It	Examples
Rewarding undesirable behaviors	• Remove the reward for the undesirable behavior.	Have Michael redo his own faulty report.
	• Increase the strength of the reward for the desirable behavior.	Offer Michael a task he likes to do after he has successfully handled the report.
	• Punish the undesirable behavior.	Withhold a task Michael likes to do until he successfully completes the report.

Dysfunctional Reward	How To Fix It	Examples
Punishing good behaviors	• Remove the punishment.	Don't assign the report to Sherry on a permanent basis.
	• Increase the strength of the reward for the desirable behavior.	If you have no choice but to make the permanent assignment, offer Sherry a task she likes to do as an additional incentive.

An account executive recently attended training in basic selling skills, but when you go with the executive on a call, you notice that he is not using what was taught in the class. The executive is not comfortable using the skills and does not want to make a fool of himself in front of the customer. Besides, the executive is still able to persuade new clients to sign up by planting seeds of doubt in the customer's mind about the competition and offering a lower price

Dysfunctional Reward	How To Fix It	Examples
Rewarding undesirable behaviors	• Remove the reward for the undesirable behavior.	Explain that offering a lower price is not the way you want business closed. Set a standard for net profitability to discourage offering lower prices.
	• Increase the strength of the reward for the desirable behavior.	Praise the executive for landing business at the same or higher price using other competitive advantages as selling points.

Dysfunctional Reward	How To Fix It	Examples
	• Punish the undesirable behavior.	Refuse to approve sales agreements below a certain price.
Punishing good behaviors	• Remove the punishment.	Have the account executive practice the skills more until he is comfortable with them.
	• Increase the strength of the reward for the desirable behavior.	Praise the executive for using the new skills.

Selecting the Right Reward

Can you think of a situation where a reward was delivered but did not work? When an employee's work is not influenced by a reward, it is probably because you are using something that is *not* a reward for *that particular* employee.

For example, someone who is on the road all the time probably will not see a dinner out at a restaurant as a reward. A person who never eats out and has to prepare meals may very well see a dinner out as a reward. Same reward; two different reactions.

When rewards don't fit, they do not work—even when you want them to. Remember, something is a reward *only* if the behaviors it follows happen more often.

How to Find Rewards That Fit

The first key to finding effective rewards is having a large number of rewards available to you. The more options you have to choose from, the better your chances are of finding something that fits the employee and the specific performance you are trying to encourage. A list of potential rewards you can use to expand your options follows. Review them for ideas you may not have thought of before.

Recognition
- Praise
- Certificate of accomplishment
- Formal public recognition
- Informal acknowledgments (pats on the back)
- Letters of appreciation
- Publicity (mention in the company newsletter)
- Awards
- Being selected to represent department at meetings

Job Tasks
- Assignment of new duties
- Relief from duties the employee does not like
- More frequent assignment of duties the employee does like
- Assignment of partners the employee likes to work with
- Approval of job-related requests
- Opportunity for advanced training

Job Responsibilities
- Opportunity for more self-management
- More authority to decide or implement
- More frequent decision making or participation in decision making
- More frequent requests to provide input for decisions
- Greater opportunity to select own goals or tasks
- Greater opportunity to set own priorities
- Greater access to information

Tangible Rewards
- Merit increases
- Cash bonuses

Prizes
- Lunch paid for by the company
- Company donations to charity in the employee's name
- Paid trips to professional meetings

Status Indicators
- Larger work area
- Promotion
- Supervision of more people
- Receipt of newer or more equipment
- Status symbols (window, carpet, nameplate, plants, better desk)
- Invitations to higher-level meetings
- New title

Personal Activities
- Taking a longer break or receiving additional breaks or longer lunch times
- Leaving work earlier
- Time off with or without pay
- Privileges (phone calls, opportunity to travel, reserved parking)
- Engaging in creative activities (work on inventions or publications)

Social Activities
- Talking to coworkers
- Going to lunch with the gang
- Going to company outings or parties
- Going to company-organized recreation activities
- Talking with the boss
- Having the boss listen with interest
- Dinner (lunch or just coffee) with the boss and spouse

Relief from Disliked Policies or Procedures
- Exempt from selected company control procedures
- Exempt from close supervision

Relief from Disliked Work Environment
- Better lighting
- Less noise
- Transfer from disliked coworkers or manager
- Move to warmer/cooler work area
- Move closer to restroom, cafeteria, or coffee facilities

If the first key to finding effective rewards is having a large number of rewards available to you, the second is knowing *what* your employees will find rewarding! There are three ways to find out what your employees would find rewarding:

- *Watch what they do.* By observing how employees spend their time when they have a chance to choose, you can learn what is important or attractive to them. You can see whom they pick to work with when they have a chance to select a work partner. You can observe how they feel about different kinds of work to learn what they like or dislike.

- *Listen to them.* By listening to what employees enjoy talking about, you can learn more about their preferences. Monday morning conversations about how a weekend was spent could lead to ideas such as a pair of tickets to a ball game or a play. Envious comments about another employee getting the chance to get advanced training might identify development as a potential reward.

- *Ask them.* If you do not know your employees well enough to guess correctly, try asking them. Asking can't hurt, and it will probably help. Asking can take the form of offering several alternative rewards instead of just one. Asking also can be used before a reward is presented to see what type of rewards are of interest to employees. Some creative managers have copied the previously described list of rewards and asked employees to check those they would find motivating.

Delivering Rewards Effectively

Selecting the right reward is only the first half of the battle. The other half is delivering the reward correctly. For example, delivering a reward nine months after the performance will not have anywhere near the effect of giving it the day following the accomplishment. In this section, you will learn about four principles for giving rewards effectively and what to say when you deliver a reward to an employee.

There are four principles for delivering rewards effectively: If-Then, ASAP, Variety, and Sometimes.

If-Then Principle

The if-then principle works like this: If an employee's performance meets or exceeds your expectations, then reward the employee. If the performance does not meet your expectations, then do not reward the employee.

For example, a supervisor wants to improve the accuracy of a new secretary's phone messages. The supervisor explains what a complete message should contain and praises the secretary for those messages that meet the standard. Incomplete messages are not praised.

If you reward performance that does not meet your expectations, you will get more of it. Rewarding below-standard performance happens more often than we would sometimes like to admit.

For example, when you have one of your best employees correct the work of a lower performer, you may be "rewarding" the lower performer for making the mistakes. Not having to correct your own errors is sometimes seen as a reward.

If you reward only those employees who meet your expectations, it will be difficult for you to improve the performance of those employees whose performance does not meet your expectations. To improve your employees' performance, reward them when their performance moves closer to your expectations.

ASAP Principle

The ASAP principle says to give the reward as soon as possible (ASAP) after the performance has occurred. For example, a manager overhears a sales representative talking to a customer on the phone. The customer must be very angry but the sales representative is doing a great job of staying calm and also diffusing the anger. Because the improvement of customer satisfaction is an important part of the representative's job, the manager compliments the employee as soon as he gets off the phone.

Rewards have their greatest effect immediately after the performance. The more time that goes by, the less the employee will be able to remember how the good performance was done. As a result, it will be harder for the employee to repeat what you want to see more of.

Variety Principle

The variety principle says you have to keep changing the reward in order to keep its effect. For example, the head of a department wants to reduce the overtime expenses in a work unit. The standard is set with the work unit's supervisor. Over the next three months, each time the standard is met the department head uses one of the following as a reward:

- Personal congratulations and praise,

- Letter of commendation and praise, or

- Praise from the department's vice president.

The same reward given ten times in a row will lose its effectiveness. Variety in your rewards will keep the motivating effect strong.

Sometimes Principle

A sometimes reward is given only some of the time when an employee's performance meets or exceeds your expectations. For example, this morning the research manager praised the analyst for handling the irate customer well. The next day the manager overhears the same analyst again handling a customer well on the phone. Since the manager had just rewarded the employee yesterday, he or she decides not to reward the analyst this time.

There are two advantages of using a sometimes reward:

- It is practical. You do not have to watch each employee constantly to reward every performance that meets or exceeds your expectations.

- You cannot always be there to reward employees and want good performance to happen in your absence. Employees who are rewarded periodically when they perform well are likely to continue performing well in the absence of rewards.

Sometimes rewards are especially suited for rewarding performances that occur frequently.

How to Deliver a Reward

Here are the steps of how to deliver a reward along with an example.

1. Describe exactly what was done well.

2. Describe how your organization or a customer benefited.

3. Deliver the reward using the if-then, ASAP, variety, and sometimes principles.

For example,

1. "Amy, your customer satisfaction index has gone up for three straight months! The more frequent visits to the problem accounts seem to be paying off."

2. "That should help us hang on to that business when renewals come due."

3. "You said you'd like to be asked for input on decisions. I'd like to get your ideas for a division-wide sales promotion program. Let's talk about it in the morning."

Application Exercise

To help you expand the reward options you can use in your work unit, review the list of potential rewards under "How to Find Rewards That Fit." Check those you would be comfortable using with your employees. Then, write down any other ideas you can think of that are not listed and use them when appropriate.

Additional reward ideas not on pages 420-421:

1. _____

   _____

2. _____

   _____

3. _____

   _____

4. _____

   _____

5. _____

   _____

6. _____

_____

7. _____

_____

8. _____

_____

9. _____

_____

10. _____

_____

Summary

A reward is something that increases the frequency of a performance it follows. Rewards make it more likely that the performance of your employees will meet your expectations.

Make sure the reward fits the employee by observing, listening to, or asking the employee. Finally, remember to follow these steps when delivering a reward:

1. Describe exactly what was done well.

2. Describe how your organization or a customer benefited from the occurrence.

3. Use the if-then, ASAP, variety, and sometimes principles discussed previously.

If an employee's performance meets or exceeds your expectations, then reward the employee. If the performance does not meet your expectations, then do not reward the employee. Give the reward as soon as possible after the performance has occurred. Or, use variety: change the reward to keep its effect. Give a sometimes reward only some of the time, when an employee's performance meets or exceeds your expectations.

Planning Change:
Past, Present, Future

Diane Dormant

Past: How We Used to Do It

Half a century ago, various professionals addressed questions such as how to get people to save scrap metal, use blackout curtains, and eat margarine instead of butter. During World War II, people made changes they were asked to make, and experts became optimistic about their change skills. In the postwar era, this optimism was especially apparent in the areas of agriculture, education, and aid to developing countries. Federal support was provided for thousands of change projects. The following is one example of such a project.

In the early 1960s, 25 percent of all tomatoes in the U.S. came from California. They were grown by 4,000 farmers and harvested by 50,000 farm workers. About that time, agricultural researchers at the University of California at Davis, funded by the Federal government, designed a mechanical tomato picker and developed a tomato variety hard enough to be harvested by machine. This innovative machine-and-seed package was marketed to California tomato farmers.

In 1962, there were a total of twenty-five tomato-picking machines; they harvested 1 percent of the tomato crop. By 1970, there were 1,521 machines and they harvested 99.9 percent of the crop. G.C. Hanna—the major planner of the change and its dissemination—was honored as the man who "saved the tomato for California."

It was common then and—in many organizations—it is still common today for planned change to mean that one group comes up with a new approach and then gets another group to accept it. In keeping with this approach, early researchers in the area of planned change (Rogers, 1962; Havelock, 1973; Zaltman, Florio, & Sikorski, 1977) looked for ways to understand users and to persuade them to adopt changes. This diffusion-and-adoption approach was compatible with the view of organizations that was predominant in the first half of the twentieth century. Organizations were seen as machine-like (Morgan, 1986), and just as one could fix a machine by inserting a new part, one could fix an organization (or industry or school system or society or developing nation) by inserting a new technology or piece of equipment. People gave little thought to the long-range impact of the change on the rest of the system.

However, if we return to our tomato farming example, we see that more is involved in long-term success than is indicated by the single measure of user acceptance.

By 1970, of the original 4,000 tomato farmers, 3,400 had been forced out of tomato farming. Of the original 50,000 farm workers, 32,000 had lost their jobs. As for consumers who liked soft, tasty tomatoes, they now found at their grocery stores only hard tomatoes with fewer vitamins.

In response to the turbulence of the 1970s—e.g., agricultural pollutants, the Vietnam War, the civil rights movement, the youth and sexual revolutions, and technological advances— change planners were less optimistic, and change planning became more complex. At the same time, the social system of the workplace, the organization, came to be viewed differently. The earlier mechanistic view of the organization was being replaced by a biological view. (The machine image of an organization is still visible today in some industries, e.g., the fast-food industry. Think of how mechanistic a local McDonald's is, by design.)

With the biological or organic view, people began to see organizations as interrelated subsystems working together (Morgan, 1986). When something new is inserted into a subsystem of a living organism, it is likely to affect other subsystems and, in the long run, the whole organism. The experts began to consider the systemic effects of a change and to expand their scope and their tools to account for such factors as organizational culture, structure, leadership, and climate of change. Even so, such long-range factors as the global economy and ecology still received little consideration.

In the 1980s, the decrease of U.S. leadership in the global marketplace took U.S. corporations by surprise. In near panic, corporate leaders cast here and there for solutions. One place they looked was at their international competitors. The Japanese, who had successfully challenged U.S. dominance of the automotive and electronics industries, were committed to the goals of quality and productivity and to various forms of worker collaboration to achieve these goals. This was a fortunate turn of events for those working in planned change. For one thing, business grew interested in change and change planning. For another thing, although change experts had always proselytized for user participation, until the 1980s, U.S. organizations had neither the commitment nor the internal mechanisms to make such participation work. Now, with growing organizational support and with such organizational mechanisms as cross-functional work groups and self-managed teams, broad-based participation was feasible. However, it is worth noting that Asian executive boards routinely give serious thought to what they want their corporations to be two hundred years in the future. Without such long-term visions and values, all organizational changes—whether efforts at quality and productivity or experiments with collaborative work modes—may be just Band Aids for organizational, economic, and social problems that require quite a different magnitude and kind of solution.

Present: A Good Way to Do It Today

Change planning has grown more complex over the years and has been applied in new organizational settings. While there are no sure-fire algorithms for complex organizational change, there are some approaches that can increase the change planner's chances of success. To begin with, it may help to think about the change situation as involving four dimensions: (1) the change itself, (2) the organization, (3) the people, and (4) the change agent (Dormant, 1986, 1992). In regard to these four dimensions, then, there are both old and newer principles that offer guidance to the change planner. Twelve such principles of change planning are offered here. The first two principles are concerned with the change itself. The next three with the organization. The next six with the significant people in the change system. And the last with the change agent.

Twelve Principles for the Change Planner

The Change
  1. Be honest about the change.
  2. Accentuate the positive; defuse the negative.

The Organization
  3. Account for the organization's culture.
  4. Account for the organization's stage of development.
  5. Account for external conditions.

The People
  6. Understand the effect change has on people.
  7. Involve key groups.
  8. Create a change team.
  9. Optimize significant group roles.
  10. Use the right strategy at the right time for all the people.
  11. Educate for change.

Principle 1. Be Honest About the Change

To be honest, a change planner must first know the change. Often this is quite difficult. For example, the person designated to manage the changeover to a corporate-wide fiber optic communication system may not have the expertise necessary to know the change technically. Given the newness of the technology, no one can know the impact that such a systemic change will have on productivity, organizational structure, and interpersonal relations. Nevertheless, the change planner can choose a position of honesty and check all plans and actions against that position.

To be honest, a change planner must know the benefits or other probable consequences of the change on the people involved, the organization, and the external world. (See Kaufman [1992] for a discussion of the micro, macro, and mega levels of planning.) Few changes are equally good for everyone. Some changes (e.g., downsizing, reorganization, forced early retirement) may have negative consequences, at least in the short run, for workers. In such cases, it is important not to misrepresent the probable impact. A better approach is to acknowledge major negatives and plan supports.

To be honest, a change planner must take responsibility. Sometimes, planners are asked to implement a change that seems to have few benefits and many shortcomings. When this happens, responsible planners diplomatically inform management of relevant concerns and suggest ways to make improvements. If management chooses to ignore such warnings, wise change planners put distance between themselves and the change because when changes fail—and "bad" changes tend to fail—change planners make handy scapegoats!

Principle 2. Accentuate the Positive; Defuse the Negative

Among change characteristics that potential adopters value are *relative advantage, simplicity, compatibility, modifiability,* and *low social impact* (Rogers, 1983). When a change is strong in these characteristics, it tends to be valued and accepted. When a change is weak or lacking in these characteristics, it tends to be devalued and rejected. Clarity about the strengths and weaknesses of a change can provide important information to guide the planner in selecting appropriate strategies and tactics. Figure 1 suggests tactics to accentuate strengths and offset weaknesses.

A change that has *relative advantage* is one that is better than the alternatives—new or old. This may seem obvious, but it is often overlooked. Even when a change is good for people, without help they may not recognize its goodness. If the change is to get a fair trial, its valued attributes must be made apparent (see Burkman, 1987). This is especially important in the early stages of acceptance when powerful, first perceptions are made.

A change that has *simplicity* is one that is easy to understand, learn, and use. In each case, "ease" must be defined from the perspective of the user or other stakeholder, not from the perspective of the designer or the technologist. Even after people have learned how-to, they may still be uncommitted if their on-the-job support system does not provide needed technical assistance and reinforcement.

A change that has *compatibility* is one that is similar to that which the person is already used to. The more easily the new system slips into the old one, the better. The change planner looks for ways in which the new is most like the old—in tasks to be performed, work patterns, outputs, worker relations, etc.,—and then communicates and builds on these similarities.

IF your change lacks...	THEN try these strategies...
Relative advantage	Know its weak and strong points. Highlight the strong; be ready to acknowledge the weak. Assess worth; have trade-offs. If more expensive, be ready with cost-effectiveness figures. Emphasize aspects that provide quick or high payoff. Appeal to team spirit.
Simplicity	Know relevant factors, advantages, disadvantages. Give a simple, bottom-line overview. Make the change "visible" through success stories, site visits, documents, peer testimonials. Know complexities of use. Highlight training or job aids available. Acknowledge potential problem areas.
Compatibility	Look for aspects, procedures, results, etc., that are similar to the way things have been done. Build on similarities. Identify and highlight values common to both old and new.
Modifiability	Know aspects adopters are most likely to want to modify, whether or not modification is possible. Highlight areas that can be modified without loss of effective functioning. Be ready to acknowledge potential problem areas.
Low social impact	Know what relationships exist among key people and key groups. Project how the change will impact these relationships. Acknowledge and empathize. Identify and communicate workable alternatives.

Figure 1. When the Change Presents Problems

A change that has *modifiability* is one that can be adapted to fit the local situation. This tends to offset the "not invented here" syndrome. The effective change planner accepts and even encourages modifications that will not destroy the critical functions or integrity of the change.

A change that has *low social impact* is one that barely affects the users' current work relationships. Effective change planners identify how the change may impact relationships. Then, they look for ways to lessen the impact of changes perceived to be negative and to emphasize changes that might be perceived as positive.

Principle 3. Account for the Organization's Culture

All organizations have their own culture, and that culture affects how, or if, a change will be accepted. When the culture and its relationship to the change are understood, the mutual impact may bde better managed.

What is organizational culture? O'Toole (1995) defines it as "...a system of beliefs and actions that characterize a particular group. Culture is the unique whole—the shared ideas, customs, assumptions, expectations, philosophy, traditions, mores, and values—that determines how a group of people will behave" (p. 72). The Vice Chairman of Alcoa, William Renner, offers an earthier definition, "It's the rules of the game; the unseen meaning between the lines in the rulebook that assures unity" (Kilmann, Saxton, Serpa, & Associates, 1985, p. 352).

Can the culture be changed? As early as the mid-1980s, culture change consultant Daryl Conner (1985) took the position that—with the right moves and support—culture can be changed. Conner's position is compatible with later, more revolutionary approaches. Waterman (1987) argues for "renewal." Hammer and Champy (1993) propose that the corporation must be completely "reengineered": "American managers must throw out their old notions about how businesses should be organized and run. They must abandon the organizational and operational principles and procedures they are now using and create entirely new ones.... Business reengineering means starting all over, starting from scratch" (pp. 1-2).

However, with all the current revolutionary discourse, it may be useful to consider several things. First, true culture runs deep and is certainly slow, if not impossible, to change. Schein (1985) believes that culture can be changed only through evolution, and that more dramatic moves are likely to destroy the culture. A second useful thing to remember is that organizational leaders—whatever they may say—cannot be counted on to support change. Argyris (1987, 1990) studied organizational defense mechanisms and found convincing evidence that while organizational leaders might publicly support a change, they often worked privately—if without awareness—to undermine the same change. Perhaps a more realistic and promising approach is that which O'Toole takes when he says, "...it is just as absurd to talk of changing the culture of a firm into something radically different as it is to talk about manipulating your personality to become someone you aren't.... Effective change builds on the existing culture" (pp. 71-73).

What if the culture and the change are a mismatch? Most experts agree that any proposed change that is in conflict with the organizational culture has a good chance of disappearing into a cultural black hole, never to be seen again. However, many if not all midsized changes can be positioned as directly supportive of the organization's strategic goals and—in this era of reinventing, if not revolutionizing the culture—its organizational survival or health. This kind of alignment not only tends to increase top level support, but—to the extent that business realities and strategic goals have been communicated and bought into by workers—also may increase support from user groups and other significant personnel.

Principle 4. Account for the Organization's Stage of Development

Organizations, like people, go through developmental stages that make up a life cycle (Sperry, Mickelson, & Hunsaker, 1977). These stages have an impact on how any proposed change will be viewed.

When an organization is new, it is usually characterized by creativity, commitment to task, cooperation, and informality. That which helps get the task done is valued. For example, in a new company that develops and manufactures microchips, the arrival of expensive, cutting-edge electronic equipment may be welcomed by the engineers who founded and control the company. In this early developmental stage, these same leaders may view a personnel accountability system as an unnecessary obstruction.

As the company grows and the demand for administrative structures and procedures also grows, the things that help management track and control what is happening are valued. The management of the microchip company now may view expensive equipment as just R&D toys, while they view the accountability system as highly valuable.

When the weight of the administrative structures becomes oppressive or when economic realities demand major change, a company tends again to decentralize and encourage individual initiative. The things that encourage creativity, support cooperation, and improve worker productivity are again valued. Participative management, self-managed teams, cross-functional groups—all of these may be indicators of organizational renewal.

An understanding of the organization's stage of development can facilitate change planning. Human performance technologists often object to management's lack of interest in instructional and performance technologies. Perhaps one reason is that until recently most of America's large corporations were in their middle years. Doing things the right way was more important than doing the right thing.

Principle 5. Account for External Conditions

There are always external conditions that influence organizations—government regulations, worker group demands, environmental controls, community standards, acts of nature, and so on. Some influences are industry-specific, e.g., airline deregulation. Others are worldwide, e.g., global competition and changing demographics. *Workforce 2000* (Johnston, 1987), oft-cited report on the socioeconomic future of the United States, predicted the following:

> The last years of this century are certain to bring new developments in technology, international competition, demography, and other factors that will alter the nation's economic and social landscape. By the end of the next decade, the changes under way will produce an America that is in some ways unrecognizable from the one that existed only a few years ago. (p. xiii)

These predictions are already coming true, and conditions are creating a new demand for the products and services of human performance professionals.

Principle 6. Understand the Effect Change Has on People

As the involved people—users, sponsors, or other stakeholders—move toward making a change, they are all affected by some of the same factors: (a) the human tendency to resist change, (b) individual style, (c) the individual's change load, and (d) whether or not enough time is allowed.

When change occurs, *resistance* is almost certain. All people resist—a little or a lot—and this is true whether or not they want the change. Regardless of what the change is, there are some losses involved, e.g., job status, a congenial work team, an office with the morning sun. The extent of people's resistance depends not only on what they are moving toward, but also on what they are leaving behind.

In addition, *individual style* affects how people move to adopt a change. Some people are adventurous; some prefer stability. Some move quickly to try new things; some try new things only after they see others try and succeed; some never try new things if they can avoid it. People live and change and grow old in ways that reflect their individuality. The wise change planner accepts this.

Whatever the style, if too many things are changing in a person's life, that person has a heavy *change load*. One well-known stress test (Holmes & Rahe, 1974) revealed the relationship between the change load and the probability of that person's hospitalization. The more changes in people's lives, the more likely they are to get sick. This is true whether the changes are perceived as good or bad. Enough is enough!

Lastly, everyone requires *time* enough to change. Whether people move rapidly or slowly to change, they all require time to become aware, to think about, to try out, to learn how-to, and to integrate. One reason that change projects fail or run over time estimates is because the change planner did not allow people the time they needed and they took it anyway.

Principle 7. Involve Key Groups

The success or failure of any change effort depends heavily on the people who are key to the process. These include the sponsors, users, bosses, technical experts, gatekeepers, and other stakeholders. Each key group should be identified and involved in the change process.

Perhaps the most important people in the change effort are the sponsors (Kotter, 1995). An effective *sponsor* has the power and influence not only to conceptualize or select the change, but also to legitimize it and provide continuing support. Generally, the higher up in the organization, the better. However, to be cost-effective, sponsorship should be leveraged down to the lowest ranking person with the authority to make the change happen. If a sponsor is weak, Conner (1983) recommends that the change planner do one of three things: (a) strengthen the sponsor, (b) find another sponsor, or (c) prepare to fail.

Obviously, the actual *users* of the change are critical. No matter how many other key personnel endorse and accept it, without effective users, the change cannot succeed. They will probably require the most extensive effort, including training and technical support.

Among other key people who can have a significant impact are users' *bosses*. In change efforts, they are often viewed as uncooperative. However, in many change efforts, the rewards for change go to top management who thought of the change and to hands-on personnel who use it, while no one considers the caught-in-the-middle managers and supervisors. Since users' bosses are essential for optimal outcomes, the effective change planner will establish a chain of support and rewards that connects sponsors, bosses, and users.

Both early and late in a change project, *technical experts* are required. In the beginning, they are essential to clarify what the change is all about. Later, as users implement the change in the workplace, experts must be available to provide technical assistance. Nothing causes a credibility gap faster than misleading or inaccurate information provided to the hands-on users.

Gatekeepers are the people throughout the organization who have no authority and often no interest in the change, but they have the power of opening or closing the gate to people, information, and resources. Gatekeepers differ from project to project but almost always include the secretaries of key personnel.

Other stakeholders are all of the other people who have a stake in whether or not the change is adopted. They may include internal constituencies, vendors, distributors, elected government officials, and employee families.

Principle 8. Create a Change Team

Almost any organizational change requires the cooperation, effort, and expertise of a number of people. Some of these may form the core change team with day-in, day-out responsibility and commitment to the project, while others may be intermittently involved, offering information, expertise, resources, and access to people as needed. Such consulting team members may be internal or external to the organization. Each has advantages and disadvantages.

Internal people tend to lack objectivity and have a limited perspective. They have a history and an existent role in the organization. Hence, they lack organizational flexibility. But, they know the system, speak the language, understand concerns, and share needs and values. By contrast, external people are strangers to the organization. They lack knowledge of its culture and language and may not even care much about what happens. But they, too, have advantages. They start fresh with the organization and its people; they are relatively independent of the power structure; they have more objectivity and a broader perspective; and they may bring new and useful expertise. In most complex change efforts, the ideal arrangement is to have both internal and external change team members.

Wherever they come from and whatever their commitment, the change team should have—in aggregate—all of the expertise required to plan and implement the specific change in the specific organization. Useful expertise includes technical information and experience related to the change itself, communication skills, data-gathering skills, information on user skills and concerns, training expertise, organizational information, and political know-how. Of course, the change planner must also have team-building and managing skills (Phillips & Elledge, 1989).

Principle 9. Optimize Significant Group Roles

Whether the change manager is dealing with the user group, a technical expert group, or other groups, it is important to recognize that certain group members have special roles and ways of influencing others in the group. The change planner who can identify specific people in these roles can better manage the change effort. Some significant group roles are those of innovators, opinion leaders, and laggards.

Of the *innovators*, Jwaideh (1976) said the following:

> Innovators are the first persons in the social system to adopt innovations. They tend to be intelligent, venturesome, eager to try new ideas, and willing to take risks. Innovators tend to be individualistic and usually not integrated into the prevailing social structure. They may be viewed as mavericks by those who are more conventional. They...have more contact with sources of information outside their own system. (p. 17)

Although the change planner may enlist the innovator to become an inside advocate for the change, care must be taken. The opinions of innovators are not always valued. After all, they tend to be oddballs. If, however, innovators who are acceptable to the group can be identified, they can become invaluable as demonstrators of the change.

Most adopters fall into the large middle group. Within this group are the *opinion leaders*. No one has ever described them better than Havelock (1973):

> Opinion leaders...are certain influential people who are held in high esteem by the majority of their fellow men.... They watch the innovator to see how the idea works, and they watch the...[laggard]...to test the social risks of adopting the idea. Indeed, in many cases they are eager to observe these changes because their continuance in power rests upon their ability to judge innovations. They want to be champions of the change whose time has come. (p. 120)

Opinion leaders represent the norms of the group. They are at the hub of the group's communications network and have considerable influence. Once identified, they can provide information about the group and, if inclined to support the change, they can be of significant help. Of course, an opinion leader for one change may not be for another.

Laggards are the last to adopt a change, and it might seem best to ignore them. However, since such people are often vocal as well as negative, they can cause damage. Laggards who get the chance to express themselves to an accepting audience (change manager) may talk less and less negatively elsewhere. Also, some of the laggard's opinions may be early indicators of what is about to go wrong. Forewarned, change managers can take appropriate action.

Principle 10. Use the Right Strategy at the Right Time for All the People

All people—whether they are sponsors, users, or others—go through stages of acceptance when they are first confronted with a new thing. Different experts propose a different number of stages and use different labels (Zaltman, Florio, &

Sikorski, 1977, p. 65). However, all experts see the stages as developmental, with each building on those that came before and each laying the groundwork for those that follow. In each stage, people evaluate the change against their needs and wants and—if the change measures up—they move on in their level of acceptance to the next stage.

Since stages are generally predictable, the change planner can select strategies and design tactics that match each stage and, in this way, can facilitate people's progress toward acceptance and manage the overall change process. Figure 2 offers a five-stage model, describes people's behavior at each stage, and suggests strategies to match.

For example, when people are entering Stage 1, Awareness, this is not the time to load them up with lots of information or catapult them into training. This is the time to get their attention. Introduce them to the change, use a once-over-lightly advertising campaign—perhaps of the "weight" of a television commercial.

After this exposure, if people feel positive toward the change, they move on to Stage 2, Curiosity. Then it is time to give them information that is relevant to their personal concerns and goals. A pamphlet on "Twenty Questions Users Most Frequently Ask" is one example.

As their personal concerns are met, they move into Stage 3, Envisioning, and they should have examples they can identify with. They are beginning to envision how the change might work in their own workplace. It is time to plant the seeds of positive images, perhaps through a visit to a successful demonstration site of similar users.

With a mental image of on-the-job success, they move into Stage 4, Tryout. For the first time, they are ready to learn the basics of how to use the new procedure, approach, or software.

IF the person is in the stage of....	THEN the strategy to use is to....
1 Awareness Passive regarding the change Little/no information about change Little/no opinion about change	**1 Advertise** Be an ad agent Be credible and positive Appeal to his or her needs and wants
2 Curiosity More active regarding change Expresses personal job concerns Asks questions about own work and change	**2 Inform** Identify specific concerns Provide clear info about concerns Emphasize pluses, acknowledge minuses
3 Envisioning Active regarding change Expresses work-related job concerns Asks questions about how change works	**3 Demonstrate** Give success images Provide demonstrations Connect with peer users
4 Tryout Active regarding change Has opinions about change Interested in learning how-to	**4 Train** Provide effective training Provide job aids, checklists Promise technical follow-up
5 Use Active regarding change Uses change on job Asks detailed questions about use	**5 Support** Provide necessary technical help Provide reinforcement Provide recognition

Figure 2. Acceptance Stages and Change Strategies

If all goes well, then they move to Stage 5, Use. It is time to support their on-the-job implementation of the change. They should have both technical information and reinforcement for effort and achievement. Nadler, Shaw, Walton, & Associates (1995) point out the organizational destructiveness of not aligning the existent reward system with the change. In particular, they note, "...promotion decisions during transitions are the most telling signal of whether 'they're serious' about the change… Typically, the promotion system continues to run as usual during the transition, resulting in promotions that send mixed signals at best, and all too often, the wrong signal… " (p. 53)

The concept of acceptance stages (with matching strategies and tactics) is a powerful tool for the planner of change. Of course, the perspective will change from group to group, e.g., from that of a group of users to that of their bosses. Hence, while general strategies remain the same, specific tactics must be designed to meet the concerns, needs, and values of the specific group.

Principle 11. Educate for Change

Whatever the change is and whatever the change manager does, people will probably feel some resistance and suffer some pain. In fact, change management is often referred to as "pain management." But, regardless of the pain, self-knowledge and coping skills can help.

When people learn that their discomfort, resistance, and anger are normal, then their load is lightened and their acceptance is facilitated. When they learn that they and their coworkers can expect to go through stages as they deal with a change, their view of the future is more optimistic. Where once they saw only problems, they may see opportunities. In *Transitions: Making Sense out of Life's Changes*, Bridges (1980) makes the following suggestions for adding value during a period of change:

1. Take your time.

2. Arrange temporary structures.

3. Don't act for the sake of action.

4. Recognize why you are uncomfortable.

---

5. Take care of yourself in little ways.

6. Explore the other side of change.

7. Get someone to talk to.

8. Find out what is waiting in the wings of your life.

9. Use this transition as the impetus to a new kind of learning.

10. Recognize that transition has a characteristic shape.

The individual, group, organization, or industry that can muster the courage to view major change in this light has the opportunity for renewal and growth.

Principle 12. Be Flexible

Probably no other characteristic is as basic to success, survival, and well-being of change managers as flexibility—flexibility in perspective, flexibility in implementation, and flexibility in self-judgment.

Change managers who can shift perspective from the micro to the macro to the mega and back again have a powerful advantage. At one moment, they may focus in on the details of the change project. At the next moment, they may turn a wide lens on the broader and longer-term views of other departments, management, global competition, and ecological impact. Effective change managers also know that different stakeholder groups have different perspectives. For example, top management may see a new computerized system as an effective way to capture critical information about costs. The company's design engineers may see it as a technical breakthrough. But, end users may see it as a cumbersome pain-in-the-neck with no recognized payoff. Appropriate data-gathering and customized tactics are necessary to integrate such diverse and apparently contradictory views into a successful change project.

In the planning phase, everything important should be accounted for. By contrast, in the implementation stage, one should "hang loose." There are at least two reasons for this. One is that, regardless of how well a person or team plans, "stuff happens." It is constructive to accept the unexpected as inevitable, to adapt, and to move on. The other reason is that some of the unexpected occurrences are actually opportunities. The change manager who can recognize an opportunity and modify the plan to take advantage of that opportunity will be more effective in implementing the change, more likely to be well thought of by top management, and better able to cope personally with the ambiguities of the job.

Change managers should try to be as flexible in self-judgments as they are in judgments of other people involved in the change project. Unexpected and unwanted things always happen. Even the role of the change manager usually turns out to be different from that planned. The effective, healthy, surviving change planner assesses the situation, does damage control where appropriate, looks for opportunities that may exist, adapts to the new conditions, and moves on without guilt but with greater wisdom. Conner, who has consulted on change projects all over the world, believes "that the single most important factor to managing change successfully is the degree to which people demonstrate resilience: the capacity to absorb high levels of change while displaying minimal dysfunctional behavior" (1993, p. 6).

Future: How We Might Do It Someday

By the year 2000, the organization will exist in a state of constant, self-aware change. Workers will be educated and supported to function in this ever-changing state. Senge (1990) calls this the "learning organization." Morgan (1986) sees the futuristic organization, not like a machine or an organism, but like a brain with each person as a cell in the thinking and planning brain.

Change planning will be less objectives-driven and more values-driven. While implementing new technology may still be the common focus, more attention will be paid to longer-term concerns. Perhaps we will be closer to asking, "What kind of company and society and world do we want in 200 years?"

References

Argyris, C. (1987). The case of the economic theory of the firm. *American Psychologist, 47*(5), 456-463.

Argyris, C. (1990). *Overcoming organizational defenses.* Boston, MA: Allyn and Bacon.

Bridges, W. (1980). *Transitions: Making sense out of life's changes.* Reading, MA: Addison-Wesley.

Burkman, E. (1987). Factors affecting utilization. In R.M. Gagne (Ed.), *Instructional technology: Foundations.* Hillsdale, NJ: Erlbaum.

Conner, D.R. (1983). *Sponsor commitment evaluation.* Atlanta, GA: OD Resources.

Conner, D.R. (1985, April). *Is your organization's culture ready for change?* Paper presented at the annual meeting of the National Society for Performance and Instruction, Chicago.

Conner, D.R. (1993). *Managing at the speed of change: How resilient managers succeed and prosper where others fail.* New York: Villard Books.

Dormant, D. (1986). The ABCD's of managing change. In M. Smith (Ed.), *Introduction to performance technology.* Washington, DC: The National Society for Performance and Instruction.

Dormant, D. (1992). Implementing human performance in organizations. In H.D. Stolovitch & E.J. Keeps (Eds.), *Handbook of human performance technology.* San Francisco, CA: Jossey-Bass.

Hammer, M., & Champy, J. (1993). *Reengineering the corporation: A manifesto for business revolution.* New York: HarperBusiness.

Havelock, R.G. (1973). *The change agent's guide to innovation in education.* Englewood Cliffs, NJ: Educational Technology.

Holmes, T., & Rahe, R. (1974). *Stress.* Chicago: Blue Cross Association.

Johnston, W.B. (1987). *Workforce 2000: Work and workers for the 21st century.* Indianapolis, IN: Hudson Institute.

Jwaideh, A. (1976). *Implementation workshop: Participants' manual.* Bloomington, IN: University Consortium for Instructional Development and Technology.

Kaufman, R. (1992). *Strategic planning plus: An organizational guide.* Newbury Park, CA: Sage.

Kilmann, R.H., Saxton, M.J., Serpa, R., & Associates. (1985). *Gaining control of the corporate culture.* San Francisco, CA: Jossey-Bass.

Kotter, J.P. (1995). Leading change: Why transformation efforts fail. *Harvard Business Review, 73*(2), 59-67.

Morgan, G. (1986). *Images of organization.* Newbury Park, CA: Sage.

Nadler, D.A., Shaw, R.B., Walton, A.E., & Associates. (1995). *Discontinuous change: Leading organizational transformation.* San Francisco, CA: Jossey-Bass.

O'Toole, J. (1995.) *Leading change: Overcoming the ideology of comfort and the tyranny of custom.* San Francisco, CA: Jossey-Bass.

Phillips, S.L., & Elledge, R.L. (1989). The team-building source book. San Diego, CA: Pfeiffer & Company.

Rogers, E.M. (1983). *Diffusion of innovations* (3rd ed.). New York: Free Press.

Schein, E.H. (1985). *Organizational culture and leadership: A dynamic view.* San Francisco, CA: Jossey-Bass.

Senge, P.M. (1990). *The fifth discipline: The art and practice of the learning organization.* New York: Doubleday Currency.

Sperry, L., Mickelson, D.J., & Hunsaker, P.L. (1977). You can make it happen: A guide to self-actualization and organizational change. Reading, MA: Addison-Wesley.

Waterman, R.H., Jr. (1987). *The renewal factor: How the best get and keep the competitive edge.* New York: Bantam Books.

Zaltman, G., Florio, D., & Sikorski, L. (1977). *Dynamic educational change: Models, strategies, tactics, and management.* New York: Free Press.

INTEGRATING PEOPLE, PLANNING, AND CHANGE

Kevin Hardy

Introduction

In a number of recent assignments, I have been called on to explore ways of creating performance cultures within the context of integrating people and planning. In these assignments changing strategies, structures, roles, and systems were rational processes that allowed the organization to advance the change process and move into a new future.

Changing the people was a more challenging exercise in paradigm shifts because the people, as is often the case, lagged behind as they struggled to find their place in the new organization and to grieve for the past, if necessary. Thus, the challenge was to bring the elements more closely together so that the best laid plans of mice and (wo)men did not lose the energy for successful, constructive change and results.

Organizations often choose a planning route that identifies internal organizational results with little conscious energy expended on planning for societal outcomes. My awareness about this was initially raised by the work of Roger Kaufman who describes organization-based planning as micro and macro levels and mega as planning at the level that demands that we take account of the external society (its needs, the usefulness and consequence of our services, and what we deliver to the world in which we live). Serving the customers and meeting their needs is critical.

Many organizations are not clear about the balance of the culture they currently have or the culture they want. Organizational leaders talk about a culture of achievement, results, and support for people but in reality are predominantly driven, for whatever reason, by the demand for excessive power and control, and in the process they create fear cultures. (Roger Harrison's and Herb Stokes's [1986] work on organization culture is a useful starting point in actually diagnosing and describing organization culture.)

Many organizations make changes at the rational levels of organizational life, for example,

- Practices and procedures (the day-to-day operations, systems, rules, regulations, structure);

- Purposes and direction (the long- and intermediate-term strategic planning for the organization).

Yet, so often they neglect the nonrational level of

- Identity and unity (the sense of shared meaning, culture, symbols, stories, corporate heroes and heroines).

Changing organizations requires both direction from above and the opportunity to collaborate and participate from below. Too many change processes falter through lack of direction during a period that is difficult for many people and through no consultation with the people that the changes affect.

Changing organizations requires front-end decisions about whether a new history is being created (which also brings forward what is valued from the past) or whether the organization is being facilitated in its evolutionary refocusing process.

Creating Performance Cultures

Frameworks

The original framework for creating performance cultures was taken from the strategic planning work of Roger Kaufman (1990) (see chapter on strategic planning) and the work of Charles Margerison and Dick McCann (1990) in team management and development. I have added the work of Tim Dalmau and Bob Dick (1987) on organizational life cycles and levels of organizational intervention.

The combination of the frameworks allows for

- Identifying where the organization is in its life cycle;

- Identifying the levels at which interventions are required to change the culture;

- Mega, macro, and micro planning with alignment of the different levels of planning; and

- Team-building activities to ensure consistently high performance, clarification of work roles, internal and external team linkages, lines of accountability, and internal team reward and recognition processes.

Bringing together the ingredients of people and planning creates an empowered critical mass of people in the organization and reduces the level of "control" in the culture.

Steps to Successful Change

Team Profiling

The framework is dominated by the planning elements that facilitate organizational alignment. However, that is not where

---

I choose to start. People are anxious about change, so experience dictates that starting with the people and building a picture/assessment of the team profile (work team role strengths and shortfalls) gives people a common base for:

- Talking about themselves;

- Appreciating their differences;

- Identifying team balance or imbalance in terms of performance, results, and processes;

- Identifying ways to best use individual work preferences; and

- Planning how to increase the "role range" of people.

Figure 1 is a diagram of the Margerison/McCann team management wheel. Some teams are "out of balance." That is, they might be good at gathering and disseminating information, thinking ahead about new business opportunities or new ideas, and selling the ideas to others, but may not be so successful at making things happen and ensuring that projects/tasks are finished completely and to an excellent performance standard. Covering all of the team role preferences either through recruitment or by individuals' increasing their repertoire around the wheel is important for success as well as high performance.

The Margerison/McCann Team Management Index gives each individual a separate comprehensive report. The sharing of this information provides a positive basis for team role changes and improvement of internal and external linkages. It also acts at the level of identity and unity in organizational life. It binds people together and readies them for the critical planning phase. It acts as a positive shared experience and reduces the level of threat, fear, and anxiety.

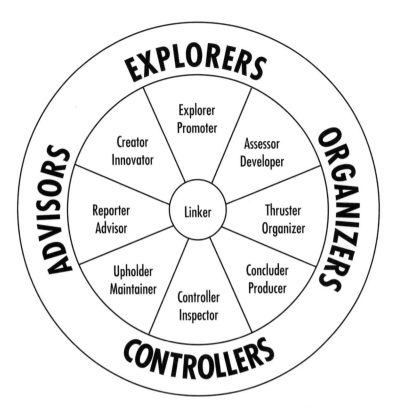

How do we meet the challenges of the team's goals?
What skills do we presently have? What is the skills gap?

Figure 1. The Margerison-McCann Team Management Wheel

Diagram used with the permission of Dick McCann, Team Management Resources, Brisbane, Australia

Life Cycles and Organizational Levels

The integrating experience of team profiling makes it easier for the team to identify where it is on the growth/decline life-cycle curve. Having done this, the team can identify the "indicators" or signs that might exist for each level of organizational life.

Groups find it easy to identify where the major problem layer is and can test their perceptions, beliefs, and data by using the Kaufman needs assessment framework to identify gaps in results (Kaufman, 1990).

A big-picture understanding of the organization gives people/teams a sense of power and understanding.

Planning

The critical piece of the jigsaw is now the planning. It is the keystone of the strategy from this point. The organization sets about establishing a hierarchy of plans—societal, corporation, divisional/regional, work team, individual (although the preparation of individual performance plans usually is undertaken after the team works on issues of responsibility, accountability, and levels of decision making). These plans have to both "roll down" and "roll up" and be based on what results would be delivered. The requirement to operate at mega, macro, and micro levels of planning causes people to shift their thinking and to be excited by the prospect of achieving significant results that give them a greater sense of pride in the organization. The significance of the Kaufman approach is its flexibility: you can adapt it to suit the situation, which proves very valuable in different organizations.

Ideally, the executive team or corporate management group drafts the three- and one-year corporate plans. This involves seeking both participation and collaboration with key people from other parts of the organization who can input constructively and again involves those people strategically placed to contribute. Planning gives direction so that the organization can move forward in times of change. It is also important to recognize that these plans are more like clay than concrete. They can be molded and changed if and when required because of legitimate demands to change during the yearly (or long-term planning cycle).

The other layers of planning are then undertaken with the other levels/groups in the organization. This creates a planning cascade and an imperative that the different levels of planning align.

The "glue" is created by every team's completion of the same process, thus ensuring a common language for team understanding, strategic thinking and planning, and cross-functional negotiation. The impact created by consistency of approach can never be underestimated.

In terms of the actual planning process, I sometimes vary the Kaufman approach but still use the core elements of his model (scope, data collection, planning, and implementation).

Scoping involves selecting the type of strategic planning from the three alternatives. Its worth is particularly in alerting people to the importance of the following scopes:

- Mega planning (focuses on the external societal impact of what the organization produces and is concerned with improving people's self-sufficiency, self-reliance, mutual interdependence, and quality of life);

- Macro planning (views "society" from the point of view of the organization's well-being with the focus on continued organizational health and survival); and

- Micro planning (functions to improve individual and/or group competence and performance, and the focus is operational rather than strategic).

My experience with scoping is that most organizations scope at the macro level until given the opportunity to think beyond the organization. Thinking beyond the organization frees up strategic thinking and seems to make organizations less risk-averse.

Also, once the organization thinks at the mega level, it is able to influence the other levels of planning so that even though people are planning at the macro and micro levels, they do it with a "mega-attitude." This shifts the focus (raises their eyes to the horizon) from operational to strategic and enables them to think beyond the confines of the past.

Data collection covers needs assessment, client/stakeholder analysis, beliefs/values, environmental scanning, and strength/weakness/opportunity/threat analysis (SWOT).

Needs Assessment

Needs assessment uses the following framework. When groups fill in the "what is" and "what should be" boxes and then have to discipline themselves to "close/eliminate the gap" in the middle, it seems to force proof or justification for their needs assessment.

The process of identifying outcomes is also useful when people get to the mission-development stage of the strategic planning process.

Clients/Stakeholders

Clients are those people who receive the service or product. Stakeholders are those people/groups/organizations that have an impact on or are impacted by the strategic planning.

Questions that organizations commonly address are "Who are our clients and stakeholders?" and "What are their stakes and interests?"

Which ones are key? (That is, clients and stakeholders have a powerful influence on your organization and your planning because they are either supportive or resistant.)

Beliefs/Values

These drive the plan. What is believed in is far more likely to motivate; therefore, it is important for organizations to be clear about their beliefs/values and also to practice acting them out. Assuredly, words relating to beliefs/values sound motivating and evocative; but, if the behavior of the organization is different from the espoused values, then the incongruity will be very apparent to the external clients and to the employees.

Environmental Scanning

Scanning the internal and external environment is undertaken to elicit key information that impacts on the strategic plan at the strategic and operational phases. Examples of internal categories would be technology, relationships, resources, political roles, and structure. Examples of external categories would be political, demographic, social, technological, economic, and relationships. Organizations can add or delete categories as appropriate.

SWOT Analysis

This process identifies the strengths, weaknesses, opportunities, and threats for the organization. Strengths and weaknesses are usually internal. Opportunities and threats are often external to the organization or work team.

It is often useful to ask, "What should be done to build or weaken SWOTs? Which are the key elements that may impact significantly on planning for change?"

Strategic Planning

Once the contextual analysis and data gathering are complete, teams move to the strategic planning stage—where do we want to get to?

It is desirable to ensure that a "mega attitude" prevails. This attitude helps teams/organizations to focus on the external consequences of what they want to achieve and prevents an internal focus that might eliminate relevance to the external world.

Kaufman's concept of establishing an "ideal vision" in terms of what our children would be proud of our achieving has the power to actually lift the quality of the desired result. This vision becomes something that people take pride in and links strongly to shared values, which mean something internally and externally.

After establishing the ideal vision, the strategic planning phase is undertaken, which includes:

- *Mission.* What the end result to be achieved is, for whom, for what purpose, and written in no more than twenty-five words. This discipline helps focus on results and cuts out the "word salad" that can disguise what teams and organizations wish to achieve.

- *Goals.* Statements of intended results that are measurable in a nominal (naming) or ordinal (ranking) scale of measurement. These are the key results critical to achieving the mission. It is customary to identify seven, plus or minus two goals (key result areas), for the mission. Goals can be of three types—maintenance (valuable continuous results to be achieved), developmental (added-value results to what has been achieved in the past), and innovation (new results that will enhance business profitability/new markets and that are aligned with the external needs of society).

- *Objectives.* Precision statements that set the performance standard for how well things will be done. For example, by June 1996, Organization Development Service will have designed and delivered two six-month corporate management programs that will return the organization an average of eight times the investment costs of full participation in the programs.

These objectives are the basis for evaluating the gap between the specific performance standard intended and the results actually achieved.

Objectives have to be given the SMART test:

Specific-results based

Measurable

Attainable

Resourced and realistic

Timebound

Finally, it is critical to test the level of objectives set because they might be too abstract or too specific.

The difficult part seems to be to set SMART objectives. My experience is that people pull back from the commitment to be specific about the standards to be achieved. This seems to be based on inexperience (not having done it before) or fear of consequences and sanctions if they set a standard and then cannot reach it. In the case of inexperience, once people have pushed through the invisible barrier and accepted the challenges they set for themselves, it often energizes and focuses them. It also clarifies what each division, group, or team will deliver.

Fear of consequences is an organizational culture and leadership style issue. You can force the situation and often have to, but people will tend to regress and protect themselves. This makes it critically important to convince leaders and managers of the strategic role they have in the whole process. If they gatekeep, block, and do not own the process, then the individuals who answer to them will protect their interests and not stretch themselves in terms of achievement and support.

Operational Planning Phase

After setting objectives, teams and organizations enter the operational planning phase—how do we want to get there? This phase includes two elements:

- Tactical activities—the major groupings of activities that will lead to the achievement of successful results. These will be the component parts and milestones that will have to be achieved to realize goals and objectives.

- Action planning—requirement that people deal in micro-specific details for each strategic activity about what has to be done, by when, how, and by whom; who else might have responsibilities, linkages, and flows.

Implementation: Putting the Nut on the Bolt

By this point, people usually have developed a stronger sense of the team. They also realize that more work has to be done to finish the plan and to ensure the alignment of plans.

People tend to want to take a deep breath and relax. Doing so leaves them at the rational levels of organizational life (practices and procedures, purpose and direction). They risk looking at structures, policies, and systems but do not dip into the third level of identity and unity in order to bind and to further develop a sense of shared meaning.

The following three questions facilitate the implementation phase of the planning process:

1. What support do we get as a team?

2. How effective are we as individuals?

3. What rewards and recognition do we get?

In answering the first question, a common process is to

- Clarify job roles in relation to those of other team members and negotiate about what they require more of, less of, the same of, none of, and instead of in order to do their job as effectively as possible (Harrison & Stokes, 1986);

- Resolve ground rules that the team will adopt to be a high-performing team;

- Clarify who is responsible and who is accountable for delivering the results; and

- Decide specifically how team performance will be monitored.

Then, a skills assessment follows:

- What skills do we require to meet the challenges of the team's goals?

- What skills do we presently have?

- What is the skills gap?

This leads to clarification of training and development needs (on-the-job, coaching, or formal courses).

How effective are we as individuals? At this point the focus then returns sharply to planning, and people develop their own individual performance agreements to answer the question.

Each member of the team is required to develop an individual performance agreement that aligns with the team's strategic and operational plans. Each individual develops key job goals, performance indicators, performance standards, training and development needs, and career goals. These are negotiated with the supervisor or manager. The sum of the individual plans should add up to the work-team plan.

What rewards and recognition do we get? This step touches the level of identity and unity in organizational life. It is often completed by varying the Kaufman needs assessment framework. Teams invariably use this framework to establish new practices to build a greater sense of shared meaning, to celebrate high performance, and to build the culture of the group as both achievement- and support-oriented.

This also means that the series of steps have allowed the team to touch each level of organizational life and to recognize that interventions are necessary for success.

Conclusion

The strong emphasis on planning encourages planning at the mega, macro, and micro levels.

High-performing teamwork and valuing people's work-preference differences create common maps and a language to affirm the desired culture.

The continual emphasis on accountability and a culture based on participation, collaboration, and results build trust, integrity, and business-like behavior.

Of course, the waves of change are continuous. Much work has to be done in many areas; however, it is encouraging to remember that large-scale change occurs when many people change just a little.

The processes outlined in this chapter are only one approach. It works because it focuses on a sequence of key events to capture the critical mass of people and to keep the change process moving forward.

I wish to thank Helen Munro, Jenny Everett, and Maureen Grear for their developmental work designed to create a performance culture in an Australian organization that operates internationally. Working in this organization provided me with the opportunity to develop the processes outlined in this chapter.

References

Dalmau, T., & Dick, R. (1987). *Interventions for community and organization change*. Brisbane, Queensland, Australia: Interchange.

Harrison, R., & Stokes, H. (1986). *Diagnosing organization culture— An instrument*. Berkeley, CA: Harrison Associations, Inc.

Kaufman, R. (1990). *Strategic planning plus: An organizational guide*. Glenview, IL: Scott Foresman.

Margerison, C., & McCann, R. *The team development manual*. Brisbane, Queensland, Australia: Team Management Resources.

PERFORMANCE IMPROVEMENT IN DEVELOPING COUNTRIES

Fred Rosensweig

This chapter describes a comprehensive approach to performance improvement in developing countries. The basic premise is that performance improvement in developing countries requires change at the mega level. Without such change any performance improvement at the macro or micro level will not last. The chapter discusses the types of performance issues that typically arise at the mega, macro, and micro levels and suggests the types of frameworks and interventions that can be used at each level.

The Need For Mega-Level Performance Interventions

The term "developing country" encompasses a wide range of countries located primarily in Africa, Latin America, and Asia that receive assistance from industrialized nations. It also includes those countries in Eastern Europe that are newly democratic. The countries range from those that are extremely poor (per capita income of $200-$300 per year) to middle-income countries (per capita income of $2,000 per year). The variety of conditions within these countries must be acknowledged and taken into account when planning a performance improvement effort.

In developing countries, the term that is commonly used for the mega level is "sector," for the macro level, "organizational or institutional," and for the micro level, "individual or unit." The "sector" refers to all those organizations that provide services and products, coordinate and regulate activities, and provide and arrange financing for a particular programmatic area. It also includes the legal and regulatory framework that determines how business is supposed to be conducted in that sector. Examples of sectors include health, water and sanitation, agriculture, housing, and energy.

Improving performance in a sector is vital to improving performance in a single organization because each organization is dependent to some extent on the other organizations operating in the sector. For example, a public utility requires a clear regulatory policy that will enable it to recover its recurrent costs and service its debt if it is to be financially self-sufficient. A water utility is also dependent on an outside organization, usually the Ministry of Health, for monitoring water quality to ensure that it meets national standards.

Focusing performance improvement efforts on the sectoral level provides greater potential for having an impact on society. If a country decides that it wants to improve environmental health, for example, it must deal with the problem on a sectoral basis. Regulations must be established, monitoring and enforcement capabilities must be developed, technical options must be explored, and financial implications must be assessed. Such change requires far more than can be achieved by strengthening a single organization.

Any approach to performance improvement in a developing country that focuses solely on improving the performance of individuals and single organizations is likely to fail. For decades, international organizations funded projects that focused on a specific geographical area, a specific organization, or in some cases a specific intervention (e.g., training). The U.S. Agency for International Development (A.I.D.), the World Bank, the United Nations Development Programme (UNDP) and other international organizations have since learned that this type of approach produces limited benefits. A.I.D., for example, has had policy reform as one of its major foci since the mid-1980s. A.I.D. now often uses its resources to stimulate developing countries to change their policies and it has funded a project whose mandate is to develop approaches to assist countries in implementing policy changes. The World Bank is using its substantial financing capability to leverage sectoral reforms. A recent $300 million loan to Mexico for water and wastewater projects is contingent on major sectoral reform. And UNDP is leading the way in international forums to promote a sectoral approach to development. A recent document on what UNDP calls "capacity-building" proposes an approach to strengthen both organizational and sectoral levels (United Nations Development Programme, 1991). All these international organizations have learned that their development efforts will not be sustainable unless they combine action at the individual and organizational levels with sectoral reform.

The sectoral approach does not address all mega-level issues, however. Other mega-level issues often constrain a country's progress. Such issues are countrywide and affect all sectors. These issues fall into three categories:

- Legal and regulatory (e.g., civil service system),

- Political (e.g., political patronage), and

- Economic and financial (e.g., tariffs and cost-recovery policy).

There are numerous examples of countries that have made limited development progress because of failure to address mega-level issues. In Latin America, for example, even mid-level managers in government agencies are replaced after elections, and agencies thus lose institutional memory every four years or so. Many countries do not allow their public utilities to charge realistic rates for water (gas, electricity) because of a belief that the service is a public one and should not be fully paid by consumers. The result is an ongoing drain on the national treasury, continuing subsidies, and an inability to extend coverage. Other countries (including developed countries) decide where to build infrastructure based on who is owed political favors. Many countries consider government service as the primary means of reducing unemployment and some even guarantee all university graduates a job. The result is serious overstaffing in many government agencies.

It is clear that mega-level changes are harder to achieve than macro- or micro-level changes. Mega-level problems that require such changes as the reform of the civil service, setting tariffs that allow for full cost recovery, reducing the political spoils system, selling off state-run companies, and reducing government payrolls are not easy. Yet, it is only such changes that can truly make a difference in developing countries. Changes within a particular sector will not address these types of mega-level issues.

Because most performance improvement practitioners work at the micro or macro level, it is critical that they understand how to diagnose individual and organizational problems and identify those problems that require attention at the mega level. The rest of this chapter focuses on providing frameworks for analyzing mega- and macro-level issues. Less attention is paid to analyzing micro-level problems because the technology is relatively well-known.

Sectoral Level

The ability to assess the effectiveness of a sector is critical to improving sectoral performance. Three areas of inquiry are essential in assessing how a sector operates (Edwards, Salt, & Rosensweig, 1992). These areas are the following:

- Sectoral context—historical, economic, political, environmental;
- Division of roles and responsibilities; and
- Allocation of major sectoral tasks.

The Sectoral Context

A sector does not operate in a vacuum. A range of factors influence the development of a sector; understanding those factors will provide insights into the feasibility of sectoral reform and how far it can go. There are four such factors: historical background, level of economic development, political system, and the population and land area of the country.

The historical background of a country greatly affects the way services are provided. A colonial history, for example, may affect land tenure, the governmental and legal system, and disposition toward hierarchy and democracy. One of the clearer examples of the impact of historical factors is Bolivia, where the population of European origin lives in urban areas located at easier-to-serve lower elevations while the Indian populations live in hard-to-serve mountainous areas. Access to the best land and services has long been a privilege of those of European origin, and any attempt to change this will meet with resistance. For another example, Guatemala's tradition of municipal government, which dates back several hundred years, provides a fertile environment for strengthening municipal government capabilities.

As for economic development, a country with a relatively high level of economic development is likely to have a decentralized system and a strong private sector. Malaysia and Chile have fairly strong economies and are giving increasing responsibility to the states or regions. Countries with a relatively high level of economic development will also have more financial resources available. Countries with a low level of economic development often do not have much capability at the local level. Most of the capability resides at the central level in the capital city.

The political system determines the degree of government control exercised over the delivery of services. It will also affect the strength of local government, the social policy behind the provision of services, and the degree of centralization. Governments have the power to constrain through law what can be done. By regulating ownership, land tenure, tariffs, and taxation, governments affect what happens. A closed political system is likely to mean an overly centralized government, limited risk-taking, and a top-down management system.

The population and land area of a country affect how a government operates. If a country is small and has a relatively small population, it might be able to operate effectively in a centralized manner. On the other hand, if a country has a large population and a moderate level of economic development, it may be able to operate effectively in a decentralized manner. The size of the country and its population will also affect the number of agencies that are involved in a particular sector. There is no sense in having a number of agencies carrying out the same function in a country with a small population, especially in a poor country. Tunisia, which has limited water resources, has a single national water authority with regional offices, a logical system for a relatively small country. Brazil, on the other hand, with a population of about 150 million, operates through a federal system. To do otherwise would be unwieldy.

Understanding these factors will enhance any performance improvement effort. Knowing why and how the current situation has evolved will provide the kind of insights that will shape a performance improvement effort.

Division of Roles and Responsibilities

The clear and rational division of responsibilities within a sector is fundamental to its performance. Take as an example the water and sanitation sector. It must be clear who is responsible for serving the urban, peri-urban, and rural areas. It must also be clear who is responsible for water and who for sanitation. In addition, the division of responsibilities between central ministries and their regional offices must be clear. It must also be clear which agencies are responsible for planning, budgeting, financing, allocating resources, setting policy, enforcing policies, and providing training. Unclear definition of sectoral roles and responsibilities can hinder the achievement of sectoral objectives. Thus, performance improvement efforts must help to rationalize the assignment of sectoral roles and responsibilities.

Allocation of Major Sectoral Tasks

Every sector must accomplish four sectoral tasks, and any sectoral analysis must determine how those tasks are handled. In many developing countries, neglect of these tasks has resulted in serious problems.

The first sectoral task is setting policies and standards. A mechanism must be in place for considering the sector as a whole and defining what is in the common interest. In the United States, the Environmental Protection Agency plays the role of setting and enforcing environmental standards within a highly decentralized system. In the absence of an effective policy-making process, a sector will find it hard to address major problems.

The second sectoral task is planning. Planning includes financial planning, master plan development, and operational planning. This is not to advocate a centralized planning system. Rather, it is to say that an effective planning process must be in place to achieve whatever goals have been set for the sector and to address major gaps. In developing countries, this usually means a planning process that involves local government, a technical agency, and a central body.

The third sectoral task is arranging financing and ensuring that the cost of capital investment is repaid. This includes deciding how much external financing is anticipated, how to service the debt, and what changes in fiscal policy are required. A developing country must have a system that provides access to capital and enables it to pay back its debts at market rates.

The fourth sectoral task is implementing programs. Typically, central ministries are not involved in program implementation although there are many exceptions to this general rule. The critical question is whether the sector provides for program implementation and how effective it is.

Organizational Level

Changes at the sectoral level are crucial to improving performance, but much of the actual effort will take place at the organizational level. Determining the needs at the organizational level requires a careful assessment of the organization. In the rest of this section, two frameworks are presented for conducting organizational needs assessment, one for private or autonomous public entities (e.g., a public utility) and the other for line government ministries (e.g., a Ministry of Health). Two approaches are necessary because the two categories of organizations are fundamentally different. Organizations in the first category have the potential to be commercially oriented in that they raise their own revenue and represent little or no cost to the general treasury. Organizations in the second category are classic government agencies. They follow the rules and regulations of the national government system and receive their funding through the national budget.

Autonomous Organizations

These types of organizations must be proficient in nine areas of performance, called performance categories (Cullivan et al., 1988). Each category should be assessed in determining the needs of a given institution. The overall assessment will provide insight into the strengths and weaknesses of an organization. A performance category is defined as a set of related skills, procedures, and capabilities. Following is a brief explanation of each performance category.

1. Organizational autonomy: the degree of independence that an organization has from the national government. No organization can operate completely independently, but it should be able to operate with minimal controls and interference in such areas as budgeting, hiring and firing, establishing pay and incentive packages, planning, and other operational matters.

2. Leadership: the capability to inspire staff to carry out the organization's mission. Leadership is the ability to make the sum of the parts greater than the whole. Leadership must reside in more than the head of the organization. It is needed at all levels of the organization.

3. Management and administration: organizing people and resources to accomplish the organization's goals. Effective management is demonstrated by having a clear sense of goals, being aware of operational details, planning, and monitoring the work. It is also character-

ized by teamwork and good communication. Administration is defined as the policies and procedures that regulate the actions of management. These include systems that handle personnel, budgeting, accounting, financial management, procurement, and management information.

4. Commercial orientation: the degree to which actions in an organization are driven by cost-effectiveness and operational efficiency. Commercially oriented organizations attempt to achieve financial equilibrium by paying attention to cost as well as quality.

5. Consumer orientation: ensuring that the products and services of an organization are directed toward consumers. Effective organizations have mechanisms in place to interact with consumers and see serving consumers as their primary function.

6. Technical capability: the ability of the organization to make sound technical decisions, control the quality of the work, complete projects on time and economically, and use appropriate technologies.

7. Developing and maintaining staff: recruiting, hiring, training, and providing adequate wages and incentives to maintain personnel. Training includes formal classroom training and other instructional methods, such as job aids, on-the-job training, self-instruction, and distance education.

8. Organizational culture: the set of values and norms that guide everyday actions. The organization's culture forms a pattern of shared beliefs that determines everyday behavior.

9. Managing the external environment: the ability to influence other entities that affect an organization's

financial, political, and legal ability to perform. This is accomplished by anticipating actions that might affect the institution and developing strategies to deal with them.

Line Ministries

Agencies that are dependent on funding through the national budget require a different assessment framework than autonomous organizations. Because they are not commercially oriented, they do not require the same degree of autonomy in their operations. They are also subject to government-wide policies and procedures. The framework for assessing this type of organization involves the following eight performance categories.

1. Providing overall direction: the development of an overall vision to guide the activities of staff. Providing overall direction requires a set of policies, along with supportive norms and standards, that offer specific guidance to units of the organization in carrying out its work.

2. Planning: the ability to develop both long-range and short-term plans that will enable the organization to achieve its vision. Planning should involve the ministry's field offices so that there is an appropriate amount of bottom-up input that ensures that planning is demand based. The central office's role in planning is generally to coordinate the planning process, make sure that the plans are supportive of the ministry's vision, and make final resource decisions.

3. Implementation: ensuring a rational approach to the conduct of projects and programs. This means use of the private sector as well as direct implementation by government ministries where appropriate.

4. Monitoring and evaluation: collecting and analyzing data on ongoing activities. This requires a management information system to enable mid-course corrections and ensure that future plans are based on real needs.

5. Resource allocation and logistical support: providing adequate human and material resources to get the job done. Public sector agencies in developing countries often suffer from either overstaffing or understaffing. Providing the right number of people with the appropriate skills is a critical function. Logistical support, especially adequate supplies and vehicle support, is essential. All too often in developing countries, staff has no money to purchase even basic office supplies.

6. Coordination: interacting with the various agencies involved in a sector. This requires a viable mechanism as well as the will to coordinate. It is rare that an agency in a developing country will not have to coordinate its actions with others to be effective. The mechanism must be formal, have high-level support, and have adequate resources.

7. Training and technical assistance: ensuring that field offices have the management and technical capabilities needed to accomplish their tasks. Field offices are usually deficient in management and technical skills, and the extent to which the central ministry can help to fill the gaps is an important factor in the success of field operations. Sometimes this assistance will take the form of training. In other cases, it will take the form of troubleshooting, problem solving, and other forms of consulting assistance.

8. Financing: obtaining the money required to fund activities. Financing can come from external sources, such as international lending institutions like the World

Bank, and/or from internal sources, such as the general treasury or the local private sector. The ability to secure adequate financing for activities is fundamental to success.

Use of one of the two assessment frameworks will result in a diagnosis of the strengths and weaknesses of an organization. An assessment framework is an important starting point in the process of organizational improvement, but by itself it is not sufficient because it does not directly address the question of strategy. Once a clear picture of the strengths and weaknesses of an organization exists, the next step is to develop a strategy for improving organizational performance in the areas of weakness.

One of the best examples of an organizational improvement effort was a seven-year A.I.D.-funded project in Sri Lanka to strengthen the National Water Supply and Drainage Board (NWSDB). The project resulted in a complete turnaround of a public utility. An indicator of the success of the project was that the utility went from collecting 12 percent of its operations and maintenance costs in 1983 before the project started to recovering 100 percent of operations and maintenance and total debt service in 1993, an astounding accomplishment for a water utility in the developing world. In the final report of the project (Bradley, 1991), a number of important lessons learned about organizational performance improvement were documented.

A few of the most important ones are the following.

- A prescriptive project design must be avoided at all costs.

- All change strategies, new procedures, and other project interventions must be owned by the organization's counterparts.

- Delegation of authority programs is essential for ensuring dissemination of new systems and ownership throughout the organization.

- Performance indicators must be developed within the institution and must be seen to be relevant to the operations being measured.

- The project should be periodically monitored by an external team to ensure that the project is focused on long-term sustainability.

- The external environment, including the political forces and external lending agencies, must be involved in support of the organizational changes.

- The consultant team should be a mix of technical specialists and organizational development experts.

The project used a number of strategies to achieve its goals of autonomy and a commercial orientation. These included the decentralization of the organization into five regional service centers, delivery of a comprehensive management development program for both senior and mid-level managers, the establishment of an effective corporate planning capability, initiation of an extensive financial viability program, development of a human resource development capability, expansion of community-based approaches to improve health education and rural sanitation services, and the strengthening of the engineering capability.

The Sri Lanka example illustrates what is possible in a developing country when a focused performance improvement effort is made over time with the assistance of skilled external consultants. Many of the approaches implied in the assessment framework discussed above became the basis for the project goals and strategies. It should be noted that all this performance improvement occurred while Sri Lanka was experiencing serious political problems and ethnic violence.

Individual Level

Although performance improvement will not come about without changes at the sectoral and organizational levels, there is, nevertheless, significant work to be done at the unit or individual level. To the extent that this work is based on an assessment of organizational needs, is part of an overall organizational improvement program, and is buttressed by supportive national policies, it will have an impact. As noted above, however, changes at the individual level cannot be sustained unless attention is also paid to policy and the overall organization.

This discussion does not go into detail about frameworks and strategies for the individual performance improvement level. For the most part, more is known about performance improvement at this level than at the sectoral or organizational level. The specific performance interventions available are similar to those used in a developed country including job aids, feedback systems, personnel recruitment and selection, and strategic planning (Rosensweig, 1992). Such instructional interventions as classroom instruction, small group instruction, self-instructional materials, on-the-job training, and distance education can be used in developing countries. However, several caveats must be kept in mind in applying these techniques.

First, cultural differences must be taken into account during the needs analysis. For example, differences in the way direct feedback is perceived, the degree to which participation in decision making is valued, and the criteria for hiring staff must be understood. Care must be taken not to impose inappropriate cultural norms.

Second, developing countries have an extreme bias toward training as the solution to all performance problems. There is generally little recognition that individual performance problems may be due to poor supervision, lack of adequate incentives, poor working conditions, or lack of resources.

Third, performance interventions must take into account the ability of the country to absorb new technologies. Instructional interventions using computers or other high-tech equipment are generally inappropriate. The technology must be consistent with the level of technology widely used in that country, and new technologies should be introduced slowly.

Conclusions

How can one expect a performance technologist to have a mega perspective? Most practitioners are trained as instructional technologists or trainers, or perhaps as organizational development specialists. To understand the mega level necessitates an interdisciplinary perspective that blends economics, political science, sociology/anthropology, and a technical area (e.g., health, agriculture). One does not have to be an expert in each of these areas, however. Rather, the effective practitioner will have a basic understanding of all these areas before planning a performance improvement project to make sure that the micro project is addressing macro needs and is not inconsistent with major goals at the mega level.

Performance improvement in developing countries requires a different perspective than in developed nations. In the United States, for example, practitioners often take for granted that the U.S. system—a coherent set of policies and sound private and public institutions—provides the necessary framework for change. Of course, many would counter that the U.S. system also has many gaps, but even if true, it is a matter of degree. In some developing countries and even in Eastern European countries, in contrast, there is no banking system. In some countries, civil servants are not paid regularly. Some countries have unemployment rates as high as 40 percent. These types of problems constrain performance improvement and must be taken into account if there is to be any chance of success. One cannot take for granted the basic soundness of the political and economic system in a developing country.

Several points should be kept in mind when applying approaches to performance-improvement in developing countries.

First, and the central thesis of this chapter, performance improvement efforts must take into account all three levels: mega, macro, and micro. Designing a performance improvement project without first assessing whether the sectoral and organizational levels will support it means the performance improvement will probably not last. This does not mean that one can never start at the individual or organization level, but it must be done with full realization of what the situation is at the mega level. This realization will probably strongly influence the nature of the intervention at the individual or organizational level.

Second, all developing countries are not the same. They are not all at the same stage of development in their ability to absorb and sustain change. A country like Brazil or Thailand has a far greater capacity to develop a computer-based management information system than would a country like Chad or Zaire. Similarly, newly emerging democracies like Hungary and Poland have a far greater human resource base than most developing countries. Flexibility in applying human performance technology is key.

Third, practitioners should have an interdisciplinary perspective that enables them to plan and implement efforts based on a sound understanding of the overall context of the performance improvement effort.

References

Bradley, R. (1991). *Executive summary final report on institutional development of the National Water Supply and Drainage Board.* United States Agency for International Development Mission to Colombo, Sri Lanka.

Cullivan, D. et al. (1988). Guidelines for institutional assessment: Water and wastewater institutions. WASH Technical Report No.37. Arlington, VA: WASH Project.

Edwards, D., Salt, E., & Rosensweig, F. (1992). *Making choices for sectoral organization in water and sanitation.* WASH Technical Report No. 74. Arlington, VA: WASH Project.

Rosensweig, F. (1992). Human performance technology in the international arena. In H. Stolovitch & E. Keeps (eds.), *Handbook of performance technology.* San Francisco, CA: Jossey-Bass.

United Nations Development Programme. (1991). *Framework document for capacity building: Guidelines for working group discussions.* Unpublished paper for symposium in Delft, Netherlands.

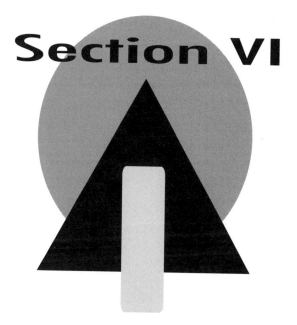

Section VI

Evaluation

EVALUATION: SEVEN DIMENSIONS, SIX STEPS, FIVE PHASES, AND FOUR GUIDELINES

Sivasailam Thiagarajan

Evaluation is the process of determining the worth of something. This chapter contains four sections that expand on the basic definition. The first section explores seven conceptual dimensions of evaluation. The second section deals with six procedural steps in evaluation. The third section synthesizes the previous two and offers practical suggestions for different phases of evaluation. The final section presents four critical guidelines.

Seven Dimensions of Evaluation

Hidden beneath the apparently simple definition of evaluation are several dimensions related to its object, purpose, focus, model, measurement strategy, types, and timing. In this section, let's explore the seven basic dimensions of evaluation and the variations in each dimension. This section should provide us with a useful framework for planning an evaluation project.

Object of Evaluation

The object of evaluation is the "something" that is found at the end of the definition. In general, the object of evaluation can be a product, a process, or a person.

A product[1] is a tangible physical article. For example, an ergonomically designed computer keyboard, a gameboard to simulate cross-cultural interactions, or a decision table to help check encoders to decide how an illegible check should be handled are all products that could be objects of evaluation.

A process is a step-by-step procedure or a series of events. For example, a team-based incentive system, a right-sizing procedure, and a sexual harassment policy are all processes that could be objects of evaluation.

People include all type of employees and performers. For example, a trainee at the completion of a workshop, an applicant during a job interview, or an employee during the annual performance appraisal are all people who could be objects of evaluation.

Most evaluation projects involve a combination of products, processes, and people. For example, in evaluating the effectiveness of an ergonomic keyboard (a product), we take into account the physical characteristics of the user (a person), and whether this person uses touch-typing (a process) or not. Similarly, in evaluating a team-based incentive system (a process), we take into account the relationships among team members (people) and the forms (products) used for recording the team's productivity. In evaluating a trainee (a person) at the end of a workshop, we have to take into consideration the training method (a process) and the test instrument (a product).

---

[1] In other chapters of this book, a product is defined as an *en route* deliverable of an organization.

In planning an evaluation project, it is critical to specify the primary object being evaluated. In addition, it is important to identify associated products, processes, and people to be included in the evaluation.

Purpose of Evaluation

Most evaluation activities in human performance technology serve one of two purposes: formative or summative. Simply put, *formative* evaluation is designed to improve the object being evaluated, while *summative* evaluation is designed to prove that the object meets certain criteria.

Here are some various examples of formative evaluation questions:

- How can we make the keyboard more suitable for left-handed employees?

- How can we make the visuals on the gameboard less culturally biased?

- How can we make the decision table easier to understand to second-language speakers of English?

- How can we reduce feelings of unfairness caused by the team-based incentive system?

- How can we reduce the guilt felt by the survivors of a rightsizing program?

- How can we give appropriate diagnostic guidance to the trainees at the end of the workshop?

Summative evaluation questions in the same situations require a yes/no or go/no-go decision. Here are some sample questions:

- Does this product meet our needs?

- Should we implement this process?

- Should we continue with this process?

- Does this person have the required skills and personal qualities?

- Can we afford to pay an appropriate salary to this person?

The same evaluation project may be used for both formative and summative purposes: in collecting formative data to improve a product, we may realize that the cost of such improvements is not worth the expected benefits. Therefore, we may make the summative decision to abort the project. Similarly, summative evaluation may indicate that we should purchase the product, implement the process, or hire a person and, at the same time, suggest some modifications. The product may require some tweaking to make it compatible with the local computer system; the process may require the elimination of a step to speed it up; or the person may require a crash course on how to handle hazardous materials. In these situations, we are adding a formative component to our summative decision.

In planning an evaluation project, it is important to specify whether our primary purpose is formative or summative. It is equally important to keep an open mind and use the same data for formative revisions or summative decisions.

Focus of Evaluation

Performance technology interventions are designed to achieve measurable goals. These goals—and specific objectives related to them—provide the criteria for making formative and summative decisions. For example, let us assume that we decide that providing customer satisfaction is our major goal and specify several performance objectives to reach this goal. To achieve this goal, we develop an incentive system based on customer ratings of employees. We evaluate the impact of the incentive system by collecting data on the achievement of each objective. If most of the data indicate increased customer dissatisfaction, we make the summative decision of abandoning the incentive system. On the other hand, if there is an increase in customer satisfaction, we may firmly implement the incentive system.

As shown in this example, most evaluation approaches compare the results with the goals. This evaluation stance, labeled the goal-based approach, is an objective approach, which increases the probability of appropriate formative and summative actions.

There are some limitations to a strict goal-free approach. Returning to our example, while the goal of increasing customer satisfaction may be achieved, we may incur several costs and face some negative consequences in areas that are not measured, but which are important. For example, our profits may go down dramatically, reminding us of critical variables other than customer satisfaction. Our customers may be satisfied, but our suppliers may become frustrated with us. Our external customers may be delighted, but our internal employees may be "at each others' throats." The incentive system may result in a short-term improvement, only to be followed by long-term customer dissatisfaction as their expectations increase.

In order to take into account expensive costs and dangerous side effects of an intervention, Scriven (1972) and others recommend a goal-free stance to evaluation. The evaluator who takes this stance collects data on the actual effects of the intervention, irrespective of its prespecified goals and objectives. To avoid selective perception, the goal-free evaluator may refuse to review the objectives for the intervention and merely measure all of its effects on all stakeholders, measuring and reporting both positive and negative outcomes of a short- and long-term nature.

Goal-based and goal-free evaluation are not alternative approaches, but rather two aspects of all evaluation. In planning for an evaluation project, you should provide for the identification and measurement of all effects.

Models of Evaluation

All evaluation is based on conceptual frameworks or models. These models provide a metaphor for guiding the evaluation activities.

Scientific Model

Most evaluation activities in human performance technology are based on the scientific model, which assumes that the best way to arrive at the truth is to conduct a controlled experiment. This model recommends that we should begin with an evaluation design that excludes irrelevant variables and controls the relevant ones. The scientific evaluator compares what happens when an intervention is implemented with what happens when it is withheld. For example, to evaluate the impact of a videotape program on employee attitudes toward physically disabled colleagues, we may assemble two equal groups of employees, ensure that the members in the groups are matched on all irrelevant variables by random assignment, measure the baseline attitudes of both groups, show the videotape program to the experimental group, show a placebo videotape on some unrelated topic to the other group, and test the two groups' attitudes again. If there is a difference, we can assume that it is due to the videotape program. With scientific modesty, we can disclaim any generalization of this result to actual changes in employees' behaviors toward their disabled colleagues in the workplace.

Ethnographic Model

Unfortunately for the scientific evaluators among us, factors that influence human performance cannot be easily isolated and experimentally manipulated. Also, results from controlled laboratory studies seldom generalize reliably to uncontrolled field conditions. An evaluation model derived from anthropology and related disciplines is now emerging as an alternative approach that is better suited to the realities of the workplace. This ethnographic model uses a variety of qualitative techniques and permits the design to emerge from the evaluation process rather than being specified at the start. The purpose of ethnographic evaluation is broadened to include a more comprehensive understanding of the object being evaluated. To achieve such understanding, the intervention is described in great detail, often from the points of view of different stakeholders.

Judicial Model

As any viewer of Perry Mason reruns can attest, truth is too complex to be determined through expert testimony. The judicial model for evaluation is based on the assumption that truth emerges from a debate between opposing points of view. For example, if we were to evaluate the effectiveness of a sexual harassment policy, the judicial evaluator would ask two groups of experts to collect data opposing and supporting the policy and to present their findings to a jury of stakeholders using the format of a formal administrative hearing. Scientific and ethnographic evaluation approaches can be incorporated within this model. Although not widely used at this time, the judicial model is especially applicable to the summative evaluation of controversial interventions.

In addition to these three, several other models or metaphors such as investigative reporting, statistical process control, architecture, literary criticism, film reviews, and consumer protection are available for evaluators (Smith, 1986). In planning an evaluation project, it is important to make an informed decision about which model to use as the guiding paradigm. There is nothing to prevent expanding our evaluation activity by including elements of several different models.

Measurement

Measurement is a necessary component of evaluation. It gives us data for determining the worth of the object being evaluated. Measuring the height of a person to be seven feet, for example, gives us an objective piece of information. But actual evaluation requires comparing this information with some criteria that will radically differ depending on whether we are recruiting a basketball center or a steeplechase jockey.

Several measuring instruments and strategies are used for collecting data during evaluation. Here are brief descriptions of some of these devices.

Tests

These paper-and-pencil instruments measure a person's mastery of such things as facts, concepts, principles, procedures, and problem-solving strategies. They can be easily administered and scored and the results can be quantified. Tests are especially useful when there is a deficit in skills and knowledge and when the appropriate intervention is instruction. Criterion-referenced tests measure the achievement of performance objectives while norm-referenced tests compare different members of the target population. Both types of tests can be constructed on the basis of guidelines for ensuring validity, reliability, and objectivity. However, paper-and-pencil tests have a serious limitation because high scores may not always correlate with high levels of actual performance in real-world situations.

Performance Tests

If we are interested in people's ability to "walk the talk" (as we should be), performance tests are superior to their paper-and-pencil counterparts. These tests require the person to actually perform in a real or simulated situation. A measurement specialist can objectively rate this performance or the resultant product. A major advantage of this measurement strategy is its high validity. A major disadvantage is the time and effort required to construct, administer, and score these tests.

Observation

This strategy can be used independently or in conjunction with a performance test to collect data related to desired performances. It involves eliciting the required behaviors or recording these behaviors as they occur naturally. The behaviors may be recorded on audio- or videotape or in the observer's log. Eventually, various elements of the behaviors are counted, classified, and organized with checklists, rating scales, or complex observation systems. Examples of this measurement strategy include analyzing a simulated cardiopulmonary resuscitation administered by a paramedic with a checklist of steps and their sequence; rating a salesperson's behavior during a typical transaction with a 5-point scale that lists different dimensions of appropriate sales techniques; and tracking the transactions during a staff meeting with an observation system that identifies who said what to whom. The advantage of this strategy is its ability to get directly to the relevant on-the-job performance. Its major disadvantages include the requirement of subject-matter expertise and the ethical issues related to unobtrusive observation.

Work Samples and Product Rating

This strategy is similar to the preceding one, except the outputs of the performance are counted or rated rather than the performance itself. It involves selecting some products (either randomly or systematically) and analyzing them against specific standards, using a checklist or a rating scale. The strategy is obviously useful in a manufacturing situation, whether the product is a hamburger, a personal computer, or an automobile. In a service industry, this strategy can be applied to paper products such as reassuring letters to irate customers, monthly bank statements, or advertisement copy. The main advantage of this strategy is the obvious relevance of the data. The main disadvantage is the possible subjectivity.

Content Analysis of Existing Records and Reports

All organizations accumulate paperwork through the years. While several memos and reports continue to be written on how to reduce this paperwork, these records provide valuable data. For example, rather than develop an elaborate survey to discover delays in filling customers' orders, we can review back-order records. Similarly, instead of interviewing people to discover if there is a gender-bias in salaries, we can examine personnel records. Standard documents such as policy manuals, organization charts, order forms, minutes of meetings, internal memos, letters to customers, production reports, and customer complaints provide valuable data on different aspects of the organization. The measurement specialist decides what types of documents are included in the archives, selects those that are relevant, and systematically analyzes the information. The advantages of this strategy include instant access and relevant data. The major disadvantages include inconsistency in record keeping over time and selective bias in the records being kept.

Interviews

An interview is a face-to-face conversation with a stakeholder. Most evaluation activities begin with an interview with the client and continue with interviews with other stakeholders. The interview can be a major measurement activity in itself, or it can be used as a preliminary activity for constructing questionnaires and designing surveys. In using this strategy, the measurement specialist prepares a set of questions, identifies appropriate stakeholders who can provide useful answers, conducts individual interviews with them, probes their responses to acquire additional insights, and summarizes the data. Throughout this process, the interviewer maintains confidentiality of sensitive information and protects the sources of information. Major advantages of this measurement strategy include involvement of the stakeholders in the evaluation process and the ability to follow up unexpected leads. Major disadvantages include the difficulties in analyzing and organizing unstructured interview data and reducing or removing the interviewer's bias.

Focus Groups

A focus group may be thought of as an interview with several people at the same time. It is a structured approach with a specific question (the focus) to be discussed by representative groups of stakeholders. For example, we can use a focus group of different types of customers to identify the impact of a customer-focus program. The major advantages of this strategy include obtaining inputs from a wide variety of people and incorporating their assistance in synthesizing and analyzing the data. The major disadvantages include the requirement for a trained facilitator and the time of several stakeholders.

Two recent developments have contributed significantly to improving the effectiveness and efficiency of focus groups.

The first of these is the availability of structured approaches (such as brainstorming, nominal group technique, and various total quality management [TQM] tools) to maximizing the quality and quantity of inputs. The second is the availability of computerized tools called group decision support systems (GDSS) that organize and display individual inputs of several participants and permit sophisticated polling and statistical computations, while maintaining the anonymity of the participants.

Measurement Types

In evaluating interventions, we measure two types of variables: *performance* and *opinion*. For example, if we have developed a job aid for constructing Pareto charts, we measure employee performance to determine the effectiveness and expert opinions to determine the accuracy of the job aid. The first type of data is collected from members of the target population through observation and testing. The second type, from different experts and stakeholders through questionnaires and interviews.

Both types of measurement are important for making formative revisions and summative decisions. Performance measurement is absolutely necessary, but not entirely sufficient. Even though performance data indicate that an intervention is effective, an expert can suggest a more effective approach, correct factual errors, or suggest strategies for improving the intervention. At the same time, measurement of opinion is not entirely sufficient in itself. These opinions have been frequently shown to be unrelated—or, worse yet, negatively correlated—to performance outcomes.

To explore the varieties of measurements under the performance and opinion categories, let us assume that we are training a group of employees to map different processes. We can measure the performance and its impact at various levels corresponding to Kaufman's classification of products, outputs, and outcomes (Kaufman, 1995). This classification is discussed in an earlier chapter on strategic planning process. Kirkpatrick (1976) uses a different scheme for levels of evaluation. Here is our recommended scheme for measuring performance and its impact at various levels.

In-Process Measurement

We can use an extended case study as a performance test during training. We can use performances of individual trainees on this test to measure intermediate performance changes. We can observe trainees as they work through these exercises to gain additional insights.

Immediate Measurement

Through a posttest, we can measure the immediate gains in learning. For example, we can use an in-basket exercise as a final test to collect useful data. We can also use other tests and questionnaires to collect additional data.

Delayed Measurement

We can administer another posttest (a parallel version of the in-basket exercise) several months later to measure any deterioration or gains in the performance. We can also use various questionnaires to probe for the reasons for these changes in the performance.

Transfer Measurement

We can use interviews, observations, and work-sample ratings to measure the application of process-mapping principles and procedures to the workplace. We can use the same techniques to identify factors that facilitate or inhibit transfer of training.

Organizational Measurement

All of the earlier measurements focused on the performance. We are now ready to shift our attention to the effects of the performance. For example, since the training topic (performance mapping) is a strategy for improving workplace processes, we can analyze organizational reports and records to measure if, and how, different processes have been made more efficient and less wasteful. We can use similar methods to measure the impact of the improved process-mapping techniques on the improvement of business strategies.

Outcome measurement. On a long-term basis, we may measure the impact of the improved performance at the community level. By collecting and analyzing long-term data, we can identify and measure data related to societal values.

In addition to measuring performance outcomes, interventions should be reviewed by different types of experts who can provide formative and summative comments. Here are brief descriptions and examples of different types of expert reviewers using the same example of a training package on process mapping.

Subject-matter experts ensure what is being presented is accurate, up-to-date, and appropriate. For example, these experts may point out that the fishbone diagram is no longer perceived as a reliable technique or recommend a process-mapping software program that should be demonstrated during training.

Target population experts ensure the appropriate match of the intervention to the characteristics of the employee group. For example, these experts may point out that the language level is too high for the trainees or that our case study ignores women employees.

Methods experts ensure that different training procedures are effectively used. For example, an expert in simulation gaming can warn us about the lack of play-balance among different roles assigned in an experiential activity.

Media experts ensure appropriate match of production quality to the preferences of the target group and industry standards. For example, a television expert may suggest that the talking-head segment should be replaced by a documentary showing a process-mapping team in action.

Language experts ensure grammatical correctness and stylistic appropriateness. For example, an editor can improve the readability and rewrite the job aid in plain English.

Depending on the type of intervention, you may require additional experts in such fields as law, ethics, public relations, and compensation. In planning an evaluation project, it is important to specify appropriate types of performance-measurement and expert-review activities. We should also plan for the availability of various experts.

Measurement Timing

Different types of measurement are undertaken before, during, and after the implementation of an intervention. As an example of a situation where measurement timing might be used, consider the following. Let's assume that we have witnessed several conflicts among the members of a team and have decided to conduct a team-building exercise to increase the cohesiveness among team members.

Output Measures

We measure immediately after its implementation to discover its probable results. In our example, these output measures will be obviously related to the goal of our project and will include recording the number and nature of conflicts among team members in simulated and real-world situations. Our tests may measure the participants' ability to identify causes of conflicts and to use a systematic conflict-resolution procedure in a positive manner.

Input Measures

We evaluate output data by comparing them with data collected *before* the implementation of an intervention. These data are collected through instruments and strategies that are labeled *input measures* and deal with the characteristics of the target population that are likely to influence the effectiveness of the intervention. In our example, such factors as age, sex, and cultural differences are likely to be critical factors in the use of team-building exercises. Another aspect of the input measures determines the baseline. In our example, we collect data on the number and nature of conflicts among team members. Other input measures include the attitudes of team members toward team-building exercises and their previous experiences with such exercises.

Process Measures

In addition to the output and input data, we collect data about what happens during the implementation of the intervention. In our example, process measures may include the amount of time spent on each team-building activity, interaction patterns during the activity, results of intermediate tests, observation and data on who talks to whom, and problems associated with the activity.

We use the measures before, during, and after the intervention to develop effective formative prescriptions and summative recommendations. For example, if output measures indicate that the desired performance is not achieved, rather than immediately rejecting the intervention, we check the input data to make sure that our assumptions about the employees are valid. If the data indicate that this group of employees has certain unique characteristics, we may revise the intervention to accommodate these characteristics. We also check the process measures to verify that the intervention was implemented the way it should have been. If the data indicate that we spent less time or more resources in some activities, we may make appropriate adjustments.

In planning an evaluation activity, it is important to specify all input, process, and output measures. It is equally important to allocate sufficient time and other resources to collect and analyze different types of data.

With our understanding of these different dimensions of evaluation, we are now ready to take a look at the steps in a typical evaluation project.

Six Steps in Conducting an Evaluation

Most evaluators use a systematic procedure for planning and conducting an evaluation. The six steps in the generic evaluation process are briefly described below.

1. Plan the evaluation project. This stage involves specifying the key questions for which evaluation is to provide the answer. Begin by identifying different stakeholders and the important issues related to each stakeholder. Specify goals to focus the evaluation and identify the relevant performance, preference, and cost factors. Convert the goals into evaluation questions.

2. Get ready for conducting the evaluation. Recruit target population representatives and experts. Obtain the products to be evaluated along with information on the relevant processes. Collect or construct measurement instruments and strategies for input, process, and output data. Whenever possible, avoid paper-and-pencil tests and use observation systems, rating scales, checklists, interviews, and other such ways of measuring performance changes and their impact on the bottom line.

3. Collect data. Use your measurement instruments and strategies to record data from experts and target population members. This task could be as simple as watching a performer working through a job aid or as complex as repeatedly administering seventeen different tests to five stratified groups of employees over a three-month period during the implementation of a new incentive system. Hire, train, and supervise data collectors to help you obtain reliable data.

4. Analyze data. Tabulate the data and compute various statistics to identify patterns of strengths and weaknesses of the intervention. Compare output data to infer probable cause of problems. Prescribe appropriate changes to eliminate the weaknesses and to exploit the strengths of the intervention. Make clear summative recommendations and support them with relevant data.

5. Help to implement the decisions. Provide additional information and suggestions on how to improve the benefits and to reduce the costs of the package. Ensure that all revisions and decisions are based on objective data and not on subjective hunches. Help decision makers to interpret the data and to justify their final decisions.

6. Repeat the process as needed. Test the revised package again to ensure that the changes have actually increased the cost-effectiveness of the package. Repeat formative evaluation procedures until the package reaches the desired level of effectiveness and efficiency. Repeat summative evaluation procedures with new interventions.

Five Phases Of Evaluation

The human performance technology model (which is based on the ISD model) consists of the stages of analysis, design, production, and implementation. Evaluation is usually inserted between the production and implementation stages as a formative loop. The implication is that the complete package of products and processes related to the intervention is produced before it is evaluated and revised. This approach to evaluation could result in complex revisions or expensive decisions that could have been avoided by conducting informal, inexpensive evaluations earlier in the analysis or design stages. For example, expert review of a set of objectives (at the end of the analysis stage) could alert us to the fact that they are unlikely to solve the performance problem. We could abort the project (or drastically modify it) at this stage rather than invest good money after a bad intervention.

Instead of treating evaluation as a discreet stage in the performance technology process, we believe that it should be integrated in all of the stages, from analysis to implementation. This results in beginning the evaluation process earlier and continuing it until later than usual. The five phases of this continuous evaluation process are described below.

1. Initial Debugging

When do you conduct this phase of evaluation? At the conclusion of the initial design stage, before work on the actual development of the package begins. You also conduct debugging later, when the rough prototype version of the package is ready.

What do you evaluate during this phase? Initial design specifications for the package. Later, the same procedure is used for evaluating the rough prototype of the package.

Evaluation   **507**

Why do you conduct this phase of evaluation?
Formative objectives:

- To improve the design specifications for the package;
- To improve the initial set of goals and objectives, overall strategy and tactics, and the choice of methods and media;
- To improve the probability that the package will reduce the performance problem within the cost restraints;
- To revise the prototype package.

Summative objectives:

- To decide whether the designer (or the design team) is capable of handling the project;
- To decide whether the goals can be realistically met within the project constraints;
- To decide whether the project should be continued after the prototype stage.

Who are the sources of data during this phase? Who are the evaluators? The designers act as both the evaluators and the sources of data. This is a preliminary, personal activity before exposing the design specifications (or the rough prototype) to the public. During the process, the designers play the roles of target-population members and experts to anticipate probable performance outcomes and provide some expert suggestions.

How do you conduct the evaluation during this phase? What are the critical steps and key success factors?

1. After the design specifications are completed, lay them aside for a few days to gain emotional detachment and objectivity.

2. Review earlier documents that summarize the results of needs assessment, task analysis, and target-population analysis. Remind yourself of the resources and constraints in the workplace where the intervention is to be implemented.

3. Prepare personal checklists based on your biases. Use them for reviewing and revising the design specifications.

4. Highlight potential problems and positive features in the design specifications. Brainstorm ways to reduce the former and to reinforce the latter. Implement suitable changes.

2. Expert Appraisal

When do you conduct this phase of evaluation? At the same stages as in the previous phase. In addition, this procedure is repeated any time the package is revised significantly.

What do you evaluate during this phase? The same elements as in the previous phase. In addition, this procedure is repeated with significant changes in the intervention.

Why do you conduct this phase of evaluation? For the same formative and summative objectives as in the previous phase.

Secondary objective:

- To improve the credibility of the package by obtaining expert certification.

Who are the sources of data during this phase? Who are the evaluators? A panel of experts to focus on different aspects of the package. This panel may include experts on the selected intervention, content, methodology, characteristics of the target population, and language.

How do you conduct the evaluation during this phase?
What are the critical steps and key success factors?

1. During initial stages of expert appraisal, use people who are familiar with your project. During later stages, use experts as far removed from the project as possible.

2. Focus different experts' reviews by using appropriate checklists and questionnaires.

3. Use two experts for each area of evaluation. Encourage one expert to undertake goal-based evaluation (by providing this person with statements of goals and objectives) and the other expert to conduct a goal-free evaluation (by focusing on the actual effects of the package).

4. Ask the experts to give you a written report. Also, conduct a debriefing interview with each expert.

5. Encourage experts to make actual revisions rather than merely identifying problem areas and potential causes of these problems.

6. Delay the work of the language expert until you have made appropriate revisions based on suggestions from the other experts.

3. Developmental Testing

When do you conduct this phase of evaluation? After the prototype package is revised on the basis of an expert review. You also conduct developmental testing after making significant changes in the intervention.

What do you evaluate during this phase? The prototype package that is revised on the basis of an expert's review. You may evaluate the entire package or different sections or different components.

Why do you conduct this phase of evaluation?

Formative objective:

- To identify and eliminate major glitches through individual or small-group testing.

Summative objective:

- To decide whether the project should be continued on the basis of reactions and responses of a few representative target-population members.

Who are the sources of data during this phase? Who are the evaluators? The major data source is a few target-population members. You conduct this phase with individuals, one at a time, unless your package is to be used by teams. You act as the evaluator at this stage to permit on-the-spot modifications to the package.

How do you conduct the evaluation during this phase? What are the critical steps and key success factors?

1. Keep the prototype package as lean as possible because it is easier to identify and to add missing elements than it is to discover and discard superfluous material.

2. To keep the costs down, use paper-and-pencil simulations of various mediated materials. For example, reproduce screens of an expert system as a printed job aid and use a storyboard to represent a motivational television program.

3. Reassure the target-population member that he or she is not being tested. Encourage this person to offer suggestions for improving the package. To prompt such suggestions, leave an obvious error near the beginning.

4. Do not prompt the target-population member. If he or she asks a procedural question, repeat appropriate instructions. However, if the target-population member asks you to assist with the content, do not explain or lecture.

5. If the target-population member appears to be completely frustrated, ask him or her to think aloud. Make on-the-spot modifications to the package and try them out immediately. If this is not possible, provide additional explanations and make a careful note of what you did.

6. Keep track of process variables. Note time spent and record indications of interest, boredom, or frustration. Capture all remarks, reactions, and responses of the target-population member.

7. Carefully observe the target-population member's final performance.

8. After the tryout, conduct a debriefing interview. Ask the target-population member to identify positive and negative features of the package and to make suggestions for improvement.

9. Make modifications to the package immediately after each developmental testing session while the feedback is still fresh in your memory.

10. Try out the revised package on another target-population member. Continue this process until you are satisfied with the results.

4. Typical-Use Testing

When do you conduct this phase of evaluation? At the conclusion of the developmental testing phase, when successive individual tests produce consistent and satisfactory results.

What do you evaluate during this phase? The complete package including instructions to the people in charge of implementation (such as trainers, facilitator, manager, administrator, or coordinator).

Why do you conduct this phase of evaluation?

Formative objectives:

- To improve the package so that it can be implemented in a typical situation;

- To improve the training and performance support provided to the implementors.

Summative objective:

- To determine if the intervention produces replicable results in the absence of the developer.

Who are the sources of data during this phase? Who are the evaluators? A large number of members from the target population are your data source. These people should be systematically selected to represent different subgroups of the target population. You also should have typical implementators of the package. The evaluator should preferably be someone who was not involved in the earlier design and development activities.

How do you conduct the evaluation during this phase? What are the critical steps and key success factors?

1. Collect or construct different measurement instruments to obtain detailed data on input, process, and output data.

2. Collect pretest data on the test subjects' entry levels and attitudes. Also collect data on the competency levels of implementors. Make sure that the implementors can fulfill their responsibilities.

3. Ask the implementors to administer the package. Observe the actual implementation. Collect process data on time requirements, interest variations, financial transactions, and administrative glitches.

4. Collect output data in terms of improved performances, transfer of these performances to the job situation, and their impact on organizational indicators.

5. Tabulate all data to identify performance patterns and outputs. If the output is less than satisfactory, analyze for causes in input and process variables.

6. Make suitable changes to the package and to implementors' manuals. Whenever possible, add additional modules and performance support systems rather than revising the basic package. If necessary, have experts review the revised version.

5. Long-Term Evaluation

When do you conduct this phase of evaluation? After the intervention has been in effect for some time and after its novelty has worn off. This phase of evaluation should be repeated every six months or so.

What do you evaluate during this phase? All components of the package and all elements of the system that influence the implementation and the impact of the package.

Why do you conduct this phase of evaluation?

Formative objectives:

- To revise the package on the basis of long-term costs and benefits;

- To identify and to incorporate local changes and adaptations to the package;

- To improve the package by updating and upgrading it to meet current realities.

Summative objective:

- To decide whether the long-term costs and benefits of the package still justify its implementation.

Who are the sources of data during this phase? Who are the evaluators? End users, implementors, and beneficiaries (customers) of the intervention are your major data sources. The evaluators are appropriate internal staff members of the organization.

How do you conduct the evaluation during this phase? What are the critical steps and key success factors?

1. Conduct this phase of evaluation as unobtrusively as possible. This will enable you to obtain information on the typical effects of the package. Incorporate data-collection activities into such existing procedures as performance appraisals, customer surveys, and production monitoring.

2. Focus on long-term productivity and payoff data.

3. Continuously check the package to make sure it is still valid. Use a panel of expert reviewers to ensure the timeliness of the content and the comparability of the procedures with the latest corporate policies.

Four Guidelines

From the preceding discussion of the dimensions, steps, and stages, evaluation may appear to be a complex undertaking. As a strategy for simplifying evaluation, we offer the following four guidelines. They have been the key success factors in my evaluation activities in the field during the past couple of decades.

1. Integrate evaluation into all other activities. Positioned as a separate function, evaluation is perceived as a wasteful embellishment. By repositioning evaluation as an integral component of all phases of performance technology—from initial front-end analysis to final implementation—we can increase its credibility and utility. This paradigm shift forces the project managers to appreciate the relevance of evaluation and the evaluators to concentrate on providing timely and practical recommendations.

2. Harness teampower. Whenever possible, use groups instead of individuals and heterogeneous groups in preference to homogenous ones. Collect data from focus groups, conduct reviews with expert panels, and derive recommendations with project teams. This team approach gives ownership of the data and of the decisions to the stakeholders. When people interact with each other, they come up with more valid information and inferences. They also buy into the wide range of opinions and values. In the short run, you spend more time with teamwork. But in the long run, this investment pays off in the utility of the results.

3. Computerize all phases of evaluation. Personal computers are not for number crunching only. They can be used in every stage of an evaluation project. For example, scheduling, budgeting, and monitoring of the project can benefit from the use of project management software. Construction and revision of questionnaires and tests can benefit from the use of word processors, style checkers, and desktop publishers. Qualitative data (such as customer complaints) can be efficiently analyzed and categorized with idea processing and personal information management (PIM) software. Quantitative data can be quickly analyzed through suitable statistical packages. Final results and recommendations can be dramatically displayed through various graphics and presentation software. In all these situations, computerization can provide significant improvements in a cost-effective fashion.

4. Get more use out of less data. There is no correlation between the quantity of data and the quality of results in an evaluation project. Too much data can be as dangerous as too little data when it comes to making valid decisions. A few pieces of relevant, reliable, and representative data can yield much more useful information than truckloads of irrelevant noise. In most formative settings, in-depth data from a few individuals have been shown to be more useful in improving the intervention than massive data from large groups.

The ultimate key to simplifying evaluation is to go back to the basic definition and recall its definition as a process of determining the worth of an intervention in order to improve it or to prove that it works.

References

Kaufman, R. (1995). *Mapping educational success* (rev.). Thousand Oaks, CA: Corwin Press.

Kirkpatrick, D.L. (1976). Evaluation of training. In R.L. Craig (ed.), *Training and development handbook* (2nd ed.) (p. 16). New York: McGraw-Hill.

Scriven, M. (1972). Pros and cons about goal-free evaluation. *Evaluation Comment*, 3(4), 1-7.

Smith, M.E. (Ed.). (1986). *Introduction to performance technology.* Washington, DC: National Society for Performance and Instruction.

PERFORMANCE IS EASY TO MONITOR AND HARD TO MEASURE

Ogden R. Lindsley

Measurement is the weakest link in performance technology. This chapter suggests why that is, lists the differences between frequency monitoring and traditional measurement, and suggests using frequency monitoring to improve and validate performance. Also offered are several examples of performance frequency monitoring at the micro, macro, and mega levels.

Pundits Say Performance Measurement Is Crucial

Most writing about performance technology preaches performance measurement and standards. This is as it should be. For example, Gilbert's (1992) six-page foreword in Stolovitch and Keeps's (1992) *Handbook of Performance Technology* tells us the following:

> Acceptable evidence about performance must rely on measurement. If science does nothing else, it measures, and we must become very good at measuring human performance. As a general rule, our clients in the workplace are not good at it, and here is where we can be of especially great help. We can

have our greatest effects on human performance just by measuring performance correctly and making the information available.

Gilbert devotes 12 percent of his earlier classic, *Human Competence* (Gilbert, 1978), to measurement. Measurement is the third of Crosby's (1984) fourteen quality-improvement steps. Although Deming (1986) did not list measurement as one of his twenty points to build an effective quality program, his crucial data-collection system is based on statistical process control (SPC) (Shewhart, 1939). SPC monitors performance over time with either continuous measurements (e.g., length or weight) or counts (e.g., number of defectives or number of defects).

So why is measurement the weak link? Perhaps because the pundits fail to provide leadership by example—to practice what they preach.

Many Words, Few Numbers

For instance, Gilbert's foreword (1992) contains no sample performance measurements; few of the other writers on performance technology provide sample measurements either. There are sixty contributors to the *Handbook of Performance Technology*, yet performance measurement is not in the handbook's 610-item index; neither are monitoring or counting (Stolovitch & Keeps, 1992). Of the sixty contributors only four (7 percent) share samples of performance data: three charts are in a chapter by one contributor, a table is in a chapter by two other contributors, and in his four-page afterword, Mager (1992) shares performance data from one of his classes.

The type of figures used by the contributors in the *Handbook of Performance Technology* are listed in the table below with their number and portion.

Figure type	Number	% Portion
Descriptive table	50	38
Diagram	44	33
Flowchart	29	22
Organizational chart	1	1
Procedure table	3	2
Checklist	1	1
Data chart	3	2
Data table	1	1
Total number of figures	132	100

The handbook contributors primarily use descriptive tables, diagrams, and flowcharts. These "what you should do" figures make up 90 percent of the figures in the handbook. Many diagrams and flowcharts might be appropriate for a theoretical handbook on general systems theory, but not for a field whose experts preach measurement as an essential component.

Another example is *Performance and Instruction*, one of two official journals of the National Society for Performance and Instruction. A frequency count of the different types of figures contained in volume 28, 1989, is shown in the table below.

Figure type	Number	Portion
Descriptive table	56	20
Diagram	169	61

Figure type	Number	Portion
Organizational chart 1	1	0
Procedure table	18	7
Checklist	27	10
Data chart	5	2
Total number of figures	276	100

Note that, as in the *Handbook of Performance Technology,* the most common figures are descriptive tables, diagrams, and flowcharts. These "what you should do" figures make up 88 percent of volume 28. The most common type of table is not a data table, but a procedure table. Practicing performance technologists tell one another how to do things but seldom report any quantitative results.

A Few Numbers with Words

Along with Mager's afterword, Daniels' (1989) *Performance Management* is an example of displaying performance measurement for the reader. Both "counting" and "measurement" appear in its 120-item index. Daniels points out that counting is the preferred performance measure because it is the simplest, easiest, and most reliable. However, he falls short of setting counting or charting standards. Four of the sixteen chapters concern performance measurement ("pinpointing," "measurement," "the right pinpoint," and "feedback in graphs"). These chapters comprise sixty-seven (26 percent) of *Performance Management*'s 259 pages. The first two of Daniels' six performance-improvement steps are "pinpoint" and "measure." The book contains forty-two figures displaying samples of performance. However, twenty-one of these are performance percentages, and the other twenty-one are only stylized (made up) curves. Real data would serve the reader better, but stylized curves are better than nothing.

These examples clearly demonstrate that measurement is the weakest link in performance technology—so weak it is almost nonexistent. What accounts for the fact that we talk measurement but do not do it? The reasons are historical, cultural, and practical. There is nothing inherent in performance that makes counting it difficult. In fact, both behavior and accomplishments are easy to count and time. Even private behaviors such as feelings, attitudes, and urges are easy to count by the person who has them, and the period over which they are counted is easy to record (Duncan, 1971). These counts per minute, per day, per week, per month, or per year give us frequencies that are the most sensitive and universal performance measures available.

Historical Reasons for Weak Measurement

There are five historical reasons for performance measurement being weak. First, performance technology was influenced by programmed instruction in the late 1950s and 1960s. Even though Skinner called frequency (rate of response) his most important contribution (Evans, 1968), he dropped both rate of response as a datum and high frequencies as goals when he turned from his free operant laboratory to develop programmed instruction. The programmed learning performances were timed but not reported as frequencies. For example, the results of using one of the first programmed texts (Holland & Skinner, 1961) in Skinner's undergraduate course (Natural Science 114) were reported by Skinner as follows:

> On the average, a student went through the set in about 14ʃ hours. The easiest disk took 8 minutes, with a range from 5 to 13 minutes, and the hardest took 28 minutes, with a range of 17 to 80 (Skinner, 1983, p. 139).

Holland or Skinner could easily have computed frequencies on these data. But neither did. As there were twenty-nine frames on each disk, the overall rate of performance was 1.7 frames per minute. The easiest disk was 3.6 frames per minute, with a range of 5.8 to 2.2, and the hardest disk was 1.0 per minute, with a range of 1.7 to 0.4 frames per minute. Almost everyone else in programmed instruction followed Skinner's lead and abandoned frequency measurements.

Second was the influence of Gilbert's book *Human Competence* (1978) throughout the late 1970s and 1980s. Gilbert defined and named performance technology, clearly separating it from the earlier programmed instruction. He set standards for performance technology but set no standards for performance-technology measurement. This was uncharacteristic. Years earlier, in 1957, Gilbert had worked on systems for standard performance measurement in my Harvard Medical School human-behavior laboratory at Metropolitan State Hospital, Waltham, Massachusetts. In the intervening years, he apparently lost what had been a strong interest in standard measurement. Gilbert's book stressed the requirement for measuring accomplishments, but he listed three classes, nine dimensions, and nineteen performance measures with no guidelines for choosing between them. He had opened a Pandora's box of different and unstandardized measures (Gilbert, 1978, pp. 43-50).

Third was the influx of trainers into performance technology during the 1970s and 1980s. These trainers came from traditional human resource or educational research departments and were schooled in using five- and ten-point rating scales (Thurstone & Chave, 1929; Likert, 1932) for measurement. Their method of analysis was the analysis of variance, and most measurement was summative—occurring after the performance intervention to determine its effect. These statistically schooled trainers so strongly believed that you must transform data before you can analyze it that they called original data "raw." They implied that raw data could make you ill, and they "cooked" all data before ingestion. The statistical methods were taught by rote memorization of formulas, from which the learners gained little real understanding. Therefore, we have a generation of performance technologists who believe we must use statistics, but who both poorly understand and frequently fear statistics. As a result, most avoid measurement entirely, unless they yield to a quick five-point rating scale.

The fourth reason is that measurement experts caution their readers about the complexity of performance measurement and urge industrialists to hire statisticians to handle this complexity. Gitlow and Gitlow's (1987) chapter 16, "How to Hire a Statistician," lists eleven requirements of an effective industrial statistician, along with 277 university statistics departments that train industrial statisticians. This effectively tells practitioners that they had better not measure performance by themselves.

The fifth and final historical reason is that measurement experts overwhelm their readers with too many options and few guidelines. Chapter 9 of the *Handbook of Human Performance Technology* covers the when, what, and who of evaluation (Geis & Smith, 1992). Then chapter 10 discusses how to measure performance but gives few guidelines. Smith and Geis include a summary table of eighteen data-collection techniques used in 331 evaluation studies to measure ten different performance dimensions, with no further description or ranking of techniques.

A Cultural Barrier to Performance Measurement

Culturally, the barrier to performance measurement is even more debilitating. For over 6,000 years we have looked at the world through our fingers. We instinctively use "add scales," in which increments of five (one hand), ten (two hands), or one hundred (percents or twenty hands) are added. The problem is that the world around us is a "multiply" world (Meadows, Meadows, Randers, & Behrens, 1972, p. 25). Everything in it grows by multiplying and decays by dividing. In distributions, performance frequencies spread by equal multiples up and down. If the middle performer produces twenty per hour, and the bottom performer produces ten per hour, the top performer should produce thirty per hour. Wrong: the top performer will produce forty per hour! The downspread is 20/10 or × 2, and the upspread is 20 × 2 = 40. When we look at our "multiply" world through base-ten add scales, we have a distorted view. We try to compensate for this distorted view, not by using standard multiply scales, but rather by using a large assortment of add scales that both complicate and distort the picture.

Two commonly used scales illustrate this cultural problem of looking at multiplying things through add scales.

Decibel Sound Intensity Scale

The first illustration is the scale of intensity used in sound research. The intensity of things around us multiplies in sound-pressure energy. A whisper is ten decibels; the noise on the flight deck of a flying B-24 bomber was 120 decibels. Now the question: what is a decibel? How many times more intense is the B-24 flight deck over a whisper? Few of us really know.

Historically, to handle the multiplying sound intensity, a times ten increase in sound pressure was set at one bel (after Alexander Graham Bell). The bel was subdivided into ten smaller steps that were called decibels but were add units on the basic multiply scale. Now the confusion: halfway up from one bel (ten decibels) to two bels (twenty decibels) is fifteen decibels. If ten decibels represents ×10 and twenty decibels represents ×100, does fifteen decibels represent ×50 as you would expect? No; fifteen decibels is ×31.6 (the square root of

10 = 3.16), a point half-way up the multiply scale from ten to one hundred.

Our B-24 flight deck sound intensity was 120 decibels, or 110 decibels greater than a whisper. Does this mean that the B-24 is 110 times more intense than a whisper? No; it is ×10 eleven times in succession, or one hundred billion times more intense. It would have been clearer to have left the intensity in actual original values. It would have been much clearer to have left the multiply scale alone and not put add values on it. It would have been clearer to say that the B-24 flight deck had the sound intensity one hundred billion times greater than a whisper. When we look at multiplying things through an add scale, we are easily confused.

Richter Scale of Earthquake Intensity

The second illustration is the Richter scale of destruction produced by earthquakes. As earthquakes increase in size, their destructive force multiplies. Rather than simply reporting the force, the quake is rated on a Richter scale. Most of us think that an earthquake of Richter 8 is much more destructive than a 7, but we are wrong. Most of us who have used logarithms think in multiples to base ten, so that a Richter 8 is ten times more destructive than a Richter 7, which is ten times more destructive than a Richter 6. By this logic, a Richter 8 is 10 × 10 or one hundred times more destructive than a Richter 6. This, too, is wrong. The Richter scale is add numbers on multiplying destructive forces—but not to base ten multiply. It was not based on the amount of force but, rather, on the amount of displacement of the needle on a standard seismograph. So, actually a Richter 8 is about thirty-five times more destructive than a 7, and a 7 is thirty-nine times more destructive than a 6 (Gere & Shah, 1984, p. 79). Therefore, a Richter 8 is 35 × 39, or 1,365 times more destructive than a Richter 6. This is thirteen times more destructive than the base-ten multiply logic of times one-hundred assumed! Once again, when we look at multiplying things through an add scale, we are easily confused.

There are many other illustrations of the confusion produced by attempting to simplify multiplying phenomena by putting them on a false add scale. Tornado intensity, hurricane intensity, hotness of pepper, and severity of an insect sting are further examples, which we cannot detail in this limited space. We can say that scale confusion is a cultural problem and definitely is not limited to performance technologists.

Practical Reasons That Traditional Measurement Cannot Be Used

There are two overbearing, practical reasons that traditional measurement techniques cannot be used easily by performance technologists. The first reason is that, simply put, clients do not like it. It is too cumbersome, and most customers react negatively to any suggestions of traditional measurement procedures. If you force clients to use them, you may get the data, but you will lose your client. About the only measurements that performance technologists can use in practice are the measurements that their clients had in place before they hired the performance technologist. These are usually reported as percentages and, therefore, are not very useful.

The second practical reason is that performance technologists are not paid for their effectiveness. We are paid by the hour, and we are paid to please our clients. If we were paid some portion of the money we saved our clients over the next five quarters, we would work harder to put measurement systems in place. We would work harder to convince our clients that a monitoring system, which they might at first dislike, will—in the longer run—make their business more profitable. We would work harder to develop comfortable, easy, nonthreatening monitoring systems. But, because we are paid primarily for the smiles we produce, we play games with our clients and ask them only if they are happy.

A Solution: Monitoring Performance

In face of these negative observations, how can performance—both behavior and accomplishments—be easily monitored at work? Although counting is common in the workplace, very little is written about it. Monitoring by counting is not seen as a substitute for traditional measurement. In fact, it is ruled out by implication—it's not "cooked."

There are measurement experts who say you must objectively define a thing before you can count it. Wrong again. You can even count unknowns. You can keep track of the time and chart the frequency of unknown things you encounter each day. The daily frequency of unknowns is very high when you are in a foreign place and very low when you are in a familiar place.

Other measurement experts say you cannot count a mix of apples and oranges. You can easily count a mix of apples and oranges; what you are counting is fresh fruit. If you are counting oranges, lemons, and limes, you are counting citrus fruits.

Skinner's Performers Monitored Their Own Performance Frequency

Although seldom identified with the field of measurement, B.F. Skinner made major measurement contributions (Lindsley, 1992c). His contributions are so novel, major, and revolutionary that most measurement experts do not see them as measurement. Skinner gave us self-recorded frequency (which he called rate of response). In his classic, *The Behavior of Organisms,* he wrote:

> All the curves given in this book (except those obtained by averaging or those extending over a number of days) are photographic reproductions of records made directly by the rats themselves (Skinner, 1938, p. 60).

Skinner Monitored with Standard Slope Charts

This frequency of responding was automatically displayed on standard charts on which the data made slopes that were represented by standard grids of one, two, four, and eight responses per minute. These standard slope charts were called cumulative response records and were produced by the rats through the automatic recording equipment. The complexity of measurement was done automatically by the recording system, not by the performers. The performers merely pressed a lever. The calculation of the frequency (number per minute) was done by the automatic recorder.

Skinner thought that frequency and the self-recorded, standard slope chart were so important that when asked what his most important contributions were he said, "My major contributions are rate of response and the cumulative response recorder" (Evans, 1968).

Self-Frequency Monitoring Is Effective in Precision Teaching

In the first systematic application of laboratory free-operant conditioning methods to humans, I restricted the measurement system to frequencies of patients' performance and symptoms. These frequencies were automatically recorded on standard slope cumulative recorders (Lindsley, 1956), just as in the rat and pigeon laboratories. When others started applying free-operant methods in more open settings such as school classrooms, they dropped both self-recorded frequency and standard slope records. They substituted in their place *observer* recorded percent-time-on-task or percent-correct and a wide range of nonstandard *stretch-to-fill* charts (Bijou & Baer, 1961).

"Stretch-to-fill" is a name I have given to the type of charts we were taught to make in school and those that most computer graphics programs make. Figure 1 is a stretch-to-fill chart (see "Percentage of Safe Acts Observed" later in this chapter). It must always be made after the data have been collected. The vertical or magnitude scale of the chart is made to encompass the range of the performance magnitudes collected. If the lowest number is 60 and the highest number is 180, the scale is stretched so that the data fit neatly inside— perhaps a scale from 50 at the bottom to 200 at the top. The horizontal or time scale is stretched to fit the data, so if the first of five observations are collected on May 8 and the last are collected on October 3, the horizontal scale would be stretched from May 1 to October 31 to include the observations. Even worse, real time might be thrown away and the time dimension completely distorted to read from one to five equally spaced observations, as was done in Figure 1. If stretch-to-fill charts were used in animal pictures, an elephant would look like a long-nosed, hairless mouse. They both would appear the same size because they had been stretched to fill the same-size rectangle.

Agreeing with Skinner that his major contributions were self-recorded frequency and standard slope recording, I closed my laboratory and went into teacher training at the University of Kansas, to secure Skinner's contributions within public school education. My students and I successfully developed self-recorded frequency monitoring by both regular and special education public school students from preschool through high school. This has been called "precision teaching." Several laws of performance and several techniques that can double performance each week have been discovered over the past twenty-five years (Lindsley, 1992).

Standard Developed to Simplify Charting by Children

Skinner's standard chart had cumulative responses up the left, and its standard slope was frequency (performance). In precision teaching, we developed a chart with frequency up the left to simplify chart making and reading. Its standard slope was acceleration in frequency (learning).

Preschoolers were taught to chart their own performance on this standard celeration chart. The daily chart covered the full range of human-performance frequencies from one per day, through one per minute, up to one thousand per minute (one million per day). The chart was designed so that a line from the lower-left corner to the upper-right corner (34 degrees) was a doubling in performance every week. The chart was also designed to cover one school semester of twenty weeks (140 days) (Pennypacker, Koenig, & Lindsley, 1972). A family of charts with the same angle slopes was made for daily performance (doubling every week), weekly performance (doubling every month), monthly performance (doubling every six months), and yearly performance (doubling every five years).[1]

Efficient Industrial Monitoring Requires Standard Charts

The value of using common performance charts across a company has been known for over thirty years, even though few companies use them today. Cordiner (1956, pp. 95-98) of

---

[1] A full complement of standard celeration charts, chart transparencies, counters, and timers is available from Behavior Research Company, Box 3351, Kansas City, KS 66103.

General Electric wrote that a common monitoring system would do the following:

1. Permit all managers to record and plan their own performance.

2. Permit each manager to detect a deviation, in time to do something about it.

3. Provide worker appraisal, selection, and compensation based on performance.

4. Motivate workers by their records of their own effectiveness.

5. Simplify business communications with common quantitative concepts and language.

6. Permit executives to evaluate performance in 100 different businesses without becoming involved in the operational details of each.

Likert (1958), known for his attitude scales, also recognized the importance of common measurements used across a company.

Charting Quality Pairs Guarantees Both Quality and Fluency

From their beginning in 1965, precision teachers always viewed their students' charts of correct frequency and error frequency. We compared frequency with percent correct in our first year of classroom research. Classroom frequencies recorded forty times more effects of curricular changes than did percent correct on the same practice sheets with the same children in the same rooms on the same days (Holzschuh & Dobbs, 1966).

In our first monitoring of outer and inner personal and social behavior, it was also clear that positive and negative outer behaviors accelerated and decelerated independent of each other. Positive and negative inner behaviors also accelerated or decelerated independently (Duncan, 1971). At the time, we called these "fair pairs," thinking it only fair to replace a negative behavior with a positive behavior.

Later, the full impact of the independence of correct and error learning became clear. If correct and errors are reciprocally related as most of us assume, there would be only three major learning patterns: (1) corrects increasing and errors decreasing, (2) corrects maintaining and errors maintaining, and (3) corrects decreasing and errors increasing. In practice, in one classroom with twenty-nine children, eleven different learning pictures were recognized by the teacher and students (All, 1977). This demonstrated the independence of correct learning from error learning and proved we must chart both independently.

In application to industrial performance, the principle of independence has held true. For this reason we must always count and chart an acceleration target/deceleration target pair to guarantee both quality and fluency.

Fluency Aims Are Successful in Education and Business

Fluency, one of precision teaching's most powerful techniques, was discovered by Haughton, his students, and his wife (Haughton, 1974). They found that when you practice performance far beyond full accuracy up to very high frequencies (for example, basic add facts to three hundred digits per minute), you get more retention, more endurance, and more generalization to other workplace situations (Haughton, 1981).

Self-recorded and self-charted performance frequencies have been combined with "direct instruction" and Tiemann-Markle instructional design to produce really powerful learning. Students at Morningside Academy in Seattle are given a money-back tuition guarantee if they do not gain over two grade levels per year. In seven years, Morningside has never had to give a refund (Johnson, 1989). With an adult literacy program for the Job Training and Partnership Act, Morningside agreed to be paid only for students who progressed two grade levels in two skills in twenty-one months. Twenty-nine of the thirty-two students exited with skills above the eighth-grade standard. Their attendance was 3.8 days per week; they spent one hour in each of two skills per day; and they gained an average of 1.7 grade levels per month. This is ten times the gain required by the U.S. government standard (Johnson & Layng, 1992).

When company product-knowledge performance is practiced beyond accuracy to high fluency, the performers not only have higher retention, endurance, and application, they also develop high self-confidence (Binder, 1990). Precision teaching to high-fluency aims has been successfully applied in sales training for new product knowledge in banking, computer software, and biomedical companies (Binder & Bloom, 1989).

Limitations of Percent

Percent is a dangerous measure. It is fine to use it as a standard in comparing two or more static portions. For this reason, I denote columns of percentages in tables as "portion," to make this clear. But percent is very misleading when used to monitor the change in magnitude or portion in a time series. Percent change is not symmetrical. For example, many of us do not realize that if you add 20 percent and then subtract 20 percent, you are not back where you started; you are actually below where you started. In fact, if you start at one hundred and add 20 percent and then subtract 20 percent ten times in a row, you will be down to 66.6.

A second problem is that percent can be very misleading in monitoring performance. For example, in using percent of calls closed to monitor life-insurance sales, salespeople with the highest percent sales often would sell a policy on their first call, then play golf for the rest of the day because they had just made 100-percent sales.

A third problem is that percent overlooks the absolute values and frequencies of performance. So the whole dimension of fluency, or speed of responding, which is important in product knowledge and other business skills, is totally lacking.

Percent is expensive because it takes time to calculate and it produces errors. There are other problems with percent too numerous to detail here.

Skinner (1969) knew of these limitations of percent when he wrote the following advice to young psychologists overcome with the expanding research literature of the late 1960s:

> Some principle of selection is required, and a useful guide is the significance of the variables studied. A glimpse of the coordinates of the graphs in an article will usually suffice. A good rule of thumb is as follows: Do not spend much time on articles in which changes in behavior are followed from trial to trial, or in which graphs show changes in the time or number of errors required to reach a criterion, or in amount remembered, or in percent of correct choices made, or which report scores, raw or standard (p. 93).

Exemplary and Lemony Days

Gilbert (1978) introduced the term "exemplar" to describe the best performers on a particular job in the workplace. The performance of these exemplars should be observed to discover the very small differences between how they do their jobs and how the other less productive workers perform. In our work in teaching people with disabilities in sheltered workshops, our attention was drawn to significantly better performance on certain days. In 1971 we called these "exceptional days." Examination of the work conditions on these exceptional days resulted in improving the performance on all the days. I later realized that we should extend Gilbert's term from exemplary workers to the exemplary days of a single worker.

In 1966, in our work with parents of disturbed children, we noticed significantly worse days with much higher frequencies of symptoms. We called these "exceptional days" also, and analyzed their conditions to improve the children's performance. In a workshop at the 1992 International Precision Teaching Conference, I named these "lemony days." In a performance distribution of workers, a significantly lower worker, whose performance should be examined for barrier conditions, would be called a "lemon."

In a performance frequency distribution of different workers, the best performer would be an "exemplar" and the worst a "lemon." In a time-series performance-frequency chart, a single performer might have unusually good "exemplary days" or unusually poor "lemony days." The words "exemplar" with "exemplary" and "lemon" with "lemony" are in the unabridged dictionary with their correct meanings (Gove, 1961).

Differences Between Monitoring and Measuring

What most of us know, dislike, and fear about measurement comes from our unpleasant experiences with hypothesis testing and normal curve statistics in university courses on measurement. We have been preached at to hypothesize, test, and measure. We have not been taught how to count and monitor. To clarify some of the differences between monitoring and measuring, here are the five "W's" of each.

Five W's	Monitoring	Measuring
Who	Self	Third party
What	Frequency, quality	Gain
Where	Workplace	Personnel center
When	Continuously	Periodic
Why	Improve, do your best	Select workers, methods

Features of Monitoring Compared with Measuring

The following features will help to further distinguish between monitoring and measuring:

Feature	Monitoring	Measuring
Data	Original	Derived (percent, mean, range, etc.)
Detail	Full	Abstractions
Appearance	Attractive	Official
Assesses	Pace, quality, and rate	Quality only and type of change
Time dimension	Continuous in real time	Brief snapshot
Performance	Constructed	Multiple choice
Forecasting	Straight line on standard chart	Not possible
Format	Developed as progress	Prepackaged
Feedback	Always continuous	Usually none
Relates to	Self	Peer normed group

Feature	Monitoring	Measuring
Failure	No failure—information only	Fail or pass criterion
Validation	Easy—at work station	Difficult
Approach	Coach	Umpire or judge
Influence	Profits	Prophets

Statistics Used in Monitoring Compared with Measuring

The statistics used in monitoring are very different from those we were taught to use in measuring. Monitoring statistics always refer to original counts taken directly from the monitoring charts. There is not space here to go into these differences in detail. However, the table that follows lists the statistical dimensions and methods used in monitoring compared with those used in traditional measuring.

Statistic	Monitoring	Measuring
Type	Descriptive	Evaluative
Parameters assumed	Nonparametric	Parametric
Evaluation	Formative	Summative
Determined by	Read standard chart	Mathematical calculation
Measurement scale	Base 10 multiply	Base 10 add
Central tendency	Middle	Mean
Daily variance	Daily bounce	Standard deviation
Distribution dispersion	Spread on chart Highest divided by lowest	Range Highest minus lowest

Statistic	Monitoring	Measuring
Outlier probability	Number of bounces away from rest of values	Standard deviations from mean
Research design	Time series	Small group
Subjects required	Single subject	Five to ten per group
Experimental controls	Each a phase in series	Control group
Accuracy	Both corrects and errors	Percent calculated
Frequency	Number per minute	Not available
Acceleration	Number per minute per week	Not available

Examples of Monitoring Compared with Measuring

Examples of the differences between monitoring and measuring pinpoints often help to clarify the differences. The table below lists pinpoint differences between monitoring and measuring for eight different business applications.

Field	Monitoring	Measuring
Air flight	Air speed, altitude, turn and bank, fuel, manifold press, etc.	Percent of flights that arrived on time.
Real estate sales	Sale closings and unsuccessful calls counted and charted each day.	Percent of calls that produced sales.
Telephone calls to service desk	Calls successfully and immediately serviced and calls not immediately serviced charted each day.	Calls rated on a scale from 1 to 10 in degree of problem and averaged each day.

Field	Monitoring	Measuring
Veterinary practice	Number of animals treated and number of treated animals that died charted each day.	Percent of customers satisfied each day.
Retail hardware store	Number of customers purchasing what they came for; customers purchasing extras; customers not finding what they came for counted and charted each day.	Percent of customers that left without purchase.
Graphic artist Logo designer	Presentable logo drafts and unprintable logo drafts counted and charted each day.	Presentable logo drafts rated on suitability scale from 1 to 10 each day.
Hotel guest service	Guests given "thank you's" and "stops" at check-in. Employees count, chart, and turn in those received from guests each day. Guests given discount for "thank you's" and "stops" used at check-out from hotel.	Guests asked to fill out service survey.
Safety program behavior	Workers given "thank you's" and "stops" to hand to other workers for safe and unsafe acts. Stubs turned in to supervisors. Workers chart safes and unsafes each day.	Percent of acts that are safe.
Safety program accomplishment	Near misses, accidents, lost time, and deaths counted and charted each day.	Percent of accidents that are lost time.

Monitoring Always Measures, Measuring Never Monitors

It is interesting to note that in monitoring you get the best of both worlds, for your monitoring data can always be used to measure the effects of your program. However, if your only data are measurements, they cannot be used to improve your program in progress.

Back Counting from Company and Personal Records

One of the nicest things about monitoring from counts is that often you can get baseline counts for previous years from clients' ordering books, service records, salespersons' appointment books, diaries, and telephone logs. It is relatively inexpensive to "back count" this information and enter it into calendar-synchronized charts. These charts provide the baseline information necessary to demonstrate the results of your performance-improvement program.

Most importantly, a couple of years of baseline charts often reveal regular rhythms in employees' performance (e.g., safety) or clients' performance (e.g., sales). Precise forecasting of these rhythms, which usually will not yield to statistical Fourier analysis, can easily be done graphically on charts. Forecasting performance rhythms is necessary to separate them from effects of the improvement program. The sales rhythms for one product (e.g., tires) usually are independent and totally different from the sales rhythms of other products (e.g., batteries) even with the same retailer, same store, and same customers. Accurate forecasting of sales rhythms also can produce real savings in interest on the inventory that must be carried.

Personal appointment books and telephone logs can be used to back count and back chart micro-level performance baselines on employees and small groups. There is a storehouse of information in those cardboard boxes in the back closets of most corporations.

Dead-Man and Leave-It Tests for Performance

There are two simple, practical tests for whether or not you have performance: the dead-man test for behavior and the leave-it test for accomplishment. I developed the dead-man test for behavior in workshops for parents of retarded children in 1965. In brief, if a dead man can do it, it is not behavior, and you shouldn't waste your client's money trying to produce it. For example, accident-free days do not pass the dead-man test. The dead never have accidents.

The leave-it test for accomplishment was developed by Gilbert in 1962 in workshops on behavioral engineering. If you can leave it behind at the plant when you go home at the end of the day, it is an accomplishment. For example, increased awareness of safety is not an accomplishment because you take it with you when you go home.

These tests, which are described in more detail in Lindsley (1991), will help your pinpointing a lot.

Micro, Macro, and Mega-Level Monitoring

Counting and charting can be used effectively to monitor all three levels of organizational contribution (Kaufman, 1992). Self-monitoring can help improve micro-level contributions to individuals and small groups within the organization. Self-monitoring can help improve macro-level products that the organization delivers to its external clients. Regular mega-level monitoring can help an organization to plan what it delivers to society at large. Examples of monitoring on standard celeration charts at these three levels of organizational contribution, along with an example of input level monitoring, follow. As mentioned in the introduction to this book, micro-level monitoring examples are much easier to find than macro- and mega-level examples.

Example of Micro-Level Monitoring: Company Safe and Unsafe Acts

The effects of a company-sponsored safety program on the safety of chemical handlers is an example of performance technology applied to benefit a group of workers within a company. Therefore, this is micro-level monitoring.

After an effective safety program was put in place, the supervisory safety team observed workplaces and recorded the number of both safe and unsafe acts. It would have been better if we had a record of the frequency of safe and unsafe acts before the safety program, but this was not available, and the client would not delay the program to collect a baseline for use in later determining program effectiveness.

Figure 1 shows a chart that the client made of observed safe acts.[2] The client's safety team converted the actual counts of safe and unsafe acts to the percentage of safe acts, thinking this would act as a reward and motivator to the workers because it showed such high percentages of safety. The team thus broke the rule to chart original frequencies.[3] Also, because the safety team was sensitive about not having made its observations regularly, it hid that fact by charting the time as order of observation rather than real time. Thus, it broke the rule to chart in real time. Obviously, it also broke the rule to use a multiply scale and standard charts.

---

[2] The source of these data is not cited in order to honor the wishes of the client.

[3] The eleven-step job aid at the end of this chapter can serve as a list of performance-monitoring rules.

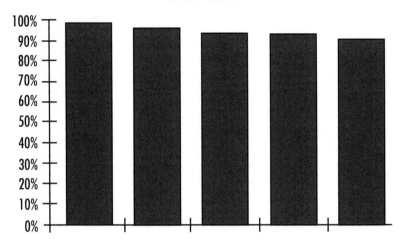

Figure 1. Percentage of Safe Acts Observed

Figure 2 shows the original frequencies of safe and unsafe acts, from which Figure 1 was derived, charted in real time on a common-standard celeration chart. Note that the frequency of unsafe acts is accelerating at a factor of ×1.4 per month. You can tell the acceleration by comparing the slope of the unsafe acts with the celeration guide (the fan of numbered slopes at the right center of the figure.)[4] Note that the unsafe line is parallel to the 1.4 line on the guide—increasing by 40 percent each month. The chart calls for rapid action to avert this acceleration. This worsening trend is not as apparent in the percent chart in Figure 1. Neither can this acceleration in unsafe acts be quantified in Figure 1.

---

[4] The celeration-guide numbers slope at ×1.1, ×1.4, ×2, ×4, and ×16 per celeration period. Once you are familiar with the standard celeration chart, these guidelines are no longer necessary because you have learned to read celerations directly. Celeration guides appear on the three other standard celeration charts that follow in this chapter.

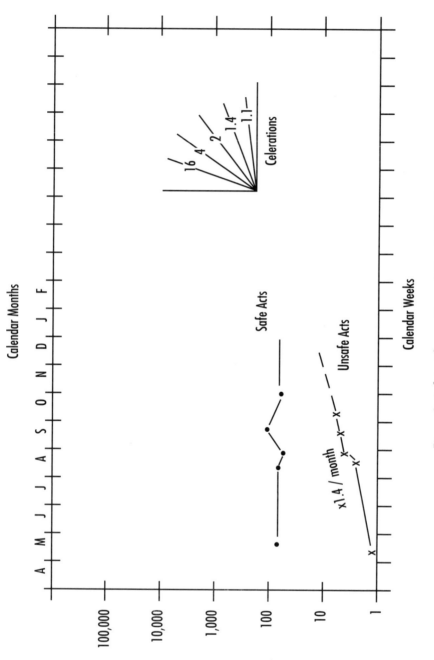

Figure 2. Safety Observations of Chemical Handlers

Charts of original frequencies should be used to inform and to improve performance. Charts should not be distorted to reward or please performers. It is important to see significant accelerations in low frequencies. Remember, it takes only one unsafe act to produce a death.

Example of Input Monitoring: Waiting Time in Hospital Admission

One of the major complaints that patients have about large urban hospitals is the long waiting time in admissions. A large Midwestern university hospital took 2.3 hours to admit patients in July, 1987. In July, 1988, the hospital's quality-improvement team put one person in charge of all admission tasks for each patient and made other administrative cutbacks.

Figure 3 shows that the admission-time reduction program divided the admission time by six from a middle of one hundred and twenty to twenty minutes in its first three months.

After this immediate deceleration, the waiting time maintained with a bounce from four to fifty minutes, with a middle at twenty minutes, for the next twenty-four months. The hospital quality team was not monitoring on charts with a multiply scale, so it was hard for it to see the variations around low values, as we can see in Figure 3. Had the team used standard celeration charts and known how to read them, it would have seen the tendency to level off at ten minutes, which was set as a goal in the quality-time reduction program. Deming (1986) is very much against quality goals for this reason.

The quality team also would have seen the exemplary months of February, 1989, and January, 1990, with five minutes, and March and May of 1990 with only four minutes waiting time. These exemplary months show clearly that because waiting times as low as four minutes occasionally occur, there is no reason they should not be produced all the time.

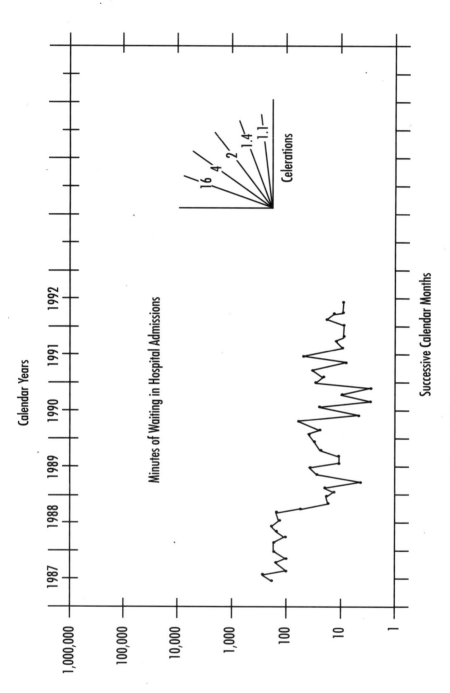

Figure 3. Monthly Average Wait Per Patient Per Visit

The exemplary months should have been examined for causal factors. Had they been, and action taken, the waiting time could have been reduced to four minutes and probably to one or two minutes.

Example of Macro-Level Monitoring: U.S. Versus Foreign-Made Cars

Perhaps the greatest economic disaster of the late 20th century is the demise of the U.S. automotive industry. It is commonplace to remark that Japanese manufacturers caught U.S. manufacturers asleep and took over their market. What is not commonplace is knowing what Detroit could have been doing to prevent this market takeover. Had U.S. manufacturers merely charted their combined annual domestic production against all foreign import on a multiply scale, they would have seen this coming by 1970 and had at least ten years to manufacture smaller, more reliable domestic cars.

Figure 4 shows U.S. automobile-factory yearly sales from 1900 to 1970, taken from the U.S. Bureau of the Census (1975, Series Q148, p. 716). The years from 1950 to 1981 of the top-line (domestics) and the entire lower line (automobiles imported into the U.S. per year from 1950 to 1981) are taken from the U.S. Bureau of the Census (1982, No. 1060, p. 615).

Note that from 1950 to 1970, the imports were accelerating by a factor of ×3.5 (250 percent increase) every five years. At that acceleration, imports would clearly have half the U.S. market by 1990. The U.S. manufacturers did not make such charts. They merely monitored their own sales, which, in spite of yearly rhythms, were actually accelerating at a factor of ×1.1 (10 percent increase) every five years—not so bad, if that is all you look at, but terrible if you realize that the competition is accelerating over three times faster!

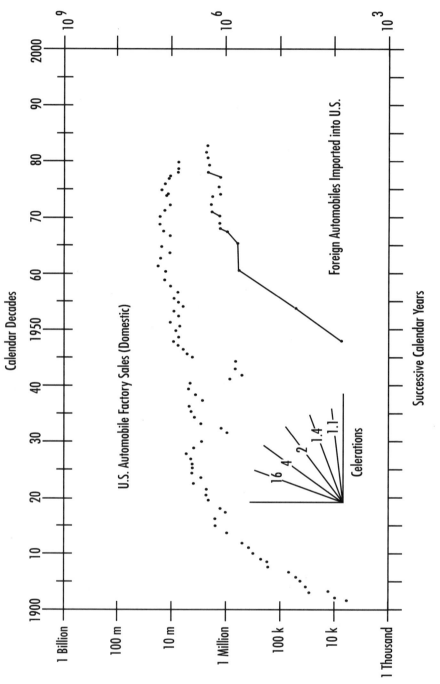

Figure 4. Number of U.S.-Manufactured Automobiles vs. Imported Automobiles

This example of back-charting an acceleration target (U.S.-made cars) with its deceleration target (foreign-made cars) shows the overall picture of automobile manufacturing on the U.S. society. It is clear that in the global marketplace it is no longer enough to monitor one's own corporate sales or even one's own and one's national competitors' sales. It is now necessary to continually monitor international competitors' sales as well to get their macro-level pictures.

This major tragedy in the U.S. economy could have been avoided if managers had monitored the macro-level impact on appropriate multiply scales, charting their own sales against those of their foreign competitors.

Example of Mega-Level Monitoring: Institutional Readmissions

From the 1960s through the 1970s, institutions for developmentally disabled individuals had a marked acceleration in residents discharged (live releases) and a marked increase in expenditures. However, their effect on society at large was worsening because their readmissions were accelerating more rapidly than their releases. The residents they released as ready for community living were not ready; as a result, more and more were being taken back to the institutions each year.

Figure 5 displays the maintenance expenditures in dollars and the total number of residents, personnel, admissions, and discharges (live resident releases) for the total number of U.S. public institutions for the developmentally disabled from 1936 through 1975 (U.S. Bureau of the Census, 1975, Series B 428-443, p. 85). These frequencies are charted on a yearly standard celeration chart. Also charted are the readmissions of former residents for 1951 through 1974 (Conroy, 1977).

As you look at this chart, squint and look at six lines at once. Notice that the top three lines are almost straight. There is almost no bounce in these frequencies, indicating that the

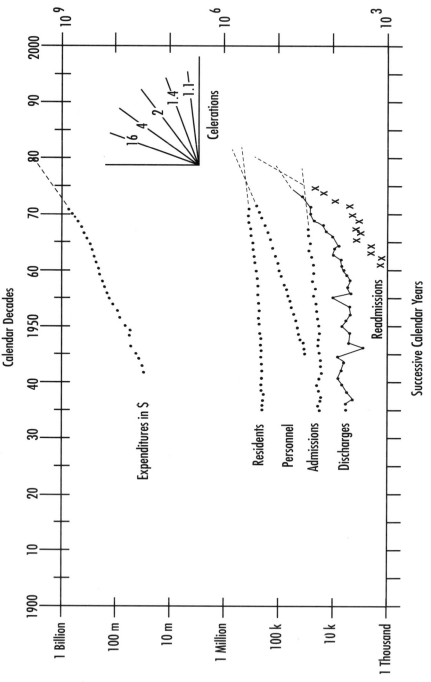

Figure 5. Discharges vs. Readmissions in U.S. Institutions for Developmentally Disabled

institutions' size (cost, residents, and staff) is regularly multi-plying. This means that these values can be projected by straight lines on the chart with high accuracy. Notice that admissions are almost as straight, with higher admissions in 1958, 1960, and 1965.

Note that residents and admissions are parallel, accelerating at ×1.1 (+10 percent) every five years, which is the same growth as for the U.S. population at large. The lines are about ×11 apart, indicating that about one out of eleven of the residents was admitted during the prior year. If we had charted the U.S. population, we would have seen that about one out of one thousand U.S. people is in an institution for the developmentally disabled because the population line would have been ×1,000 above the residents line.

Note that the expenditures line is much steeper (×1.8) than the residents line, indicating that the cost of personnel is probably a major factor in expenditures, as the number of residents is not parallel with expenditures. The distance of the expenditures line above the residents line has increased from 1947 to 1970, indicating a higher cost per resident. The distance increased from ×300, or $300 per resident, in 1947 to ×5,000, or $5,000 per resident, in 1970.

Note that the personnel line (×1.5) is steeper than the residents line (×1.1). This means that the number of staff per patient is multiplying at 1.5, divided by 1.1, equals ∞1.4, every five years (+40 percent). The ratio went from one staff for seven patients in 1945 to one staff for two patients in 1965. Is this due to inexorable, creeping bureaucracy, or is it actually an improvement in the quality of treatment? An actual improvement in treatment would produce more discharges. By looking at the discharges, we can answer this question.

The next-to-the-bottom connected line is discharges (called "live releases" in the U.S. handbook). Note that the line is bouncier than the other lines. This indicates that the production of the institutions is not regular and could be subject to political pressures (other than financial). It could not be due to financial causes or the expenditures line would also bounce proportionally. The discharges have bounced as high as ×2.5 from lowest to highest years. There is an unexplained lemony year in 1947 and an unexplained exemplary year in 1956. These should have been examined for special causes, but obviously were not.

From 1939 to 1965, the discharges multiplied by ×1.1 every five years—parallel with admissions, residents, and the general population growth. This represents stable institutional production. During this time, personnel were multiplying at ×1.3, but they had no effect on discharges. This favors the creeping-bureaucracy theory rather than the increased-quality-of-treatment interpretation. Discharge acceleration shifted abruptly in 1965 from ×1.1 to ×1.3, which was maintained through 1970. As there was no change in personnel at this time, the shift is probably owed to the "deinstitutionalization, community treatment" push that started in 1965. How effective was the increased acceleration in discharges that now seems to parallel personnel?

The quality of the institutions' production is revealed by comparing discharges with readmissions. The bottom line of small "X's" is readmissions. The readmissions are not regularly reported to the government and were obtained from a different source (Conroy, 1977). If readmissions also go up with discharges, the treatment is not of a higher quality, for the institutions are merely pushing more residents out their doors who cannot survive in society at large, and who later must be readmitted.

Note that from 1960 to 1969, readmissions accelerated at ×1.3—parallel with discharges—showing that the quality of discharges was maintained. The readmission line was about ×5 below the discharge line, showing that for every five discharges there was one readmission. Then, in 1969, the readmissions abruptly increased to ×6 every five years. There was no concomitant turn or jump in discharges or personnel. By 1972, for every two discharges, there was one readmittance. This rapid decrease in the quality of discharge is unexplained.

If you have followed this text and Figure 5, you have understood the five hundred numbers in sixteen columns and thirty-five rows of the table on page 85 of the U.S. statistical handbook.

Any way you look at it, the production track record of the institutions is very poor. How could it be any different, as we pay them for number of residents warehoused? It would be very different if institutions were paid for number of residents permanently discharged. Here again, it looks as if society gets what it pays for!

Quality Navigation™

Precision teachers and learners have self-monitored academic performance on standard celeration charts in classrooms and learning centers since 1965. Over 32,000 learning charts collected in a mainframe computer demonstrated that human-performance frequencies increase by multiplying and decrease by dividing. A large number of laws and rules of teaming were discovered over these twenty-five years of standard charting of academic performance.

We have long known that business-performance frequencies (attributes) follow the same rules. In 1991, I found that business-product continuous values (e.g., ohms resistance) also follow the same rules and can be charted easily on the same standard acceleration chart. The chart we had developed for preschoolers could be used by blue-collar workers to monitor both values and attributes more easily and more quickly than statistical process control, and with much less training. These methods are available to industry for quality control under the trademark "Quality Navigation™."

Job Aid for Monitoring Performance

This chapter closes with a procedure table to serve as your job aid for monitoring performance frequencies.

Step	Action
1	List your products that help your customers do *their* jobs
2	Reword list to noun-past tense verb form (e.g., debts paid)
3	Discard all behaviors that do not pass the "dead-man test"
4	Discard all accomplishments that do not pass the "leave-it test"
5	Pinpoint acceleration/deceleration counting pairs
6	Count each in real time (minutes, days, weeks, months, or years)
7	Chart original frequencies in real time on standard multiply charts
8	Monitor for "exemplary" and "lemony" outliers
9	Analyze the workplace for outlier causes
10	Institute exemplary causes. Eliminate lemony causes
11	Monitor for early signs of trend changes

References

All, P. (1977). *From get truckin' to jaws, students improve their learning picture.* Unpublished master's thesis, University of Kansas, Lawrence, Kansas.

Bijou, S.W., & Baer, D.M. (1961). *Child Development: Vol 1. A systematic and empirical.* New York: Appleton-Century-Crofts.

Binder, C.V. (1990, September). Closing the confidence gap. *Training,* pp. 49-56.

Binder, C.V., & Bloom, C. (1989, February). Fluent product knowledge: application in the financial services industry. *Performance and Instruction, 28*(2), 17-21.

Conroy, J.W. (1977, August). Trends in deinstitutionalization *Mental Retardation, 15*(4), 44-46.

Cordiner, R.J. (1956). *New frontiers for professional managers.* New York: McGraw-Hill.

Crosby, P.A. (1984). *Duality without tears: The art of hassle-free management.* New York: McGraw-Hill.

Daniels, A.C. (1989). *Performance management.* Tucker, GA: Performance Management Publications.

Deming, W.E. (1986). *Out of the crisis.* Cambridge, MA: Massachusetts Institute of Technology, Center for Advanced Engineering Study.

Duncan, A.D. (1971). The view from the inner eye: personal management of inner and outer behaviors. *Teaching Exceptional Children, 3*(3), 152-156.

Evans, R.I. (1968). *B.F. Skinner: The man and his ideas.* New York: E.P. Dutton.

Geis, G.L., & Smith, M.E. (1992). Chapter 9: The function of evaluation. In H.D. Stolovitch & E.J. Keeps (Eds.), *Handbook of human performance technology* (pp. 130-150). San Francisco, CA: Jossey-Bass.

Gere, J.M., & Shah, H.C. (1984). *Terra non firma.* Stanford, CA: Stanford Alumni Association.

Gilbert, T.F. (1978). *Human competence: Engineering worthy performance.* New York: McGraw-Hill.

Gilbert, T.F. (1992). Foreword. In H.D. Stolovitch & E.J. Keeps (Eds.), *Handbook of human performance technology* (pp. xiii-xviii). San Francisco, CA: Jossey-Bass.

Gitlow, H.S., & Gitlow, S.J. (1987). *The Deming guide to quality and competitive position.* Englewood Cliffs, NJ: Prentice-Hall.

Gove, P.B. (Ed.). (1961). *Webster's third new international dictionary of the English language* (unabridged). Springfield, MA: G. & C. Merriam Co.

Haughton, E.C. (1974). Define your act and set your fluency goals in personal, social, and academic areas. *Special Education in Canada, 48*(2), 10-11.

Haughton, E.C. (1981, March). REAPS. *Data Sharing Newsletter.* Waltham, NM: Behavior Prosthesis Laboratory.

Holland, J.G., & Skinner, B.F. (1961). *The analysis of behavior.* New York: McGraw-Hill.

Holzschuh, R.D., & Dobbs, D. (1966). *Rate correct vs. percentage correct.* Unpublished manuscript, University of Kansas Medical Center, Lawrence.

Johnson, K.R. (1989). *Executive summary.* Seattle, WA: Morningside Corporation.

Johnson, K.R., & Layng, T.V.J. (1992). Breaking the structuralist barrier: Literacy and numeracy with fluency. *American Psychologist, 47*(11), 1475-1490.

Kaufman, R. (1992). *Strategic planning plus.* Newbury Park, CA: Sage.

Likert, R. (1932). A technique for the measurement of attitudes. *Archives of Psychology, 22*(140), 1-55.

Likert, R. (1958). Measuring organizational performance. *Harvard Business Review, 36*(2), 41-50.

Lindsley, O.R. (1956). Operant conditioning methods applied to research in chronic schizophrenia. *Psychiatric Research Reports, 5*, 118-139.

Lindsley, O.R. (1991). From technical jargon to plain English for application. *Journal of Applied Behavior Analysis, 24*, 449-458.

Lindsley, O.R. (1992). Precision teaching: Discoveries and effects. *Journal of Applied Behavior Analysis, 25*, 51-57.

Lindsley, O.R. (1992c). *Skinner on measurement.* Kansas City, KS: Precision Media.

Mager, R.F. (1992). Afterword. In H.D. Stolovitch & E.J. Keeps (Eds.), *Handbook of human performance technology* (pp. 743-746). San Francisco, CA: Jossey-Bass.

Meadows, D.H., Meadows, D.L., Randers, J., & Behrens, W.W. (1972). *The limits to growth.* New York: Universe Books.

Pennypacker, H.S., Koenig, C.H., & Lindsley, O.R. (1972). *Handbook of the standard behavior chart.* Kansas City, KS: Precision Media.

Shewhart, W.A. (1939). *Statistical method from the viewpoint of quality control.* Washington, DC: United States Department of Agriculture, Graduate School. (Reprint edition, 1986, New York: Dover.)

Skinner, B.F. (1938). *The behavior of organisms.* Englewood Cliffs, NJ: Prentice-Hall.

Skinner, B.F. (1969). *Contingencies of reinforcement: A theoretical analysis.* New York: Appleton-Century-Crofts.

Skinner, B.F. (1983). *A matter of consequences.* New York: Alfred A. Knopf.

Smith, M.E., & Geis, G.L. (1992). Chapter 10: Planning an evaluation study. In H.D. Stolovitch & E.J. Keeps (Eds.). *Handbook of human performance technology* (pp. 151-166). San Francisco, CA: Jossey-Bass.

Stolovitch, H.D., & Keeps, E.J. (Eds.). (1992). *Handbook of human performance technology.* San Francisco, CA: Jossey-Bass.

Thurstone, L.L., & Chave, E.J. (1929). *The measurement of attitude.* Chicago, IL: University of Chicago Press.

U.S. Bureau of the Census. (1975). *Historical statistics of the United States, Colonial times to 1970, Bicentennial edition, Part 1.* Washington, DC: Author.

U.S. Bureau of the Census. (1982). *Statistical abstract of the United States: 1982-83 edition.* Washington, DC: Author.

DEVELOPING TEST AND ASSESSMENT ITEMS

Jeffrey A. Cantor

Testing and assessment is the cornerstone for appropriate planning in human performance technology. Through well-constructed test items, we are able to ensure that a worker is either competent for a job or receives appropriate interventions: training, counseling, reassignment, or termination.

Test-item writing (and associated test development) should be an integral part of the overall instructional systems process. Systematic planning is required for developing test items within the overall framework of human performance technology.

Test-item technology has come a long way. Yes, test-item development is an art; however, there are certain rules and practices that should be followed to construct structurally sound test items. This chapter discusses and describes these rules and practices.

To understand the requirement for skills in test-item writing, one should fully understand the role of testing and assessment of human performance. Why do we evaluate?

The Role of Evaluation

Evaluation is a necessary component of human performance technology. Test-item writing is a critical skill that is necessary to ensure that the test instrument is both valid and a reliable measure. Therefore, we evaluate for several purposes.

- To determine a person's occupational competence:
  We evaluate as a means to measure job readiness. We do this at various times: at predetermined intervals in critical-skills occupations, prior to job assignments, or prior to making promotion decisions. Sometimes we do this before commencing formal instruction as a pre-test baseline measure.

- To determine progress or growth in formal learning activities:
  When a pretest measure is followed at the end of a course with a parallel posttest, an assessment of an individual learner's progress or growth is possible. This permits us to certify personnel as job ready or to design appropriate performance interventions to correct behavior.

- To determine organizational climate and readiness:
  Often testing is also used to assess the overall climate of an organization in terms of worker performances and/or departmental/work/group/divisional functions. Sometimes safety and readiness can only be assessed as a group function.

- To determine an organization's effect on its society:
  In many occupations (e.g, nuclear power generating facilities), external entities (e.g., the Nuclear Regulatory Commission) use tests of human performance as a means to determine the organization's level of safety. Hence, its effects on society are assessed.

Two Essential Elements of a Test

The process of designing and developing a test instrument—whether for assessment of knowledge or motor skills—involves the writing of multiple items. Most jobs or tasks demand competence in more than one set of skills or behaviors. You will ultimately piece together a number of items that indicate total mastery of a subject area. This will ensure a test's validity and reliability.

Validity refers to the test instrument's content; in other words, the test should measure what it claims to measure. The test should assess the knowledge, skills, and abilities required to function competently on a job. Any effort on your part to measure more or less than is required to do the job diminishes the validity of the test.

As validity determines whether or not a test measures what it is designed to measure, *reliability* determines the degree to which it does so consistently. A test, like any other measuring instrument, is useless unless it can produce results consistently.

Developing Test Items

Test-item development is part of a three-phase test-development process. In the first phase, the test developer gathers all the information necessary to identify the performance or behaviors to be tested, the conditions under which these behaviors should be demonstrated (and therefore tested), and the degrees or standards of required performance.

Integral in this phase of test development is development of a *test-design specification*. A test-design specification identifies what is to be tested. I adopted the concept of test design from the work of Popham (1975), wherein he suggested using a test item specification as an outline to guide development of each test item, ensuring congruity between performance objective conditions, standards, and behaviors and associated test items. In the test-design specification, I identify the purpose of the test, the specific behaviors to be tested, conditions under which the behaviors are to be performed, and standards to which the behaviors must be performed. This information should come from the task analysis data and from the written performance objectives. The test-design specification will also specify which behaviors will be tested by written test and which will be tested by performance test. The specification will also list what equipment, tools, and materials will be required in the test process.

The next phase is the item writing process—the actual drafting of the test items. Again, item writing is an art. Successful item writers must possess a unique combination of abilities. There is no specific set of rules to follow to ensure good test items; however, some general principles can help. The degree to which you apply these principles will determine the quality of the item and the integrity of the ensuing test as a useful measurement instrument. Of course, you must know the subject matter or work with subject-matter experts. And, you should listen well and ask appropriate questions.

In this phase you might be developing tests of information to be responded to in writing and/or tests of physical or motor skills to be performed by the examinee that you work into a checklist form. Just as you developed a test-design specification listing the requirements for the whole test, each test item should have a specification detailing the behavior, conditions, and standards for examinee performance. Your development of the item should be based on this specification.

Multiple-Choice Items

Multiple choice is, by far, the most popular format for written tests because it can determine mastery of many different subject-matter areas and assess a variety of cognitive processes, from straightforward factual knowledge to complex thinking processes. This format is also supported by the computer for both test development and actual on-line testing. Multiple-choice tests contain series of questions that we call test items. Each item measures a particular competence, providing specific information about what a person knows about a specific topic. To be valid and accurate, a good test must rely on well-written items.

Format of Multiple-Choice Items

A multiple-choice item consists of two parts: (1) a stem; and (2) a set of distractors or responses, one of which is correct. The example below represents a typical multiple-choice item.

The stem has a single central theme, in this case the name of the second president of the United States. It asks a question, presents a problem, or takes the form of an incomplete statement.

Who was the second President of the United States? (stem)

A. George Washington	(distractor)
B. John Adams	(correct answer)
C. James Madison	(distractor)
D. Abraham Lincoln	(distractor)

I find that most item writers prefer the question form because it presents the central theme clearly and avoids cuing the correct answer. The distractors are possible answers to the problem or question. Here they provide a variety of choices of the second president of the United States. Notice that the correct answer and the three distractors are similar, both in terms of tense and grammatical structure. This illustrates a very important point: all distractors must be plausible as correct responses and must be written in a way that prevents examinees from guessing the correct answer simply on the basis of the distractors' format.

If, for example, distractor B read, "John Adams, who followed George Washington," examinees probably would have little difficulty choosing it as the correct response. It is so different from the other distractors that it cues itself. Similarly, if distractor C said, "Richard Nixon," examinees would probably rule it out because it is not plausible compared to the other distractors.

If you can remember this basic format—a stem with one central theme, a correct answer, and several plausible and similar distractors—you are on your way to constructing good test items. Now, before you can begin writing the test, you have to decide what kind of specific information or content the test should cover.

Central Theme and Possible Distractors

You have to identify the central themes to be tested. You will not develop the test in isolation. Of course, you must be familiar with the subject; and if the test supports a training course, you probably will have had a part in developing the course itself. Refer to your test-design specification at this point. Also be sure you have all the necessary job or course technical references at hand. Use these documents to identify the aspects, concepts, and facts that are critical to the mastery of the subject-matter area. These critical skills or knowledge form the core of your test, and each of them represents a possible central theme for a test item.

Now ask yourself some questions. How can an examinee demonstrate knowledge of this theme? In what sort of circumstances might it be important to understand these concepts (e.g., on the job)? What might be the consequence of an examinee's not knowing or understanding these concepts? What are common misconceptions or misunderstandings about this subject? These questions and their answers help you to fine-tune the test items and the manner in which you will construct them.

For example, suppose the subject area is emergency medical procedures and your test design centers on the treatment of shock. Ask yourself, "If someone did not know the proper treatment for shock, what steps might he or she take?" Write down the answers that occur to you and then all the correct responses to your test. This information becomes part of your test item specification. This makes a good preliminary set of distractors.

At this point, do not be overly concerned about proper wording or format: you are only trying to create a first draft of the items, like the one shown below:

An accident victim is in shock. Which one of the following actions should be taken for the victim?

A. Cover the victim to keep him/her warm.   (correct answer)

B. Raise victim's head above his/her knees.   (distractor)

C. Position the victim's head on a pillow.   (distractor)

D. Put an ice pack on the victim's head.   (distractor)

E. Give the victim a cool drink.   (distractor)

Write the stem to present a discrete central theme. Although the example above asks its question in two separate sentences, it presents only one theme: What should you do to treat someone in shock? Now arrange all of the distractors and the correct response below the stem and letter them consecutively. If more than four choices occur to you, that's OK. You can decide later which are the best or use all of them. There is no rule limiting the choices to four. While the test item above could use some work, you now have a base from which to construct your final version of the item.

Item Format and Stem Revision

Multiple-choice items can take any one of four forms: correct answer, best answer, negative, and combined response. The type of item you select will depend on the content to be tested and the complexity of the process that indicates an examinee's mastery. For example, learner behaviors that call for decision making based on varying sets of circumstances may be better tested by best-answer types of items. Alternatively, straightforward but more complex behaviors are probably better tested with combined-response type items. In general, though, the simpler and clearer the item, the better.

The correct-answer form poses a question requiring the examinee to identify the correct response. One answer choice must be absolutely correct and the others incorrect, as shown below.

In what year did Ponce de Leon discover Florida?

A. 1394   (distractor)

B. 1513   (correct answer)

C. 1588   (distractor)

D. 1742   (distractor)

The stem asks a clearly worded question, based on a well-defined central theme, and the examinee selects an answer from the list of distractors. This item format works best for testing facts—where there is little room for debate about the correctness of the response. Examinees either recall the information or they do not.

The correct-answer format also lends itself to completion items such as:

"Ponce de Leon discovered Florida in_____."

In this form the distractors complete the sentence begun in the stem.

The best-answer format tests higher-order cognitive processes because it presents more than one "correct" answer. Examinees must then select the best correct answer; some or all of the distractors may be appropriate in varying degrees, but only one is the best correct response. The sample below illustrates one way of using the best-answer format.

What is the fundamental purpose of law enforcement in the U.S.?

A. To arrest criminals.

B. To maintain order without loss of liberty.

C. To control citizens' conduct through the impartial enforcement of detectable violations.

D. To obtain a balanced program of criminal and civil enforcement.

The best-answer format works well here because the primary goal of a police department cannot be stated with absolute certainty. However, the classroom instructor probably stressed one particular goal, and this test item asks the examinee to recall it.

Even if the instructor did not specifically offer the answer to the question, the item may still be valid if the training gave the examinee enough skills and information to evaluate this issue and draw the appropriate conclusions. I suggest that you should avoid this situation by including additional clarifying information in the stem. This will protect you from challenges to the test later on. The item in the above sample could be restated like this: "According to Kane's analysis in *Police Science*, which of the following...." The specific reference to a source with which the examinees should be familiar eliminates any ambiguities that might cause confusion and invalidate the item. This information should be identified on the test item specification as a source of authority for the performance standard. For all best-answer items, make sure that all competent experts will agree on the "best" answer.

The negative form instructs the examinee to choose the answer that is incorrect. The distractors include three or more true answers and one that is incorrect or definitely weaker than the others. This is the one that examinees are supposed to identify and select. The next sample exemplifies the negative form.

All the following are desirable practices when preparing multiple-choice test items except:

A. Stating the stem positively.

B. Using a stem suitable for a short-answer item.

C. Underlining certain words in the stem for emphasis.

D. Shortening the premise by lengthening the distractors. (correct answer)

Negative items are appropriate when knowing the exception is as important as knowing the rule. However, take special care to avoid confusing your examinees. Avoid double negatives: a negative stem with instructions to find the exception. An example of this poor pattern might be:

"None of the following are undesirable practices when preparing multiple-choice items except...."

You can also steer examinees in the right direction by underlining or capitalizing the negative qualifier, in this case *except*. Examinees correctly answering the above item tell you more about their patience in decoding gibberish than their understanding of the central theme.

The combined-response form uses a stem followed by several numbered answer choices, one or more of which may be correct. A second set of code letters lists various possible combinations of correct responses. The examinee chooses the letter that designates the correct response or responses, as in the following example.

An officer posed with a life-threatening situation discharged her service revolver. Her partner had drawn his weapon but had not fired it. Two other officers were present at the discharge and had drawn their weapons. Three more officers reported to the scene after the discharge. The weapons of which of the individuals listed below should be preserved for processing?

I. The officer who discharged the service revolver.
II. The partner who drew his weapon.
III. The two officers present at the discharge who drew their weapons.
IV. The three officers who arrived after the discharge.

A. I only
B. I and II only
C. I, II, and III only
D. I, II, III, and IV

Combined-response form items can also be employed to assess an examinee's ability to arrange material in sequences such as chronological order, order of importance, and the like. It permits the assessment of complex cognitive skills, such as organizational ability and the ability to apply and evaluate facts, values, and concepts. Exercise care to keep it from becoming a multiple "true-false" item.

Again, no matter what format you choose for your test items and their stems, keep a few general rules in mind. Be sure to include only one central theme in each stem. This permits the examinees to zero in on the exact information you seek. Clearly and concisely word each stem to help avoid confusion. If there are any words or phrases common to all distractors, place them in the stem instead. Also include in the stem any qualifying words that limit or isolate the possible responses. Look at the sample below.

John Adams was the:

A. second Vice President of the United States.

B. second member of the Continental Congress.

C. second President of the United States.

D. second general in the Continental Army.

The word "second," which appears at the beginning of each distractor, really belongs in the stem. Thus, the stem would read "John Adams was the second:" This construction lets examinees know right away that they have to recall something that John Adams did second.

Developing and Writing Distractors

You have written a good stem, formulated a correct response, and developed a list of possible distractors. Review that list. Remember that all distractors must be plausible and fit the grammatical structure of the stem. Here are some general guidelines to help you review your distractors.

Avoid using "none of the above" or "all of the above" as distractors. They are often confusing. Also avoid obviously incorrect responses. Both of these devices destroy plausibility.

Define the class of things to which all of the answer choices should belong to make sure your distractors are plausible. Refer to the second example, which asks what you should do to treat someone in shock. The class of possible answers might be defined as "first-aid measures." This process gives you distractors A, B, and C—all of which seem to be valid first-aid procedures.

Think of things closely associated with the terms in the stem as well as some misconceptions people may hold about the subject in question. Distractors D and E are based on the premise that an uninformed person might think the most important factor is making the victim comfortable. Therefore, all the distractors in this example are plausible. Since most test items contain only three distractors plus the correct response, you can throw out one of the distractors.

Write distractors so that they make grammatical sense. That means making them correspond to the verbal structure of the stem. Be sure that the beginning of each distractor logically follows the last word in the stem. For example, if the stem ends with the word "an," examinees will probably assume that the correct response is a singular noun beginning with a vowel; make sure all the distractors have this pattern. When using items that ask examinees to complete a sentence, ensure that all the distractors do, in fact, complete the sentence. Also, all the distractors should begin with uppercase letters and end with periods. Finally, place all distractors in logical order if they are numerically or sequentially related. The third sample illustrates this principle; the dates appear in chronological order.

The most effective distractors are clearly and concisely written without excess information that could confuse the examinee. A good test item measures an examinee's ability to recall a central theme, not his or her ability to take tests.

Matching-Test Items

Matching-test items can condense the testing of a relatively large amount of information. These tests require information sequencing and assimilating. When the facts are selected carefully, the chance of guessing is greatly reduced. Matching-test items cannot effectively test higher-order intellectual skills, and their content must have relational association (i.e., cause and effect, term and definition).

Matching-test items (shown below) are related to multiple-choice test items in that many of the latter can be combined into one matching-test item. They are good for testing content that includes classifying, sequencing, labeling, or defining (i.e., defined concepts). While matching items is an acceptable method of assessment, avoid overuse of this particular format.

Directions: Match the type of test on the left with the disadvantages of using the method on the right.

_____ 1. Multiple-choice	a. Can't test higher levels of learning.
_____ 2. True/False	b. Takes time to construct effective test.
_____ 3. Matching	c. Questions can be too broad or ambiguous.
_____ 4. Short Answer	d. Can only test factual information.
_____ 5. Essay	e. Questions must be carefully phrased to avoid leading examinee to a specific answer.

In structuring matching-test items, give directions that describe the matching task to be performed. Use a set of four-to-twelve problems to be performed. Place the terms on the left and the alternative responses on the right; capitalize the first letter of the word in each item to identify where it starts.

All components of a given matching item should be contained on a single page to avoid flipping back and forth.

A well-constructed, matching-test item contains clear instructions stating how the items are to be matched and whether responses are to be used only once. Each question should have a central theme with parallel problems and parallel responses; this parallelism will help prevent guessing. If used, distractors should be plausible. Make sure there are no grammatical clues (e.g., "a" or "an") in the items. Arrange options in logical order, for instance, alphabetically or numerically. This ordering makes it easier to locate options and reduces the chance of giving subtle clues.

Short Answer/Completion Items

Short-answer/completion-items tests allow a large amount of information to be condensed into a few questions. Because the examinee must write something, you can make a clear assessment of what has been mastered. However, these items are limited to recall of specific facts. The items must be carefully phrased to avoid directing the examinee to a specific answer.

List the steps performed in connecting an ohmmeter to a circuit.

1. _____

2. _____

3. _____

4. _____

Short answer/completion items are easy to construct and may be used to test recall of specific facts, concepts, or principles (as shown above). When constructing completion items, be certain that there is only one answer that will complete the statement. Answers should require no more than a few words; if more are required, it will be hard to grade the answers objectively.

A common structure for the short answer/completion item is an incomplete statement. In this form, a significant word or two is left out and the examinee must complete the statement. Each test item should be matched to a performance objective.

Essay-Test Items

Essay-test items (see following sample) can test for higher-order intellectual skills and cognitive strategies. They allow examinees to display mastery of an entire range of knowledge about a subject. There are, however, several disadvantages associated with essay tests. First, it is often difficult to write question items that are not too broad or ambiguous; this in turn makes scoring difficult. Second, only a limited number of concepts and principles can be tested. Essay tests are not fair to examinees with poor writing skills. From an instructor's point of view, essays are very time-consuming to assess.

- Discuss the four primary advantages of an incident command system and compare these advantages to the alternatives of not using an incident command system. (Each advantage and alternative discussed will be worth 4 points.)

Although essay-test items are excellent for evaluating higher levels of learning and application of principles, they are difficult to construct in a way that limits subjectivity. In a well-constructed essay test, complete directions are given, questions are clearly and unambiguously written, model responses are used in grading, and components and their weighing are identified. Ample space is provided for the answer, or directions are given for using additional space. You must allow examinees enough time to formulate and construct their answers.

Skills-Performance Checklists

Skills-performance checklists are the assessment devices for identifying and recording data about skill performances in specific motor skills areas. By first analyzing the purpose of the performance test and the behaviors (specific performance objectives) to be measured, a determination of the best approaches for testing can be made. Two types of performance tests are commonly used: product or process. A product performance test requires the examinee to actually produce an item or perform a series of tasks associated with the job from start to finish. A process performance test requires only a series of steps or tasks to be demonstrated.

A test-design specification for a skills-performance test must indicate the performance-based behaviors to be tested. To do this and to be able to identify the motor skills, abilities, and associated knowledge critical to carrying out the work, it is necessary to analyze all pertinent instructional objectives in detail. This analysis is an important part of establishing the content validity of the test. The test-design specification should identify the following:

- Specific behavioral elements that should be measured;

- Whether a performance test, written test, or both are more appropriate for the measurement; and

- The number of questions or trials required to establish proficiency on a task.

Measurement Points

Ask several qualified experts to review and agree on the critical measurement points (based on the instructional objectives and task analysis data) to be used. Establish a process for recording relevant work and training experience of the people who will judge test content. This helps to support a test's content validity. Each expert should record which task-analysis components are important to the overall purpose of the test and should be measured. These components include duties, tasks, task elements, and knowledge, skills, and abilities. For example, to measure an examinee's performance on a specific task, such as overhauling a computer mother board, tasks and task elements probably would be rated as more important to the end product than to the analysis. If overall job performance is to be measured, then the knowledge, skills, and abilities would be rated higher. The level of detail in the analysis only has to be deep enough to satisfy the intended purpose of the test.

The Checklist

Once the test-design specification is completed, you have to decide how much time will be required to compile testing materials and processes to complete the test. Record all such information to ensure test validity. Testing materials might include a proctor's or supervisor's guide, directions, information sheets, drawings, tools, and machines. The test will also include a checklist to record the examinee's performance. Write notes (such as technical standards, safety measures, constraints, and scoring methods) on the test-item form or checklist as appropriate. Figure 1 is a skills-performance checklist.

Name: _____

Trade Machinist   Title: Slotted Block

Step	Checkpoints	Checkpoint Performance		Required Step Score	Maximum Possible Score	Actual Score	Step	
							Pass	Fail
A.	Set Up Vise	Totals		5.5	11			
	1. Mount Vise: Depth 1-7/8	Sat.	Unsat.		2			
	2. Indicate vise parallel to table slots	Sat.	Unsat.		7			
	a. Secure indicator (dial test) to machine quill using drill chuck. b. Snug nuts holding vise to table. c. Bring quill down to touch solid jaw of vise, putting about .005 pressure on indicator. Set indicator to 0. d. Rapid traverse table longitudinally. Read indicator. Tap vise to remove any differences in reading. Rapid traverse in opposite direction. When a zero reading on indicator is achieved, tighten nuts holding vise. e. Reindicate to ensure that vise has not moved while tightening.							
	3. Scale block to be machined to determine if adequate material is available.	Sat.	Unsat.		2			

Figure 1. Sample Assessment Checklist

Step	Checkpoints	Checkpoint Performance		Required Step Score	Maximum Possible Score	Actual Score	Step Pass	Fail
B.	Set Block in Vise	Totals		4	8			
	1. Use parallels of same height (approximately 1") against solid movable chuck jaws.	Sat.	Unsat.		2			
	2. Lay down block on parallels with 1" dimension up and about 1/2" extending beyond end of vise.	Sat.	Unsat.		3			
	3. Tighten vise.	Sat.	Unsat.		2			
	4. Tap block down on top.	Sat.	Unsat.		1			
C.	Insert End Mill.	Totals		3	6			
	1. Sleect 1" diameter end mill.	Sat.	Unsat.		1			
	2. Measure cutter shank and install proper collet in quill.	Sat.	Unsat.		2			
	3. Install cutter shank into collet and tighten drawbar.	Sat.	Unsat.		1			
	4. Make sure quill is completely withdrawn.	Sat.	Unsat.		1			
	5. Lock quill.	Sat	Unsat.		1			
	Evaluation Sheet Totals							

Figure 1 (continued). Sample Assessment Checklist

The Guidebook for Performance Improvement

Review the Test Item

Now that you have fine-tuned your draft item, you have to review it. Ask yourself the following questions:

- Does the item measure what I am trying to measure?

- Does the stem contain just one central theme? (If not, you may have to reword it or split it into more than one item.)

- Do the examinees have all the information they require to answer the item?

- Will the item's intent be clear to someone reading it for the first time?

- Is the wording as clear and concise as possible? If not, can the item be revised and still be understood?

- Are the distractors plausible and do they make sense grammatically? Are any of the distractors clearly inappropriate?

- Is the correct answer clearly correct and up-to-date according to recognized experts in the field?

If your test item satisfies all these standards, it is a good one.

Test Validity and Reliability

A test must reflect only the competencies identified as critical in the job or task analysis—and as reflected in the performance objectives. This is why I advocate development of test items immediately following the writing of performance objectives—while the conditions, behaviors, and standards (or degrees of proficiency) are fresh in your mind. Make sure you have a test item for each critical aspect of the job to be measured. Once you have arranged all the items into a complete test, you should have subject-matter experts review it for content accuracy: this is phase three of the test development process. You will pilot the test using actual workers. Their feedback will give you an idea of the test's ability to measure actual on-the-job competence requirements.

Several factors influence a test's reliability. The most important is the appropriateness and technical accuracy of the test items. They must evaluate realistic and practical aspects of the job performance. The number of test items is also important; while there must be at least one item for each performance objective (including each enabling objective) in the training plan for a particular job, the more test items you include in the test, the better it will measure true competence. This should not be deemed a license to overkill: a four-step procedure does not warrant a one-hundred question test. However, be sure you adequately and completely test all critical skills and knowledge.

Also, the order in which you present the items can affect test reliability. Just as improper distractors can cue the correct response, improper sequencing of items may give away correct behaviors or answers. Make sure item 1 does not give away the answer to item 2. Also make sure that the correct response to number 2 is not dependent on knowing the correct response to number 1. Each item must present an independent problem.

You may not be able to control some of the factors affecting reliability, but you should be aware of them. Try to create a consistent atmosphere for test taking. Uniformity of the examination environment is important. The same test administered once in a noisy and poorly lit factory area and again in a quiet classroom will probably yield very different results. Also realize that cheating will skew test results. You should arrange for as much test security and exam proctoring as is necessary.

Summary

If you follow these general principles of test-item writing, you will be off to an excellent start. Remember, base your items on the critical job-performance criteria identified in your test-design specification. Choose an item format that suits the nature and complexity of the central theme you want your examinees to recall or demonstrate. Develop item stems that focus on one central theme and provide examinees with all the information necessary to address the item. Create plausible distractors that make grammatical sense. Finally, be sure that the correct answer is totally correct. Item writing is an art that you can learn. Practice it, and you will have valid and reliable tests.

Reference

Popham, W.J. (1975). *Educational evaluation.* Englewood Cliffs, NJ: Prentice-Hall.

QUALITY MANAGEMENT/ CONTINUOUS IMPROVEMENT

Roger Kaufman and Douglas Zahn

Human performance and organizational improvement is not a one-shot process. Internal and external clients must be satisfied with the immediate product, but the process is ongoing. Quality management is a process for the continuous improvement of everything an organization uses, does, produces, and delivers including the external payoffs and consequences (Kaufman & Zahn, 1993). It is far more than improving one's isolated processes or simply complying with existing procedures or methods. It is a way of thinking and acting that allows an organization not only to do things right but also to do the right things (as noted in a different context by Peter Drucker, 1973). The continuous improvement/quality management process is vital; an organization's survival depends on it being done correctly and consistently.

There is nothing more natural—and ethical—than delivering goods and services that are both satisfying and useful. Quality resides in satisfying clients and assisting them to be successful. Quality management/continuous improvement (QM/CI) is designed to satisfy the client—an essential ingredient in making a contribution—but current QM/CI approaches should be extended to deliver both satisfaction and continual well-being.

QM/CI: Doing It Right the First Time and Moving Continuously Toward Perfection

Delivering quality is sensible and very practical. Increasing numbers of organizations are starting quality initiatives to "do it right the first time and every time." Quality programs usually target similar elements as they move continuously toward their vision (see Figure 1).

Figure 1. Linked Elements in a Conventional TQM Program

Everything an organization uses, does, and produces—including organizational and human performance improvement—must be based on ever-improving efficiency, quality, and a useful deliverable. Organizations must train their associates to "do it right the first time and every time." Everyone should hold the same vision: move toward total quality to the customer. Good intentions and slogans are not sufficient to deliver quality.

Deming (1982) provides fourteen principles to guide a quality process. Joiner (1986) suggests that these steps form three clusters:

- Everyone on one team,
- A passion[1] for quality, and
- Data-based decision making.

Before making decisions, we must take the following steps to generate specifics:

- Define quality objectives,
- Develop criteria for measuring accomplishments, and
- Identify what has to be done to get us from where we are to our vision.

Data-Based Decisions: Doing a Needs Assessment for Quality Initiatives

Needs are gaps between current results and desired ones (Kaufman, 1996). For each element in a quality-management process, the gaps in results between "what is" and "what should be" are determined so that useful ways of meeting needs can be selected. A sample format for this is shown in Table 1.

---

[1] Joiner uses the term "obsession," but we prefer "passion."

Table 1. Needs Assessment Format for a TQM Program

	Current Results	Current Consequences	Desired Results	Desired Consequences
MEGA LEVEL Customer satisfaction				
No loss of life No harmful pollutants				
Profits over time				
MACRO LEVEL Output quality				
Delivery schedule met				
Return/Rejection rate(s)				
MICRO LEVEL Product/ Unit quality				
Unit rejection rate(s)				
Timeliness				
Job/Performance levels				
PROCESS LEVEL (Quasi-needs) Production methods				

The Guidebook for Performance Improvement

	Current Results	Current Consequences	Desired Results	Desired Consequences
INPUT LEVEL (Quasi-needs) Quality of vendor resources				
Funding availability				
Availability of human resources				
Facilities				
Equipment				
Clarity of objectives				
Attitude/ Motivation				

The needs—gaps in results—are placed in priority order, based on what it costs, directly and indirectly, to meet the needs versus what it costs to ignore them (Kaufman, 1992, April, 1996). These criteria relate costs to payoffs and the costs of action compared to inaction.

After the needs are identified, the best ways and means (which could include training, new production methods, and job redesign) to achieve total quality are chosen. This process also includes comparing costs to consequences.

Selecting the Methods and Means for Quality

Rather than rushing to use familiar or popular methods, we may be creative and select how-to-do-its—techniques, resources, and means—on the basis of the costs and consequences that they will deliver. We take the needs selected and identify possible methods and means (e.g., human resources development, benchmarking, reengineering, workplace redesign, work simplification, automation) for meeting them. No tool, technique, or procedure is selected unless it will efficiently close the results gaps between what exists and what is desired. Possible synergies with other organizational activities also are considered. Table 2 provides a sample methods-means selection format.

Evaluating Results and Payoffs

Evaluation shows us what worked and what did not. It compares our accomplishments with our objectives. Based on the evaluation results, we choose what to change and what to keep.

The criteria for evaluation come directly from the "what should be or desired results" column of Table 1. So needs assessment not only provides the objectives for quality, it also produces the criteria for evaluation. Evaluation data must be used only for fixing, never for blaming. Evaluation data will allow you to move continuously toward the goal of quality: satisfying the client.

Plotting Continuous Improvement

Quality management requires that all involved keep track of what is moving everyone toward quality and where changes might be made. Some tools for "keeping score" so that data-based decisions may be made include the following:

- Sampling
- Descriptive Statistics
    sequence plots
    bar charts

Reprinted, with permission, from Kaufman, Herman, & Watters, 1996.

Table 2. Sample Methods-Means Selection Format

| Need* | Current Performer Skills, Knowledge and Abilities | Identify Possible Ways and Means to Close the Gaps in Results | | Cost/Consequences Analysis | |
		Required Performer Skills, Knowledge and Abilities	Possible Interventions	Advantages	Disadvantages

*Needs may be clustered; several might deal with some common gaps in results

histograms (side-by-side, stacked bar)
scattergrams
cause-and-effect diagrams
control charts
pie charts
Pareto diagrams
flowcharts

Do Quality Programs Go Far Enough?

When Customer Satisfaction Is Not Enough

All organizations are means to societal ends; they all have external clients. To keep those external clients satisfied and returning, organizations have to provide value-added products or services. What organizations use, do, develop, and deliver to clients are evaluated on the basis of both customer satisfaction and the usefulness of what is delivered.

Usefulness is based on sustained value and worth both to the client and to the world. Table 1 shows the basic questions any organization asks and answers, whether it does so formally or not.

Conventional total-quality approaches focus only on one part of the mega/outcomes level: client satisfaction. Figure 2 shows the general rolling-up of the typical TQM program elements, as they move from quality resources ("all resources will be right") to processes ("all know their jobs and can be depended on to do them right") to results ("the product is right the first time and every time"). The vision—where we want to be and what we want to deliver—is focused on the output and the satisfied-customer levels.

Of course, satisfied clients are crucial to a business. But there is more.

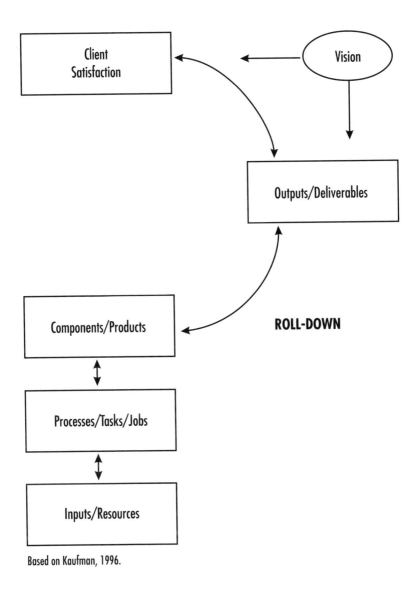

Based on Kaufman, 1996.

Figure 2. Conventional TQM Elements and Their
Roll-Up Sequence

Quality Management/Continuous Improvement "Plus"

Beyond Client Satisfaction

Peter Drucker (1973) reminds us that doing things right is not as important as doing the right things. Quality management, as usually practiced, concentrates on doing things right.

But what about the contributions and usefulness of what pleases the clients? We can think of many things that make customers happy that might not be helpful or even safe: plastic bags, styrofoam cups/plastic packaging and utensils, chemicals (DDT, Chlordane, Alar), marbled beef, fried chicken with its skin on, cigarettes/tobacco products, disposable diapers, newspaper inks, aerosol/fluorocarbon sprays, leaded gasoline, asbestos insulation, loud rock music, leaf blowers, sun tans, and phosphates in detergents. The development and marketing of each of these items could be the subject of a conventional QM/CI program. The producer of any of them might win a Deming Prize or a Malcolm Baldrige Award, and each could bring client satisfaction without total quality usefulness (to the client and the world).

The missing component in conventional quality programs is the delivery of results that move society toward a vision, not just of a successful company and a satisfied client, but of a safe and satisfying world, one we would be proud to leave for our children. Only with this end will the client be happy and also well-served (Drucker, 1993; Kaufman & Zahn, 1993; Popcorn, 1991).

Figure 3 provides a Quality Management/Continuous Improvement Plus (QM/CI+) framework. The QM/CI+ process begins outside the organization with identification of what is required for societal usefulness (the mega level), then rolls down to create what should be delivered to the client, then meets with the roll-up contributions of conventional quality management. QM/CI+ integrates with conventional quality management; it takes a good idea and extends it.

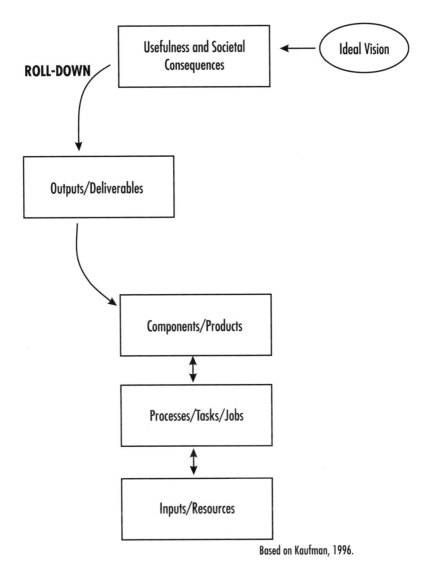

Based on Kaufman, 1996.

Figure 3. Elements of Quality Management/Continuous Improvement Plus (QM/CI+)

The first element, the primary focus of the vision, is determining what would create a better world as well as client satisfaction. It then rolls down until it meets with a conventional quality management roll-up cycle.

This Is Practical and Profitable

More and more organizations are finding that it is practical, ethical, and profitable to please clients and to help ensure that they will be well-served. Organizations that do not serve their clients well will not survive the next decade. Delivering things that provide societal good is, increasingly, both profitable and ethical.

Total Quality Management Planning Question	Type of Planning	Primary Client
1. Are we to be concerned with the current and future survival, health, well-being, self-sufficiency, and quality of life of the world in which we and our clients live?	Mega	Society
2. Are we to be concerned with the quality of that which our organization delivers to its clients?	Macro	Our external clients
3. Are we to be concerned with the quality of that which is turned out within our system and is used by internal clients as they do the business of the organization?	Micro	Individuals or small groups within our organization

Based on Kaufman, 1995, 1996.

Figure 4. Basic Questions for Putting QM/CI+ to Work

What Can You Do?

Performance-improvement professionals are often the first to realize that something is missing from organizational missions, capabilities, and methods. They see the link between people, productivity, satisfaction, continued health, and organizational success. When developing a quality-management program, open a dialogue with executive management about going beyond the conventional framework by adding societal payoffs to customer satisfaction. Figure 4 provides some questions and considerations that you might use with your quality partners in working toward an extended total quality management needs assessment.

Doing a Needs Assessment for a QM/CI+ Activity

When doing QM/CI+, the information from a conventional needs assessment, such as that shown in Table 1, is augmented by harvesting the gaps in results at the full *mega* level, such as the additional elements shown in Table 3.

Much is to be gained by using QM/CI+. Not only do organizations have to be competitive, they also must contribute to our future societal well-being. Futurists (Naisbitt & Aburdene, 1990; Toffler, 1991) agree that a new world is coming our way, ready or not. Other experts assert that the paradigm (Barker, 1989, 1993) relating to how we view and interact with the world has already shifted (Block, 1993; Drucker, 1993; Marshall & Tucker, 1992). To be responsive to that new reality, we should become active players in creating the kind of world in which we (1) want our children to live, (2) can make a contribution, (3) will get a return on our investment for what we do and deliver, and (4) can be accountable for useful results.

Table 3. A Needs-Assessment Format for a QM/CI+ Activity

	Current Results	Current Consequences	Desired Results	Desired Consequences
MEGA LEVEL				
Sustained profits				
Environmental Sustainability				
Safety				
Health & Well-being				
Quality of life				
Image/ Reputation				
MACRO LEVEL				
Output quality				
Delivery sched- ule met				
Return/Rejection rate(s)				

Based on Kaufman, 1996.

By using a societal-payoffs dimension when setting our targets—moving beyond just client satisfaction to also include client and societal well-being—we can not only be responsive to our coming world, we can also be the masters of it. A delighted customer is not enough. A healthy, safe, *and* satisfied one is better.

References

Barker, J.A. (1989). *The business of paradigms: Discovering the future* [Videotape]. Burnsville, MN: ChartHouse Learning.

Barker, J.A. (1993). *Paradigm pioneers.* Burnsville, MN: ChartHouse Learning.

Block, P. (1993). *Stewardship.* San Francisco, CA: Berrett-Koehler.

Deming, W.E. (1982). *Quality, productivity, and competitive position.* Cambridge, MA: Massachusetts Institute of Technology, Center for Advanced Engineering Study.

Drucker, P.F. (1973). *Management: Tasks, responsibilities, practices.* New York: Harper & Row.

Drucker, P.F. (1993). *Post-capitalist society.* New York: HarperBusiness.

Joiner, B.L. (1986, May). Using statisticians to help transform industry in America. *Quality Progress*, pp. 46-50.

Kaufman, R. (1992). *Strategic planning plus: An organizational guide.* Newbury Park, CA: Sage.

Kaufman, R. (1992, April). The challenge of total quality management in education. *International Journal of Educational Reform.*

Kaufman, R. (1995, May-June). Quality management plus: Beyond standard approaches to quality. *Educational Technology.*

Kaufman, R. (1996). *Strategic thinking: Identifying and solving problems.* Washington, DC: International Society for Performance Improvement / Alexandria, VA: American Society for Training and Development.

Kaufman, R., Herman, J., & Watters, K. (1996). *Educational planning: Strategic, tactical, operational.* Lancaster, PA: Technomic.

Kaufman, R., & Zahn, D. (1993). *Quality management plus: The continuous improvement of education.* Thousand Oaks, CA: Corwin Press.

Marshall, R., & Tucker, M. (1992). *Thinking for a living: Education & the wealth of nations.* New York: Basic Books.

Naisbitt, J., & Aburdene, P. (1990). *Megatrends 2000: Ten new directions for the 1990's.* New York: William Morrow.

Popcorn, F. (1991). *The Popcorn report.* New York: Doubleday.

Toffler, A. (1991). *Powershift: Knowledge, wealth, and violence at the edge of the 21st century.* New York: Bantam.

PERFORMANCE APPRAISAL

John F. Fox

Introduction

If we share a concern for organizational and human performance, it naturally follows that we must assess that performance. Historically, the measurement of human and organizational performance has been the subject of many articles, and a variety of models are applied in the workplace. Success of any model or system depends on how well the model fits (or can be modified to fit) the organization to which it is being applied. Levels of success have varied as widely as the models and organizations applying them. The fundamental question remains: Can human systems engineers, developing performance assessment systems, find an approach that builds on proven techniques to assess human and organizational performance? I think we can!

Industrial engineers have been telling us, "You can't evaluate what you can't measure and you can't manage what you can't evaluate." Then what should you measure? Brown (1990, p. 11) states, "When it comes time to decide what to measure in an organization, it's tempting to measure everything." Some of us have yielded to just such a temptation. In *The Fifth Discipline*, Peter Senge (1990) relates, "Perhaps for the first time in history humankind has the capacity to create far more information than we can possibly absorb." Are we guilty of collecting as many measures as possible with the false hope that all this information will be able to support our decisions?

Evaluation systems depend on meaningful, accurate measurement of the information we require. Accurate is defined as deviating only slightly from a standard. Therefore, the accuracy of an organization's measurements is directly related to the standards set by the organization. Standards are defined within the organizational context. Laws and regulations imposed from external sources are turned into organizational policies and procedures. Necessity and good business practice also dictate internally imposed standards and rules.

Many organizations integrate a futurist orientation. Anticipatory goals can result in additional standards being developed or can influence current standards. The policies and rules developed reflect not only the external environment but also the internal organizational culture and the level of maturity.

Organizational maturity (Fox, 1990) plays an important role in establishing the performance goals of an organization. Kaufman (1989) categorizes planning and goal setting into *mega, macro,* and *micro* levels. Figure 1 shows graphically how an organization's maturity is reflected through its planning and goal setting.

A mature organization's goals and performance expectations are often in the mega level, and evaluation of successes in reaching these goals is correspondingly difficult to quantify. These obstacles pressure organizations into spending an inordinate amount of time and money in focusing on that which is easy to measure and quantify.

Using these data, organizations extrapolate to how successful they have been in reaching the goals that are difficult to measure. Or, worse, they focus all evaluation efforts on easy-to-measure indicators and direct all improvement efforts to a limited set of organizational functions.

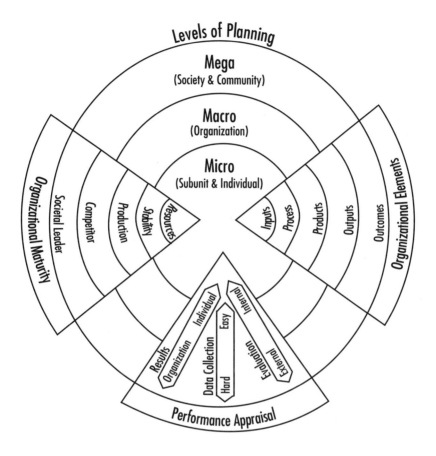

Figure 1. Performance-Appraisal Model

Changes based on these data are done so at the expense of rigorous examination of organizational goals. It is no wonder that individuals and subgroups caught in such a system have a difficult time figuring out what the organization truly requires of them.

Managers assigned to assess individuals' performance have addressed this task through the setting of performance goals and standards. To assess individual performance against these goals, managers have resorted to management by objectives and other systems designed to highlight individual contribution and worth to the organization. Superior performance can be achieved only when organizational goal achievement is consistent with personal goal achievement. An excellent performer who fails to notice changes in the organization's requirements can become obsolete and quickly lose the excellent ratings.

The problem is one of assessing organizational performance, subunit performance, and individual performance. Once we decide what performance is required, we can determine the appropriate measures of that performance. Applying those measures, we can assess where we are in relation to a goal and then institute the changes required to move closer to the goal.

This chapter is about creating an integrated approach for designing effective performance-appraisal systems. It examines organizational maturity as a means of establishing what is important to the organization. It discusses how a subunit determines what it can contribute to the organization's performance, and it tells how individuals can contribute to the organization's performance.

The Impact of Organizational Maturity on Performance

By modifying the maturation model developed by Maslow (1943, 1954) and substituting organizational characteristics for personal traits, we can create a model that is useful in predicting organizational maturity (see Figure 1).

The resources level represents the lowest level of organizational maturity, roughly equivalent to Maslow's basic needs. Each successive level—stability, productivity, competitor, and societal leader—represents significant growth in the organization's maturity.

Estimating the organizational maturity level is useful in understanding what the organization is likely to value. Such values provide the context for determining what is important to the organization and, thus, what to measure in order to assess how well the organization is performing.

If an organization is in its infancy, it is unlikely that it can afford to concern itself with the societal impact of its product or service. This organization would be represented at the resources and stability levels on the model. Basic needs of the organization are revealed by answering these questions: Can it meet the payroll? Does it have the essential tools and equipment? Should it hire full-time staff? The organization may be characterized as struggling for existence. As such, its planning focuses on tactical levels through the fine-tuning of a process or system. Measures of performance are found in the inputs and process levels of the organizational-elements section of Figure 1.

As the organization becomes productive, the focus begins to shift to productivity measures (e.g., whether its products meet the clients needs). Efficiency and effectiveness of the product are of primary concern.

Results can be attributed not to any one individual but rather/ to the organizational subunit. Products are combined with others to constitute organizational outputs that now bridge the *macro* and *mega* levels. Measures of performance move to external sources and become increasingly difficult to collect. The organization must become proactive in addressing future needs.

As the organization continues to mature, it becomes recognized in its industry or business field. The organization's goals may now be affected by the organization's relative ranking with its competitors.

Status, in the organizational sense, may result in expansion of product lines or other modifications of the business related to outputs and products. Planning and organizational goals are evolving from *macro* to *mega* levels.

Further maturity produces an increased interest in organizational outcomes. Keep in mind that all the lower-level needs must also be met if the organization is to be allowed to concern itself with outcomes. Mature organizations look far beyond institutional boundaries. Internal needs are combined with societal needs, placing more emphasis on outputs that result in positive societal outcomes. The organization now becomes a societal leader, diverting a portion of its resources to helping solve societal problems.

Divisions, departments, groups, or other subunits within the organization are chartered to support the organization's goals and must be evaluated within this context.

Organizational Subunits

Organizational subunits can use this model to examine their maturity as they grow within the overall organization. Applying these same questions to an organizational unit can result in that immature unit being classified as reactive. The subunit may be struggling with identifying its mission and attempting to carve its niche in the organization. At this stage, the subunit must demonstrate that it belongs in the organization and that it makes a significant contribution to organizational productivity. Subunit employees will likely be focusing their efforts on assessing productivity in terms of inputs and processes. Projects involving current job requirements, safety, and identified employee and organizational deficiencies that can be resolved at the tactical level will be highlighted in the workload. Subunit problems may span the resources, stability, and production levels of the model.

As a subunit matures, its employees increasingly will be called on to participate in higher-level decision making within the organization. They will gain esteem and status from their abilities to respond effectively to their internal clients' needs. At this stage, the subunit becomes more future oriented and proactive in responding to the needs of the organization. Continued success is determined by the subunit's ability to work effectively within the plexus of organizational units. Joint efforts with other organizational subunits moves the performance measures beyond a single unit's products and into the higher level of organizational outputs. Performance appraisal goes beyond the boundaries of any one subunit and becomes increasingly complex.

With continued growth, the subunit's maturity bridges the production and competitor levels. Further growth may not be possible while the subunit remains within the boundaries of the overall organization. As the subunit's reputation and status grow, the likelihood of its becoming a separate, stand-alone organization increases. As occasionally happens, an internal organization is severed from the mother company to begin the maturation process once again. Reorganization is likely at this time. Major sections of the subunit may become new subunits or merge with others to form a new subunit. In each of these cases, the maturation process begins anew, impacting the design of the organizational performance assessment.

Possibly the smallest subunit within the organization is the individual. Human performance is the building block for all organizational performance. When the human performance supports the organizational goals, the organization is successful. However, when human performance is not aligned with organizational needs, the organization suffers.

Individual Performance

In assessing an individual's performance, how someone does his or her job (process) is at least as important as the results. Often we see employees who, charging toward an objective, succeed in meeting the goal but leave a path of broken glass. Cleaning up the broken glass takes money and individual effort and, most significantly, can permanently damage essential working relationships among work groups.

Performance-appraisal systems can be designed to focus on process and/or result. Process-centered systems are characterized by performance indicators and standards. An example of an indicator for a secretarial function might be answering the phone; the standard might be answering before the fourth ring 80 percent of the time. This is measurable. It could be considered an effective performance measure. An advantage is that the employee knows what is expected for satisfactory performance.

These well-defined tasks and subtasks usually result in the development of a plethora of data. For these data to be useful in measuring the individual's performance, the data splinters must be bundled and tied to results. In the above example, knowing how often the telephone answerers meet or exceed the standard may not be as significant as the results of how they answer the phone. Results may take the form of irritated customers, lost sales, and missed opportunities.

Purely results-oriented human-performance systems can have a negative effect. An employee may meet or exceed a results target at the expense of relationships, equipment, or tools. Shortcuts also may place workers in physical danger or create an unsafe work environment. The damage and potential damage are considered in evaluating the individual's performance. By combining results targets with a process-centered evaluation, an effective human-performance measurement system can be designed that will satisfy both organizational and individual needs.

Individual and organizational needs can be satisfied simultaneously. On the other hand, individual needs can be unrelated to organizational needs. In this case, the individual succeeds and the organization suffers. When the needs of the organization are known and are linked to the individual employees' needs, individual success yields organizational benefits. When this is designed into the performance-measurement system, organizational performance can be attributed directly to employee performance.

Rewards for successful performance must be consistent with the organization's goals. Recognition systems can have negative consequences. One public school system implemented a merit-pay component in its compensation system. One of the high school industrial-arts teachers was recognized for merit pay based on the long hours he was found to be working in his shop. School board members reportedly had seen the lights on in the high school shop late into the evening and had seen the teacher working on weekends. They did not know that he was building kitchen cabinets for his new house. Of course, the other teachers in the system responded negatively when he was recognized with a merit-pay reward.

When employees are allowed to abuse a system and win, it can damage organizational performance. Employees expect discipline from the managers in an organization. When one is not held accountable for one's actions, how can one feel good about an accomplishment?

Individual performance-appraisal systems must link subunit and organizational goals to individual performance. Employees who understand how their personal performance impacts the subunit and organizational performance are more likely to continue to be productive.

A variety of appraisal techniques are useful in collecting meaningful data about individual and organizational performance. These techniques are often used selectively and are seldom used simultaneously.

Additional Appraisal Techniques

Peer review can be an effective technique for providing a measurement of where one is relative to his or her peers. Presentations at conferences can often result in a form of peer review. Within an organization these reviews can be informal or structured to provide a formal feedback mechanism. In either case, these reviews provide employees direct feedback on their performance.

Some organizations use an evaluation committee from outside the organization. The committee consists of individuals who are experienced and knowledgeable in the organization's field or business and are deemed expert in evaluating the organization's contributions and abilities. The value of these committees and their contribution varies. Evaluation committees most often examine organizational goals and overall organizational performance and seldom directly evaluate individual performance.

Unobtrusive indicators of performance also can be valid performance measurements (e.g., whether clients arrive on time, whether one is called on for consultation before a decision is made, whether people are excited about an idea or proposed project). Although subject to criticism by measurement experts, such indicators are sometimes sufficient. Occasionally, they will point to areas where a more sophisticated system of measurement should be applied.

Checklists for managers and employees allow for the self-assessment of a subunit of the organization against performance standards. When the standards change, the system in place must also reflect those changes. At the product level in the organization, checklists are relatively easy to develop and understand. They tend to be concrete indicators that can be observed or easily measured with standard techniques and tools. As you move toward the outcome level, checklists may lose some of their effectiveness, and other methods should be considered.

Audits, as measurement tools, can be both internal and external and provide additional information about organizational performance. External auditors are generally considered more objective than individuals from within an organization. External audits can be expensive and are used less frequently than internal audits. Internal audits can be conducted by independent assessment subgroups within the organization. They have the advantage of more extensive knowledge of the structure and goals of the organization. On occasion, however, this internal knowledge can bias the audit.

Many industries have internal self-assessment programs wherein the staff in a subunit of the organization assesses its own function. It is then audited by the organization's internal auditors and, ultimately, by external auditors. This process gives the organization a feel for how accurately and objectively it is completing a self-assessment.

Agreement on the audit's measures and standards is crucial to the success of an assessment. Audit teams can be divided into subteams to look at the different levels of performance of an organization. Outcome measures can be examined by a mega-team, while organizational outputs can be measured by a macro-team, and the product-level measures can be evaluated by a micro-team. It is necessary to measure what is important at each level of the organization if one is to have a complete performance-measurement system. Individuals at all levels of an organization must understand how their productivity contributes to the organization's outcomes.

Conclusion

Measurement systems and evaluation techniques can be restrictive and inhibit an organization's ability to respond to change. Therefore, we must be prudent in selecting and designing the measurement systems that we put in place. Our focus must be on simple, easily understood systems that are flexible enough to meet the challenge of fast-paced change. We must abandon complex, sophisticated systems wherever possible.

Performance measurement can be accomplished through the systematic matching of organizational goals and individual goals, both of which are designed in light of the organization's culture. Engineering a system characterized by simple, efficient measurement maintains the organization's ability to take action.

Sharing the information about organizational results and goals empowers employees at all levels of the organization to direct their efforts in support of the organization's results. As the acceleration of change continues to create increasing levels of uncertainty within organizations, let us be brave enough to suggest more streamlined systems that will enable us to keep pace.

Organizations traditionally have used seven criteria for measuring performance: quality, effectiveness, efficiency, market share, financial resources, quality of work life, and innovation. These and any other criteria must be placed into the organizational context as the measurement system is designed. Just as strategic planning through tactical planning is a process yielding goals and objectives for the organization, so should be the design of the measurement system. As we approach the mega-level outcomes (Figure 1), the less defined the measure becomes and the less objective we are in measuring the outcome. Here our customers or clients must be called on to provide evaluation data.

As we move to the output level in the hierarchy, the picture of what to measure becomes clearer, and we increase our objectivity through better definition of the measures. Continuing to the product level increases our objectivity, and measurement at this level becomes fairly easy to accomplish.

Figure 1 shows the relationship that exists between organizational maturity, levels of planning, organizational elements, and performance appraisal. Individual and subunit performance measures are based in the micro level; the organizational performance measures are in the macro level; and the societal performance measures are in the mega level.

Once we have selected what to measure and how to measure it and feel that we know the data required to measure organizational success, we face the problem of keeping up with organizational change. In some ways, organizations can resist change. In other ways, changes can occur in startlingly short periods of time. The performance-assessment system must be an integral part of the planning and goal-setting process for the organization. Systems must be installed to provide the appropriate feedback and initiate the necessary change before the crisis.

In an era of continued cultural change, organizations are challenged to examine their progress and be prepared to respond quickly. Human-systems professionals, responsible for designing systems for measuring organizational and individual performance, must remain adroit. Flexibility and the ability to assess change and deal effectively with it are essential for continued organizational success. Performance-system dynamics (the integration of organizational needs, subunit needs, and individual needs) will help to ensure that one is measuring the right things.

As Jim Popham of UCLA once said, if you are not going to use the data to make a decision, don't collect them! The best advice for any systems designer is "keep it simple." Measure only what is important at each level in the organization. Employees at all levels want to know how they're doing, so make the performance measures visible and as easily understood as possible.

The following Performance-Appraisal Checklist (Figure 2) is included to provide "food for thought" as you consider what to include in an appraisal system.

Organizational Checks

Internal
- Documented mission and goals/Documented procedures
- Adherence to procedures
- Self-assessment
- Support and tracking systems/Verification functions
- Lessons-learned programs
- Quality programs
- Peer reviews
- Standing committees

External
- Program drivers
- Regulations and laws
- Good business practices
- Anticipatory-needs-assessment review systems
- Audits
- Review committees
- Rewards
- Recognition programs
- Disciplinary actions/Penalties

Individual Checks
- Employee involvement
- Employee empowerment
- Rewards/Recognition
- Discipline programs

Performance-Appraisal System
- Individual-results targets/Performance indicators
- Performance standards

Figure 2. Performance-Appraisal Checklist

- Product evaluations
- Developmental plans
- Peer reviews
- Upward-evaluation system

Support Systems
- Training programs
- Leave programs

Other Indicators
- Unobtrusive indicators
- Morale

Figure 2 (continued). Performance-Appraisal Checklist

References

Brown, M.G. (1990, May/June). You get what you measure: Engineering a performance measurement system. *Performance & Instruction Journal.*

Fox, J.F. (1990, September). Applied models in HRD: Maslow and mega planning. *Performance & Instruction Journal.*

Kaufman, R. (1989, February). Selecting a planning mode: Who is the client? Who benefits? *Performance & Instruction Journal.*

Maslow, A.H. (1943). A theory of human motivation. *Psychological Review, 50,* 370-396.

Maslow, A.H. (1954). *Motivation and personality.* New York: Harper & Row.

Senge, P. (1990). *The fifth discipline.* New York: Doubleday.

About the Editors

Roger Kaufman, Ph.D.
Professor and Director, Center for Needs Assessment and Planning
Learning Systems Institute, Florida State University
Tallahassee, Florida 32306-2022

Roger Kaufman is a professor and director of the Center for Needs Assessment and Planning at the Florida State University. He is also a research professor of engineering management at Newark College of Engineering, New Jersey Institute of Technology. He received an M.A. in industrial psychology engineering from Johns Hopkins University and a Ph.D. in communications from New York University. Roger specializes in needs assessment, quality management and strategic planning and is the author of 31 books and more than 160 articles. He is a past president and life member of ISPI.

Sivasailam Thiagarajan, Ph.D.
Workshops by Thiagi
4423 East Trailridge Road
Bloomington, Indiana 47408-9653

Sivasailam "Thiagi" Thiagarajan is the principal of Workshops by Thiagi, which designs and delivers training workshops. He is the editor of ISPI's *Performance & Instruction Journal,* adjunct professor of instructional systems technology at Indiana University, and vice president of the Institute for International Research, Inc. He received a Ph.D. in instructional systems technology from Indiana University. He is the author of 12 books and more than 150 articles on human performance technology.

Paula W. MacGillis, Ph.D.
Research Associate
Center for Needs Assessment and Planning
Learning Systems Institute, Florida State University
Tallahassee, Florida 32306-2022

Paula W. MacGillis is a research associate at the Center for Needs Assessment and Planning at the Florida State University, formerly at the Florida Department of Labor and Employment Security. Since 1969, she has worked as a performance technologist in human services agencies. She presents at state and national conferences on governmental applications of performance technology. Paula re-ceived her Ph.D. in instructional systems from the Florida State University.

ABOUT THE CONTRIBUTORS

Frank W. Banghart, Ph.D.
3374 Lake Shore Drive
Tallahassee, Florida 32312

Frank W. Banghart received his doctorate degree from the University of Virginia. He has held professorships at the University of Virginia, Harvard University, and Florida State University. He initiated the first Ph.D. program in the United States in educational policy analysis based on systems theory. He has served as a consultant to nine countries. He is the author of five books and numerous articles in national and international journals.

Adrian Bell, CMAHRI.
Leaderskill Group
P.O. Box 6
West Lindfield, New South Wales 2070, Australia

Adrian Bell established Beta Training Services Pty Ltd in 1982. He has worked in many areas of personnel/human resource management as a training and development manager and personnel manager and as a consultant with public and private organizations. He is a founding member of the New South Wales Small Business Agency. Adrian also maintains a personal commitment to improving opportunities for Australia's Aboriginal people.

Margie Bluett
Acumen Human Resource Consultancy
16 Seabeach Avenue
Mona Vale, New South Wales 2103, Australia

Margie Bluett is the managing director of Acumen Human Resource Consultancy in Sydney, which specializes in organizational change and human resource development in Pacific Rim countries. Margie has a background in psychology and 20 years' experience as a management and organizational consultant. She recruits internationally and arranges partnerships, mergers, and joint ventures. She also trains professional recruiters and line managers in recruitment and retention techniques.

Dale M. Brethower, Ph.D.
8190 Two Mile Road, N.E.
Ada, Michigan 49301

Dale M. Brethower is a professor of psychology at Western Michigan University. He is a licensed clinical psychologist and has been a consultant for 30 years. He is a consulting editor for the *Performance Improvement Quarterly,* and the editor or a guest editor of several other journals. Dale is the author or coauthor of 8 books. He received a Lifetime Achievement Award in organizational behavior management from IABA.

Jeffrey A. Cantor, Ph.D.
City University of New York
25 Judith Drive
Danbury, Connecticut 06811

Jeffrey A. Cantor is an associate professor of adult education and corporate training with Lehman College of The City University of New York. He teaches courses and conducts research in the areas of training evaluation and instructional systems design. He also has provided consultative services to the commercial nuclear power industry and to the U.S. Government, including the U.S. Navy.

Richard A. Cornell, Ph.D.
University of Central Florida
Education, Room 310
Orlando, Florida 32816

Richard A. Cornell is an associate professor in instructional systems in the College of Education at the University of Central Florida. He was the university's first director of instructional media. He is a past president of the International Division of AECT, is a co-founder of the Central Florida AECT, and has served as vice president of the Paris-based International Council of Educational Media—a nongovernmental organization of UNESCO.

Diane Dormant, Ph.D.
Dormant & Associates, Inc.
316 N. Hillsdale Dr.
Bloomington, Indiana 47408

Diane Dormant directs Dormant & Associates, Inc., consultants in management communication and organizational change. Their Change Mapping^{SM} Workshop is based on twenty years of Diane's consulting, publishing, and teaching experience. She has a Ph.D. in instructional systems technology from Indiana University where she is an adjunct professor. Diane is a past president of the International Society of Performance Improvement (ISPI).

Ahmad K. Elshennawy, Ph.D.
Department of Industrial Engineering and Management
  Systems
University of Central Florida
P.O. Box 162450
Orlando, Florida 32816-2450

Ahmad K. Elshennawy is an associate professor in the department of industrial engineering and management systems at the University of Central Florida. He received a Ph.D. in industrial engineering from the Pennsylvania State University. He is a senior member of ASQC, a member of ASQC's Quality Press Standing Review Board, a certified quality engineer (CQE), and a certified reliability engineer (CRE).

Ron Forbes, Ph.D.
Leaderskill Group
P.O. Box 6
West Lindfield, New South Wales 2070, Australia

Ron Forbes is founder of the Leaderskill Group, which specializes in communication and win-win conflict resolution. Ron has lived among the indigenous peoples of many countries and has served as education specialist for the Organization of American States. He has led projects ranging from scientific and educational research to systems consulting. He received his Ph.D. from UCLA. Ron is an associate fellow of the Australian Institute of Management.

John Fox
Los Alamos National Laboratory
Mail Stop K-491
Los Alamos, New Mexico 87545

John Fox is the chief of staff for the Environment, Safety, and Health Division of the Los Alamos National Laboratory, where his research has supported management's understanding of technical-staff career development. As a research advisor, he mentored M.S. and Ph.D. students in education and applied psychology. John is known internationally for his management training programs. He received his masters degree from State University of New York, Oswego.

Judith Hale, Ph.D.
Hale Associates
4365 Lawn Avenue
Suite #6
Western Springs, Illinois 60558

Judith Hale, Ph.D., is a management and training consultant and president of Hale Associates. Her firm does needs assessment and designs performance management systems and certification programs. The firm offers customized workshops on testing, certification, and needs assessment. Judith is a speaker, facilitator, and author. Her latest book, *Achieving a Leadership Role for Training*, is a university text. Judith received her Ph.D. in Instructional Technology from Purdue University. She is a member of ASTD and ISPI.

Wallace Hannum, Ph.D.
University of North Carolina at Chapel Hill
School of Education
Chapel Hill, North Carolina 27597-3560

Wallace Hannum is an associate professor in the School of Education at the University of North Carolina at Chapel Hill. He teaches graduate-level courses in learning theory, instructional design, ISD, and multimedia. He regularly consults with governmental agencies and private corporations. He specializes in training and performance-support programs, task analysis, and instructional design. He has written several books and numerous articles.

Ronald L. Jacobs, Ph.D.
The Ohio State University
Graduate Program in Human Resource Development
325 Ramseyer Hall
Columbus, Ohio 43210-1177

Ronald L. Jacobs is an associate professor and the coordinator of the graduate specialization in human resource development, College of Education, The Ohio State University. His Ph.D. is from Indiana University in instructional systems technology and organizational behavior. Ronald has done award-winning research on systems theory applied to HRD and structural on-the-job training. He is involved with several professional journals and has written numerous journal articles and book chapters.

Randolph I. James
James and Associates
P.O. Box 1408
Orangevale, California 95662

Randolph I. James has worked in the field of performance technology for over fourteen years, in both the public and private sectors. He received a masters degree in industrial organizational psychology from California State University, Sacramento. He is the author of *The No-Nonsense Guide to Common Sense Management* and has published several articles on improving performance. He is a member of the International Society for Performance Improvement and has presented at several international conferences.

Michael J. Jones
Human Resource Development Manager
Kenworth Truck Company
7327 Marietta Road
Chillicothe, Ohio 45601

Michael J. Jones is the manager of human resource development at Kenworth Truck Company. He has been a manager of training in the automotive industry for 15 years. He has authored books and articles on structured OJT, employee development, and organizational change in the new economy. Michael is a member of ISPI and a past president of the Heartland Central Ohio Chapter. He also presents at national professional conferences.

Danny G. Langdon
International Technology Corporation
17461 Derian Avenue
Irvine, California 92714

Danny G. Langdon specializes in instructional design and performance technology. He is the principal of Performance International, a management-consulting firm in Santa Monica, California. Danny is the author of several books and articles in the field of human performance technology. He is a former president of ISPI and he has presented at the White House.

Seth Leibler, Ph.D.
The Center for Effective Performance
4250 Perimeter Parks South
Suite 131
Atlanta, Georgia 30341

Seth Leibler is the president and CEO of the Center for Effective Performance (CEP). Seth has been an executive and consultant in the business of improving human performance for 25 years. For eight years, he has managed the Center for Professional Development and Training within the Centers for Disease Control.

He has a doctorate in educational psychology from the University of Rochester. He is a past president of ISPI.

Odgen R. Lindsley, Ph.D.
Behavior Research Company
366 N. 1600 Rd.
Lawrence, Kansas 66049-9199
[olindsley@aol.com]

Odgen R. Lindsley is the president and founder of Behavior Research Co., a provider of performance tracking and change-charting systems. He also is chairman of the Lindsley Group, which installs corporate change-tracking and managing systems. Ogden founded the first human operant laboratory, coined the term "behavior therapy," and developed "precision teaching" and "standard celeration charting." He is a Professor Emeritus, Kansas University.

Bette Madson, Ph.D.
Senior Instructional Technologist, AT&T
111 N. Fourth Street, Room 1102
Columbus, Ohio 43215

Bette Madson is a performance technologist with Lucent Technologies, formerly a part of AT&T. She supports trainers at a national technical training center and has created and conducted courses throughout AT&T on course development, instruction, hypertext design, and management. She founded ISPI's Performance Technology in the Community Committee. She has a Ph.D. in Instruction from The Ohio State University.

Jeffrey J. Nelson, Ph.D.
Jeffrey J. Nelson & Association, Inc.
780 Pilot House Drive, Suite 500-C
Newport News, Virginia 23606-4415
[eojt@widomaker.com]

Jeffrey J. Nelson: The editors have been unable to locate a current address and biography for this contributor.

Carol M. Panza
66 Fanok Road
Convent Station, New Jersey 07961

Carol M. Panza is the president of CMP Associates, an independent management consulting firm with a client list representing a broad range of industries and functions. CMP Associates was founded in 1985 and specializes in analysis and custom design of performance effectiveness systems. Carol regularly delivers presentations to national organizations on performance and is the author of a book entitled *Picture This... Your Function, Your Company...* as well as several articles on performance improvement.

Ann W. Parkman
The Center for Effective Performance
4250 Perimeter Park South
Suite 131
Atlanta, Georgia 30341

As executive vice president, managing partner, and co-founder of the Center for Effective Performance, Ann manages the research and development of new products and works with clients worldwide to identify strategies for improving performance. The work of Ann and her staff has been recognized by many professional organizations and has received numerous national awards. She has more than 20 years' experience working with organizations to improve workforce performance.

Richard B. Perlstein, Ph.D.
U.S. Senate
734 Sonata Way
Silver Spring, Maryland 20901

Richard B. Pearlstein is the manager of computer training at the United States Senate Computer Center and is the president of Dyad Corporation. His background is in experimental and humanistic psychology, and he has worked as a performance technologist since 1969. Richard also is the past vice president for research and development of ISPI.

Fred Rosensweig
Technical Director for Human Resources and
  Institutional Development
Environmental Health Project
1611 N. Kent Street, Suite 300
Arlington, Virginia 22209

Fred Rosensweig is the vice president and managing partner of Training Resources Group. He also serves as technical director for human resources and institutional development on the USAID-funded Environmental Health Project. He has worked in over thirty countries.

William W. Swart, Ph.D.
University of Central Florida
Department of Industrial Engineering
4000 Central Florida Boulevard
Orlando, Florida 32816

William W. Swart is a professor and chair of the department of industrial engineering at the University of Central Florida. A specialist in productivity and quality, he has had academic experience at several universities and has held positions in a number of major corporations. He is the director of the UCF/NASA-KSC M.S. program in Engineering Management and holds research contracts to implement TQM in NASA/KSC.

Odin Westgaard, Ed.D.
Hale Associates
4365 Lawn Avenue
Suite #6
Western Springs, Illinois 60558

Odin Westgaard is a human performance technologist and senior associate with Hale Associates, where he specializes in performance measurement and evaluation. He has developed industrial training, set quality standards, and consulted with management on the design, development, delivery, and evaluation of interventions. He is the author of several books and articles and has served on several committees of ISPI and the board of IBSTPI.

x

Douglas A. Zahn, Ph.D.
249 Timberlane Road
Tallahassee, Florida 32312

Douglas A. Zahn is a professor of statistics and director of the Statistical Consulting Center in the Department of Statistics at Florida State University. He is the founder of the nonprofit Center for Quality and Learning in Tallahassee, Florida. He received his Ph.D. from Harvard University.

Jack Zigon
Zigon Performance Group
604 Crum Creek Road
Media, Pennsylvania 19063-1646

Jack Zigon is the president of Zigon Performance Group, a management consulting firm near Philadelphia. His work as manager of human resource development at Yellow Freight Systems, Inc., earned national recognition as one of the ten most outstanding examples of human factors work. Jack has designed thirteen performance-appraisal systems and coauthored twenty major training programs and nine books about improving employee performance.

Index

of product quality information,
220
in project development, 396
Communications experts, 207
Company-wide communication,
232
Competence. *See also*
Performance
individual, 7
monitoring, 345
Competence modeling, 387
Competency assessment, 342
Competitiveness, 1
Computers
as a model for cognition, 37
project management and, 408
Computer "shareware," 408
Conflict resolution, 293-294
Conner, Daryl, 436, 449
Consensus, seeking, 294-297
Consequences, fear of, 463
Constructivism, 5
Consulting
client agreement form for, 288
in organizational development,
286-287
performance technology and,
22
Consulting relationships, closing,
298-302
Consumer orientation, 478
Content analysis, 187, 498
Continuous improvement, 64, 220,
228-229, 380
defined, 15
evaluations for, 101-102
plotting, 590-592
Shewhart's Cycle for, 222
Continuous improvement
monitoring procedure, 83-84
Control Data Corporation, 52
"Core values," 71, 86
Cornell, Richard A., 393, 620
Corporate culture, risk and,
372-373, 387-388
Corporate social policy process,
50-51

Corporate social responsibility
(CSR), 45-57
benefits of, 49
literature on, 55
program for, 50
suggestions for, 55-56
viewpoints on, 46-51
Corporate values, 49
socially responsible, 54
Corporations, social partnerships
of, 48
Correct-answer test item format,
568-569
Costs-consequences analysis, 125
Counseling
employee, 386
as an intervention, 216
Craft system, 246-247
Criterion-referenced tests, 496
Critical path management (CPM),
403
Critical skills, testing, 566
Critical theory, 5
Cultural differences, in
developing countries, 483
Cumulative response records, 530
Current mission, identifying and
defining, 72-73
Customer, demands for quality by,
219-220. *See also* Clients
"Customer driven" organizations,
376
Customer expectations, 375-376
Customer focus, 376
Customer satisfaction, 220, 592.
See also Quality
measures of, 153-154

D

Data. *See also* Measurement
disagreement in, 122
internal- and external-needs,
118-121
mapping process for, 172-173
merging process for, 123

Expert judgments, on job
   candidates, 319
Experts
   as an information source, 183
   task analysis of, 193-194
Extended task analysis procedure
   model, 191
External audits, 611
External clients
   gathering data from, 312
   satisfying, 592
   serving, 95
External consultants, 284, 285
External environmental
   management, 478-479
External needs data, 118-121
External partners, 86
External performance data, 119

F

"Fashions," defined, 373
Feedback
   quality assurance and, 219
   upward, 377, 388
Feigenbaum, Armand V., 226
Field trips, 257-258
Fifth Discipline, The (Senge),
   601-602
Financing, 480-481.
   See also Profitability
Finnegan, Greg, 23
Flowcharts, task-analysis, 190-191
Fluency technique, 534-535
Focus, narrow versus broad, 35
Focus groups, 499-500
Forbes, Ron, 371, 621
Forecasting. *See also*
   Measurement
   accuracy in, 398
   of performance rhythms, 542
Formative evaluation, 491
Fox, John F., 601, 621
Friedman, Milton, 46
Front-end analysis, 9
Front-line employee development
   system (FEDS), 248-252

Front-line employees, 241-259
   defined, 242-244
   developing, 241-259, 247-258
   multiskilled, 244-247
   role transformations for,
      243-244
   technological advancements
      and, 243
Functions, setting, 79
Fundamentalist viewpoint, 46-47
Future, creating, 1, 12

G

Gantt Charts, 403, 408
Gatekeepers, 441-442
General systems theory (GST), 33,
   37-38, 283
Gestalt psychology, 3, 21
Global thinking, 63
Goal analysis, 322
Goal-free evaluation, 493-494
Goals
   in the Hale Hierarchy Model,
      209
   support for, 159-160
   types of, 462
Goal setting, levels of, 602
Government, systems approach
   to, 134-136
Government regulation, 46
Group decision support systems
   (GDSS), 500
Group performance, 6
Group-process skills, 282-283
Guatemala, historical background
   of, 473

H

Hale, Judith A., 22, 23, 24, 205,
   621-622
Hale Associates, 24
Hale Hierarchy Model, 205-217
   development of, 208, 217
   interventions used in, 2143

M

MacGillis, Paula W., 617-618
Machiavelli, Niccolo, 24
Macro-level monitoring, 549-551
Macro-level outcomes, 290-291
Macro-level planning, 8, 9, 15, 52, 96, 111, 459
Madson, Bette, 45, 624
Mager, Bob, 25
Management. *See also* Managers; Performance management; Program management; Quality management
  authoritarian, 146
  in autonomous organizations, 477-478
  commitment of, 231-232
  creativity in, 56
  effect of change on, 441
  elements of, 394
  employee terminations and, 331-332
  employee turnover and, 331
  humane side of, 4
  role of, 387
  supervision of, 224
  training and education of, 233
Management Competencies Development Program, 336
Management experts, 207
Management plans, 110
Management views, 47, 160-164
Manager checklists, 610-611
Manager group process, as an intervention, 215
Managerial behavior, performance and, 383-387
Managerial processes, 226
Managers
  developing, 241
  as a source of task inventory data, 182
  staff turnover accountability and, 357
  turnover activities of, 356
Manpower plan, 337

Manufacturers, as an information source, 182-183
Manufacturing
  macro-level planning in, 111
  mega-level planning in, 111
Margerison, Charles, 455
Margerison-McCann Team Management Index, 384, 456
Margerison-McCann team management wheel, 456, 457
Markle, Susan, 25
Marriott Corporation, 54, 55, 358
Maslow maturation model, 604
Mass production systems, 247
Mathematical models, 137
Mathematical problem solving, 193
Mathematical techniques, 132
McCann, Dick, 455
McDonald's Corporation, 47
Means, 96
  defined, 15
  performance indicators and, 94
  selection of, 68, 97-98
Means/ends relationship, 97, 375-377
Measurement. *See also* Evaluation; Performance measurement
  accuracy in, 602
  performance technology and, 145
  timing of, 503-505
  traditional, 528-529
  types of, 500-503
  versus monitoring, 537-543
  weak, 523-529
Measurement experts, 525
Measurement scales, 76, 98-99
Measurement systems, care in choosing, 611-612
Measurement theory, 22
Media experts, 503
Meetings, with key players, 292-294
"Mega, macro, and micro analysis," 34

Systems approach, 132-138
Systems design, 84
Systems flow format, 165
Systems study, schema for, 131-139
Systems thinking, 378
System subcomponents, training in, 298
Systems work, performing, 136-138
Systems worker, tasks of, 131

T

Tactical plan, developing, 79
Tactical planning, 5, 52, 61, 72, 79
Taguchi, Genichi, 227-228
"Talk through" approach, 195
Target population experts, 502
Task analysis, 9, 180, 187-188. *See also* Job-task analysis
cognitive, 194-200
procedural, 190-194
recent developments in, 191-194
Task analysis models, 180, 185, 187
Task description model, 189
Task inventories, 180-184
flawed, 183-184
Tasks
questioning, 377
rating scale for, 186
Task selection, 180, 184-187
criteria for, 185
Taylor, F. W., 35, 39
Team balance, 336-337, 343
Team-building sessions, 296
Team culture, 336
Team development, 344, 384
Team goals, 333
Team life cycles, 457-458
Teampower, harnessing, 516
Team profiling, 455-456
Team role preference, 384
Teams, self-managing, 382-383
Teamwork, 38

Teamwork achievements, recognizing, 237
Technical capability, 478
Technical experts, change and, 441
Technology
changes in, 395-396
in developing countries, 484
Terrell, Thomas, 398
Test-design specifications, 563-564, 577
Test-development process, 563-572
Test instruments, elements of, 563
Test items
appropriateness of, 582
central theme of, 566-568
developing, 561-583
essay, 576-577
format and revision of, 568-572
matching, 574-575
reviewing, 581
short answer/completion, 575-576
writing distractors for, 572-577
writing process for, 564
Test reliability
defined, 563
factors in, 582
Tests
evaluative, 4976-497
validity and reliability of, 563, 581-582
Theory
misapplication of, 32-34
understanding, 34-35
Thiagarajan, Sivasailam, 22, 489, 617
"Think-aloud" method, 195-196
Tiemann, Phil, 25
Tiemann-Markle instructional designs, 534
"Tiger teams," 229
Tom Peters Award, 358
Top-down directives, 231
Top-performers management, 365
Total cost, minimizing, 224

Total quality, organizational
effectiveness and, 219-239
Total quality control (TQC),
226-227
Total quality management
(TQM), 9, 87, 144-145
attributes of, 228-230
implementing, 221
organizational development
and, 281-282
organizational performance
and, 220-230
tools used in, 221-222
Total quality management (TQM)
program
linked elements in, 586
needs assessment format for,
588-589
Total-quality programs,
conventional, 592-593
Trainees, costs of losing, 349
Training, 9. *See also* Job aids; Job-
task analysis
apprenticeship, 254
in developing countries,
483-484
in the Hale Hierarchy Model,
212
in line ministries, 480
management, 233
on-the-job, 224, 253
tasks selection for, 184-187
in total quality management
(TQM), 229
Training cycle time, 261
Training needs assessment, 73, 126
Training programs, 87
packaging, 262
Training requirements analysis, 9,
74
Transfer measurement, 501
*Transitions: Making Sense Out of
Life's Changes* (Bridges), 447
Turnover committees, 364
Turnover competitions, 365-366

Turnover costing
implementing, 367-368
methodology in, 364
Turnover level, optimum, 357
Turnover meetings, 366-367
Turnover performance bonus, 365
Two-Tiered Organizational
Elements Model, 117
Type I indicators, 94, 95, 103
Type R indicators, 94, 103
Typical-use testing, 512-514

U

U.S. Agency for International
Development (A.I.D.), 471
Unemployment benefits, 330
United Nations Development
Programme (UNDP), 471

V

Value-added products, 592
Values, 71
corporate, 49
Variability reduction, 229
Variety principle, 424
Vendors, involvement in statistical
process control, 234
Vertical integration, 83
Victories, celebrating, 300-3031
Videotape task analysis method,
197
Virtue ethics approach, 48
Vision, common, 14
Vocabulary, common, 16

W

Wants, defined, 15
Watkins, C. L., 36
Wells, Fred, 22
Westgaard, Odin, 21, 626
"What should be" criteria, 74
White-collar employee turnover,
328-329, 330